APR 2004

917.8043 DOUBLE V. 2
The double eagle guide to
camping along the Lewis and
Clark Trail. Volume 2--Return
from the distant sea, 1805-
1806 33241003966553

WITHDRAWN

Y0-BZY-756

Double Eagle Guides™

The Double Eagle Guide to

CAMPING
ALONG
the
LEWIS *and* CLARK
TRAIL

VOLUME 2

RETURN FROM THE DISTANT SEA
1805-1806

Illinois   Missouri   Kansas   Iowa   Nebraska
South Dakota   North Dakota   Montana
Idaho   Washington   Oregon

Lewis and Clark Bicentennial Edition

A DOUBLE EAGLE GUIDE™

DISCOVERY PUBLISHING BILLINGS, MONTANA USA

ALAMEDA FREE LIBRARY
2200-A CENTRAL AVENUE
ALAMEDA, CA 94501

The Double Eagle Guide to
Camping Along the Lewis and Clark Trail
Volume 2 Return from the Distant Sea 1805-1806

Lewis and Clark Bicentennial Edition

Copyright © 2004 by Thomas and Elizabeth Preston

All Rights Reserved.

Selected readings from the text of the Journals of Lewis and Clark, (public domain) edited by the authors.

No part of this book may be reproduced or transmitted in any form or by any means without the written permission of the publisher.

Published by:

Discovery Publishing
Post Office Box 50545
Billings, Montana 59105 USA

Discovery Publishing is an independent, private enterprise. The information contained herein should not be construed as reflecting the publisher's approval of the policies or practices of the public agencies listed.

Information in this book is subject to change without notice.

Front jacket: Confluence of the Missouri and Yellowstone Rivers,
        Montana-North Dakota, from William Clark's map;
        William Clark's signature, Pompeys Pillar National Monument, Montana

Frontispiece: Ecola State Park, Oregon

10 9 8 7 6 5 4 3 2 1

March 9, 2004 4:00 PM Mountain Time

Produced, printed, and bound in the United States of America.

ISBN 1-932417-06-0

ALAMEDA FREE LIBRARY
2200-A CENTRAL AVENUE
ALAMEDA, CA 94501

TABLE OF CONTENTS

Volume 2: Return from the Distant Sea

Double Eagle™ Guides

🦅 INTRODUCTION TO THE *Double Eagle*™ SERIES 🦅

What is perhaps the greatest saga of discovery in North American history has inspired the creation of the latest volumes in the widely read and enjoyed *Double Eagle*™ series of travel and recreation guidebooks.

Whether you're a veteran of many Western trips or are planning your first visit, this series is for you.

In *The Double Eagle Guide to Camping Along the Lewis and Clark Trail*, Lewis and Clark Bicentennial Edition, we've fully described recreation areas directly along or conveniently near the route of Lewis and Clark's Corps of Discovery through lands which now are within 11 contiguous Mid-Western and Western United States. Our goal is to provide you with accurate, detailed, and yet concise, *first-hand* information about the recreation areas you're most likely to want to know about. Camping areas you can reach in a standard car, pickup, van or recreational vehicle. Camps worth going out of your way to visit and to spend some time in.

In *The Double Eagle Guide to Camping Along the Lewis and Clark Trail*, we've included virtually all public campgrounds along the Expedition's route: From simple, free camps with terrific scenery, to campgrounds with higher levels of comfort and convenience. Only public camping areas along the way are described. After all, the Expedition camped on public lands, not in posh, private rv parks decorated with astro turf and plastic palms.

The volumes which comprise the *Double Eagle*™ series constitute a significant departure from the sketchy, plain vanilla approach to recreation information provided by so many other guidebooks. Here is the most *useful* information about the West's most *useable* public recreation areas.

The name for this critically acclaimed series was suggested by the celebrated United States twenty-dollar gold piece—most often called the "*Double Eagle*"—the largest and finest denomination of coinage ever issued by the U.S. Mint. The *Double Eagle* has long been associated with the history of the West, as a symbol of the West's abundant resources, and of traditional Western excellence.

So, too, the *Double Eagle*™ series seeks to provide you with information about what are perhaps the finest of all the West's treasures—its public recreational lands.

We hope you'll enjoy reading these pages, and come to use the information in the volumes to enhance your own appreciation for the outstanding camping opportunities available along the Lewis and Clark Trail.

We truly hope that you'll enjoy your adventure!

Tom and *Liz Preston*
Publishers

🏠 CONVENTIONS USED IN THIS SERIES Å

The following conventions or standards are used throughout the *Double Eagle*™ series as a means of providing a sense of continuity between one recreation area and the next.

State Identifier: The state name and number combination in the upper left corner of each destination's description provides an easy means of cross-referencing the written information to the numbered locations on the maps in the Appendix.

Campground Name: The officially designated name for the camping area is listed in boldface, followed by the specific category in which it is classified ("National Forest", "State Park", "Corps of Engineers Park", "County Park", and so forth.) In most instances, the name was transcribed directly from the signpost planted at the recreation area entrance; it may (and often does), vary slightly from the name as it appears in other printed sources, (especially in 'official' literature). One example: Throughout the West, it's quite common to find places with a 'possessive' noun in their names to be spelled without the possessive apostrophe ("Clarks Camp" vs "Clark's Camp"). We have retained that convention whenever we determined it to be historically appropriate. Evidently, the apostrophe was considered a grammatical frill by many of our forebears.

Larger recreation areas with distinctively different major units may be divided into two or more separate descriptions. For example, if "Big River Regional Park" has two large camp areas, the "Mountain Valley" unit and the "Great Plains" unit, each with different access, facilities, and natural features, the two sections might be titled:

MOUNTAIN VALLEY
BIG RIVER REGIONAL PARK

GREAT PLAINS
BIG RIVER REGIONAL PARK

Location: This section allows you to obtain a quick approximation of a place's location in relation to nearby key communities, as depicted on the maps in the appendix.

Access: Our *Accurate Access* system makes extensive use of highway mileposts in order to pinpoint the location of access roads, intersections, and other major terminal points. (Mileposts are about 98 percent reliable—but occasionally they are mowed by a snowplow or an errant motorist, and may be missing; or, worse yet, the mileposts were replaced in the wrong spot!) In some instances, locations are noted primarily utilizing mileages between two or more nearby locations—usually communities, but occasionally key junctions or prominent landmarks.

Since everyone won't be approaching a camping area from the same direction, we've provided access information from two, sometimes three, points. In all cases, we've chosen the access points for their likelihood of use. Distances from communities are listed from the approximate **midtown** point (very often the city hall, courthouse, or post office), unless otherwise specified. Mileages from Interstate highways and other freeway exits are usually given from the approximate center of the interchange. Mileages from access points usually have been rounded to the nearest mile, unless the exact mileage is critical. All instructions are given using the *current official highway map* available free from each state.

Directions are given using a combination of compass and hand headings, i.e., "turn north (left)" or "swing west (right)". This isn't a bonehead navigation system, by any means. When the sun is shining or you're in a region where moss grows on tree trunks, it's easy enough to figure out which way is north. But anyone can become temporarily disoriented on an overcast day or a moonless night while looking for an inconspicuous park turnoff, or while being buzzed by heavy traffic at a key intersection, so we built this redundancy into the system.

Camping and Day Use Facilities: The items in this section have been listed in the approximate order in which a visitor might observe them during a typical swing through a campground. Following the total number of individual camp units, items pertinent to the campsites themselves are listed, then information related to 'community' facilities. It has been assumed that each campsite has a picnic table.

Site types: (1) Standard—no hookup; (2) Partial hookup—water, electricity; (3) Full hookup—water, electricity, sewer.

We have extensively employed the use of *general* and *relative* terms in describing the size, separation, and levelness of campsites ("medium to large", "fairly well separated", "basically level", etc.). Please note that "separation" is a measure of relative privacy and is a composite of both natural visual 'screens' and spacing between campsites. The information is presented as an *estimate* by highly experienced observers. Please allow for variations in perception between yourself and the reporters.

Parking Pads: (1) Straight-ins, (sometimes called "back-ins" or "spurs")—the most common type, are just that—straight strips angled off the driveway; (2) Pull-throughs— usually the most convenient type for large rv's, they provide an in-one-end-and-out-the-other parking space; pull-throughs may be either arc-shaped and separated from the main driveway by some sort of barrier or 'island' (usually vegetation), or arranged in parallel rows, somewhat like a parking lot; (3) Pull-offs—essentially just wide spots adjacent to the driveway. Pad lengths have been categorized as: (1) Short—a single, large vehicle up to about the size of a standard pickup truck; (2) Medium—a single vehicle or combination up to the length of a pickup towing a single-axle trailer; (3) Long—a single vehicle or combo as long as a crew cab pickup towing a double-axle trailer. Normally, any overhang out the back of the pad has been ignored in the estimate, so it might be possible to slip a crew cab pickup hauling a fifth-wheel trailer in tandem with a ski boat into some pads, but we'll leave that to your discretion.

Fire appliances have been categorized in three basic forms: (1) Fireplaces—angular, steel or concrete, ground-level, usually open at both ends; (2) Fire rings—circular, steel or concrete, ground-level or below ground-level; (3) Barbecue grills—angular steel box, supported by a steel post about 36 inches high. This may seem to some to be a superfluous detail. However, in our experience it's easier to keep a fire going in a 'fireplace' than in either of the other two 'field ranges' because of the draft created through the typical open-ended fireplace. Barbecue grills are often used in areas where ground fires are a problem, as when charcoal-only fires are permitted. The trend is toward installing steel fire rings, since they're durable, relatively inexpensive—60 to 80 dollars apiece—and easy to install and maintain.

Toilet facilities have been listed thusly: (1) Restrooms—'modern', i.e., flush toilets and usually a wash basin; (2) Vault facilities—'simple', i.e., outhouses, pit toilets, call them what you like. (A rose by any other name.....).

Campers' supply points have been described at five levels: (1) Camper Supplies—buns, beans and beverages; (2) Gas and Groceries—a 'convenience' stop; (3) Limited—at least one store which approximates a small supermarket, more than one fuel station, a general merchandise store, hardware store, and other basic services; (4) Adequate— more than one supermarket, (including something that resembles an IGA or a Safeway), a choice of fuel brands, and several general and specialty stores and services; (5) Complete—they have a major discount store.

♿ Recreation areas reported by public agencies to have facilities for physically challenged persons that conform to the requirements of the Americans with Disabilities Act of 1990 (ADA) have been highlighted with this familiar symbol. In most places, a minimum you can expect is equal access to restrooms. In many areas, special handicapped-access picnic or camp sites, fishing piers and other recreational facilities are also provided, especially in larger parks. Some places which are not listed as having handicapped access may indeed have some facilities that offer it on a limited basis, usually at restrooms, but they may not technically conform to the rigid standards of the ADA. If you rely on these facilities, it might be a good idea to double check for their existence and condition prior to visiting the area, using the ☎ information.

Recreation area managers, attendants and camp hosts can be expected to be on-site or readily available during the regular season in more than two-thirds of the listed areas.

Activities & Attractions: As is mentioned a number of times throughout this series, the local scenery may be the principal attraction of the recreation area (and, indeed, may be the *only* one you'll need). Other nearby attractions/activities have been listed if they are low-cost or free, and are available to the general public. An important item: *Swimming and boating areas usually do not have lifeguards.*

Natural Features: Here we've drawn a word picture of the natural environment in and around each camp area. Please remember that seasonal, even daily, conditions will affect the appearance of the locale. A normally "sparkling stream" can be a muddy torrent for a couple of weeks in late spring; a "deep blue lake" might be a nearly empty hole in a drought year; "lush vegetation" may have lost all its greenery by the time you arrive in late October. In the interest of simplicity and easy readability, we list broadleaf trees (i.e., "deciduous" trees, such as cottonwood, maple, oak) as "hardwoods"; cone-bearing needle trees (pine, Western cedar, spruce, etc.) as "conifers". We typically call the relatively small Eastern redcedar and Western junipers "evergreens". This information might be especially helpful to you in determining the amount of shade you can expect to find to help cool you in midsummer. Elevations above 500´ are rounded to the nearest 100´; lower elevations are rounded to the nearest 50´. (Some elevations are estimated, but no one should develop a nosebleed or a headache because of a 100´ difference in altitude.)

Season, Fees & Phone: Seasons listed are approximate, since weather conditions, particularly in mountainous or hilly regions, may require adjustments in opening/closing dates. Campground entrance gates are usually unlocked from 6:00 a.m. to 10:00 p.m. Fee information listed was obtained directly from the responsible agencies a few hours before press time. Costs for recreation area *entry permits* are given if applicable. Otherwise, listed fees should be considered minimum fees per vehicle for *camping*. They are always *subject to adjustment* by agencies or legislatures. Discounts and special passes are usually available for seniors and disabled persons. A local telephone number is listed which can be called in order to obtain information about current conditions in that recreation area. We've accented the phone number with a ☎ symbol for quick reference. It could be very helpful while you're in a highwayside phone booth fumbling for a quarter or your 'calling card', poking the buttons on the touch-tone pad, and simultaneously trying to hold the handset up to your ear as you're calling about campsite availability, current weather info, or whatever.

Camp Journal: Consider this section to be somewhat more subjective in nature than the others. In order to provide our readers with a well-rounded report, we have listed personal comments, as well as miscellaneous items of local historical, ecological, or geographical interest, related to our field observations. (Our enthusiasm for the West is, at times, unabashedly proclaimed. So if the text sometimes reads a bit like a tourist promotion booklet, please bear with us—there's a lot to be enthusiastic about!)

Throughout the series, certain small 'satellite' areas are given abbreviated 'thumbnail' descriptions in the *Camp Journal* section of a principal recreation area. Since these spots often are little-used outback hideouts, it might pay to check them out if you're in the neighborhood and looking for a simple, tranquil place to sit or stay for a while.

Editorial remarks (Ed.) occasionally have been included.

Itinerary...

After a great deal of thought and discussion over *who* would be using this guide and *how* they would be using it, we decided to follow a straightforward pattern in assembling the camping information. The Expedition mainly followed two great river systems in their remarkable journey to the Pacific Ocean and back again: The Missouri and the Columbia. Both outbound and homebound, they camped on whatever riverbank offered the best campsite at the time. However, modern travelers are unlikely to want to (or be able to) continually criss-cross the streams in order to precisely follow the Expedition's campsites. So, with some expeditious exceptions, we've settled on listing the modern camping areas in a north-bank-westward/south-bank-eastward pattern.

The camping areas are located directly along the main route traveled by the Corps of Discovery, or within a 20-mile 'corridor' along either side of the main route. Side trips were part of the daily routine practiced by the Expedition's members. The Journals mention numerous day-long and overnight explorations of tributaries and overland routes. Captains Lewis and Clark themselves were especially eager to see what was on 'the other side of the hill'. So it seemed logical to include camps in outlying areas which may very well have been visited by members of the expedition. Also included are a number of "Side Trips" related to the travels of the Corps of Discovery.

Lewis and Clark Journal Entries...

The readings have been selected and edited from the original Journals. It should be remembered that the Journals are 'field notes' written while swatting squads of "musqueters", engulfed in billowing clouds of campfire smoke, or being drenched by rain dripping down through the thatched roof of a log hut. Lewis and Clark were complying with President Jefferson's mandate to record whatever they observed or experienced. They often wrote in their own form of shorthand (including generous use of the ampersand–&), never thinking that the Journals would ever be published, let alone in their rough-hewn version. Therefore, original punctutation, capitalization, and spelling have been moderately edited to be generally consistent with the *Linqua Americana* of that era, while continuing to reflect each Captain's individual expressions of thought. For the most part, sentence syntax has been left undisturbed. In any event, we have endeavored to retain the authentic 'tone' or 'charm' of the original Journals intact, while allowing for easy campfire or armchair reading. We have associated the Journal entries as closely as possible to the camping areas along the route. We have let this great adventure story unfold in the words of its authors. Occasionally, interlinear notes in squared brackets [∗] within the selected readings, as well as more lengthy, explanatory or 'bridge' paragraphs, indicated by ☀ , were added by the editors.

Style...

Throughout the *Double Eagle*™ series, we've utilized a free-form writing style. Complete sentences, phrases, and single words have been incorporated into the place descriptions as appropriate under the circumstances. We've adopted this style in order to provide our readers with detailed information about each item, while maintaining conciseness, clarity, and conversationality.

Print...

Another departure from the norm is our use of print sizes which are 10 percent larger (or more) than ordinary guidebooks. We also use more efficient page layouts for less paper waste. It's one thing to read a guidebook in the convenience and comfort of your well-lit living room. It's another matter to peruse the pages while you're bounding and bouncing along in your car or camper as the sun is setting; or by a flickering flashlight inside a breeze-buffeted dome tent. We hope this works for you, too.

Maps...

After extensive tests of the state maps by seasoned campers, both at home and in the field, we decided to localize all of the maps in one place in each book. Travelers felt that, since pages must be flipped regardless of where the maps are located, it would be more desirable to have them all in one place. We're confident that you'll also find this to be a convenient feature. Likewise, we determined that states should be shown in their entirety, rather than fragmented into regions. Although this makes for 'cramped quarters' in a few high-density recreation areas, map readers preferred the overall 'big picture' approach. Cities shown on the maps are keyed to the cities listed in the *Location* and *Access* sections of the text.

Furthermore, details on the maps have been limited not only for clarity, but to discourage blatant mass photocopying and wholesale distribution of access information. You or your library paid with someone's hard-earned greenbacks for this book. You'll probably not want to compete with hordes of 'second-hand' users for what you hope is a tranquil outdoor recreation experience.

And a Final Note...

We've tried very, very hard to provide you with accurate information about the West's great recreation opportunities. But occasionally, all is not as it's supposed to be.....

If a campground's access or facilities have been changed, please let us know. We'll try to pass along the news to other campers.

If the persons in the next campsite keep their generator poppety-popping past midnight so they can cook a turkey in the microwave, blame the bozos, not the books.

If the beasties are a bit bothersome in that beautiful camp down by the bog, note the day's delights and not the difficulties.

Thank you for using, and enjoying, our books. We hope you'll have a terrific time following the footsteps of Lewis and Clark!

Winter at Fort Clatsop 1805-1806

Looking across the Columbia Bar from Cape Disappointment, Fort Canby State Park, Washington

Forward...

The Corps of Discovery has arrived at what Captain Clark described as a place where the Columbia River "widens into kind of a bay" above the open shores of the Pacific Ocean.

(Some scholars dispute Clark's "Ocian in view" statement of November 7th, claiming he was premature in his enthusiasm. But it is really a matter of judgement as to where the "ocian" begins in the vast Columbia estuary. Clark did indeed later refine his commentary, making reference to shores which they would explore in succeeding days as being on the "main" part of the ocean.)

We pick up the Expedition's epic saga, with the entire group still intact and relatively well, but eager to move on to the open shores of the Pacific, where hopefully they will find a ship to transport them home. They are encamped on the north bank (Washington side) of the Columbia River, a few miles above the open sea.

> **⚑ *Fort Clatsop***
> ***November-December 1805***

📖 *November 8, 1805*

A cloudy morning. Some rain. We did not set out untill 9 oClock, having changed our clothing. Three Indians in a canoe overtook us

with salmon to sell. We came to at the remains of an old village and dined. Here we saw great numbers of fowl. Sent out 2 men and they killed a goose and two canvas back ducks. Here we found great numbers of fleas, which we treated with the greatest caution and distance.

After dinner the Indians left us and we took the advantage of a returning tide and proceeded on to the second point on the starbd. Here we found the swells or waves so high that we thought it imprudent to proceed; we landed, unloaded, and drew up our canoes.

Some rain all day at intervals. We are all wet and disagreeable, as we have been for several days past, and our present situation a verry disagreeable one inasmuch as we have not leavel land sufficient for an encampment, and for our baggage to lie clear of the tide. The high hills jutting in so close and steep that we cannot retreat back, and the water of the river too salt to be used. Added to this, the waves are increasing to such a height that we cannot move from this place. In this situation, we are compelled to form our camp between the height of the ebb and flood tides, and raise our baggage on logs. We are not certain as yet if the white people who trade with those people, or from whom they procure their goods, are stationary at the mouth, or visit this quarter at stated times for the purpose of traffic, &c. I believe the latter to be the most probable conjecture. The seas rolled and tossed the canoes in such a manner this evening that several of our party were seasick.

—*Captain Clark*

📖 *November 9, 1805*

The tide of last night obliged us to unload all the canoes, one of which sank, before she was unloaded, by the high waves or swells which accompanied the returning tide. The others we unloaded, and 3 others were filled with water soon after by the swells or high seas which broke against the shore immediately where we lay.

Rained hard all the forepart of the day. The tide, which rose untill 2 oClock P.M. today, brought with it such emence swells or waves, added to a hard wind from the South which loosened the drift trees, which are verry thick on the shore, and tossed them about in such a manner, as to endanger our canoes verry much. Every exertion and the strictest attention by the party was scarcely sufficient to defend our canoes from being crushed to pieces between those emencely large trees, many of them 200 feet long and 4 feet through.

Notwithstanding the disagreeable time of the party for several days past, all are cheerfull and full of anxiety to see further into the ocian.

—*Captain Clark*

♣ Washington 93

CHINOOK
Pacific County Park

Location: Southwest corner of Washington east of Illwaco.

Access: From U.S. Highway 101 at milepost 3.8 (on the east edge of the town of Chinook, 3.5 miles west of the Columbia River bridge from Astoria, Oregon), turn south onto Chinook Park Road (paved) and go 0.1 mile to the park.

Camping Facilities: Approximately 60 campsites, including some with partial hookups; sites are small to small+, level, with nominal separation; parking surfaces are grass, mostly medium to long straight-ins; large areas for tents; random parking on the grass for standard tent sites; fire rings; b-y-o firewood; water at several faucets; restrooms with showers; paved driveways; gas and groceries+ in Chinook; limited+ to adequate supplies and services are available in Illwaco.

Day Use Facilities: Small parking area.

Activities & Attractions: Small boat launch area in the park (usable at high tide); large boat launch 1 mile west; boat fishing for salmon; bank fishing for perch and flounder; playground; Fort Columbia State Park, 1 mile east.

Natural Features: Located on a flat along the north bank of the Columbia River a few miles upriver of the Pacific Ocean; sites are lightly to moderately sheltered/shaded, mostly by hardwoods; bordered by dense vegetation and a rock sea wall; sea level.

Season, Fees & Phone: Open all year; $12.00 for a standard site, $15.00 for a hookup site; 14 day limit; park manager ☎(360) 777-8442 or

Pacific County Public Works Department, Long Beach, (360) 642-9300, ext. 273.

Camp Journal: Chinook serves as a simple fishing camp for hundreds of Columbia River anglers each year. If you're not a boater of fisherman and would like some diversion, pleasant surroundings and scenery, Fort Columbia could easily occupy a couple of hours. The nearby state park features the well-preserved buildings and grounds of a harbor defense post that dates back to the early 1900's.

📖 *November 10, 1805*

Rained verry hard the greater part of last night & continues this morning. The wind has layed and the waves are not high. We loaded our canoes and proceeded on. Passed several small and deep niches on the starboard side. We proceeded on about 10 miles; saw great numbers of sea gulls.

The wind rose from the N.W., and the waves became so high that we were compelled to return about 2 miles to a place we could unload our canoes, which we did in a small niche at the mouth of a small run, on a pile of drift logs, where we continued untill low water. When the river appeared calm, we loaded and set out, but were obliged to return, finding the waves too high for our canoes to ride. We again unloaded the canoes and stowed the loading on a rock above the tide water, and formed a camp on the drift logs which appeared to be the only situation we could find to lie, the hills being either a perpendicular clift or steep ascent, rising to about 500 feet. Our canoes we secured as well as we could. We are all wet, the rain having continued all day, our bedding and many other articles. Employ ourselves drying our blankets. Nothing to eate but dryed fish, pounded, which we brought from the falls. We made 10 miles today.

—*Captain Clark*

📖 *November 11, 1805*

A hard rain all the last night. During the last tide the logs on which we lay was all afloat.

About 12 oClock 5 Indians came down in a canoe, the wind verry high from the S.W.,with most tremendous waves breaking with great violence against the shores, rain falling in torrents. We are all wet as usial, and our situation is truly a disagreeable one, our canoes at one place, our baggage at another; and ourselves and party scattered on floating logs and such dry spots as can be found on the steep hill sides and crevices in the rocks.

We purchased of the Indians 13 red charr, which we found to be an excellent fish. One of those men had on a sailor's jacket and pantaloons, and made signs that he got his clothes from the white people who lived below the point, &c. Those people left us and crossed the river (which is about 5 miles wide at this place), through the highest waves I ever saw a small vessel ride. Those Indians are certainly the best navigators I ever saw.

—*Captain Clark*

📖 *November 12, 1805*

A tremendous wind from the S.W. about 3 oClock this morning, with lightening and hard claps of thunder and hail, which continued untill 6 oClock A.M., when it became light for a short time; then the heavens became suddenly darkened by a black cloud from the S.W. and rained with great violence untill 12 oClock, the waves tremendous, breaking with great fury against the rocks and trees on which we were encamped.

Our situation is dangerous. We took the advantage of a low tide and moved our camp around a point to a small wet bottom, at the mouth of a brook, which we had not observed when we came to this cove, from it's being verry thick and obscured by drift trees and thick bushes. It would be distressing to see our situation, all wet and cold, our bedding also wet (and the robes of the party which compose half the bedding is rotten, and we are not in a situation to supply their places), in a wet bottom scarcely large enough to contain us, our baggage half a mile from us, and canoes at the mercy of the waves, altho' secured as well as possible, sunk with emence parcels of stone to weight them down to prevent their dashing to pieces against the rocks. One got loose last night and was left on a rock a short distance below, without receiving more damage than a split in her bottom. Fortunately for us, our men are healthy.

—*Captain Clark*

📖 *November 14, 1805*

Rained all the last night without intermission, and this morning the wind blows verry hard, but our situation is such that we cannot tell from what point it comes. One of the canoes is much broken by the waves dashing it against the rocks.

5 Indians came up in a canoe, thro' the waves which are verry high and roll with great fury. They made signs to us that they saw our 3 men we sent down yesterday. Only 3 of those

Indians landed; the other 2, which was women, played off in the waves, which induced to to suspect that they had taken something from our men below.

At this time, one of the men, Colter, returned by land and informed us that those Indians had taken his gig & basket. I called to the squars to land and give back the gig, which they would not do untill a man run with a gun, as if he intended to shoot them when they landed, and Colter got his gig & basket.

Colter informed us that it was but a short distance from where we lay around to a beautifull sand beach, which continued for a long way; that he found a good harbor in the mouth of a creek near 2 Indian lodges; that he had proceeded in the canoe as far as he could for the waves; the other two men, Willard & Shannon, had proceeded on down.

Capt. Lewis concluded to proceed on by land & find, if possible, the white people the Indians say are below, and examine if a bay is situated near the mouth of this river, as laid down by Vancouver, in which we expect, if there are white traders, to find them &c. At 3 oClock, he set out with four men, Drewyer, Jos. & R. Fields, and R. Frazier, in one of our large canoes, and 5 men to set them around the point on the sand beach. This canoe returned nearly filled with water at dark, which it received by the waves dashing into it on it's return, having landed Capt. Lewis & his party safe on the sand beach. The rain &c., which has continued without a longer intermission than 2 hours at a time for a time ten days past, has destroyed the robes and rotted nearly one half of the fiew clothes the party has, particularly the leather clothes. If we have cold weather before we can kill & dress skins for clothing, the bulk of the party will suffer verry much.

—*Captain Clark*

📖 *November 15, 1805*

Rained all the last night at intervals of sometimes 2 hours. This morning it became cold & fair. I prepared to set out, at which times the wind sprung up from the S.E. and blew down the river & in a fiew minits raised such swells and waves breaking on the rocks at the point as to render it unsafe to proceed. I went to the point in an empty canoe and found it would be dangerous to proceed even in an empty canoe.

The sun shown untill 1 oClock P.M., which gave an opportunity for us to dry some of our bedding & examine our baggage, the greater part of which I found wet. Some of our pounded fish spoiled .I had all the arms put in order & amunition examined.The rainey weather continued without a longer intermission than 2 hours at a time—from the 5th in the morning untill the 16th is eleven days rain—and the most disagreeable time I have experenced, confined on a tempest coast, wet, where I can neither get out to hunt, return to a better situation, or proceed on; in this situation have we been for six days past.

Fortunately, the wind lay about 3oclock. We loaded in great haste and set out, past the blustering point below, which is a sand beach, with a small marshy bottom, for 3 miles on the starbd. side, on which is a large village of 36 houses deserted by the Indians & in full possession of the fleas. A small creek falls in at this village, which waters the country for a few miles back.

Shannon & 5 Indians met me here. Shannon informed me that he met Capt. Lewis some distance below & he took Willard & sent him to me. The Indians were rogues; they had the night before stolen both his and Willards guns from under their heads. Capt. Lewis & party arived at the camp of those Indians at so timely a period that the Indians were allarmed & delivered up the guns &c. I told those Indians who accompanied Shannon that they should not come near us, and if anyone of their Nation stole anything from us, I would have him shot, which they understood verry well.

The tide, meeting of me and the emence swells from the main Ocian (immediately in front of us), raised to such a height that I concluded to form a camp on the highest spot I could find in the marshey bottom, and proceed no further by water, as the coast becomes verry dangerous for crafts of the size of our canoes, and as the Ocian is immediately in front and gives us an extensive view of it from Cape Disappointment to Point Adams, except 3 small islands off the mouth and S.W. of us. My situation is in the upper part of Haleys Bay.

4 Indians in a canoe came down with wappato roots to sell, for which they asked blankets or robes, both of which we could not spare. I informed those Indians, all of which understood some English, that if they stole our guns &c the men would certainly shoot them. I treated them with great distance, & the sentinel which was over our baggage allarmed them verry much, they all promised not to take any things, and if any thing was taken by the

squars & bad boys, to return them &c. The waves became verry high; evening fair & pleasant, our men all comfortable in the camps they have made of the boards they found at the town above.

–Captain Clark

📖 *November 17, 1805*

A fair cool morning, wind from the East. The tide rises at this place 8 feet 6 inches and comes in with great waves breaking on the sand beach on which we lay, with great fury. Six hunters out this morning in search of deer & fowl.

At half past 10 Clock Capt. Lewis returned, having traversed Haley Bay to Cape Disappointment and the sea coast to the North for some distance. Several Chinnook Indians followed Capt. L., and a canoe came up with roots, mats &c. to sell. Those Chinnooks made us a present of a root boiled, much resembling the common liquorice in taste and size; in return for this root we gave more than double the value to satisfy their craving disposition. It is a bad practice to receive a present from those Indians, as they are never satisfied for what they receive in return, if ten times the value of the articles they gave.

This Chinnook Nation is about 400 souls, inhabit the country on the small rivers which run into the bay below us and on the ponds to the N.W. of us; live principally on fish and roots; they are well armed with fusees and sometimes kill elk, deer and fowl.

Our hunters killed today 3 deer, 4 brant and 2 ducks, and inform me they saw some elk sign. I directed all the men who wished to see more of the main Ocian to prepare themselves to set out with me early on tomorrow morning.The principal Chief of the Chinnooks &his family came up to see us this evening.

–Captain Clark

📖 *November 18, 1805*

I set out at daylight with 10 men and my man York, and proceeded on a sandy beach to a rock island at 3 miles, past a nitch. This rock island is small and at the South of a deep bend in which the nativs inform us the ships anchor, and from whence they receive their goods in return for their peltries and elk skins &c. This appears to be a very good harbor for large ships. Here I found Capt. Lewis name on a tree. I also engraved my name, & by land, the day of the month and year, as also several of the men. Men appear much satisfied with their trip, beholding with astonishment the high waves dashing against the rocks & this emence Ocian.

—*Captain Clark*

⚐ Washington 94 ♿

FORT CANBY
Fort Canby State Park

Location: Southwest Washington west of Illwaco.

Access: From U.S. Highway 101 in midtown Illwaco at the corner of First Street and Spruce Street, head west on Spruce Street (Fort Canby Road) and out of town on a winding, hilly road for 3.4 miles to the park

Camping Facilities: 250 campsites, including 60 with full hookups; sites are small to small+ in size, essentially level, with fair to very good separation; parking pads are paved, short to medium-length, mostly straight-ins; adequate space for medium to large tents; b-y-o firewood is recommended; water at several faucets; restrooms with showers; holding tank disposal station; paved driveways; camper supplies at the park concession; limited+ to adequate supplies and services are available in Illwaco.

Day Use Facilities: Several small picnic areas: at the beach, near the end of the jetty, at the interpretive center, and in the north end of the park near the North Head Lighthouse; drinking water; restrooms; small to medium-sized parking lots at the beach, at the boat launch, at the end of the jetty and at the interpretive center.

Activities & Attractions: Lewis and Clark Interpretive Center; swimming/wading in a small cove on Waikiki Beach (really); Cape Disappointment Lighthouse, constructed in the 1850's, is the oldest West Coast lighthouse still in operation; four hiking trails; good beachcombing, particularly in winter; boat launch; fishing.

Natural Features: Located on more than 1700 acres along the Pacific Ocean at the mouth of the Columbia River; picnic sites vary from unsheltered to moderately sheltered; campsites receive light to moderately dense shade/shelter by medium-high shrubbery and bushy pines, and some large hardwoods; sea level to 100′.

Season, Fees & Phone: Open all year; interpretive center open daily during the summer, and weekends by appointment during the winter; $16.00 for a standard site, $22.00 for a hookup site; campsite reservations accepted, recommended for anytime during the summer, contact the park office for reservation procedures; ☎(360) 642-3078 or ☎(360) 642-3029.

Camp Journal: Fort Canby was operated as a Columbia River defense post from the 1870's to the end of World War II. The interpretive center features exhibits about frontier foods, early medicine, trade goods, biographical information about Lewis and Clark and other principal members of the Corps of Discovery, and info about the Expedition. Lewis and Clark spent most of their time on the Coast at their winter home at Fort Clatsop in Oregon. Fort Canby is large enough, though, and has enough items of interest, that you'll probably spend more time than Meriwether & William did on this side of the Columbia.

Essentially, the Corps of Discovery had completed their primary mission—to determine if there was indeed a Northwest Passage from the Mississippi-Missouri to the Columbia and thence to the Pacific. Having determined that there was not a feasible route, Lewis and Clark had hoped to find a ship which would take them home, 'round Cape Horn, thus avoiding a long, arduous trek back from whence they came. Finding no such ship, they named this headland Cape Disappointment.

📖 *November 19, 1805*
Cape Disappointment at the enterance of the Columbia River into the Great South Sea, or Pacific Ocean

I arose early this morning from under a wet blanket caused by a shower of rain which fell in the latter part of the last night, and sent two men on ahead with directions to proceed on near the seacoast and kill something for brakfast, and that I should follow myself in about half an hour. After drying our blankets a little, I set out with a view to proceed near the coast, the direction of which induced me to conclude that at the distance of 8 or 10 miles, the bay was no great distance across. I overtook the hunters at about 3 miles. They had killed a small deer, on which we brakfasted. It commenced raining and continued moderately untill 11 oClock A.M.

After taking a sumptuous brakfast of venison, which was roasted on sticks exposed to the fire, I proceeded on through rugged country of high hills and steep hollows to the commencement of a sandy coast which extended N. from the top of the hill above the sand shore to a point of high land, distant near

20 miles. This point I have taken the liberty of calling after my particular friend, Lewis.

After dining on the remains of our small deer, I proceeded on to a bay about 2 miles, thence up the mouth of Chinnook River 2 miles and encamped.

–Captain Clark

📖 *November 20, 1805*

On my way back up to our main camp, I met several parties of Chinnooks; they were on their return from our camp. All those people appeared to know my determination of keeping every individual of their Nation at a proper distance, as they were guarded and reserved in my presence &c.

Found many of the Chinooks with Capt. Lewis, of whom there were 2 Chiefs, Com-com-mo-ly and Chil-lar-la-wil, to whom we gave medals, and to one a flag. One of the Indians had on a robe made of two sea otter skins. The fur of them was more beautifull than any fur I had ever seen. Both Capt. Lewis & myself endeavoured to purchase the robe with different articles. At length, we procured it for a belt of blue beeds which the squar wife of our interpreter Shabono wore around her waist.

–Captain Clark

📖 *November 21, 1805*

Most of the Chinnooks leave our camp and return home. Several Indians visit us today of different nations or bands: Some of the Chiltz Nation who reside on the sea coast near Point Lewis, several of the Clatsops who reside on the opposit side of the Columbia immediately opposit to us, and a Chief from the grand rapid, to whome we gave a medal.

An old woman and wife to a Chief of the Chinooks came and made a camp near ours. She brought with her 6 young squars, (her daughters and nieces), I believe for the purpose of gratifying the passions of the men of our party and receiving for those indulgences such small presents as she (the old woman) thought proper to accept of.

Those people appear to view sensuality as a necessary evil, and do not appear to abhor it as a crime in the unmarried state. The young females are fond of the attention of our men, and appear to meet the sincere approbation of their friends and connections for thus obtaining their favours.

The women of the Chinook Nation have handsome faces, low and badly made with large legs and thighs, which are generally swelled from a stoppage of the circulation in the feet (which are small) by many strands of beeds or curious strings which are drawn tight around the leg above the ankle. Their legs are also tattooed with different figures. I saw on the left arm of a squar the following letters: "J. Bowman". All those are considered by the nativs of this quarter as handsome decorations, and a woman without those decorations is considered as among the lower class. The men are low, homely and badly made, small crooked legs, large feet; and all of both sex have flattened heads. many of the Chinnooks appear to have venerious and pustulous disorders.

We gave to the men each a piece of ribbon to bestow on their favourite lasses. We purchased cranberries, mats verry neatly made of flags and rushes, some roots, salmon; and I purchased a hat made of splits and strong grass, which is made in the fashion which was common in the U. States two years ago; also small baskets to hold water, made of split and straw; for those articles we gave high prices.

—Captain Clark

📖 *November 22, 1805*

A little before daylight the wind, which was from the S.S.E., blew with such violence that we were almost overwhelmed with water blown from the river. This storm did not cease at day, but blew with nearly equal violence throughout the whole day, accompanied with rain. O! How horrible is the day—waves breaking with great violence against the shore, throwing the water into our camp &c. All wet and confined to our shelters, several Indian men and women crowding about the mens shelters today. We purchased a fiew wappato roots, for which we gave arm bands & rings to the old squar; those roots are equal to the Irish potato, and is a tolerable substitute for bread.

The threat which I made to the men of this nation whome I first saw, and an indifference towards them, is, I am fully convinced, the cause of their conducting themselves with great propriety towards ourselves & party.

—Captain Clark

📖 *November 23, 1805*

Capt. Lewis branded a tree with his name, date, &c. I marked my name, the day and year, on an alder tree. The party all cut the first letters of their names on different trees in the bottom.

In the evening, seven Indians of the Clatsop Nation came over in a canoe. They brought with them 2 sea otter skins, for which they asked blue beeds &c., and such high prices that we were unable to purchase them without reducing our small stock of merchandize on which we depended for subsistence on our return up this river. Merely to try the Indian who had one of those skins, I offered him my watch, handkerchief, a bunch of red beeds, and a dollar of the American coin, all of which he refused and demanded *ti-a-co-mo-shack*, which is "chief beeds", and the common blue beeds, but fiew of which we have at this time.

—*Captain Clark*

📖 *November 29, 1805*

The wind being high, the party were unable to proceed with the perogues. I determined, therefore, to proceed down the river on it's East side in search of an eligible place for our winter's residence, and accordingly set out early this morning in the small canoe, accompanied by 5 men.

—*Captain Lewis*

🌿 Before leaving Cape Disappointment and the storm-lashed north (Washington) shore of the Columbia to winter in what were more favorable surroundings on the south (Oregon) side, Captain Clark used his belt knife to inscribe this celebrated mark:

📖 *December 3, 1805*

I marked my name & the day of the month and year on a large pine tree on this peninsula:

Capt William Clark   December 3rd 1805.
By Land. U. States in 1804 & 1805

—*Captain Clark*

📖 *December 7, 1805*

We set out at 8 oClock down to the place Capt. Lewis pitched on for winter quarters when he was down. We stopped and dined in the commencement of a bay, after which we proceeded on around the bay to S.E. and ascended a creek 8 miles to a high point and camped. At this place of encampment we propose to build and pass the winter. The situation is in the center of, as we conceive, a hunting country.

—*Captain Clark*

🌿 This long-term encampment site would soon become Fort Clatsop (named for a local tribe), the first U.S. military post west of the Great Plains. Lewis chose a location several miles up the Netul (now Lewis and Clark) River on a little knoll, south-southwest of present-day Astoria, Oregon. The site had a number of 'pluses' going for it: Well-sheltered from ocean storms by a dense stand of pine, a good source of fresh water, and, according to the Indians, plenty of game.

🌲 **Oregon Side Trip** ♿

FORT CLATSOP
Fort Clatsop National Memorial

Location: Northwest corner of the Oregon Coast south of Astoria.

Access: From U.S. Highways 101 & 26 at milepost 6 +.4 (on the northeast edge of the city of Warrenton near the south end of the bridge/causeway which crosses Youngs Bay, 5 miles southwest of Astoria), turn south-easterly onto U.S. 101 Business Route and proceed 2 miles; turn south (right) onto the park access road and proceed 0.3 miles to the park.

Camping Facilities: None; nearest public campground is in Fort Stevens State Park.

Day Use Facilities: Picnic area; shelters; drinking water, restrooms; large parking lot.

Activities & Attractions: Interpretive center with displays and audio-visual presentations especially related to the Corps of Discovery's 'wintering over' at Fort Clatsop; log replica of the original Fort Clatsop; living history presentations; interpretive trails.

Natural Features: Located along the west bank of Lewis and Clark River about 2 miles south of Youngs Bay of the Pacific Ocean; most of the park is densely forested with stands of conifers and hardwoods over a carpet of ferns and shrubs; elevation 50´.

Season, Fees & Phone: Open all year; nominal entry fee charged; park office ☎(503) 436-2844.

Camp Journal: .The original Fort Clatsop (vs the modern interpretation here) wasn't much. The 'physical plant' consisted of a perimeter of pine trunks sunk upright into the earth to form a stockade about 50 feet square, bordering two parallel rows of tiny cabins—three in one row facing four in another line. A small parade ground for musters and military drills lay between the rows of cabins.

December 8, 1805

We having fixed on this situation as the one best calculated for our winter quarters, I determined to go as direct a course as I could to the seacoast, which we could hear roar and appeared to be at no great distance from us. My principal object is to look out a place to make salt, blaze the road or rout that the men out hunting might find the direction to the fort if they should get lost in cloudy weather; and see the probability of game in that direction, for the support of the men we shall send to make salt.

—*Captain Clark*

December 9, 1805

I set out in a westerly direction, crossed 3 slashes, and arived at a creek. Met 3 Indians loaded with fresh salmon. Those Indians made signs that they had a town on the seacoast at no great distance, and invited me to go to their town. They had a canoe hid in the creek; we crossed in this little canoe. After crossing, 2 of the Indians took the canoe on their shoulders and carried it across to the other creek, about 1/4 of a mile. We crossed the 2nd creek and proceeded on to the mouth of the creek, which makes a great bend. Above the mouth of this creek, or to the South, are 3 houses and about 12 families of the Clatsop Nation. We crossed to those houses.

Those people treated me with extraordinary friendship. One man attached himself to me as soon as I entered the hut, spread down new mats for me to sit on, gave me fish, berries, roots, etc. All the men of the other houses came and smoked with me. In the evening an old woman presented in a bowl made of a light-coloured horn, a kind of syrup made of dried berries which the nativs call *shale-well*. They gave me a kind of soup made of bread of the shale-well berries mixed with roots, which they presented in neat trenchers made of wood.

When I was disposed to go to sleep, the man who had been most attentive, named Cus-ca-lah, produced 2 new mats and spread them near the fire, and directed his wife to go to his bed, which was the signal for all to retire. I had not been long on my mats before I was attacked most violently by the fleas, and they kept up a close siege during the night.

—*Captain Clark*

December 10, 1805

One of the Indians pointed to a flock of brant sitting in the creek a short distance below and requested me to shoot one. I walked down with my small rifle and killed two at about 40 yards distance. On my return to the houses, two small ducks sat at about 30 steps from me. The Indians pointed at the ducks. They were near together. I shot at the ducks and accidentally shot the head of one off.

This duck and brant were carried to the house, and every man came around, examined the duck, looked at the gun, the size of the ball, which was 100 to the pound, and said in their own language, "*Clouch musket, wake, coin-ma-tax, musket, Kloshe musket, wake kumtaks musket*", which is, "A good musket, do not understand this kind of musket", &c. I entered the same house I slept in; they immediately set before me their best roots, fish, and syrup. I attempted to purchase a small sea otter skin for red beeds which I had in my pockets. They would not trade for those beeds, not prizing any other colour than blue or white. I purchased a little of the berry bread and a fiew of their roots for which I gave small fishhooks, which they appeared fond of.

—*Captain Clark*

December 12, 1805, Fort Clatsop

All hands that are well employed in cutting logs and raising our winter cabins. Detached two men to split boards. Some rain at intervals all last night and today. The fleas were so troublesome last night that I made but a broken night's rest. We find great difficulty in getting those troublesome insects out of our robes and blankets. In the evening, two canoes of Clatsops visited us. They brought with them wappato, a black sweet root they call *sha-na-ta-que*, and a small sea otter skin, all of which we purchased for a fiew fishing hooks and a small sack of Indian tobacco which was given us by the Snake Indians.

Those Indians appear well disposed. We gave a medal to the Principal Chief, named Con-ny-au or Com-mo-wol, and treated those with him with as much attention as we could. I can readily discover that they are close dealers, and stickle for a verry little, never close a bargain except they think they have the advantage; value blue beeds highly, white they also prize, but no other colour do they value in the least.

—*Captain Clark*

📖 *December 24, 1805, Fort Clatsop*

Cuscalah, the Indian who had treated me so politely when I was at the Clatsops' village, came up in a canoe with his young brother and two squars. He laid before Capt. Lewis and myself each a mat and a parcel of roots. Some time in the evening, two files were demanded for the presents of mats and roots. As we had no files to part with, we each returned the present which we had received, which displeased Cuscalah a little. He then offered a woman to each of us, which we also declined accepting of, which displeased the whole party verry much. The female party appeared to be highly disgusted at our refusing to accept of their favours.

—*Captain Clark*

📖 *Christmas, December 25, 1805*

At daylight this morning, we were awoke by the discharge of the firearms of all our party & a salute, shouts, and a song which the whole party joined in under our windows, after which they retired to their rooms. Were cheerfull all the morning.

After brakfast we divided our tobacco, which amounted to 12 carrots, one half of which we gave to the men of the party who used tobacco, and to those who do not use it we made a present of a handkerchief.

The Indians leave us in the evening. All the party snugly fixed in their huts. I received a present of Capt. L. of a fleece hosiery shirt, drawers and socks; a pair of mockersons of Whitehouse, a small Indian basket of Goodrich, two dozen white weasels tails of the Indian woman, & some black root of the Indians before their departure. The day proved showery, wet, and disagreeable.

We would have spent this day, the nativity of Christ, in feasting, had we had anything either to raise our spirits or even gratify our appetites. Our dinner consisted of pore elk, so much spoiled that we ate it thro' mere necessity, some spoiled pounded fish, and a fiew roots.

—*Captain Clark*

📖 *December 27, 1805*

Rained last night as usial, and the greater part of this day, the men complete chimneys & bunks today.

We sent out R. Fields & Collins to hunt, and order Drewyer, Shannon & Labiche to set out early tomorrow to hunt, Jo. Fields, Bratten, & Gibson to make salt at Point Adams, Willard

& Wiser to assist them in carrying the kittles &c. to the Ocian, and all the others to finish the picquits and gates. Warm weather. I saw a musquetor, which I showed Capt. Lewis.

In the evening a Chief and 4 men come of the Clotsop Nation, Chief Co-ma-wool. Those Indians gave us, a black root they call *Shan-na-tah-que,* a kind of licquorice which they roast in embers and call *Cul-ho-mo*; a black berry the size of a cherry & dried, which they call *Shel-well-all* , of which they prize highly and make use of as food to live on, for which Capt. Lewis gave the Chief a cap of sheep skin and I his son, earbobs, piece of ribbon, a piece of brass, and 2 small fishing hooks, of which they were much pleased. Those roots & berries are gratefull to our stomachs, as we have nothing to eate but pore elk meat nearly spoiled; & this accident of spoiled meet is owing to warmth & the repeated rains, which cause the meat to taint before we can get it from the woods. Musquetors troublesome.

—*Captain Clark*

📖 *December 28, 1805. Fort Clatsop*

Directed Drewyer, Shannon, Labiche, Reuben Fields, and Collins to hunt; Joseph Fields, Bratton, Gibson to proceed to the ocean, at some convenient place form a camp, and commence making salt with 5 of the largest kittles, and Willard and Wiser to assist them in carrying the kittles to the sea coast. All the other men to be employed about putting up picquits and making the gates of the fort. My man York verry unwell from a violent cold, and strain by carrying meat from the woods and lifting the heavy logs on the works, &c.

—*Captain Clark*

🔆 The salt-making camp was about 20 miles down the coast, near present-day Seaside, Oregon. Besides giving the men something constructive to occupy themselves during the long, wet winter, it would provide a seasoning to enhance the flavor of their meals, plus a greatly needed mineral for processing skins, as well as being a possible trade good.

📖 *December 30, 1805, Fort Clatsop*

Our fortification is completed this evening, and at sunset we let the nativs know that our custom will be in the future to shut the gates at sunset, at which time all Indians must go out of the fort and not return into it untill next morning after sunrise, at which time the gates will be opened.

—*Captain Clark*

⚐ Oregon 95 ♿

FORT STEVENS

Fort Stevens State Park

Location: Northwest corner of Oregon southwest of Astoria.

Access: From U.S. Highways 101 & 26 (southbound) at milepost 6 +.4 (on the northeast edge of the city of Warrenton near the south end of the bridge/causeway which crosses Youngs Bay, 5 miles southwest of Astoria), turn west onto East Harbor Drive; proceed toward midtown Warrenton, then pick up North Main Avenue and continue generally northwesterly (toward the community of Hammond) as North Main curves and becomes NW Warrenton Drive, and finally Pacific Drive for a total of 4.4 miles from U.S. 101; at the intersection of Pacific Drive and Ridge Road, continue ahead (west) to the historic areas; or turn south (left) onto Ridge Road to the day use areas and the campground.

Alternate Access: From U.S. 101 & 26 (northbound) at milepost 9 +.2 on the north edge of the Camp Rilea Military Reservation, turn west, then immediately north and proceed (on what should be a well-signed route to the park) northwesterly on Ridge Road for a total of 4.6 miles to the campground entrance, on the west (left) side of the road; or continue ahead for 1 mile to the day use and historical areas, on the west (left) side of Ridge Road.

Camping Facilities: 605 campsites, including 130 with partial hookups and 213 with full hookups, in 15 loops; (8, small group tent camps are also available); sites are generally small, level, with minimal to fair separation; parking pads are paved, short to medium-length straight-ins or medium to long pull-throughs; medium to large tent areas; water at sites and at several faucets in each loop; restrooms with showers; paved driveways; adequate+ supplies and services are available in the Warrenton/Hammond area.

Day Use Facilities: 2 picnic areas with shelters and large parking lots at Coffenbury Lake; beach access is provided from 4 large parking lots situated just off of the main road which leads to the tip of the point at the mouth of the river.

Activities & Attractions: Fort Stevens Historical Center features self-guided tours of the shore batteries which defended the mouth of the Columbia River from the War Between the States to World War II; museum with military items and interpretive exhibits; several miles of ocean beach; 7 miles of paved bicycle trails; 5 miles of hiking trails; wreck of the Peter Iredale, a sailing ship which ran aground in 1906 on what is now the park's beach; 2 swimming areas, fishing for trout and perch, and limited (10 mph) boating on Coffenbury Lake; watching ships cross the Columbia Bar and fishing at the South Jetty on the northwest tip of the park.

Natural Features: Located on 4000 acres on a peninsula near and along the Pacific Ocean at the mouth of the Columbia River; park vegetation consists of dense stands of hardwoods, conifers and shrubbery in the camping and picnicking areas; remaining sections of the park consist mostly of grass-covered dunes and miles of beach; small Coffenbury Lake is adjacent to the picnic areas and campground; sea level.

Season, Fees & Phone: Open all year; $16.00 for a standard site, $22.00 for a partial hookup site, $22.00 for a full hookup site; 10 day limit; ☎ (503) 861-1671.

Camp Journal: Fort Stevens is the largest piece of real estate in the Oregon State Park System. Detailed park maps are displayed at several points in order to help you get your bearings once you arrive. Chances are, you'll run out of time before you run out of things to see and do here. One of the shore gun emplacements, Battery Russell, which was shelled by a Japanese sub in WWII, is the only installation on the U.S. mainland to have been attacked by a foreign power since the War of 1812.

📖 *December 31, 1805*

With the party of Clatsops who visited us last was a man of much lighter colour than the nativs are generally. He was freckled, with long, dusky red hair, about 25 years of age, and must certainly be half white at least. This man appeared to understand more of the English language than the others of his party, but did not speak a word of English. He possessed all the habits of the Indians.

—Captain Clark

Ⓐ *Fort Clatsop*
January-March 1806

📖 *January 1, 1806*

This morning I was awakened at an early hour by the discharge of a volley of small arms, which was fired by our party in front of our quarters to usher in the New Year. This was the only mark of respect which we had it in our power to pay this celebrated day. Our repast of this day, tho' better than that of Christmas, consisted principally in the anticipation of the 1st day of January, 1807, when, in the bosom of our friends, we hope to participate in the mirth and hilarity of the day; and when, with the zest given by the recollection of the present, we shall completely, both mentally and corporally, enjoy the repast which the hand of civilization has prepared for us. At present we were content with eating our boiled elk and wappato, and solacing our thirst with our only beverage, pure water. Two of our hunters who set out this morning returned in the evening having killed two buck elk. They presented Capt. Clark and myself each a marrow bone and tongue, on which we supped.

We were uneasy with respect to two of our men, Willard and Wiser, who were dispatched on the 28th with the salt makers, and were directed to return immediately; they not having returned induces us to believe it probable that they have missed their way.

—*Captain Lewis*

📖 *January 1, 1806*

A list of the names of sundry persons who visit this part of the coast for the purpose of trade &c. &c. in large vessels; all of which speak the English language &c., as the Indians inform us:

Moore	Visits them in a large 4 masted ship, they expect him in 2 moons to trade
1-Eyed Skellie	In a large ship, long time gone
Youin	In a large ship, and they expect him in 1 moon to trade with them
Swepeton	In a ship, they expect him in 3 months back to trade
Mackey	In a ship, they expect him back in 1 or 2 moons to trade with them
Meship	In a ship, they expect him 2 moons to trade
Jackson	Visit them in a ship and they expect him back in 3 months to trade
Balch	In a ship, and they expect him in 3 months to trade
Mr. Haley	Visits them in a ship & they expect him back to trade with them in 3 moons to trade. He is the favourite of the Indians (from the number of presents he gives) and has the trade principally with all the tribes
Washilton	In a schooner, they expect him in 3 months to return and trade with them—a favourite
Lemon	In a sloop, and they expect him in 3 moons to trade with them
Davidson	Visits this part of the coast and river in a brig for the purpose of hunting the elk, returns when he pleases, he does not trade any, kills a great many elk &c. &c.
Fallawan	In a ship with guns, he fired on & killed several Indians, he does not trade now and they do not know when he will return

📖 *January 3, 1806, Fort Clatsop*

Our party, from necessity having been obliged to subsist some length of time on dogs, have now become extreemly fond of their flesh. It is worthy of remark that while we lived principally on the flesh of this animal, we were much more healthy, strong, and more fleshy than we had been since we left the buffaloe country. For my own part, I have become so perfectly reconciled to the dog that I think it an agreeable food and would prefer it vastly to lean venison or elk.
—*Captain Lewis*

📖 *January 3, 1806*

At 11 A.M. we were visited by our near neighbour, Chief Co-mo-wool, alias Conia, and six Clatsops. They brought for sale some roots, berries and 3 dogs, also a small quantity of fresh blubber. This blubber, they informed us, they had obtained from their neighbours, the Cal-la-mox, who inhabit the coast to the S.E. Near one of their villages a whale had recently perished. This blubber the Indians eat and esteem it excellent food. Our party, from necessity have been obliged to subsist some length of time on dogs, have now become extreemly fond of their flesh; it is worthy of remark that, while we lived principally on the flesh of this animal we were much more healthy, strong and more fleshy then we have been since we left the buffalow country. As for my own part, I have not become reconciled to the taste of this animal as yet.

Sent Sergt. Gass and G. Shannon to the salt makers, who are on the sea coast to the S.W. of us, to enquire after Willard & Wiser, who have not yet returned. R. Field, Potts & Collins, the hunters who set out on the 28th, returned this evening after dark. They reported that they had been about 15 miles up the river which falls into Meriwethers Bay to the East of us, and had hunted the country a considerable distance to East, and had proved unsuccesfull, haveing killed one deer and a fiew fowls, barely as much as subsisted them. Capt. Lewis gave the Chief Conia a pair of satin breeches, with which he appeared much pleased.

—Captain Clark

📖 *January 4, 1806*

Comowooll and the Clatsops who visited us yesterday left us in the evening. These people, the Chinnooks and others residing in this neighbourhood, and speaking the same language, have been very friendly to us; they appear to be a mild, inoffensive people, but will pilfer if they have an opportunity to do so, where they conceive themselves not liable to detection. They are great haglers in trade, and if they conceive you anxious to purchase, will be a whole day bargaining for a handfull of roots; this I should have thought proceeded from their want of knowledge of the comparitive value of articles of merchandize and the fear of being cheated; did I not find that they invariably refuse the price first offered them and afterwards very frequently accept a smaller quantity of the same article.

In order to satisfy myself on this subject, I once offered a Chinnook my watch, two knives and a considerable quantity of beads for a small inferior sea otters skin, which I did not much want. He immediately conceived it of great value, and refused to barter, except I would double the quantity of beads; the next day, with a great deal of importunity on his part, I received the skin in exchange for a few strands of the same beads he had refused the day before. I therefore believe this trait in their character proceeds from an avaricious, all-grasping disposition. In this respect they differ from all Indians I ever became acquainted with, for their dispositions

invariably lead them to give whatever they are possessed of, no matter how usefull or valuable, for a bauble which pleases their fancy, without consulting it's usefullness or value.

—Captain Lewis

📖 *January 5, 1806. Fort Clatsop*

At 5 P.M., Willard and Wiser returned. They had not been lost as we expected. They informed us that it was not untill the fifth day after leaving the fort that they could find a convenient place for making salt; that they had at length established themselves on the sea coast about 15 miles S.W. from this, near the houses of some Clatsop and Killamuck families; that the Indians were verry friendly and had given them a considerable quantity of the blubber of the whale which perished on the coast some distance S.E. of them. It was white and not unlike the fat of pork, tho' the texture was more spongy and somewhat coarser. We had part of it cooked and found it verry palatable and tender. It resembles the beaver in flavour.

Those men also informed us that the salt makers, with their assistance, had erected a comfortable camp, killed an elk and several deer and secured a good stock of meat. They commenced the making of salt and found that they could make from 3 quarts to a gallon a day. They brought with them a specimen of the salt of about a gallon. We found it excellent, white, and fine, but not so strong as the rock salt, or that made in Kentucky or the western parts of the U. States. This salt was a great treat to most of the party, having not had any since the 20th of December. As to myself, I care but little whether I have any with my meat or not, provided the meat is fat, having from habit become entirely careless about my diet.

I determined to set out early tomorrow with two canoes and 12 men in quest of the whale, or at all events to purchase from the Indians a parcel of the blubber. For this purpose I made up a small assortment of merchandize and directed the men to hold themselves in readiness.

—Captain Clark

📖 *January 6, 1806*

Set out after an early brakfast. The last evening Shabono and his Indian woman were verry impatient to be permitted to go with me and were therefore indulged. She observed that she had traveled a long way with us to see the great waters and, now that monstrous fish was also to be seen, she thought it verry hard that she could not be permitted to see either. (She had never yet been to the ocian.)

—Captain Clark

📖 *January 6, 1806*

The Clatsops, Chinnooks, Killamucks &c. are very loquacious and inquisitive; they possess good memories and have repeated to us the names, capacities of the vessels &c of many traders and others who have visited the mouth of this river; they are generally low in stature, proportionably small, reather lighter complected and much more illy formed than the Indians of the Missouri and those of our frontier; they are generally cheerfull but never gay. With us their conversation generally turns upon the subjects of trade, smoking, eating or their women; about the latter they speak without reserve in their presence, of their every part, and of the most familiar connection. They do not hold the virtue of their women in high estimation, and will even prostitute their wives and daughters for a fishing hook or a strand of beads.

In common with other savage nations, they make their women perform every species of domestic drudgery. But in almost every species of this drudgery, the men also participate; their women are also compelled to gather roots, and assist them in taking fish, which articles form much the greatest part of their subsistence; notwithstanding the servile manner in which they treat their women, they pay much more rispect to their judgment and opinions, in many rispects, than most Indian nations; their women are permitted to speak freely before them, and sometimes appear to command with a tone of authority; they generally consult them in their traffic and act in conformity to their opinions.

I think it may be established as a general maxim that those nations treat their old people and women with most deference and rispect where they subsist principally on such articles that these can participate with the men in obtaining them; and that that part of the community are treated with least attention when the act of procuring subsistence devolves entirely on the men in the vigor of life. It appears to me that nature has been much more deficient in her filial tie than in any other of the strong affections of the human heart, and therefore think our old men, equally with our women, indebted to civilization for their ease and comfort.

Among the Siouxs, Assinniboins and others on the Missouri who subsist by hunting, it is a custom when a person of either sex becomes so old and infirm that they are unable to travel on foot from camp to camp as they roam in search of subsistence, for the children or near relations of such person to leave them without compunction or remorse; on those occasions they usually place within their reach a small peace of meat and a platter of water, telling the poor old superannuated wretch for his consolation that he or she had lived long enough, that it was time they should die and go to their relations who can afford to take care of them much better than they could.

I am informed that this custom prevails even among the Minnetares, Arwaharmays and Ricaras when attended by their old people on their hunting excursions; but, in justice to these people, I must observe that it appeared to me at their villages that they provided tolerably well for their aged persons; and several of their feasts appear to have principally for their object a contribution for their aged and infirm persons.

This day I overhauled our merchandize and dryed it by the fire, found it all damp; we have not been able to keep anything dry for many days together since we arrived in this neighbourhood; the humidity of the air has been so excessively great. Our merchandize is reduced to a mere handfull, and our comfort during our return the next year much depends on it; it is therefore almost unnecessary to add that we much regret the reduced state of this fund.

—Captain Lewis

📖 *January 7, 1806, Fort Clatsop*

Near the base of a high mountain, I found our salt makers, and with them Sergt. Gass. Geo. Shannon was out in the woods assisting Jo. Fields and Gibson to kill some meat. The salt makers had made a neat, close camp, convenient to wood, salt water, and the fresh water of the Clatsop River, which at this place was within 100 paces of the ocian. They were also situated near four houses of Clatsops and Killamucks, who, they informed me, had been verry kind and attentive to them.

I hired a young Indian to pilot me to the whale, for which service I gave him a file in hand and promised several other small articles on my return. Left Sergt. Gass and one man of my party, Warner, to make salt, and permitted Bratten to accompany me.

We proceeded on the round slippery stones under a high hill [Tillamook Head] which projected into the ocian about 4 miles further than the direction of the coast . After walking for 2 1/2 miles on the stones, My guide made a sudden halt, pointed to the top of the mountain, and uttered the word *"Pe shack"* which means bad, and made signs that we could not proceed any further on the rocks, but must pass over that mountain.

I hesitated a moment & view this emence mountain, the top of which was obscured in the clouds, and the ascent appeared to be almost perpindecular; as the small Indian path along which they had brought emence loads but a fiew hours before, led up this mountain and appeared to ascend in a sideling direction. I thought more than probable that the ascent might be tolerably easy, and therefore proceeded on.

I soon found that the path become much worse as I ascended, and at one place we were obliged to support and draw ourselves up by the bushes & roots for near 100 feet; and after about 2 hours labour and fatigue we reached the top of this high mountain, from the top of which I looked down with astonishment to behold the height which we had ascended, which appeared to be 10 or 12 hundred feet up a mountain which appeared to be almost perpendicular. Here we met 14 Indians, men and women loaded with the oil and blubber of the whale.

—*Captain Clark*

⚕ **Oregon 96** ♿

SADDLE MOUNTAIN
Saddle Mountain State Park

Location: Northwest Oregon southeast of Seaside.

Access: From U.S. Highway 26 at milepost 10 +.15 (10 miles southeast of the junction of U.S. 26 & U.S. 101 south of Seaside, 11 miles northwest of Elsie) turn north onto the paved park access road and proceed 7.1 miles to the park.

Camping Facilities: 10 park n' walk tent sites scattered about the hillside; sites are small+ to medium+, with minimal to good separation; medium to large, generally level, space for tents; fireplaces; ample firewood is available for gathering along the access road, but may be wet; water at several faucets; restrooms; gas and groceries are available in Elsie.

Day Use Facilities: Medium-sized picnic area; drinking water; restrooms; large parking lot.

Activities & Attractions: 4-mile hiking trail to the summit of Saddle Mountain.

Natural Features: Located near the base of 3283´ Saddle Mountain in the Coast Range; park vegetation consists of tall conifers and hardwoods, and some underbrush which provide adequate shelter/shade for picnic and camp sites; a small creek flows through the picnic area; elevation 1650´.

Season, Fees & Phone: Open all year, subject to weather conditions; $9.00; 10 day limit; phone c/o Fort Stevens State Park ☎(503) 861-1671.

Camp Journal: The road to the park passes through sections of superb forest. (Although some logged-off sections aren't so superb.) Many, perhaps a majority, of visitors come here to take the trail up Saddle Mountain. The trail isn't the West's best for a casual hiker: Much of the route to the summit is steep and precarious. A good hiker's efforts, however, will be rewarded with compelling views of Northwest Oregon, Southwest Washington and the Pacific Ocean.

Saddle Mountain is several miles inland and almost due east of the Expedition's salt-making camp and Tillamook Head, which was climbed by Clark and Bratton.

This and the other state parks along this section of the coast might be considered as being on a southerly 'spur' of the Lewis and Clark Trail.

📖 *January 8, 1806*

We arived on a beautifull sand shore. Found only the skeleton of this monster on the sand; the whale was already pillaged of every valuable part by the Killamuck Indians, in the vicinity of whose villages it lay on the strand where the waves and tide had driven up & left it. This skeleton measured 105 feet.

I returned to the village of 5 cabins on the creek, which I call Ecola or Whale Creek. Found the nativs busily engaged boiling the blubber, which they performed in a large, square wooden trough, by means of hot stones. The oil, when extracted, was secured in bladders and the guts of the whale; the blubber, from which the oil was only partially extracted by this process, was laid by in their cabins, in large flitches for use; those flitches they usually expose to the fire on a wooden spit, untill it is pretty well warmed through, and then eate it either alone or with roots of the rush dipped in the oil.

The Killamucks, altho' they possessed large quantities of this blubber and oil, were so penurious that they disposed of it with great reluctance, and in small quantities only; insomuch that my utmost exertions, aided by the party, with the small stock of merchandize I had taken with me, were not able to procure more blubber than about 300 lbs. and a fiew gallons of oil. Small as this stock is, I prize it highly; and thank Providence for directing the whale to us; and think Him much more kind to us than He was to Jonah, having sent this monster to be swallowed *by* us, instead of swallowing *of* us, as Jonah's did.

—*Captain Clark*

▲ Oregon Side Trip &

ECOLA
Ecola State Park

Location: Northern Oregon Coast south of Seaside.

Access: From U.S. Highway 101 at milepost 28 +.1 (at the north edge of the community of Cannon Beach) turn west onto North U.S. 101A and proceed 0.2 mile to the bottom of the hill; turn northwest (right) onto 5th St. for 0.2 mile, then north for 1.6 miles on a narrow, curving and, steep paved access road to the park.

Camping Facilities: None; nearest public campgrounds are in Oswald West State Park (walk-in tent camping only) and Fort Stevens State Park.

Day Use Facilities: Picnic area, drinking water, restrooms, medium-sized parking area, and beach access at Ecola Point and at Indian Beach.

Activities & Attractions: Ocean beaches; hiking trails; Tillamook Head National Recreation Trail passes through the park.

Natural Features: Located on the south side of Tillamook Head on the Pacific Ocean; most of the park is steep, hilly, and densely forested with stands of conifers and hardwoods over steep hillsides carpeted with ferns; rocky headlands frame the beaches; elevation varies from sea level to 200´.

Season, Fees & Phone: Open all year; daily park entry fee $5.00; park office ☎(503) 436-2844.

Camp Journal: Just the drive on the park road along the exquisitely forested hillsides is worth the trip, let alone the views of the beaches, offshore rocks, and headlands! Ecola is one of the best spots on this segment of the North Coast to watch for gray whales during their annual migrations from December to May.

The sandy beach in the vicinity of this park was where Captain Clark found the whale which had been washed ashore and whose blubber had been utilized by the Killamucks.

Oregon 97 &

OSWALD WEST
Oswald West State Park

Location: Northern Oregon Coast north of Manzanita.

Access: From U.S. Highway 101 at milepost 39 +.3 (4 miles north of Manzanita, 10 miles south of Cannon Beach) turn west off the highway into the campground parking lot.

Camping Facilities: 36 walk-in tent campsites, accessible via a somewhat steep, paved, 0.3-mile trail from the parking lot; (hand carts are available to help pack equipment up and down the trail); adequate space for medium to large tents; water at several faucets; restrooms; limited supplies and services are available in Manzanita.

Day Use Facilities: A few picnic tables are located on the edge of the forest near the parking lot; small, walk-in picnic area on the beach; drinking water; restrooms; large parking lot.

Activities & Attractions: Trail to the beach (approximately 0.7 mile) from the campground; Oregon Coast Trail extends north and south from here for a total of 64 miles along the Pacific Ocean; good views of the Cape Falcon area from the beach.

Natural Features: Located in a coastal rain forest near the Pacific Ocean; Sand Creek flows along the north side of the campground; sea level.

Season, Fees & Phone: April to October; $14.00; 10 day limit; park office ☎(503) 368-5153.

Camp Journal: The park's major recreational item of interest is its strikingly beautiful and unique campground, and the hiking trails provide plenty of exploring opportunities on the beach. "Os West" (named for an Oregon governor of the early 1900's), was one of the first parks developed in the state. Neat place.

This camp is at the southern tip of the coastal 'spur' of the Lewis and Clark Trail; it is less than a dozen miles south of Clark's Ecola Beach. If you're a tent camper traveling the Trail, this simple spot would be a terrific place to achieve a certain appreciation for the coastal wilds on which the Expedition camped so long ago.

January 8, 1806

The Clatsops, Chinnooks and others inhabiting the coast and country in this neighbourhood are excessively fond of smoking tobacco. In the act of smoking, they appear to swallow it as they draw it from the pipe, and for many draughts together you will not perceive the smoke which they take from the pipe; in the same manner also, they inhale it in their lungs untill they become surcharged with this vapour, when they puff it out to a great distance through their nostrils and mouth.

I have no doubt the smoke of the tobacco in this manner becomes much more intoxicating, and that they do possess themselves of all it's virtues in their fullest extent; they frequently give us sounding proofs of it's creating a dismorality of order in the abdomen; nor are those light matters thought indelicate in either sex, but all take the liberty of obeying the dictates of nature without reserve.

These people do not appear to know the use of spirituous liquors, they never having once asked us for it; I presume, therefore, that the traders who visit them have never indulged them with the use of it; from whatever cause this may proceed, it is a very fortunate occurrence, as well for the natives themselves, as for the quiet and safety of those whites who visit them.

—*Captain Lewis*

January 9, 1806, Fort Clatsop

The persons who usually visit the entrance of this river for the purpose of traffic or hunting, I believe are either English or Americans; the Indians inform us that they speak the same language with ourselves, and give us proofs of their veracity by repeating many words of English, as "musket", "powder", "shot", "knife", "file", "damned rascal", "son of a bitch", &c. Whether these traders are from Nootka Sound, from some other late establishment on this coast, or immediately from the U'. States or Great Britain, I am at a

loss to determine, nor can the Indians inform us.

The Indians whom I have asked in what direction the traders go when they depart from hence or arrive here, always point to the S.W., from which it is presumable that Nootka cannot be their destination; and as, from Indian information, a majority of these traders annually visit them about the beginning of April and remain with them six or seven months, they cannot come immediately from Great Britain or the U. States, the distance being too great for them to go and return in the ballance of the year. From this circumstance I am sometimes induced to believe that there is some other establishment on the coast of America, southwest of this place, of which little is but yet known to the world, or it may be perhaps on some little island in the Pacific Ocean, between the continents of Asia and America, to the southwest of us.

This traffic on the part of the whites consists in vending guns (principally old British or American muskets), powder, balls and shot, copper and brass kettles, brass teakettles and coffee pots, blankets from two to three points, scarlet and blue cloth (coarse), plates and strips of sheet copper and brass, large brass wire, knives, beeds, and tobacco, with fishing hooks, buttons, and some other small articles; also a considerable quantity of sailors clothes, as hats, coats, trousers, and shirts. For these they receive in return from the natives dressed and undressed elk skins, skins of the sea otter, common otter, beaver, common fox, spuck, and tiger cat; also dryed and pounded salmon in baskets, and a kind of bisquit which the natives make of roots, called by them *shappellel*. The natives are extreemly fond of the most common, cheap, blue and white beads, of moderate size; the blue is usually preferred to the white

—*Captain Lewis*

January 9, 1806, Fort Clatsop

Last night about 10 oClock, while smokeing with the nativs, I was allarmed by a loud, shrill voice from the cabins on the opposit side. The Indians all run immediately across to the village. My guide, who continued with me, made signs that someone's throat was cut. By enquiry, I found that one man, McNeal, was absent. I immediately sent off Sergt. N. Pryor & 4 men in quest of McNeal, who they met coming across the creek in great haste, and informed me that the people were allarmed on the opposit side at something, but what he could not tell. A man had verry friendly envited him to go and eate in his lodge; that the Indian had locked arms with him and went to a lodge in which a woman gave him some blubber; that the man envited him to another lodge to get something better, and the woman, knowing his design, held him (McNeal) by the blanket which he had around him. He, not knowing her object, freed himself and was going off, when this woman (a Chinnook, an old friend of McNeal) and another, ran out and helloed, and his pretended friend disappeared.

I immediately ordered every man to hold themselves in a state of readiness, and sent Sergt. Pryor and 4 men to know the cause of the allarm, which was found to be a premeditated plan of the pretended friend of McNeal to assassinate him for his blanket and what fiew articles he had about him, which was found out by a Chinnook woman, who allarmed the men of the village who were with me, in time to prevent the horrid act. This man was of another band, at some distance, and ran off as soon as he was discovered.

We have now to look back and shudder at the dreadful road on which we have to return, of 45 miles S.E. of Point Adams and 35 miles from Fort Clatsop. I had the blubber and oil divided among the party, and set out about sunrise and returned by the same rout we had gone out. Met several parties of men and women of the Chinnook and Clatsop Nations on their way to trade with the Killamucks for blubber and oil.

On the steep descent of the mountain, I overtook five men and six women with emence loads of the oil and blubber of the whale. Those Indians had passed by some rout by which we missed them as we went out yesterday. One of the women, in the act of getting down a steep part of the mountain, her load by some means had slipped off her back, and she was holding the load by a strap which was fastened to the mat bag in which it was in, in one hand and holding a bush by the other. As I was in front of my party, I endeavoured to relieve this woman by taking her load untill she could get to a better place a little below, and to my astonishment found the load as much as I could lift, and must exceed 100 pounds. The husband of this woman, who was below, soon came to her relief.

Those people proceeded on with us to the salt works, at which place we arived late in the evening. Found them without meat, and three of the party, J. Fields, Gibson, and Shannon,

out hunting. As I was excessively fatigued, and my party appeared verry much so, I determined to stay untill the morning and rest ourselves a little.

—*Captain Clark*

📖 *January 13, 1806*

This evening we exhausted the last of our candles, but fortunately had taken the precaution to bring with us moulds and wick, by means of which, and some elk's tallow in our possession, we do not yet consider ourselves destitute of this necessary article; the elk we have killed have a very small portion of tallow.

—*Captain Lewis*

📖 *January 14, 1806*

From the best estimate we were able to make as we descended the Columbia, we conceived that the natives inhabiting that noble stream, for some miles above the great falls to the grand rapids, inclusive, annually prepare about 30,000 lbs. of pounded salmon for market. But whether this fish is an article of commerce with the whites, or is exclusively sold to, and consumed, by the natives of the sea coast, we are at a loss to determine. The first of those positions I am disposed to credit most; but, still, I must confess that I cannot imagine what the white merchant's object can be in purchasing this fish, or where they dispose of it. And on the other hand, the Indians in this neighbourhood, as well as the Skillutes, have an abundance of dryed salmon which they take in the creeks and inlets, and I have never seen any of this pounded fish in their lodges, which I presume would have been the case if they purchased this pounded fish for their own consumption.

The Indians who prepared this dryed and pounded fish informed us that it was to trade with the whites, and showed us many articles of European manufacture which they obtained for it. It is true they obtain those articles principally for their fish, but they trade with the Skillutes for them and not immediately with the whites; the intermediate merchants and carryers, the Skillutes, may possibly consume a part of this fish themselves and dispose of the ballance of it to the natives of the sea coast, and from them obtain such articles as they again trade with the whites.

—*Captain Lewis*

📖 *January 16, 1806*

We have plenty of elk beef for the present and a little salt, our houses dry and comfortable, and having made up our minds to remain until the 1st of April, everyone appears content with his situation and his fare.

It is true that we could even travel now on our return as far as the timbered country reaches, or to the falls of the river; but further it would be madness for us to attempt to proceed untill April, as the Indians inform us that the snows lie knee deep in the plains of Columbia during the winter, and in these plains we could scarcely get as much fuel of any kind as would cook our provision as we descended the river; and even were we happily over these plains and again in the woody country at the foot of the Rocky Mountains, we could not possibly pass that immence barrier of mountains on which the snows lie in winter to the depth in many places of 20 feet.

In short, the Indians inform us that they are impracticable untill about the 1st of June, at which time even there is an abundance of snow, but a scanty subsistence may be obtained for the horses. We should not, therefore, forward ourselves on our homeward journey by reaching the Rocky Mountains earlier than the 1st of June, which we can easily effect by settng out from hence on the 1st of April.

—*Captain Lewis*

📖 *January 20, 1806*

Visited this morning by three Clatsops who remained with us all day; the object of their visit is merely to smoke the pipe. On the morning of the eighteenth we issued 6 lbs. of jerked elk per man; this evening the Sergt. reported that it was all exhausted; the six lbs. have therefore lasted two days and a half only. At this rate our seven elk will last us only 3 days longer, yet no one seems much concerned about the state of the stores; so much for habit.

We have latterly so frequently had our stock of provisions reduced to a minimum, and sometimes taken a small touch of fasting, that three days full allowance excites no concern. In those cases our skill as hunters affords us some consolation, for if there is any game of any description in our neighbourhood, we can track it up and kill it. Most of the party have become very expert with the rifle.

The Indians who visited us today understood us sufficiently to inform us that the whites did not barter for the pounded fish; that it was

purchased and consumed by the Clatsops, Chinnooks, Cathlahmahs and Skillutes. The native roots which furnish a considerable proportion of the subsistence of the Indians in our neighbourhood are those of a species of thistle, fern, and rush; the liquorice, and a small cylindric root, the top of which I have not yet seen; this last resembles the sweet potatoe very much in it's flavour and consistency.

—*Captain Lewis*

📖 *January 24, 1806*

Drewyer and Baptiste La Page returned this morning in a large canoe with Comowooll and six Clatsops. They brought two deer and the flesh of three elk & one elk's skin, having given the flesh of one other elk which they killed and three elk skins to the Indians as the price of their assistance in transporting the ballance of the meat to the fort; these elk and deer were killed near Point Adams, and the Indians carried them on their backs about six miles, before the waves were sufficiently low to permit their being taken on board their canoes. The Indians remained with us all day.

The Indians witnessed Drewyer's shooting some of those elk, which has given them a very exalted opinion of us as marksmen, and the superior excellence of our rifles compared with their guns; this may probably be of service to us, as it will deter them from any acts of hostility if they have ever meditated any such. My air gun also astonishes them very much; they cannot comprehend it's shooting so often and without powder; and think that it is great medicine which comprehends every thing that is to them incomprehensible.

—*Captain Lewis*

📖 *January 27, 1806*

Goodrich has recovered from the Louis Veneri which he contracted from an amorous contact with a Chinnook damsel. I cured him as I did Gibson last winter by the use of mercury. I cannot learn that the Indians have any simples [medicinal plants] which are sovereign specifics in the cure of this disease; and indeed, I doubt very much whether any of them have any means of effecting a perfect cure. When once this disorder is contracted by them, it continues with them during life; but always ends in decripitude, death, or premature old age; tho' from the use of certain simples, together with their diet, they support this disorder with but little inconvenience for many years, and even enjoy a tolerable share of health; particularly so among the Chippeways, who I believe to be better skilled in the use of those simples than any nation of savages in North America.

The Chippeways use a decoction of the Lobelia, and that of a species of sumac common to the Atlantic states, and to this country near and on the western side of the Rocky Mountains. These decoctions are drank freely and without limitation. The same decoctions are used in cases of the gonorrhea and are efficacious and sovereign. Notwithstanding that this disorder does exist among the Indians on the Columbia, yet it is witnessed in but few individuals, at least the males who are always sufficiently exposed to the observations or inspection of the physician. In my whole rout down this river, I did not see more than two or three with the gonorrhea and about double that number with the pox.

—*Captain Lewis*

January 29, 1806

Nothing worthy of notice occurred today. Our fare is the flesh of lean elk boiled with pure water, and a little salt. The whale blubber, which we have used very sparingly, is now exhausted. On this food I do not feel strong, but enjoy the most perfect health; a keen appetite supplies in a great degree the want of more luxurious sauces or dishes, and still renders my ordinary meals not uninteresting to me, for I find myself sometimes enquiring of the cook whether dinner or breakfast is ready.

—*Captain Lewis*

February 1, 1806

The Indians have but few axes among them, and the only tool usually employed in felling the trees or forming the canoe, carving &c, is a chisel formed of an old file about an inch or an inch and a half broad. This chissel has sometimes a large block of wood for a handle; they grasp the chisel just below the block with the right hand, holding the edge down, while with the left they take hold of the top of the block and strike back-handed against the wood with the edge of the chissel. A person would suppose that the forming of a large canoe with an instrument like this was the work of several years; but these people make them in a few weeks. They prize their canoes very highly; we have been anxious to obtain some of them for our journey up the river, but have not been able to obtain one as yet from the natives in this neighbourhood.

Today we opened and examined all our ammunition, which had been secured in leaden canisters. We found twenty seven of the best rifle powder, 4 of common rifle, three of glazed and one of the musket powder in good order, perfectly as dry as when first put in the canisters, altho' the whole of it from various accidents has been for hours under the water.

These cannisters contain four lbs. of powder each and 8 of lead. Had it not have been for that happy expedient which I devised of securing the powder by means of the lead, we should not have had a single charge of powder at this time. Three of the canisters had been accidentally bruised and cracked, one of which was carelessly stopped, and a fifth that had been penetrated with a nail, were a little damaged; these we gave to the men to make dry; however, exclusive of those five, we have an abundant stock to last us back; and we always take care to put a proportion of it in each canoe, to the end that, should one canoe or more be lost, we should still not be entirely bereft of ammunition, which is now our only hope for subsistence and defence in a rout of 4000 miles through a country exclusively inhabited by savages.

—*Captain Lewis*

February 7, 1806

This evening we had what I call an excellent supper; it consisted of a marrow bone apiece, and a brisket of boiled elk that had the appearance of a little fat on it. This, for Fort Clatsop, is living in high stile.

The small pox has destroyed a great number of the natives in this quarter. It prevailed about 4 years since among the Clatsops and destroyed several hundred of them; four of their cheifs fell victims to it's ravages. Those Clatsops are deposited in their canoes on the bay a few miles below us. I think the late ravages of the small pox may well account for the number of remains of villages which we find deserted on the river and sea coast in this quarter.

—*Captain Lewis*

February 12, 1806

This morning we were visited by a Clatsop man who brought with him three dogs as a remuneration for the elk which himself and nation had stolen from us some little time since; however, the dogs took allarm and ran off; we suffered him to remain in the fort all night.

—*Captain Lewis*

📖 *February 13, 1806*

Yesterday we completed the operation of drying the meat, and think we have a sufficient stock to last us this month. The Indians inform us that we shall have great abundance of a small fish in March, which from their description must be the herring. These people have also informed us that one Captain Moore, who sometimes touches at this place and trades with the natives of this coast, had on board of his vessel three cows; and that, when he left them, he continued his course along the N.W. coast. I think this strong circumstantial proof that there is a settlement of white persons a Nootka Sound or some point to the N.W. of us on the coast.

—*Captain Lewis*

📖 *February 14, 1806, Fort Clatsop*

I completed a map of the country through which we have been passing from the Mississippi, at the mouth of the Missouri, to this place. On the map, the Missouri, Jefferson's River, the S.E. branch of the Columbia or Lewis's River, Kooskooskee, and Columbia from the enterance of the S.E. fork to the Pacific Ocian, as well as a part of Clark's River and our track across the Rocky Mountains, are laid down by celestial observations and survey. The rivers are also connected at their sources with other rivers, agreeably to the information of the nativs, and the most probable conjecture, arising from their capacities and the relative positions of their respective enterances, which last have, with but fiew exceptions, been established by celestial observations.

We now discover that we have found the most practicable and navigable passage across the Continent of North America; it is that which we have traveled, with the exception of that part of our rout from the foot of the Falls of the Missouri, or in neighbourhood of the enterance of the Rocky Mountains, untill we arive on Clark's River at the enterance of Travellers Rest Creek. The distance between those two points would be travelled more advantageously by land, as the navigation of the Missouri above the Falls is crooked, laborious, and 521 miles distant, by which no advantage is gained, as the rout which we are compelled to travel by land from the source of Jeffersons River to the enterance of Travellers Rest Creek is 220 miles, being further by about 600 miles than that from the Falls of the Missouri to the last mentioned point (Travellers Rest Creek), and a much worse rout, if Indian information is to be relied on,

which is from the Shoshone or Snake Indians, and the Flatheads of the Columbia [Nez Percé] West of the Rocky Mountains.

From the same information, Clark's River [Bitterroot River], like that of the S.E. branch of the Columbia which heads with Jeffersons and Madisons Rivers, cannot be navigated thro' the Rocky Mountains, in consequence of falls and rapids; and as a confirmation of the fact, we discovered that there were no salmon in Clark's River, which is not the case in the S.E. branch of the Columbia, altho' it is not navigable. Added to this, the Indians of different quarters further inform us, that Clark's River runs in the direction of the Rocky Mountains for a great distance to the North before it discharges itself into the Columbia River.

From the same information, the Columbia, from the enterance of the S.E. branch to the enterance of Clark's River, is obstructed with a great number of difficult and dangerous rapids (and the place Clark's River comes out of the Rocky Mountains is a tremendous fall &c. [possibly Thompson Falls in N.W. Montana], which there is no possibility of passing the mountains either by land or water.)

Considering, therefore, the dangers and difficulties attending the navigation of the Columbia in this part, as well as the circuitous and distant rout formed by itself and that of Clark's River, we conceive that, even admitting that Clark's River, contrary to information, to be as navigable as the Columbia below it's enterance, that the tract by land over the Rocky Mountains usually travelled by the nativs from the enterance of Travellers Rest Creek to the Forks of the Kooskooske, is preferable; the same being a distance of 184 miles.

The inference, therefore, deduced from these premises are that the best and most practicable rout across the Continent is by way of the Missouri to the Falls; thence to Clark's River at the enterance of Travellers Rest Creek; from thence up Travellers Rest Creek to the forks, from whence you pursue a range of mountains which divides the waters of the two forks of this creek, and which still continues it's westwardly course on the mountains which divide the waters of the two forks of the Kookooske River to their junction; from thence to decend this river to the S.E. branch of the Columbia [Snake River], thence down that river to the Columbia, and down the latter to the Pacific Ocian.

There is a large river which falls into the Columbia on it's South side, at what point we could not learn; which passes thro' those extensive Columbian Plains from the southeast, and, as the Indians inform us, heads in the mountains South of the head of Jeffersons River and at no great distance from the Spanish settlements, Multnomah; and that that fork which heads with the River Rochejhone and waters of the Missouri passes through those extensive plains in which there is no wood, and the river crowded with rapids & falls many of which are impassable.

The other, or westerly fork, passes near a range of mountains, and is the fork on which live great numbers of Indian bands of the Shoshone or Snake Indians. This fork most probably heads with North River or the waters of California. This river may afford a practicable land communication with New Mexico by means of it's western fork. This river cannot be navigable, as an impracticable rapid is within one mile of it's enterance into the Columbia, and we are fully pursuaded that a rout by this river, if practicable at all, would lengthen the distance greatly and encounter the same difficulties in passing the Rocky Mountains with the rout by way of Travellers Rest Creek & Clark's River.

—*Captain Clark*

🐾 Whew! Clark must have a lot of time on his hands this day. Probably most of the foregoing comments are self-evident, but perhaps a bit of additiional information about the last couple of paragraphs might be helpful.

The "Multnomah" River he mentions is basically the Willamette River, which enters the Columbia at Portland, although the information Clark received was not very accurate. The Expedition didn't see that sizeable river on the way down the Columbia because of an intervening island which blocked its view from their passage, which was closer to the north bank of the main stream. The deduction that "This river cannot be navigable, as...a rapid is within one mile of its enterence" was essentially correct, owing to Willamette Falls and other swift stretches. Because of the faulty 'intelligence' handed down to Clark by numerous Indian sources, his conjectures about there being a water route to California and New Mexico weren't valid. Good try, though!

📖 *February 15, 1806*
The quadrupeds of this country from the Rocky Mountains to the Pacific Ocean are, 1st, the domestic animals, consisting of the horse and the dog only; 2ndly, the native wild animals.

The horse is confined principally to the nations inhabiting the great plains of Columbia, extending from Latitude 40° to 50°. N., and occupying the tract of country lying between the Rocky Mountains and a range [Cascade] of mountains which pass the Columbia River about the great falls or from Longitude 116 to 121 West.

In this extensive tract of principally untimbered country, so far as we have learnt, the following natives reside , viz, the Shoshone or Snake Indians, the Chopunnish, Sokulks, Cutssahnims, Chymnapums, Echelutes, Eneshuh & Chilluckkittequaws. All of whom enjoy the bennefit of that docile, generous and valuable animal, the horse; and all of them except the three last have immence numbers of them. Their horses appear to be of an excellent race; they are lofty, elegantly formed, active and durable; in short, many of them look like the fine English coursers and would make a figure in any country. Some of those horses are pied with large spots of white, irregularly scattered and intermixed with the black brown bay or some other dark colour [Appaloosas], but much the larger portion are of an uniform colour, with stars, snips and white feet, or, in this rispect, marked much like our best blooded horses in Virginia, which they resemble as well in fleetness and bottom as in form and colours.

The natives suffer them to run at large in the plains, the grass of which furnishes them with the only subsistence, their masters taking no trouble to lay in a winters store for them, but they even keep fat if not much used on the dry grass of the plains during the winter. No rain scarcely ever falls in these plains and the grass is short and but thin. The natives (except those near the R. Monts.) appear to take no pains in selecting their male horses from which they breed; in short, those of that description which I have noticed appeared much the most indifferent.

Whether the horse was originally a native of this country or not, it is out of my power to determine, as we cannot understand the language of the natives sufficiently to ask the question. At all events, the country and climate appears well adapted to this animal. Horses are said to be found wild in many parts of this extensive plain country. The several tribes of Shoshones who reside towards Mexico on the waters of the Multnomah River, or particularly one of them called Shabo-bo-ah, have also a great number of mules, which among the Indians I find are much more highly prized than horses.

An elegant horse may be purchased of the natives in this country for a few beeds or other paltry trinkets, which in the U' States would not cost more than one or two dollars. This abundance and cheapness of horses will be extreemly advantageous to those who may hereafter attempt the fur trade to the East Indies by way of the Columbia River and the Pacific Ocean. The mules in the possession of the Indians are principally stolen from the Spaniards of Mexico; they appear to be large and fine, such as we have seen. Among the Shoshones of the upper part of the S. E. fork of the Columbia, we saw several horses with Spanish brands on them, which we supposed had been stolen from the inhabitants of Mexico.

—*Captain Lewis*

February 20, 1806

This forenoon we were visited by Tah-cum, a principal Chief of the Chinnooks, and 25 men of his Nation. We had never seen this Chief before. He is a good-looking man of about 50 years of age, reather larger in stature than most of his Nation; ss he came on a friendly visit, we gave himself and party something to eat and plyed them plentifully with smoke. We gave this Cheif a small medal, with which he seemed much gratified.

In the evening at sunset we desired them to depart, as is our custom, and closed our gates. We never suffer parties of such number to remain within the fort all night; for, notwithstanding their apparent friendly disposition, their great avarice and hope of plunder might induce them to be treacherous. At all events, we determined always to be on our guard as much as the nature of our situation will permit us, and never place ourselves at the mercy of any savages. We well know that the treachery of the aborigines of America and the too great confidence of our countrymen in their sincerity and friendship has caused the destruction of many hundreds of us.

So long have our men been accustomed to a friendly intercourse with the natives, that we find it difficult to impress on their minds the necessity of always being on their guard with rispect to them. This confidence on our part we know to be the effect of a series of uninterupted friendly intercourse, but the well-known treachery of the natives by no means

entitles them to such confidence; and we must check it's growth in our own minds, as well as those of our men, by recollecting ourselves, and repeating to our men, that our preservation depends on never losing sight of this trait in their character, and being always prepared to meet it in whatever shape it may present itself

—*Captain Lewis*

February 22, 1806

We were visited today by two Clatsop women and two boys, who brought a parcel of excellent hats made of cedar bark and ornamented with beargrass. Two of these hats had been made by measures which Capt. Clark and myself had given one of the women some time since, with a request to make each of us a hat; they fit us very well, and are in the form we desired them. We purchased all their hats and distributed them among the party. The woodwork and sculpture of these people, as well as these hats and their waterproof baskets, evince an ingenuity by no means common among the aborigines of America.

In the evening, they returned to their village and Drewyer accompanied them in their canoe in order to get the dogs which the Clatsops have agreed to give us in payment for the elk they stole from us some weeks since. These women informed us that the small fish began to run, which we suppose to be herring from their description. They also informed us that their Chief Conia or Comowooll, had gone up the Columbia to the valley in order to purchase wappato, a part of which he intended trading with us on his return.

Our sick, consisting of Gibson, Bratton, Sergt. Ordway, Willard and McNeal, are all on the recovery. We have not had as many sick at any one time since we left Wood River. The general complaint seams to be colds and fevers, something I believe of the influenza.

—*Captain Lewis*

February 25, 1806

This evening we were visited by Comowooll the Clatsop Chief and 12 men, women & children of his Nation. The Chief and his party had brought for sale a sea otter skin, some hats, sturgeon, and a species of small fish which now begin to run, and are taken in great quantities in the Columbia R. about 40 miles above us by means of skimming or scooping nets. On this page I have drawn the likeness of them as large as life; it is as perfect as I can make it with my pen and will serve to give a general idea of the fish. The rays of the fins are boney but not sharp, tho' somewhat pointed. All the fins are of a white colour. The back is of a blueish dusky colour, and that of the lower part of the sides and belly is of a silvery white. No spots on any part. It has no teeth. The scales of this little fish are so small and thin that, without minute inspection, you would suppose they had none. They are filled with roes of a pure white colour and have scarcely any perceptable alimentary duct. The bones are so soft and fine that they form no obstruction in eating this fish

I found them best when cooked in Indian stile, which is by roasting a number of them together on a wooden spit without any previous preparation whatever. They are so fat that they require no additional sauce, and I think them superior to any fish I ever tasted, even more delicate and luscious than the white fish of the Great Lakes, which have heretofore formed my standard of excellence among the fishes. I have heard the fresh anchovey much extolled, but I hope I shall be pardoned for believing this quite as good.

—*Captain Lewis*

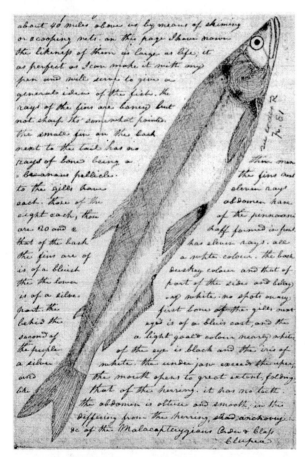

Lewis's rendition of the candlefish or eulachon

The fish described by Lewis is the candlefish, or the Chinook name, *eulachon*. It is related to the smelt, and arrived in overwhelming numbers in the Columbia River during brief periods. To the Indians, the *eulachon*'s importance as a food source and as a trade item was second only to the salmon.

For the next several weeks, each day's entry of both Lewis and Clark Journals consists mostly of routine remarks relating to the activities of hunting parties, visits of Indians, caring for the infirmed, and pages of detailed information relating to the flora and fauna of the Pacific Northwest

📖 *March 15, 1806*

This morning at 11 oClock the hunters arrived, having killed four elk only. Labiche, it seems, was the only hunter who fell in with the elk; and having by some accident lost the fore sight of his gun, shot a great number of times but killed only the number mentioned. As the elk were scattered, we sent two parties for them; they returned in the evening with four skins and the flesh of three elk, that of one of them having become putrid from the liver and pluck having been carelessly left in the animal all night.

We were visited this afternoon by Delashshelwilt, a Chinnook Chief, his wife and six women of his Nation which the Old Bawd, his wife, had brought for market. This was the same party that had communicated the venereal to so many of our party in November last, and of which they have finally recovered.

I therefore gave the men a particular charge with rispect to them, which they promised me to observe. Late this evening we were also visited by Catel, a Clatsop man, and his family. He brought a canoe and a sea otter skin for sale, neither of which we purchased this evening. The Clatsops who had brought a canoe for sale last evening left us early this morning.

—*Captain Lewis*

📖 *March 16, 1806*

The Indians remained with us all day, but would not dispose of their canoes at a price which it was in our power to give, consistently with the state of the stock of our merchandize. Two handkerchiefs would now contain all the small articles of merchandize which we possess; the ballance of the stock consists of 6 blue robes, one scarlet do., one unifom coat and hat. On this stock we have wholly to depend for the purchase of horses and such portion of our subsistence from the Indians as it will be in our powers to obtain.

—Captain Lewis

📖 *March 17, 1806*

Catel and his family left us this morning. Old Delashelwilt and his women still remain. They have formed a camp near the fort and seem to be determined to lay close seige to us, but I believe, notwithstanding every effort of their winning graces, the men have preserved their constancy to the vow of celibacy which they made on this occasion to Capt. C. and myself. We have had our perogues prepared for our departure, and shall set out as soon as the weather will permit.

Drewyer returned late this evening from the Cathlahmahs with our canoe, which Sergt. Pryor had left some days since, and also a canoe which he had purchased from those people. For this canoe he gave my uniform laced coat and nearly half a carrot of tobacco. It seems that nothing except this coat would induce them to dispose of a canoe, which, in their mode of traffic, is an article of the greatest value except a wife, with whom it is equal, and is generally given in exchange to the father for his daughter. I think that the U' States are indebted to me another uniform coat, for that of which I disposed on this occasion was but little worn.

—Captain Lewis

📖 *March 18, 1806*

Several of the men are complaining of being unwell. It is truly unfortunate that they should be sick at the moment of our departure. We directed Sergt. Pryor to prepare the two canoes which Drewyer brought last evening for his mess. Comowooll and two Cathlahmahs visited us today; we suffered them to remain all night.

This morning we gave Delashelwilt a certificate of his good deportment, &c., and also a list of our names, after which we dispatched him to his village with his female band. These lists of our names we have given to several of the natives, and also pasted up a copy in our room. The object of these lists we stated in the preamble of the same, as follows:

"The object of this list is that, through the medium of some civilized person who may see the same, it may be known to the informed world that the party consisting of the persons whose names are hereunto annexed, and who were sent out by the government of the U'. States in May 1804 to explore the interior of the continent of North America, did penetrate the same by way of the Missouri and Columbia Rivers, to the discharge of the latter into the Pacific Ocean, where they arrived on the 14th of November, 1805, and from whence they departed in March, 1806, on their return to the United States by the same rout they had come out."

On the back of some of these lists we added a sketch of the connection of the upper branches of the Missouri with those of the Columbia, particularly of it's main S.E. branch, on which we also delineated the track we had come out and that we meant to pursue on our return where the same happened to vary. There seemed so many chances against our government ever obtaining a regular report through the medium of the savages and the traders of this coast, that we declined making any. Our party are also too small to think of leaving any of them to return to the U'. States by sea, particularly as we shall be necessarily divided into three or four parties on our return in order to accomplish the objects we have in view, and at any rate, we shall reach the United States, in all human probability, much earlier than a man could, who must in the event of his being left here, depend for his passage to the United States on the traders of the coast who may not return immediately to the U'. States, or if they should, might probably spend the next summer in trading with the natives before they would set out on their return.

—Captain Lewis

📖 *March 19, 1806*

It continued to rain and hail today in such manner that nothing further could be done to the canoes. We gave Commorwool, alias Cania, a certificate of his good conduct and the friendly intercourse which he has maintained with us during our residence at this place.

The Killamucks, Clatsops, Chinnooks, Cathlahmahs and Wac-ki-a-cums resemble each other as well in their persons and dress as in their habits and manners. Their complexion is not remarkable, being the usual copper brown of most of the tribes of North America. They are low in stature, reather diminutive, and illy shapen, possessing thick, broad, flat feet, thick ankles, crooked legs wide mouths, thick lips, nose moderately large, fleshey, wide at the extremity with large nostrils, black eyes and black, coarse hair. Their eyes are sometimes of a dark yellowish brown, the pupil black.

The most remarkable trait in their physiognomy is the peculiar flatness and width of forehead, which they artificially obtain by compressing the head between two boards while in a state of infancy, and from which it never afterwards perfectly recovers. This is a custom among all the nations we have met with West of the Rocky Mountains. I have observed the heads of many infants, after this singular bandage had been dismissed, or about the age of 10 or eleven months, that were not more than two inches thick about the upper edge of the forehead, and reather thinner still higher. From the top of the head to the extremity of the nose is one straight line. This is done in order to give a greater width to the forehead, which they much admire. This process seems to be continued longer with their female than their male children, and neither appear to suffer any pain from the operation. It is from this peculiar form of the head that the nations East of the Rocky Mountains call all the nations on this side, except the Aliahtans or Snake Indians, by the generic name of "Flat heads". I think myself that the prevalence of this custom is a strong proof that those nations having originally proceeded from the same stock.

The nations of this neighbourhood wear their hair loosely flowing on the back and shoulders; both men and women divide it in the center of the crown in front and throw it back behind the ear on each side. They are fond of combs and use them when they can obtain them; and even without the aid of a comb, keep their hair in better order than many nations who are in other rispects much more civilized than themselves.

The large or apparently swollen legs, particularly observable in the women, are obtained in a great measure by tying a cord tight around the ankle. Their method of squatting or resting themselves on their hams, which they seem from habit to prefer to sitting, no doubt contributes much to this deformity of the legs by preventing free circulation of the blood.

The dress of the man consists of a small robe, which reaches about as low as the middle of the thigh, and is attached with a string across the breast, and is at pleasure turned from side to side as they may have occasion to disencumber the right or left arm from the robe entirely, or when they have occasion for both hands; the fixture of the robe is in front, with it's corners loosly hanging over their arms. A mat is sometimes temporarily thrown over the sholders to protect them from rain. They have no other article of clothing whatever, neither winter nor summer. And every part except the sholders and back is exposed to view. They are very fond of the dress of the whites, which they wear in a similar manner when they can obtain them, except the shoe, which I have never seen worn by any of them.

The dress of the women consists of a robe, tissue, and sometimes, when the weather is uncommonly cold, a vest. Their robe is much smaller than that of the men, never reaching lower than the waist, nor extending in front sufficiently for to cover the body. It is, like that of the men, confined across the breast with a string and hangs loosely over the sholders and back. The most esteemed and valuable of these robes are made of strips of the skins of the sea otter, net together with the bark of the white cedar or silk-grass. These strips are first twisted and laid parallel with each other a little distance assunder, and then net or wove together in such a manner that the fur appears equally on both sides, and unites between the strands. It makes a warm and soft covering. Other robes are formed in a similar manner of the skin of the raccoon, beaver &c.

The vest is always formed in the manner first described of their robes and covers the body from the armpits to the waist, and is confined behind, and destitute of straps over the sholder to keep it up. When this vest is worn, the breast of the woman is concealed. But without it, which is almost always the case, they are exposed; and from the habit of remaining loose and unsuspended, grow to great length, particularly in aged women, in many of whom I have seen the bubby reach as low as the waist. The garment which occupys the waist, and from thence as low as nearly to the knee before and the ham behind, cannot properly be denominated a petticoat, in the common acceptation of that term; it is a tissue of white cedar bark, bruised or broken into small shreds, which are interwoven in the middle by means of several cords of the same materials, which serve as well for a girdle as to hold in place the shreds of bark which form the tissue, and which shreds confined in the middle hang with their ends pendulous from the waist, the whole being of sufficient thickness when the female stands erect to conceal those parts usually covered from familiar view; but when she stoops or places herself in many other attitudes, this battery of Venus is not altogether impervious to the inquisitive and penetrating eye of the amorite.

The favorite ornament of both sexes are the common coarse blue and white beads which the men wear tightly wound around their wrists and ankles many times untill they obtain the width of three or more inches. They also wear them in large rolls loosly around the neck, or pendulous from the cartilage of the nose or rims of the ears, which are perforated for the purpose. The women wear them in a similiar manner, except in the nose, which they never perforate. They are also fond of a species of wampum which is furnished them by a trader whom they call Swipton. It seems to be the native form of the shell without any preparation. The men sometimes wear collars of bears claws, and the women and children the tusks of the elk variously arranged on their necks, arms &c. Both males and females wear bracelets on their wrists of copper, brass or iron in various forms.

—*Captain Lewis*

📖 *March 20, 1806*

It continued to rain and blow so violently today that nothing could be done towards forwarding our departure. We have yet several days provision on hand, which we hope will be sufficient to subsist us during the time we are compelled by the weather to remain at this place.

Altho' we have not fared sumptuously this winter and spring at Fort Clatsop, we have lived quite as comfortably as we had any reason to expect we should; and have accomplished every object which induced our remaining at this place, except that of meeting with the traders who visit the entrance of this river. Our salt will be very sufficient to last us to the Missouri, where we have a stock in store. It would have been very fortunate for us had some of those traders arrived previous to our departure from hence, as we should then have had it in our power to obtain an addition to our stock of merchandize, which would have made our homeward-bound journey much more comfortable.

—*Captain Lewis*

Ascending the Columbia 1806

Columbia River Gorge National Scenic Area

X *Fort Clatsop to Beacon Rock*

📖 *March 23, 1806*

The rain ceased and it became fair about Meridian, at which time we loaded our canoes, & at 1 P.M. left Fort Clatsop on our homeward bound journey. At this place we had wintered and remained from the 7th of December, 1805, to this day, and have lived as well as we had any right to expect, and we can say that we were never one day without 3 meals of some kind a day, either pore elk meat or roots, notwithstanding the repeated fall of rain which has fallen constantly since we passed the long narrows of November last. Indeed, we have had only a fiew days fair weather since that time. Soon after we had set out from Fort Clatsop, we were met by Delashelwilt and 8 men of the Chinnook and Delashelwilt's wife, the Old Bawd, and his six girls. They had a canoe, a sea otter skin, dryed fish, and hats for sale. We purchased a sea otter skin, and proceeded on.

—*Captain Clark*

📖 *March 29, 1806*

We set out early this morning and proceeded along the side of Deer Island; halted at 10 A.M. near it's upper point and breakfasted. After breakfast we proceeded on, and at the distance of 14 miles from our encampment of last night we passed a large inlet. This inlet or arm of the river extends itself South 10 or 12 miles to the hills on that side of the river and passes out of the Columbia about 20 miles above; the large island thus formed we call Wappato Island.

—*Captain Lewis*

In the above paragraph "Deer Island" retains the same name today; it's along the south-west bank of the Columbia just offshore of Columbia City, Oregon. "Wappato Island", by far the largest landmass wholly within the river, is now named Sauvie Island. The island's southern tip extends into the mouth of the Willamette River at Portland. Lewis estimated that Wappato (now Sauvie) Island was 20 miles long and 5-10 miles wide.

Early in the afternoon of March 30th, they passed the vicinity of today's downtown Portland.

▲ **Oregon Side Trip** &

LEWIS AND CLARK
Lewis and Clark State Park

Location: Northern Oregon border east of Troutdale.

Access: From Interstate 84 Exit 18 on the east edge of Troutdale, turn south onto Columbia River Scenic Highway, U.S. 30, and proceed 0.25 mile; turn east (left) into the park..

Camping Facilities: None; nearest public campground is in Ainsworth State Park.

Day Use Facilities: Large picnic area; drinking water; restrooms; large parking lot.

Activities & Attractions: Swimming, wading; tubing, floating, canoeing; fishing.

Natural Features: Located on a grassy flat well-sheltered by large hardwoods, at the west edge of the Columbia River Gorge; the Sandy River flows past the park, on the opposite side of U.S. 30; elevation 50´.

Season, Fees & Phone: Open all year; phone c/o Rooster Rock State Park ☎ (541) 695-2261.

Camp Journal: Although it doesn't offer camping, this quick n' easy swing off the ol' Interstate offers a convenient spot to gather your wits about you, either before or after the mad dash past Portland. Would the distinguished explorers of the Western Wilderness, whose names appear on the signboard, approve of this park and what's become of the south bank of the Columbia?

📖 *March 31, 1806*

We continued our rout along the North side of the river, passed Diamond Island and Whitebrant Island, to the lower point of a handsome prarie opposite the upper entrance of Quicksand River; here we encamped, having traveled 25 miles today.

We determined to remain at our present camp a day or two for the purposes of examining Quicksand River, making celestial observations, and procuring some meat to serve us as far as the falls or through the western mountains, where we found game scarce as we descended.

—Captain Lewis

🌿 In the preceeding entry, "Diamond Island" is essentially the presently named Government Island; "Quicksand River" is now Sandy River; both are northeast of metro Portland. The Expedition's camp, at which they were to spend the following five days, was near the mouth of Washington State's Washougal River.

📖 *April 1, 1806*

We were visited by several canoes of natives in the course of the day, most of whom were decending the river with their women and children. They informed us that they resided at the great rapids [at The Dalles] and that their relations at that place were much strained at that place for want of food; that they had consumed their winter store of dried fish and that they did not expect the salmon to arrive untill the full of the next moon, which happens on the 2d of May.

This information gave us much uneasiness with rispect to our future means of susbsistence. above the falls or through the plains from thence to the Chopunnish [Nez Percé] there are no deer, antelope nor elk on which we can depend for subsistence; their horses are very poor most probably at this season, and if they have no fish their dogs must be in the same situation.

Under these circumstances there seems to be but a gloomy prospect for subsistence on any

terms; we therefore took it into serious consideration what measures we were to pursue on this occasion. It was at once deemed inexpedient to wait the arrival of the salmon, as that would detain us so large a portion of the season that it is probable we should not reach the United States before the ice would close the Missouri; or at all events would hazard our horses which we left in charge of the Chopunnish who informed us they intended passing the Rocky Mountains to the Missouri as early as the season would permit them, which is as we believe about the begining of May. Should these people leave their situation near Kooskooske before our arrival, we may probably find much difficulty in recovering our horses, without which there will be little possibility of repassing the mountains. We are therefore determined to loose as little time as possible in getting to the Chopunnish Village.

I purchased a canoe from an Indian today for which I gave him six fathoms of wampum beads; he seemed satisfied with his bargain and departed in another canoe, but shortly after returned and canceled the bargain, took his canoe and returned the beads. This is frequently the case in their method of trading and is deemed fair by them.

—Captain Lewis

📖 *April 2, 1806*

This morning we came to a resolution to remain at our present encampment, or somewhere in this neighbourhood, untill we had obtained as much dryed meat as would be necessary for our voyage as as far as the Chopunnish; to exchange our perogues for canoes with the natives on our way to the great falls of the Columbia, or purchase such canoes from them for elk skins and merchandize as would answer our purposes. These canoes we intend exchanging with the natives of the plains for horses as we proceed, untill we obtain as many as will enable us to travel altogether by land.

At some convenient point, perhaps at the entrance of the S.E. branch of the Columbia [Snake River], we propose sending a party of four or five men ahead to collect our horses, that they may be in readiness for us by our arrival at the Chopunnish; calculating by thus acquiring a large stock of horses, we shall not only secure the means of transporting our baggage over the mountains, but that we will also have provided the means of subsisting; for we now view the horses as our only certain resource for food; nor do we look forward to it with any detestation or horror, so soon is the mind which is occupied with any interesting object, reconciled to it's situation.

We now informed the party of our intention of laying in a store of meat at this place, and immediately dispatched two parties consisting of nine men to the opposite side of the river. We also sent out three others on this side, and those who remained in camp were employed in collecting wood, making a scaffoald and cutting up the meat in order to dry it.

—*Captain Lewis*

April 2, 1806

This morning we informed the party of our intention to lay in a store of meat at this place. About that time, several canoes of the nativs arived at our camp, among others two from below with eight men of the Sha-ha-la Nation. Those men informed us that they reside on the opposit side of the Columbia near some pine trees which they pointed to, in the bottom South of the Diamond Island. They singled out two young men who, they informed us, lived at the falls of a large river which discharges itself into the Columbia on it's South side, some miles below us.

We readily prevailed on them to give us a sketch of this river, which they drew on a mat with a coal. It appeared that this river, which they call Mult-no-mah [today's Willamette], discharged itself behind the island we call the Image Canoe Island, and, as we had left this island to the South in descending & ascending the river, we had never seen it. They informed us that it was a large river, and runs a considerable distance to the South between the mountains.

I determined to take a small party and return to this river and examine it's size, and collect as much information of the nativs on it or near it's enterance into the Columbia of it's extent; the country which it waters; and the nativs who inhabit it's banks, &c. I took with me six men: Thompson, J. Potts, Peter Cruzat, P. Wiser, T. P. Howard, Joseph Whitehouse, & my man York, in a large canoe, with an Indian whome I hired for a sun glass to accompany me as a pilot.

At 11:30 A.M., I set out and had not proceeded far, ere I saw 4 large canoes, at some distance above, descending and bending their course toward our camp, which at this time is verry weak, Capt. Lewis having only 10 men with him. I hesitated for a moment whether it would not be advisable for me to return and delay untill a part of our hunters

should return to add more strength to our camp; but on a second reflection, and reverting to the precautions always taken by my friend Capt. Lewis on those occasions, banished all apprehensions, and I proceeded on down.

At 3 P.M. I landed at a large double house of the Ne-er-che-ki-oo tribe of the Sha-ha-la Nation. I entered one of the rooms of this house and offered several articles to the nativs in exchange for wappato. They were sulky, and they positively refused to sell any.

I had a small piece of port-fire match in my pocket, off of which I cut a piece one inch in length & put it into the fire, and took out my pocket compass and sat myself down on a mat on one side of the fire, and also showed a magnet, which was in the top of my ink stand. The port-fire caught and burned vehemently, which changed the colour of the fire. With the magnet I turned the needle of the compass about verry briskly, which astonished and allarmed these nativs, and they laid several parcels of wappato at my feet, & begged of me to take out the bad fire; to this I consented. At this moment, the match being exhausted was of course extinguished, and I put up the magnet, &c. This measure allarmed them so much that the womin and children took shelter in their beds, and behind the men. All this time, a very old blind man was speaking with great vehemence, apparently imploring his god.

I lit my pipe and gave them a smoke, & gave the womin the full value of the roots which they had put at my feet. They appeared somewhat pacified, and I left them and proceeded on along the South side of Image Canoe Island, which I found to be two islands [present Hayden and Tomahawk Islands]. At the distance of thirteen miles below the last village and at the place I had supposed was the lower point of Image Canoe Island, I entered this river which the nativs had informed us of, called Mult-no-mah River, so called by the nativs from a Nation who reside on Wappato Island a little below the enterance of this river. Multnomah discharges itself in the Columbia on the S.E., and may be justly said to be 1/4 the size of that noble river. From the enterance of the river, I can plainly see Mt. Jefferson, which is high and covered with snow S.E., Mt. Hood East, Mt. St. Helens and a high humped mountain [Mount Adams] to the East of Mt. St. Helens.

—*Captain Clark*

📖 *April 3, 1806*

I set out and proceeded up a short distance and attempted to fathom the river with my cord of 5 fathoms, but could find no bottom. The mist was so thick that I could see but a short distance up this river. When I left it, it was bending to the East of S.E.; being perfectly satisfied of the size and magnitude of this great river which must water that vast tract of country between the western range of mountains and those on the sea coast, and as far South as the waters of California about Latd. 37° North, I determined to return.

At 7 oclock A.M. set out on my return. The men exerted themselves and we arived at the Neerchokioo house in which the nativs were so illy disposed yesterday, at 11 A.M. I prevailed on an old man to draw me a sketch of the Multnomah River and give me the names of the nations residing on it, which he readily done, and gave me the names of 4 nations who reside on this river, two of them very numerous. The enterance of Multnomah river is 142 miles up the Columbia River from it's enterance into the Pacific Ocian.

I purchased 5 dogs of those people, for the use of their oil on the plains; and at 4 P.M. left the village and proceeded on to camp.

—*Captain Clark*

📖 *April 6, 1806*

This morning we had the dryed meat secured in skins and the canoes loaded; we took breakfast and departed at 9 A.M. We continued up the N. side of the river nearly to the place at which we had encamped on the 2nd of Nov. From the appearance of a rock near which we were encamped on the 2nd of November last, I could judge better of the rise of the water than I could at any point below. I think the flood of this spring has been about 12 feet higher than it was at that time; the river is here about 1 1/2 miles wide; it's general width from the Beacon Rock, which may be esteemed the head of tide water, to the marshy islands is from one to 2 miles, tho' in many places it is still wider. It is only in the fall of the year, when the river is low, that the tides are perceptable as high as the Beacon Rock. This remarkable rock, which stands on the North shore of the river, is unconnected with the hills and rises to the height of seven hundred feet; it has some timber on it's northern side; the southern is a precipice of it's whole height. It rises to a very sharp point and is visible for 20 miles below on the river.

—*Captain Lewis*

🦫 The party spent the next two days in this location near Beacon Rock, hunting and waiting for a break in the weather.

⛺ **Oregon 98** ♿

AINSWORTH
Ainsworth State Park

Location: Northern Oregon border east of Portland.

Access: From Interstate 84 Exit 35 (9 miles west of Cascade Locks, 18 miles east of Troutdale), turn south, then west, onto the Columbia River Scenic Highway, U.S. 30; proceed west 0.5 mile to the campground entrance, on the south (left) side of the highway.

Camping Facilities: 45 campsites with full hookups in 2 loops; sites are generally medium-sized, with fair to good separation; parking pads are paved, and many are pull-throughs long enough for very large rv's; some additional leveling may be required; adequate space for a small to medium sized tent in most sites; fireplaces; b-y-o firewood; water at sites; restrooms with showers; paved driveways; limited supplies in Cascade Locks; adequate supplies and services are available in Troutdale and Hood River.

Day Use Facilities: 2 small, roadside picnic areas; drinking water; restrooms; small parking areas.

Activities & Attractions: A 4-mile section of the Columbia Gorge Trail links Ainsworth to John Yeon State Park, east of here; Horsetail Falls (176´ high) is a half-mile west of the campground on the Scenic Highway.

Natural Features: Located on a forested slope a short distance from the south bank of the Columbia River, in the Columbia Gorge (although there is no river access from the park); campground vegetation consists of mown grass, medium-height conifers, and tall hardwoods; elevation 100´.

Season, Fees & Phone: April to October; $20.00; 10 day limit; phone c/o Rooster Rock State Park ☎ (541) 695-2261.

Camp Journal: John Yeon State Park, mentioned above, is a small natural area on the south slopes of the Gorge. Trails lead up the densely forested slopes to Elowah Falls (0.8 mile) and Upper McCord Creek Falls (1.1 miles). Beacon Rock, a celebrated Columbia River landmark mentioned as far back in recorded history as the Lewis and Clark Journals, can be viewed from Yeon's trailhead and parking lot.

▲ *Beacon Rock to the Great Falls*

📖 *April 9, 1806*

At 2 oClock P.M. we set out and passed under the Beacon Rock on the North side of two small islands. We arived at the first rapid at the head of Strawberry Island. As we could not pass with the large canoes up the N.W. side for the rocks, the wind high and a rainey disagreeable evening. Our smallest canoe being too low to cross through the high waves, we sent her up on the N W. side with Drewyer and the two Fields and crossed into the sluce of a large high Island separated from the S.E. side by a narrow channel. In this channel we found a good harbour and encamped on the lower side. evening wet & disagreeable.
—*Captain Clark*

🏕 **Oregon 99** ♿

EAGLE CREEK
Mount Hood National Forest

Location: Northern Oregon border west of Hood River.

Access: From Interstate 84 eastbound, take Exit 41 (3 miles west of Cascade Locks, 24 miles east of Troutdale); proceed east 0.2 mile on the off-ramp to the fish hatchery; turn south (right) into the recreation area entrance, then east (left) on a fairly steep, paved road for 0.4 mile to the campground. (Note: Exit 41 is an eastbound exit only; if westbound, take Exit 44 at Cascade Locks and proceed 3 miles west on a frontage road to the recreation area.)

Camping Facilities: 19 campsites; most sites are medium-sized and moderately well separated; parking pads are paved, fairly level, medium-length straight-ins; adequate space for medium-sized tents in most sites; fireplaces, plus a few barbecue grills; a small quantity of firewood is available for gathering in the vicinity, b-y-o is suggested; water at several faucets; restrooms; paved driveway; limited supplies and services are available in Cascade Locks.

Day Use Facilities: Small parking area.

Activities & Attractions: Shady Glen Interpretive Trail leads off from an associated day use area; suspension bridge over the creek; Eagle Creek Trailhead, 0.5 mile south.

Natural Features: Located on a densely forested hill overlooking the Columbia River; campground vegetation consists of alder, maple, Douglas fir, and ferns; Eagle Creek enters the Columbia River below the campground, a short distance to the north; elevation 200´.

Season, Fees & Phone: Late-May to October; $12.00; 7 day limit; Columbia Gorge Ranger District ☎ (541) 695-2276.

Camp Journal: Eagle Creek is an historic campground of the first order of magnitude. Set your WayBack™ Time Machine to the year *1915* and you'll see Eagle Creek Campground being built. It is considered to be the *first national forest public campground* constructed in the United States. Want another 'first'? The restrooms here were the first with flusheroos installed in a Forest Service campground. Neat, huh? A number of the campsites have very impressive views of the Columbia Gorge.

📖 *April 10, 1806*

At 6 A M we set out and proceeded to the lower point of the island from whence we were compelled to draw our canoes up a rapid for about 1/4 mile, which we soon performed. In crossing the river which at this place is not more than 400 yards wide, we fell down a great distance owing to the rapidity of the current. We continued up on the N. side of the river with great difficulty, in consequence of the rapidity of the current and the large rocks which form this shore; the South side of the river is impassable. As we had but one suffecent toe rope and were obliged to employ the cord in getting on our canoes the greater part of the way, we could only take them one at a time, which retarded our progress very much.

By evening we arived at the portage on the N. side, where we landed and conveyed our baggage to the top of the hill about 200 paces distant, where we formed a camp. We had the canoes drawn on shore and secured. The small canoe got loose from the hunters and went adrift with a tin cup & a tomahawk in her; the Indians caught her at the last village and brought her up this evening, for which we gave them two knives; the canoe overset and lost the articles which were in her.
—*Captain Clark*

📖 *April 11, 1806*

As the tents and skins which covered both our men and baggage were wet with the rain which fell last evening, and as it continued still raining this morning, we concluded to take our canoes first to the head of the rapids, hoping that by evening the rain would cease and afford us a fair afternoon to take our baggage over the portage. This portage is two thousand eight hundred yards along a narrow, rough, and slippery road. The duty of getting the canoes above the rapid was, by mutual consent, confided to my friend Capt. C., who took with him for that purpose all the party except Bratton, who is yet so weak he is unable to work, three others who were lamed by various accidents, and one other to cook for the party.

A few men were absolutely necessary, at any rate, to guard our baggage from the Wah-clel-lahs, who crowded about our camp in considerable numbers. These are the greatest thieves and scoundrels we have met with. By the evening, Capt. C. took 4 of our canoes above the rapids, tho' with much difficulty and labour. The canoes were much damaged by being driven against the rocks in spite of every precaution which could be taken to prevent it. The men complained of being so much fatigued in the evening that we postponed taking up our 5th canoe untill tomorrow.

These rapids are much worse than they were in the fall when we passed them. At that time there were only three difficult points within seven miles. At present the whole distance is extreemly difficult of ascent, and it would be impracticable to descend except by letting down the empty vessels by a cord, and even then the risk would be greater than in taking them up by the same means. The water appears to be considerably upwards of 20 feet higher than when we descended the river. The distance by way of the river between the points of the portage is 3 miles.

Many of the natives crowded about the bank of the rivers where the men were engaged in taking up the canoes. One of them had the insolence to cast stones down the bank at two of the men who happened to be a little detached from the party at the time. On the return of the party in the evening from the head of the rapids, they met with many of the natives on the road, who seemed but illy disposed. Two of these fellows met with Jo. Shields, who had delayed some time in purchasing a dog and was a considerable distance behind the party on their return with Capt. C.. They attempted to take the dog from

him and pushed him out of the road. He had nothing to defend himself with, except a large knife which he drew with an intention of putting one or both of them to death before they could get themselves in readiness to use their arrows; but, discovering his design, they declined the combat and instantly fled through the woods.

Three of this same tribe of villains, the Wah-clel-lahs, stole my dog this evening, and took him toward their village. I was shortly afterward informed of this transgression by an Indian who spoke the Clatsop language (some of which we had learned from them during the winter), and sent three men in pursuit of the thieves with orders, if they made the least resistance or difficulty in surrendering the dog, to fire on them. They overtook these fellows, or reather came within sight of them, at the distance of about 2 miles. The Indians, discovering the party in pursuit of them, left the dog and fled. They also stole an ax from us, but scarcely had it in their possession before Thompson detected them and wrested it from them.

We ordered the sentinel to keep them out of camp, and informed them by signs that if they made any further attempts to steal our property, or insulted our men, we should put them to instant death. A Cheif of the Wah-clel-lah tribe informed us that there were two very bad men among the Wah-clel-lahs who had been the principal actors in these scenes of outrage of which we complained, and that it was not the wish of the Nation by any means to displease us. We told him that we hoped it might be the case, but we should certainly be as good as our word if they persisted in their insolence. I am convinced that no other consideration but our number at this moment protects us. The Cheif appeared mortified at the conduct of his people, and seemed friendly disposed toward us. As he appeared to be a man of consideration, and we had reason to believe much rispected by the neighbouring tribes, we thought it well to bestow a medal of small size upon him.

The Cheif had in his possession a very good pipe tomahawk, which he informed us he had received as a present from a trader who visited him last winter over land, pointing to the N.W., whom he called Swippeton. He was pleased with the tommahawk of Capt.C. in consequence of it's having a brass bowl, and Capt. C. gratified him by an exchange. As a further proof of his being esteemed by this white trader, he gave us a well baked sailor's bisquit, which he also informed us he had received from Swippeton.

From these evidences, I have no doubt but the traders who winter in some of the inlets to the N. of us visit this part of the Columbia by land at certain seasons, most probably when they are confined to their winter harbour. And if so, some of those inlets are probably at no great distance from this place, as there seems to be but little inducement to entice the trader hither from any considerable distance, particularly as the difficulty in traveling on the borders of this mountainous country must be great at that season; as the natives informed me, their snows were frequently breast deep. I observe snow shoes in all the lodges of the natives above the Columbian Valley. I hope that the friendly interposition of this Chief may prevent our being compelled to use some violence with these people; our men seem well disposed to kill a few of them. We keep ourselves perefectly on our guard.

—*Captain Lewis*

📖 *April 12, 1806*

It rained the greater part of last night and still continued to rain this morning. I therefore determined to take up the remaining perogue this morning, for which purpose I took with me every man that could be of any service. A small distance above our camp there is one of the most difficult parts of the rapid. At this place the current sets with great violence against a projecting rock. In hauling the perogue arround this point, the bow, unfortunately took the current at too great a distance from the rock; she turned her side to the stream and the utmost exertions of all the party were unable to resist the force with which she was driven by the current. They were compelled to let loose the cord and, of course, both perogue and cord went adrift with the stream. The loss of this perogue will, I fear, compel us to purchase one or more canoes of the Indians at an extravagant price.

After breakfast, all hands were employed in taking our baggage over the portage. We caused all the men who had short rifles to carry them, in order to be prepared for the natives, should they make any attempts to rob or injure them. I went up to the head of the rapids and left Capt. C. below. By 5 P.M. we had brought up all our baggage and Capt. C. joined me from the lower camp with the Wahclellah Cheif. I employed Sergt. Pryor the greater part of the day in repairing and corking the perogue and canoes. It continued to rain by showers all day. As the evening was

rainy cold and far advanced and ourselves wet we determined to remain all night.

—*Captain Lewis*

🏕 **Oregon 100** ♿

WYETH
Mount Hood National Forest

Location: Northern Oregon border west of Hood River.

Access: From Interstate 84 Exit 51 (13 miles west of Hood River, 6 miles east of Cascade Locks), turn south off the Interstate, then head immediately west (right) onto Herman Creek Road (paved); continue west for 0.1 mile to the campground, on the south (left) side of the road.

Camping Facilities: 14 campsites; (6 small group sites are also available; most units are spacious, with fair separation; parking pads are paved, long, wide, level straight-ins; generally good areas for tents, but a few spots might be slightly off-level; fire rings; some firewood is available for gathering in the area; water at faucets throughout; restrooms; paved driveways; limited supplies at Cascade Locks; adequate supplies and services are available in Hood River.

Day Use Facilities: Small parking area.

Activities & Attractions: Trailhead parking at the south end of the campground; museum and visitor center in Cascade Locks.

Natural Features: Great views of the Columbia River Gorge from the campground area; tall pine and spruce forest, along with big leafy hardwoods; very little low-level vegetation other than ferns; set against the south face of the gorge; elevation 150´.

Season, Fees & Phone: Mid-May to October; $12.00; 7 day limit; Columbia Gorge Ranger District ☎ (541) 695-2276.

Camp Journal: An extensive landscaping project accomplished by various government and volunteer groups has turned Wyeth into one of the most attractive campgrounds in this part of the country. The rockwork alone is worth a king's ransom. Definitely worth the stop—even if it's just to take a look. Taking a good look just about everywhere in this region is mandatory. Wyeth and the other parks and camps in this vicinity are within the Columbia River Gorge National Scenic Area. This unique, quarter-million-acre scenic entity was established by Act of Congress in 1986 and transcends national, state, local and private boundaries. It is the first creation of its kind in the United States.

📖 *April 13, 1806*

The loss of one of our perogues rendered it necessary to distribute her crew and cargo among the 2 remaining perogues and 2 canoes, which we loaded and set out at 8 A.M.

We passed the village immediately above the rapids where only one house at present remains entire, the other 8 having been taken down and removed to the oposite side of the river. We found the additional loading, which we had been compelled to put on board, rendered our vessels extreemly inconvenient to manage and, in short, reather unsafe in the event of high winds. I therefore left Capt. C. with the two perogues to proceed up the river on the N. side, and with the two canoes and some additional hands, passed over the river above the rapids to the Y-eh-huh village in order to purchase one or more canoes.

I found the village, consisting of 11 houses, crowded with inhabitants; it appeared to me that they could have mustered about 60 fighting men, then present. They appeared very friendly disposed, and I soon obtained two small canoes from them, for which I gave two robes and four elk skins. I also purchased four paddles and three dogs from them with deer skins. The dog now constitutes a considerable part of our subsistence and, with most of the party, has become a favourite food; certain, I am, that it is a healthy strong diet, and from habit it has become by no means disagreeable to me. I prefer it to lean venison or elk, and it is very far superior to the horse in any state.

After remaining about 2 hours at this village, I departed and continued my rout with the four canoes along the S. side of the river, the wind being too high to pass over to the entrance of Cruzats [Wind] River, where I expected to have overtaken Capt. C. Not seeing the perogues on the opposite side, I ascended the river untill one oClock or about 5 miles above the entrance of Cruzats River. Being convinced that the perogues were behind, I halted and directed the men to dress the dogs and cook one of them for dinner. A little before we had completed our meal, Capt. C. arrived with the perogues and landed opposite to us. After dinner I passed the river to the perogues and found that Capt. C. had halted for the evening and was himself hunting with three of the party.

—*Captain Lewis*

♠ Oregon 101 ♿

VIENTO
Viento State Park

Location: Northern Oregon border west of Hood River.

Access: From Interstate 84 Exit 56 for Viento Park (8 miles west of Hood River, 39 miles east of Troutdale), proceed to the north side of the freeway, then 0.1 mile east on a park access road to the main campground; a second camp loop for standard/tent camping is located on the south side of the freeway, 0.3 mile east of the exit.

Camping Facilities: 75 campsites, including 58 with partial hookups; sites are small to medium-sized, with nominal to fair separation; parking pads are paved, short to medium length straight-ins, and are fairly well leveled; adequate space for medium to large tents; fireplaces or fire rings; firewood is usually for sale, or b-y-o; water at faucets in most sites; restrooms with showers; paved driveways; adequate supplies and services are available in Hood River.

Day Use Facilities: Small picnic area; vault facilities; (restrooms are in the campground).

Activities & Attractions: Hiking trails in this park and in several other small state parks in the vicinity; limited river access.

Natural Features: Located on a hillside above the south bank of the Columbia River; the heavily forested south walls of the Columbia Gorge rise steeply, directly behind the park; grassy campsites are quite well shaded/sheltered by tall conifers, hardwoods, and shrubbery; elevation 100´.

Season, Fees & Phone: April to October; $14.00 for a standard site, $16.00 for a hookup site; 10 day limit; park office ☎(541) 374-8811.

Camp Journal: Viento is more of a 'sitting' campground rather than a 'doing' camp—and that's just fine. However, the park is situated between the Interstate and a very active railroad line, so one or the other could be a bit of a bother at times. But the grounds are grassy and inviting and provide a verdant stop for Interstate travelers. Views of the Columbia River and the Columbia Gorge along this stretch are fabulous!

During April 14th & 15th, the Expedtion laboriously continued upstream, passing the vicinity of the present-day town of Hood River, Oregon.

📖 *April 16, 1806*

About 8 oclock this morning, I passed across the river with the two interpreters and nine men in order to trade with the nativs for their horses, for which purpose I took with me a good part of our stock of merchindize. Capt L. sent out the hunters and set several men at work making pack saddles. Twelve horses will be sufficient to transport our baggage and some pounded fish with our dried elk, which we intend taking with us as a reserved store for the plains & Rocky Mountains.

I formed a camp on the N. side and sent Drewyer & Goodrich to the Skillute Village, and Shabono & Frazier down to the Chilluckkitequaw Village, with directions to inform the nativs that I had crossed the river for the purpose of purchasing horses; and if they had horses to sell us, to bring them to my camp. Great numbers of Indians came from both villages and delayed the greater part of the day without trading a single horse.

Drewyer returned with the principal Chief of the Skillutes, who was lame and could not walk. After his arrival, some horses were offered for sale, but they asked nearly half the merchindize I had with me for one horse. This price I could not think of giving. The Chief informed me if I would go to his town with him, his people would sell me horses. I therefore concluded to accompany him to his village 7 miles distant.

We set out and arived at the village at sunset. After some ceremony, I entered the house of the Chief. I then informed them that I would trade with them for their horses in the morning, for which I would give for each horse the articles which I had offered yesterday. The Chief set before me a large platter of onions which had been sweated. I gave a part of those onions to all my party and we all ate of them; in this state the root is very sweet and the tops tender. The nativs requested the party to dance, which they very readily consented, and Peter Cruzat played on the violin and the men danced several dances & retired to rest in the houses, of the 1st and second Chief.

We observed many stacks of fish remaining untouched on either side of the river. This is the great mart of all this country. Ten different tribes visit those people for the purpose of purchasing their fish, and the Indians on the Columbia and Lewis's River quite to the Chopunnish Nation visit them for the purpose of trading horses, buffalow robes, for beeds and such articles as they have not. The Skillutes procure the most of their cloth, knives, axes & beeds from the Indians from the North of them, who trade with white people who come into the inlets to the North at no great distance. Their horses, of which I saw great numbers, they procure from the Indians who reside on the banks of the Columbia above, and what fiew they take from the Towarnihiooks or Snake Indians. I smoked with all the principal men of this nation in the house of their great Chief, and lay my self down on a mat to sleep, but was prevented by the mice and vermin with which this house abounded and which was very troublesome to me.

—*Captain Clark*

📖 *April 17, 1806*

I rose early after a bad nights rest, and took my merchindize to a rock which afforded an eligible situation for my purpose, and divided the articles of merchindize into parcels of such articles as I thought best calculated to please the Indians. And in each parcel I put as many articles as we could afford to give, and thus exposed them to view, informing the Indians that each parcel was intended for a horse.

They tantalized me the greater part of the day, saying that they had sent out for their horses and would trade as soon as they came. Several parcels of merchindize were laid by for which they told me they would bring horses. I made a bargain with the Chief for 2 horses. About an hour after, he canceled the bargain, and we again bargained for 3 horses, which were brought forward. Only one of the 3 could be possibly used, the other two had such intolerable backs as to render them entirely unfit for service. I refused to take two of them, which displeased him, and he refused to part with the 3rd.

I then packed up the articles and was about setting out for the village above, when a man came and sold me two horses, and another man sold me one horse, and several others informed me that they would trade with me if I would continue untill their horses could be drove up. This induced me to continue at this village another day. Maney of the nativs from different villages on the Columbia above offered to trade, but asked such things as we had not, and double as much of the articles which I had as we could afford to give. This was a very unfavourable circumstance, as my dependence for procuring a sufficiency of horses rested on the suckcess above, where I had reasons to believe there was a greater abundance of those animals, and was in hopes of getting them on better terms. I purchased 3 dogs for the party with me to eate, and some chap-pa-lell for myself.

Before procuring the three horses, I dispatched Cruzat, Willard, and McNeal and Peter Wiser to Capt. Lewis with a note informing him of my ill success in procuring horses, and advised him to proceed on to this place as soon as possible.That I would, in the meantime, proceed on to the Enesher Nation, above the Great Falls, and try to purchase some horses of that people.

Soon after I had dispatched this party, the Chief of the Eneshers and 15 or 20 of his people visited me, and appeared to be anxious to see the articles I offered for the horses. Several of them agreed to let me have horses if I would add sundry articles to those I offered, which I agreed to do, and they layed those bundles by and informed me they would deliver me the horses in the morning. I proposed going with them to their town. The Chief informed me that their horses were all in the plains with their womin gathering roots. They would send out and bring the horses to this place tomorrow.

This intelligence was flattering, tho' I doubted the sincerity of those people, who had several times disappointed me in a similar way. However, I determined to continue untill tomorrow. In the meantime, industriously employed ourselves with the great mulitude of Indians of different nations about us, trying to purchase horses. Shabono purchased a verry fine mare for which he gave ermine, elk's teeth, a belt, and some other articles of no great value. No other purchase was made in the course of this day.

In the evening, I received a note from Capt. Lewis by Shannon, informing me that he should set out early on tomorrow morning, and advising me to double the prices which we had first agreed on for each horse. I was envited into the house of the 2nd Chief, where I concluded to sleep. This man is pore, nothing to eat but dried fish, and no wood to burn. Altho' the night was cold, they could not raise as much wood as would make a fire.

—*Captain Clark*

📖 *April 18, 1806*

Early this morning I was awakened by a man of the Choppunish Nation who delivered me a bag of powder and ball which he had picked up this morning at the place the goods were exposed yesterday. I had a fire made of some poles purchased of the nativs a short distance from the houses and the articles exposed as yesterday. Collected the four horses purchased yesterday, and sent Frazier and Shabono with them to the basin, where I expected they would meet Cap L., and commence the portage of the baggage on those horses.

About 10 A.M. the Indians came down from the Enesher villages and I expected would take the articles which they had laid by yesterday. But to my astonishment, no one would make the exchange today. Two other parcels of goods were laid by, and the horses promised at 2 P.M. I paid but little attention to this bargain; however, suffered the bundles to lie.

I dressed the sores of the principal Chief, gave some small things to his children, and promised the Chief some medicine for to cure his sores. His wife, who I found to be a sulky bitch, was somewhat afflicted with pains in her back. This I thought a good opportunity to get her on my side, giving her something for her back. I rubbed a little camphor on her temples and back and applied warm flannel to her back, which, she thought had nearly restored her to her former feelings. This I thought a favourable time to trade with the Chief, who had more horses than all the Nation besides. I accordingly made him an offer, which he accepted, and sold me two horses. Great numbers of Indians from different directions visited me at the place,but none of them appeared willing to part with their horses.

At 3 P.M. Sergt. Ordway and three men arived from Cap Lewis. They brought with them several elk skins, two of my coats, and four robes of the party, to add to the stores I had with me for the purchase of horses. Sergt. O. informed me that Cap L. had arived with all the canoes into the basin 2 miles below, and wished some dogs to eate. I had 3 dogs purchased and sent down. At 5 P.M. Capt. Lewis came up. He informed me that he had passed the river to the basin with much difficulty and danger, having made one portage.

I deturmned to proceed with Capt. L. down to camp at the basin. I left the articles of merchandize &c. with Drewyer, Warner, Shannon & Goodrich untill morning. At the basin we cut up two of our canoes for fire wood, very much to the chagrin of the nativs, notwithsanding that they would give us nothing for them. Capt. Lewis gave a large kittle for a horse which was offered to him at the basin this evening.

—*Captain Clark*

50

⚕ Oregon 102 ♿

MEMALOOSE
Memaloose State Park

Location: Northern Oregon border east of Hood River.

Access: From Interstate 84, (westbound) at milepost 73 (9 miles east of Hood River, 12 miles west of The Dalles), take the exit for "Rest Area, Memaloose Park"; continue west through the rest area parking lot to the park entrance and the campground. **Alternate Access:** From I-84, eastbound, take Exit 76, backtrack on I-84 westbound to the "Rest Area" exit at milepost 73, then continue as above.

Camping Facilities: 110 campsites, including 43 with full hookups; most sites are average-sized, with fair separation; parking pads are paved, reasonably level, and some are large enough for very large rv's; adequate space for medium to large tents; fireplaces; b-y-o firewood is recommended; water at faucets throughout; restrooms with showers; holding tank disposal station; adequate supplies in Hood River; complete supplies and services are available in The Dalles.

Day Use Facilities: Several picnic tables and restrooms in the rest area adjacent to the park.

Activities & Attractions: Large, grassy area for general recreation.

Natural Features: Located on a mown, grassy flat above the south bank of the Columbia River; assorted conifers, hardwoods, and bushes dot the park area; elevation 100´.

Season, Fees & Phone: April to October; $16.00 for a standard site, $20.00 for a hookup site; 10 day limit; phone c/o Rooster Rock State Park ☎ (541) 695-2261.

Camp Journal: The park's name was derived from an island in the Columbia River which was used as a burial ground by Indians. The nearby town of Hood River bills itself as the "Windsurfing Capitol of the World".

📖 *April 19, 1806*

This morning we had our small canoes drawn out, and employed all hands in transporting our baggage on their backs, and by means of the four pack horses, over the portage. This labour we had accomplished by 3 P.M. and established our camp a little above the Skillute village.

There was great joy with the natives last night, in consequence of the arrival of the salmon; one of those fish was caught; this was the harbinger of good news to them. They informed us that these fish would arrive in great quantities in the course of about 5 days. This fish was dressed and, being divided into small pieces, was given to each child in the village. This custom is founded on a superstitious opinion that it will hasten the arrival of the salmon. With much difficulty we obtained four other horses from the Indians today. We were obliged to dispense with two of our kettles in order to acquire those. We now have only one small kettle to a mess of 8 men.

In the evening Capt. Clark set out with four men to the Enesher village at the grand falls in order to make a further attempt to procure horses. These people are very faithless in their contracts. They frequently receive the merchandize in exchange for their horses and, after some hours, insist on some additional article being given them or revoke the exchange. They have pilfered several small articles from us this evening.

I directed the horses to be hobbled and suffered to graize at a little distance from our camp under the immediate eye of the men who had them in charge. One of the men, Willard, was negligent in his attention to his horse and suffered it to ramble off; it was not to be found when I ordered the others to be brought up and confined to the picquits. This, in addition to the other difficulties under which I laboured, was truly provoking. I reprimanded him more severely for this piece of negligence than had been usual with me. I had the remaining horses well secured by picquits; they were extreemly restless, and it required the attention of the whole guard through the night to retain them, notwithstanding they were hobbled and picquited. All except one were stallions, for the people in this neighbourhood do not understand the art of gelding them, and this is a season at which they are most vicious.

—*Captain Lewis*

📖 *April 20, 1806*

This morning I was informed that the natives had pilfered six tomahawks and a knife from the party in the course of the last night. I spoke to the cheif on this subject. He appeared angry with his people and addressed them, but the property was not restored. One horse which I had purchased and paid for yesterday and which could not be found when I ordered the horses into close confinement yesterday, I was now informed had been gambled away by the rascal who had sold it to me, and had been taken away by a man of another nation. I therefore took the goods back from this fellow. I purchased a gun from the cheif, for which I gave him 2 elk skins.

In the course of the day I obtained two other indifferent horses, for which I gave an extravagant price. I found that I should get no more horses, and therefore resolved to proceed tomorrow morning with those which I had, and to convey the baggage in two small canoes that the horses could not carry. For this purpose I had a load made up for seven horses, the eighth Bratton was compelled to ride as he was yet unable to walk. I bartered my elk skins, old irons and 2 canoes for beads. One of the canoes for which they would give us but little I had cut up for fuel. I had the horses graized untill evening and then picquited and hobbled within the limits of our camp. I ordered the Indians from our camp this evening and informed them that, if I caught them attempting to purloin any article from us, I would beat them severely. They went off in reather a bad humour and I directed the party to examine their arms and be on their guard. They stole two spoons from us in the course of the day.

—*Captain Lewis*

📖 *April 21, 1806*

Notwithstanding all the precautions I had taken with respect to the horses, one of them had broken his cord of five strands of elk skin and had gone off. I sent several men in search of the horse, with orders to return at 10 A.M., with or without the horse, being determined to remain no longer with these villains. They stole another tomahawk from us this morning. I searched many of them but could not find it. I ordered all the spare poles, paddles, and the ballance of our canoe put on the fire, as the morning was cold, and also that not a particle should be left for the benefit of the Indians.

I detected a fellow in stealing an iron socket of a canoe pole, and gave him several severe blows, and made the men kick him out of camp. I now informed the Indians that I would shoot the first of them that attempted to steal an article from us, that we were not afraid to fight them; that I had it in my power at that moment to kill them all and set fire to their houses, but it was not my wish to treat them with severity, provided they would let my property alone. That I would take their horses if I could find out the persons who had stolen the tomahawks, but that I had reather lose the property altogether than take the horse of an innocent person. The chiefs who were present hung their heads and said nothing.

At 9 A.M. Windsor returned with the lost horse. The others who were in search of the horse soon after returned also. The Indian who promised to accompany me as far as the Chopunnish [Nez Percé] country produced me two horses, one of which he politely gave me the liberty of packing. We took breakfast and departed, a few minutes after 10 oClock, having nine horses loaded, and one which Bratton rode, not being able as yet to march. The two canoes I had dispatched early this morning.

At 1 P.M., I arrived at the Enesher village, where I found Capt. Clark and party. After dinner, we proceeded on about four miles to a village of 9 mat lodges of the Enesher, a little below the entrance of Clark's [Deschutes] River and encamped. We obtained two dogs and a small quantity of fuel of these people, for which we were obliged to give a higher price than usual.

Our guide continued with us. He appears to be an honest, sincere fellow. He tells us that the Indians a little above will treat us with much more hospitality than those we are now with. We purchased another horse this evening, but his back is in such a horrid state that we can put but little on him. We obtained him for a trifle, at least for articles which might be procured in the U' States for 10 shillings Virginia Currency

—*Captain Lewis*

♠♠ **Oregon 103**

DESCHUTES RIVER
Deschutes River State Recreation Area

Location: North-central Oregon east of The Dalles.

Access: From Interstate 84 (eastbound) Exit 97, (12 miles east of The Dalles, 7 miles west of the junction of U. S. 97 with I-84), turn east onto Oregon State Highway 206; continue for 3.2 miles (Highway 206 parallels I-84), and over the Deschutes River Bridge; turn south (right) into the park. From I-84 (westbound) Exit 104 (at the junction of I-84 with U.S 97), turn west onto State Highway 206; continue 4.5 miles, then turn south (left) into the park.

Camping Facilities: 34 electrical hookup campsites; (25 primitive sites and group camps are also available); hookup sites are small, with nominal separation; parking pads are paved, fairly level, short+ to medium-length straight-ins; gently sloping grassy areas for tents; fireplaces; b-y-o firewood is recommended; water at several faucets; restrooms; paved driveways; gas and groceries in Celilo Village, 5 miles west; complete supplies and services are available in The Dalles.

Day Use Facilities: Medium-sized picnic area and parking lot.

Activities & Attractions: Fishing and floating on the Deschutes River; The Dalles Dam Visitor Center, 15 miles west.

Natural Features: Located along the east bank of the Deschutes River; the campground is situated in a grove of tall hardwoods and a few evergreens; the Deschutes enters the Columbia River just downstream of this point; the park is bordered by fairly steep and rocky canyon walls and rolling, grassy hillsides; elevation 150´.

Season, Fees & Phone: April to October; $8.00 for a primitive site, $16.00 for a hookup; 10 day limit; park office ☎ (541) 739-2322.

Camp Journal: Actually, there are more complete camping facilities in a Washington state park (Maryhill) just across the river But Deschutes River SRA does provide a strong motivator for sportsmen—the park's namesake. Fishing and floating/boating are usually good on the Deschutes.

▲ *Great Falls to the Land of the Wallawallahs*

📖 *April 22, 1806*

At 7 A.M. we set out, having previously sent on our small canoe with Colter and Potts. We had not arrived at the top of a hill over which the road leads, opposite the village, before Charbono's horse threw his load and, taking fright at the saddle and robe which still adhered, ran at full speed down the hill. Near the village he disengaged himself from the saddle and robe. An Indian hid the robe in his lodge. I sent our guide and one man who was with me in the rear to assist Charbono in retaking his horse, which, having done, they returned to the village on the track of the horse, in search of the lost articles. They found the saddle but could see nothing of the robe. The Indians denied having seen it. They then continued on the track of the horse to the place from whence he had set out with the same success.

Being now confident that the Indians had taken it, I sent the Indian woman on, to request Capt. Clark to halt the party and send back some of the men to my assistance, being determined either to make the Indians deliver the robe or burn their houses. They have vexed me in such a manner by such repeated acts of villainy that I am quite disposed to treat them with every severity; their defenseless state pleads forgiveness so far as rispects their lives. With this resolution, I returned to their village, which I had just reached when Labiche met me with the robe, which, he informed me, he found in an Indian lodge hidden behind their baggage. I now returned and joined Capt. Clark who was waiting my arrival with the party.

We now made the following regulations as to our future order of march, viz., that Capt. C. & myself should divide the men who were disencumbered by horses and march alternately each day, the one in front and the other in rear. Having divided the party agreeably to this arrangement, we proceeded on through an open plain country about 8 miles to a village of 6 houses of the Enesher Nation. Here we observed our two canoes passing up on the opposite side. The wind being too high for them to pass the river, they continued on. We halted at a small run just above the village, where we dined on some dogs which we purchased of the inhabitants and suffered our horses to graize about three hours.

After dinner we proceeded on up the river about 4 miles to a village of 7 mat lodges of the last mentioned nation. Here our Chopunnish guide informed us that the next village was at a considerable distance, and that we could not reach it tonight. A man belonging to the next village above proposed exchanging a horse for one of our canoes. Just at this moment one of our canoes was passing. We hailed them and ordered them to come over, but the wind continued so high that they could not join us untill after sunset, and the Indian who wished to exchange his horse for the canoe had gone on. We obtained 4 dogs and as much wood as answered our purposes on moderate terms. We can only afford ourselves one fire, and are obliged to lie without shelter. The nights are cold and days warm.

—*Captain Lewis*

📖 *April 23, 1806*

At daylight this morning we were informed that the two horses of our interpreter

Charbono were absent; on enquiry it appeared that he had neglected to confine them to picquits, as had been directed last evening. We immediately dispatched Reuben Fields and Labiche to assist Charbono in recovering his horses. One of them was found at no great distance and the other was given over as lost.

We continued our march along a narrow rocky bottom on the N. side of the river about 12 miles to the Wah-how-pum village of 12 temporary mat lodges near the Rock Rapid. These people appeared much pleased to see us, sold us 4 dogs and some wood for our small articles which we had previously prepared as our only resource to obtain fuel and food through those plains. These articles consisted of pewter buttons, strips of tin, iron and brass, twisted wire &c.

Here we met with a Chopunnish man on his return up the river with his family and about 13 head of horses, most of them young and unbroken. He offered to hire us some of them to pack as far as his Nation, but we prefer buying, as by hiring his horses we shall have the whole of his family most probably to maintain. At a little distance below this village, we passed five lodges of the same people who, like those below, were waiting the arrival of the salmon.

After we had arranged our camp, we caused all the old and brave men to set around and smoke with us. We had the violin played and some of the men danced; after which the natives entertained us with a dance after their method. This dance differed from any I have yet seen. They formed a circle and all sung, as well the spectators as the dancers who performed within the circle. These placed their shoulders together with their robes tightly drawn about them and danced in a line from side to side, several parties of from 4 to seven will be performing within the circle at the same time. The whole concluded with a promiscuous dance in which most of them sung and danced. These people speak a language very similar to the Chopunnish, whome they also resemble in their dress. After the dance was ended, the Indians retired at our request and we retired to rest. We had all our horses side hobbled and turned out to graize.

—*Captain Lewis*

⚐ Oregon 104 ♿

LEPAGE
Lake Umatilla/Corps of Engineers Park

Location: Northern Oregon border east of The Dalles.

Access: From Interstate 84 Exit 114 for Le Page Park/John Day River Recreation Area, (5 miles east of Rufus, 29 miles east of The Dalles, 24 miles west of Arlington), at the south side of the freeway proceed south on a paved access road for 0.3 mile (past the day use area) to the campground.

Camping Facilities: 22 campsites with partial hookups; sites are small+ to medium-sized, level, with nominal to fair separation; parking pads are gravel, medium to long straight-ins or pull-offs; enough space for a small tent; restrooms with showers nearby, plus vault facilities; disposal station; complete supplies and services are available in The Dalles.

Day Use Facilities: Medium-sized picnic area with several small shelters; drinking water; restrooms; medium-sized parking lot.

Activities & Attractions: Designated swimming area; boating; boat launch; fishing.

Natural Features: Located near the mouth of a canyon along the bank of the John Day River at its confluence with the Columbia River; this segment of the Columbia has been dammed to form Lake Umatilla; sites are lightly shaded by large hardwoods; about half of the sites are riverside; bordered by dry, rocky hills and bluffs; elevation 200´.

Season, Fees & Phone: Open all year, limited swervices October to April; $16.00; 14 day limit; Corps of Engineers John Day Project Office, The Dalles, ☎ (541) 506-7816.

Camp Journal: Great little freewayside stop. The terrific day use area has watered/mown lawns dotted with hardwoods. From near here are commanding views down through the Columbia Gorge and of Mount Hood rising prominently (on a clear day) in the distance. This recreation area is named for Jean Baptiste Lepage, a member of the Corps of Discovery. Lewis and Clark had named what is now John Day River, "River LaPage". The Corps camp on the night of April 23 1806, was on the north side of the Columbia, just upstream of here.

📖 *April 24, 1806*
Rose early this morning and sent out after the horses, all of which were found except

McNeals, which I hired an Indian to find and gave him a tomahawk. Had 4 pack saddles made ready to pack the horses which we may purchase. We purchased 3 horses, and hired 3 others of the Chopunnish man who accompanies us with his family, and at 1 P.M. set out and proceeded on through a open country, rugged & sandy, between some high lands and the river, to a village of 5 lodges of the Met-cow-we band. Great numbers of the nativs pass us on horse back, many meet us and continued with us to the lodges. We purchased 3 dogs which were pore, but the fattest we could procure, and cooked them with straw and dry willow.

We sold our canoes for a fiew strands of beeds. The nativs had tantalized us with an exchange of horses for our canoes in the first instance, but when they found that we had made our arrangements to travel by land, they would give us nothing for them. We sent Drewyer to cut them up. He struck one and split her. They discovered that we were determined to destroy the canoes and offered us several strands of beeds, which were accepted. Most of the party complain of their feet and legs this evening being very sore. It is no doubt caused by walking over the rough stone and deep sand after being accustomed to a soft soil. My legs and feet give me much pain. I bathed them in cold water from which I experienced considerable relief.

—*Captain Clark*

❧ The Expedition now continued east afoot or on horseback for the next two days, until they met up with an old friend in present southeast Washington State, near the confluence of the Columbia and Walla Walla Rivers:

📖 *April 27, 1806*
This morning we were detained untill 9 A.M. in consequence of the absence of one of Charbono's horses. The horse at length being recovered, we set out, and at the distance of fifteen miles, passed through a country similar to that of yesterday; the hills at the extremity of this distance again approach the river and are rocky, abrupt and 300 feet high. We ascended the hill and marched through a high plain 9 miles when we again returned to the river.

I now thought it best to halt, as the horses and men were much fatigued. Altho' we had not reached the Wallahwallah villages, we had been led to believe by our guide, who informed us that the village was at the place we should next return to the river, and the consideration of our having but little provision had been our inducement to make the march we had made this morning. We collected some of the dry stalks of weeds and the stems of a shrub which resembles the southern wood, made a small fire and boiled a small quantity of our jerked meat on which we dined.

While here, the principal Cheif of the Wallahwallahs joined us with six men of his Nation. This Cheif, by name Yellepit, had visited us on the morning of the 19th of October last, at our encampment a little below this place. We gave him at that time a small medal and promised him a larger one on our return. He appeared much gratified at seeing us return, invited us to remain at his village three or four days, and assured us that we should be furnished with a plenty of such food as they had themselves, and some horses to assist us on our journey. After our scanty repast we continued our march, accompanied by Yellepit and his party, to the village.

This Cheif is a man of much influence, not only in his own Nation but also among the neighbouring tribes and nations. Yellepit harangued his village in our favour, entreated them to furnish us with fuel and provision, and set the example himself by bringing us an armful of wood and a platter of three roasted mullets. The others soon followed his example with rispect to fuel, and we soon found ourselves in possession of an ample stock. We purchased four dogs of these people on which the party supped heartily, having been on short allowance for near two days. The Indians retired when we requested them this evening, and behaved themselves in every rispect extreemly well.

The Indians informed us that there was a good road which passed from the Columbia opposite to this village to the entrance of the Kooskooske on the S. side of Lewis's [Snake] River; they also informed us, that there were a plenty of deer and antelopes on the road, with good water and grass. We knew that a road in that direction of the country would permit us to shorten our rout at least 80 miles. The Indians also informed us that the country was level and the road good. Under these circumstances we did not hesitate in pursuing the rout recommended by our guide, whose information was corroborated by Yellepit and others.

—*Captain Lewis*

⚕ Oregon 105 ♿

SAND STATION

Lake Wallula/Corps of Engineers Recreation Area

Location: Northeast Oregon northeast of Hermiston

Access: From U.S Highway 730 near milepost 194 +.5 (18 miles east of Interstate 82 Exit 1 at Umatilla, 9 miles southwest of the Oregon-Washington border south of Wallula, WA) turn north into the recreation area at either of 2 entrances 0.1 mile apart.

Camping Facilities: 17 campsites in 2 sections; sites are small, with minimal separation; parking pads are gravel, essentially level, short to medium-length straight-ins; small areas for tents; sun shelters for· a few sites; barbecue grills and fire rings; b-y-o firewood; no drinking water; vault facilities; gravel driveway; limited supplies and services are available in Umatilla.

Day Use Facilities: Small picnic area; medium-sized parking lot; other facilities are shared with campers.

Activities & Attractions: Sandy gravel swimming beach; fishing; boating.

Natural Features: Located on a moderate slope above the south-east shore of Lake Wallula, a reservoir on the Columbia River formed by McNary Dam; most sites are located along the beach, a few sites are higher up on the slope; sites are lightly to moderately sheltered by medium to large hardwoods; the lake is bordered by high, rocky, treeless bluffs; elevation 350´.

Season, Fees & Phone: Open all year, with limited services October to April; 14 day limit; no fee; McNary Dam CoE Project Office, Plymouth WA, ☎(509) 922-3211

Camp Journal: Great, distant views both upriver and downriver (or uplake and downlake, as it were) from here. At any rate, most of the sites are near the water's edge. The mighty Columbia Basin wind blusters through here on an almost daily basis. But the sites are somewhat sheltered by the surrounding terrain and the large hardwoods within the recreation area.

📖 *April 28, 1806*

This morning early the Great Chief Yellepit brought a very elegant white horse to our camp and presented him to me, signifying his wish to get a kittle; but being informed that we had already disposed of every kittle we could possibly spare, he said he was content with whatever I thought proper to give him. I gave him my swoard, 100 balls & powder and some small articles, of which he appeared perfectly satisfied.

It was necessary before we entered on our rout through the plains, where we were to meet with no lodges or resident Indians, that we should lay in a stock of provisions and not depend altogether on the gun. We directed R. Frazier, to whome we have entrusted the duty of making the purchases, to lay in as many fat dogs as he could procure; he soon obtained 10.

Being anxious to depart, we requested the Chief to furnish us with canoes to pass the river, but he insisted on our remaining with him this day at least, that he would be much pleased if we would consent to remain two or 3 days, but he would not let us have canoes to leave him this day, that he had sent for the Chim-na-pums, his neighbours, to come down and join his people this evening and dance for us. We urged the necessity of our proceeding on immediately, in order that we might the sooner return to them with the articles which they wished brought to them, but this had no effect; he said that the time he asked could not make any considerable difference. At length we urged that there was no wind blowing and that the river was consequently in good order to pass our horses, and if he would furnish us with canoes for that purpose, we would remain all night at our present encampment. To this proposition he assented and soon produced a canoe.

I saw a man who had his knee contracted who had previously applyed to me for some medicine, that if he would furnish another canoe I would give him some medecine. He readily consented and went himself with his canoe, by means of which we passed our horses over the river safely and hobbled them as usial.

We found a Sho-sho-ne woman, prisoner among those people by means of whome and Sah-cah-gah-weah, Shabono's wife, we found means of conversing with the Wallahwallahs. We conversed with them for several hours and fully satisfied all their enquiries with rispect to ourselves and the objects of our pursuit. They were much pleased.

They brought several disordered persons to us, for whome they requested some medical aid. To all of whome we administered, much to the gratification of those pore wretches. We gave them some eye water, which I believe will render them more essential service than any other article in the medical way which we had it in our power to bestow on them. Sore eyes seem to be a universal complaint among those people; I have no doubt but the fine sands of those plains and the river contribute much to the disorder. A man who had his arm broken had it loosely bound in a piece of leather without any thing to surport it. I dressed the arm which was broken short above the wrist & supported it with broad sticks to keep it in place, put it in a sling and furnished him with some lint bandages &c. to dress it in future.

A little before sunset the Chimnahpoms arived; they were about 100 men and a fiew women; they joined the Wallahwallahs, who were about 150 men, and formed a half circle around our camp where they waited verry patiently to see our party dance. The fiddle was played and the men amused themselves with dancing about an hour.

We then requested the Indians to dance, which they verry cheerfully complyed with; they continued their dance untill 10 at night. The whole assemblage of Indians, about 350 men women and children, sung and danced at the same time. Most of them danced in the same place they stood and merely jumped up to the time of their music. At 10 P.M. the dance ended, and the nativs retired; they were much gratified in seeing some of our party join them in their dance. One of their party who made himself the most conspicious character in the dance and songs, we were told was a medicine man & could foretell things. That he had told of our coming into their country and was now about to consult his God the Moon if what we said was the truth &c. &c.

—*Captain Clark*

📖 *April 29, 1806*

This morning Yelleppit furnished us with 2 canoes, and we began to transport our baggage over the river; we also sent a party of the men over to collect our horses. We purchased some dogs and shappellell this morning. We had now a store of 12 dogs for our voyage through the plains.

By 11 A. M. we had passed the river with our party and baggage, but were detained several hours in consequence of not being able to collect our horses. Our guide now informed us that it was too late in the evening to reach an eligible place to encamp; that we could not reach any water before night. We therefore thought it best to remain on the Wallahwallah River about a mile from the Columbia untill

the morning, and accordingly encamped on that river near a fish weir.

The Wallahwallah River discharges itself into the Columbia on it's S. side 15 miles below the entrance of Lewis's River, or the S.E. branch. This is a handsome stream about 4 1/2 feet deep and 50 yards wide. The Indians inform us that it has it's source in the range of mountains [Blue Mountains] in view of us to the E. and S.E.

The Snake Indian prisoner informed us that at some distance in the large plains to the South of those mountains there was a large river running to the N.W. which was as wide as the Columbia at this place which is nearly one mile. This account is no doubt somewhat exaggerated, but it serves to evince the certainty of the Multnomah being a very large river and that it's waters are separated from the Columbia by those mountains, and that with the aid of a Southwardly branch of Lewis's River which passes around the Eastern extremity of those mountains, it must water that vast tract of country extending from those mountains to the waters of the Gulf of California.

We gave small medals to two inferior cheifs of this Nation, and they each presented us with a fine horse; in return we gave them sundry articles, and among others, one of my case pistols and several hundred rounds of ammunition.

There are 12 other lodges of the Wallahwallah Nation on this river a little distance below our camp. Those people, as well as the Chymnapos, are very well dressed, much more so particularly their women, than they were as we decended the river last fall. Most of them have long shirts and leggings, good robes and mockersons. Their women wear the truss when they cannot procure the shirt, but very few are seen with the former at the moment. I presume the success of their winters hunt has produced this change in their attire. They insisted on our dancing this evening, but it rained a little, the wind blew hard, and the weather was cold; we therefore did not indulge them.

—*Captain Lewis*

📖 *April 29, 1806*

Several applyed to me today for medical aide, one a broken arm, another inward fevers and several with pains across their loins, and sore eyes. I administered as well as I could to all. In the evening a man brought his wife and a horse both up to me. The horse he gave me as a present, and his wife, who was verry unwell, the effects of violent colds, was placed before me. I did not think her case a bad one and gave such medicine as would keep her body open and wrapped her in flannel. Left some simple medicine to be taken. We also gave some eye water.

—Captain Clark

📖 *April 30, 1806*

This morning we had some difficulty in collecting our horses, notwithstanding we had hobbled & picqueted those we obtained of those people. We purchased two other horses this morning and 4 dogs. We exchanged one of our most indifferent horses for a very good one with the Choponnish man who has his family with him. This man has a daughter now arived at the age of puberty, who being in a certain situation, is not permited to associate with the family, but sleeps at a distance from her father's camp, and when traveling, follows at some distance behind. In this state I am informed that the female is not permited to eat, nor to touch any article of a culinary nature or manly occupation.

At 10 A.M. we had collected all our horses, except the white horse which Yellepit the Great Chief had given me. The whole of the men having returned without being able to find this horse, I informed the Chief and he mounted Capt. Lewis's horse and went in search of the horse himself. About half an hour after the Chopunnish man brought my horse. We determined to proceed on with the party, leaving one man to bring up Capt L.'s horse when Yellepit should return. We took leave of those honest and friendly people, the Wallahwallahs, and departed at 1 A.M., accompanied by our guide and the Chopunnish man and family.

—Captain Clark

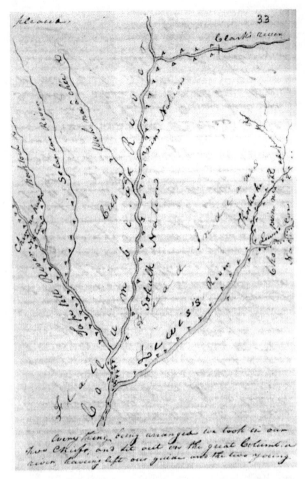

Lewis's map of the middle segment of the Columbia River and its principal tributaries

Kooskooskee Encampment *1806*

⚑ *Overland to the Forks of the Kooskooskee*

The Expedition now headed eastward overland, back to the confluence of Lewis's (Snake) River and the Kooskooskee (Clearwater) River at today's twin cities of Lewiston-Clarkston. It was deemed considerably easier to walk and ride instead of plying their oars against the Snake River's swift current. Washington State Highway 124 to Waitsburg, then U.S. Highway 12 to Clarkston pretty much follow the route along the Indian roads traveled by the Corps on this leg of the journey.

📖 *May 1, 1806*

We made a total of 26 miles today. Some time after we had encamped, three young men arrived from the Wallahwallah village bringing with them a steel trap belonging to one of our party which had been negligently left behind; this is an act of integrity rarely witnessed among Indians. During our stay with them, they several times found the knives of the men which had been carelessly lost by them and returned them. I think we can justly affirm to the honor of these people that they are the most hospitable, honest, and sincere people that we have met with in our voyage.

—Captain Lewis

⚑ Washington 106 ♿

LEWIS AND CLARK TRAIL
Lewis and Clark Trail State Park

Location: Southeast Washington north of Walla Walla.

Access: From U.S. Highway 12 at milepost 362 (5 miles west of Dayton, 4.5 miles east of Waitsburg), turn north into the campground.

Camping Facilities: 30 campsites; (4 hike-bike/primitive sites and a group camp are also available); most sites are small to medium-sized, level, with fair to excellent separation; parking pads are gravel/earth, medium-length straight-ins; small to medium-sized tent areas;

fireplaces; b-y-o firewood; water at several faucets; restrooms with showers; holding tank disposal station; paved driveways; limited+ supplies and services are available in Dayton and Waitsburg.

Day Use Facilities: Medium-sized picnic area; 3 medium or large shelters (2 are reservable by groups); drinking water; restrooms; medium-sized parking lot.

Activities & Attractions: Self-guiding three-quarter mile nature trail with the theme "Food, Fuel and Medicine"; (a good guide pamphlet is available); 1 mile of hiking trails; sports field; amphitheater for summer campfire programs.

Natural Features: Located along and near the south bank of the Touchet River; campsites are generally well-shaded/sheltered and some are tucked into their own little alcoves of hardwoods and some conifers and lots of underbrush; bordered by grassy, rolling hills and agricultural land; elevation 1000´.

Season, Fees & Phone: Open all year, with limited services October to April; $14.00; 10 day limit; park office ☎ (509) 337-6457.

Camp Journal: The Lewis and Clark Expedition traveled through this valley in May of 1806, thus the name for the park. The park is about midway between their camps of May 1st and May 2nd. The setting for this campground is really a surprise, considering the comparatively barren hillsides of the surrounding terrain. The dense vegetation along the river, particularly around some of the campsites, might remind you of parks much closer to the Coast.

📖 *May 3, 1806*

This morning we set out at 7 A.M. We met with We-ark-koomt, whom we have usually distinguished by the name of the Bighorn Chief, from the circumstance of his always wearing a horn of that animal suspended by a cord to the left arm. He is the 1st Chief of a large band of the Chopunnish Nation. He had 10 of his young men with him. This man went down Lewis's River by land as we descended it by water last fall, quite to the Columbia, and I believe was very instrumental in procuring us a hospitable and friendly reception among the natives. He had now come a considerable distance to meet us. We came 28 miles today.

We divided the last of our dryed meat at dinner when it was consumed, as well as the ballance of our dogs nearly. We made a scant supper and not anything for tomorrow; however, We-ark-koomt consoled us with the information that there was an Indian lodge on the river at no great distnace, where we might supply ourselves with provision tomorrow. Our guide and the three young Wallahwallahs left us this morning reather abruptly and we have seen nothing of them since.

—*Captain Lewis*

📖 *May 4, 1806*

Collected our horses and set out early; the morning was cold and disagreeable. We ascended through a high level plain to a ravine which forms the source of a small creek, thence down this creek to it's entrance into Lewis's River, 7 1/2 miles below the entrance of the Kooskooske [Clearwater]. On the river a little above this creek we arrived at a lodge of 6 families of which We-ark-koomt had spoken. We halted here for breakfast and with much difficulty purchased 2 lean dogs. The inhabitants were miserably poor. We obtained a few large cakes of half cured bread made of a root which resembles the sweet potatoe; with these we made some soup and took breakfast.

A great portion of the Chopunnish, we are informed, are now distributed in small vilages through this plain, collecting the quawmash and cowse [camas and cowas, both having edible bulbs or roots], the salmon not yet having arrived to call them to the river.

The hills of the creek which we decended this morning are high, and in most parts rocky and abrupt. One of our pack horses slipped from one of those heights and fell into the creek with it's load, consisting principally of ammunition; but fortunately neither the horse nor load suffered any material injury. The ammunition being secured in canisters, the water did not affect it.

After dinner, we continued our rout up the West side of the river 3 miles opposite to 2 lodges, the one containing 3 and the other 2 families of the Chopunnish Nation. Here we met with Te-toh-ar-sky, the youngest of the two Cheifs who accompanied us last fall to the great falls of the Columbia. We also met with our pilot who descended the river with us as far as the Columbia. These Indians recommended our passing the river at this place and ascending the Kooskooske on the

N.E. side. They said it was nearer and a better rout to the forks of that river where the Twisted Hair resided, in whose charge we had left our horses; thither they promised to conduct us.

We determined to take the advice of the Indians and immediately prepared to pass the river, which, with the assistance of three Indian canoes, we effected in the course of the evening; purchased a little wood and some bread of cowse from the natives and encamped, having traveled 15 miles only today. We-ark-koomt, whose people resided on the West side of Lewis's River above, left us when we determined to pass the river, and went on to his lodge. The evening was cold and disagreeable; the natives crowded about our fire in great numbers, insomuch that we could scarcely cook or keep ourselves warm.

At all these lodges of the Chopunnish, I observe an appendage of a small lodge with one fire, which seems to be the retreat of their women in a certain situation. The men are not permitted to approach this lodge within a certain distance, and if they have anything to convey to the occupants of this little hospital, they stand at the distance of 50 or 60 paces and throw it towards them as far as they can and retire.

—*Captain Lewis*

Washington 107 ♿

CHIEF TIMOTHY
Snake River/Corps of Engineers PArk

Location: Southeast corner of Washington west of Clarkston.

Access: From U.S. Highway 12 at milepost 425 +.9 (8 miles west of Clarkston, 21 miles east of Pomeroy), turn north, proceed across the causeway to the park.

Camping Facilities: 66 campsites, including 33 with full hookups and 16 park 'n walk tent sites; sites are medium-sized, with minimal separation; most parking pads are paved, level, long pull-throughs; excellent, grassy tent sites; fireplaces; firewood is usually for sale, or b-y-o; water at hookups and at several faucets; restrooms with showers; holding tank disposal station; paved driveways; complete supplies and services are available in Lewiston-Clarkston.

Day Use Facilities: Medium-sized picnic area; small shelters; drinking water; restrooms; 2 medium-sized parking lots.

Activities & Attractions: Alpowai Interpretive Center features exhibits related to local Native American lore and legend; boating; boat launch and docks; really nice playground ("Tot Lot"); pebble and sand swimming beach.

Natural Features: Located on an island in Lower Granite Lake, an impoundment on the Snake River; planted pines and hardwoods on watered and mown lawns provide very light to light-medium shade; bordered by high, rocky hills and bluffs; elevation 700´.

Season, Fees & Phone: Open all year; $17.00 for a standard site, $24.00 for a hookup site; park office ☎ (509) 758-9580.

Camp Journal: The island on which the park stands was formerly a high spot in the Lewis and Clark Valley before the area was flooded by the man-made lake. Displays and a-v programs in the interpretive center will give you the history of the area which the Indians called *Alpowai*. Chief Timothy was one of the first Christians among the Nez Percé chiefs. All picnic and camp sites have quite a spectacular view. In summer, the park stands in rich green contrast to the rugged, nearly treeless bluffs which border the river. The campground stretches for nearly a half mile along the south shore of the island. Several docks are located along the shore of the island, so you can tie-up to within arm's length of your site.

📖 *May 5, 1806*

Collected our horses and set out at 7 A.M. At 4 1/2 miles we arrived at the entrance of the Kooskooskee, up the N. Eastern side of which we continued our march 12 miles to a large lodge of 10 families, having passed two other large mat lodges; but not being able to obtain any provision at either of those lodges, continued our march to the third, where we arrived at 1 P.M., & with much difficulty obtained 2 dogs and a small quantity of root bread and dried roots.

At the second lodge, we passed an Indian man who gave Capt. C. a very elegant gray mare, for which he requested a phial of eye-water, which was accordingly given him. While we were encamped last fall at the entrance of the Chopunnish [N. Fork Clearwater] River, Capt. C. gave an Indian man some volatile liniment to rub his knee and thigh for a pain of which he complained. The fellow soon after recovered, and has never ceased to extol the virtues of our medicines, and the skill of my friend Capt. C. as a physician. This occurrence, added to the benefit which many of them experienced from the eye-water we gave them about the same time, has given them an exalted opinion of our medicine.

My friend Capt. C. is their favourite physician and has already received many applications. In our present situation, I think it pardonable to continue this deception, for they will not give us any provision without compensation in merchandize, and our stock is now reduced to a mere handfull. We take care to give them no article which can possibly injure them. We found our Chopunnish guide at this lodge with his family.

While at dinner, an Indian fellow very impertinently threw a poor, half-starved puppy nearly into my plate, by way of derision for our eating dogs, and laughed very heartily at his own impertinence. I was so provoked at his insolence that I caught the puppy and threw it with great violence at him and struck him in the breast and face, seized my tomahawk, and showed him by signs, if he repeated his insolence, I would tomahawk him. The fellow withdrew, apparently much mortified, and I continued my repast on dog without further molestation.

After dinner, we continued our rout 4 miles to the entrance of Colter's Creek [now Potlatch River]. We encamped on the lower side of the creek, at a little distance from 2 lodges of the Chopunnish, having traveled 20 1/2 miles today. We arrived here extreemly hungry and much fatigued, but no articles of merchandize in our possession would induce them to let us have any article of provision, except a small quantity of bread of cowse and some roots dried.

We had several applications to assist their sick, which we refused, unless they would let us have some dogs or horses to eat. A Cheif, whose wife had an abscess formed on the small of her back, promised a horse in the morning, provided we would administer to her. Accordingly, Capt. C. opened the abscess, introduced a roll of linen, and dressed it with ointment. Capt. C. soon had more than 50 applications. I prepared some doses of flower of sulphur and creme of tartar, which were given with directions to be taken on each morning. A little girl and sundry other patients were offered for cure, but we postponed our operations untill morning. They produced us several dogs, but they were so poor that they were unfit for use.

This is the residence of one of the 4 principal Cheifs of the Nation, whom they call Neesh-ne-park-ke-ook, or The Cut Nose, from the circumstance of his nose being cut by the

Snake [Shoshone] Indians with a lance in battle. To this man we gave a medal of the small size, with the likeness of the President. He may be a great Cheif, but his countenance has but little intelligence, and his influence among his people seems but inconsiderable. A number of Indians besides the inhabitants of these lodges gathered about us this evening and encamped in the timbered bottom on the creek near us.

We met with a Snake Indian man at this place, through whome we spoke at some length to the natives this evening with rispect to the objects which had induced us to visit their country. This address was induced at this moment by the suggestions of an old man who observed to the natives that he thought we were bad men and had come, most probably, in order to kill them. This impression, if really entertained, I believe we effaced; they appeared well satisfied with what we said to them, and, being hungry and tired, we retired to rest at 11 oClock.

—*Captain Lewis*

📖 *May 6, 1806*

This morning the husband of the sick woman was as good as his word. He produced us a young horse in tolerable order, which we immediately had killed and butchered. The inhabitants seemed more accommodating this morning; they sold us some bread. We received a second horse for medicine & prescription to a little girl with the rheumatism, whome I had bathed in warm water, and anointed her a little with balsam. I dressed the woman again this morning who declared that she had rested better last night than she had since she had been sick. I was busily employed for several hours this morning in administering eye water to a crowd of applicants. We once more obtained a plentiful meal, much to the comfort of all the party.

Capt. Lewis exchanged horses with We-ark-koomt and gave him a small flag with which he was much pleased and gratifyed. The sorrel which Cap. L. obtained is a strong, active, well-broke horse. The Kooskooske River may be safely navigated at present; all the rocks of the shoals and rapids are perfectly covered; the current is strong, the water clear and cold. This river is rising fast.

It was 2 P.M. before we could collect our horses. At 3. P.M. we set out accompanied by the brother of the Twisted Hair and We-ark-koomt. We directed the horse which I had

obtained for the purpose of eating to be led, as it was unbroken. In performing this duty, a quarrel ensued between Drewyer and Colter. We continued our march along the river on it's North side. A little after dark our young horse broke the rope by which he was confined and made his escape, much to the chagrin of all who recollected the keenness of their appetites last evening.

—*Captain Clark*

Special Note: *Ten camping areas lie along either side of U.S. Highway 12 in Montana and Idaho. The Expedition traveled this same basic route through Lolo Pass both westward in 1805 and eastward in 1806. So we have listed these ten highwayside camps in an alternating pattern—five campgrounds in the eastbound section that follows, the remaining five along the westbound trek in Volume 1.*

⛺ Idaho 108 ♿

PINK HOUSE
Public Lands/BLM Recreation Site

Location: Northern Idaho east of Lewiston.

Access: From U.S Highway 12 at milepost 39 +.1 (5 miles west of Orofino, 39 miles east of Lewiston), turn north and go 0.1 mile to the recreation area.

Camping Facilities: Approximately 12 campsites in a park-'em-and-pitch-'em-wherever arrangement around the perimeter of the large parking area; tent and parking spots are level, gravel, with enough space for small to large outfit, depending upon the individual spots; no tables; fire rings; some firewood is available for gathering in the general vicinity; no drinking water; vault facilities; gravel driveway; limited to adequate supplies and services are available in Orofino.

Day Use Facilities: Large parking area; other facilities are shared with campers.

Activities & Attractions: Rafting, floating; launch area; steelhead and trout fishing.

Natural Features: Located on a large riverside flat in a canyon along the south bank of the Middle Fork of the Clearwater River; sites receive light to medium shade/shelter from conifers and hardwoods; a few sites are riverside; closely bordered by hills and low mountains, with light to moderately timbered area interspersed with open, grassy sections; elevation 1300´.

Season, Fees & Phone: Open all year, subject to weather conditions; principal season is April to November; no fee (subject to change); 14 day limit; (no phone).

Camp Journal: An old, pink-painted house once stood on this locale. The recreation site is also called "Pink House Hole", depending upon which local sign you heed. The 'hole" refers to a deep section on the river that's a favorite fishing spot. This is more or less an 'official' jackcamping area (which is somewhat of a contradiction in terms), rather than a full-fledged camp and picnic ground. But it works if you bring along everything you need.

This small BLM site is a couple of miles from the Corps camps near the confluence of the North Fork of the Clearwater (Chopunnish River) and the main stream of the Clearwater (Kooskooskee River).

▲ *Kooskooskee Forks to the Camp on the Kooskooskee*

📖 *May 7, 1806*

This morning we collected our horses and set out early, accompanied by the brother of the Twisted Hair as a guide. We-ark-koomt and his party left us. We proceeded up the river 4 miles to a lodge of 6 families just below the entrance of a small creek. Here our guide recommended our passing the river. He informed us that the road was better on the South side, and that game was more abundant also on that side near the entrance of the Chopunnish River. We determined to pursue the rout recommended by the guide, and accordingly unloaded our horses and prepared to pass the river, which we effected by means of one canoe in the course of 4 hours.

A man of this lodge produced us two canisters of powder, which he informed us he had found by means of his dog where they had been buried in a bottom near the river some miles above. They were the same which we had buried as we descended the river last fall. As he kept them safe and had honesty enough to return them to us, we gave him a fire steel by way of compensation.

The Shoshone man of whom I have before made mention overtook us this evening with Neeshneparkkeook, and remained with us this evening. We supped this evening, as we had dined, on horse beef. We saw several deer this evening, and a great number of the tracks of

these animals. We determined to remain here untill noon tomorrow in order to obtain some venison, and accordingly gave orders to the hunters to turn out early in the morning.

The spurs of the Rocky Mountains which were in view from the high plain today were perfectly covered with snow. The Indians inform us that the snow is yet so deep on the mountains that we shall not be able to pass them untill the next full moon, or about the first of June; others set the time at still a more distant period. This is unwelcome intelligence to men confined to a diet of horse beef and roots, and who are anxious as we are to return to the fat plains of the Missouri and thence to our native homes.

—*Captain Lewis*

📖 *May 8, 1806*

Most of the hunters turned out by light this morning; a few others remained without our permission or knowledge untill late in the morning. We chided them severely for their indolence and inattention to the order of last evening. About 8 oClock Shields returned with a small deer, on which we breakfasted. By 11 A.M. all our hunters returned. Drewyer and Cruzatte brought each a deer. Collins wounded another, which my dog caught at a little distance from the camp. Our stock of provision now consisted of 4 deer and the remnant of the horse which we killed at Colter's Creek.

At half after 3 P.M., we departed for the lodge of the Twisted Hair, accompanied by the Cheif and sundry other Indians. The relation of the Twisted Hair left us. The road led us up a steep and high hill to a high and level plain mostly unlimbered, through which we passed parallel with the river about 4 miles when we met The Twisted Hair and a party of six men. To this Cheif we had confided the care of our horses and a part of our saddles when we descended the river last fall.

The Twisted Hair received us very coolly, an occurrence as unexpected as it was unaccountable to us. He shortly began to speak with a loud voice and in an angry manner. When he had ceased to speak, he was answered by the Cutnose Cheif, or Neeshneparkkeook. We readily discovered that a violent quarrel had taken place between these Cheifs but at that instant knew not the cause; we afterwards learned that it was on the subject of our horses. This controversy between the Cheifs detained us about 20 minutes. In order to put an end to this dispute, as well as to relieve our horses from the embarrassment of their loads, we informed the Cheifs that we should continue our march to the first water and encamp.

Accordingly, we moved on and the Indians all followed. About two miles on the road, we arrived at a little branch which ran to the right. Here we encamped for the evening, having traveled 6 miles today. The two Cheifs with their little bands formed separate camps a short distance from ours; they all appeared to be in an ill humor. We had been informed some days since that the natives had discovered our deposit of saddles and taken them away, and that our horses were much scattered. To obtain our horses and saddles as quickly as possible is our wish, and we are somewhat apprehensive that this difference which has taken place between these Cheifs may militate against our operations in this rispect. We were therefore desirous to bring about a good understanding between them as soon as possible.

The Shoshone boy refused to speak. He alleged it was a quarrel between two Chiefs, and that he had no business with it. It was in vain that we urged that his interpreting what we said on this subject was not taking the responsibility of the interference on himself. He remained obstinately silent.

About an hour after we had encamped, Drewyer returned from hunting. We sent him to The Twisted Hair to make some enquiries relative to our horses and saddles, and to ask him to come and smoke with us. The Twisted Hair accepted the invitation and came to our fire.

The Twisted Hair informed us that, according to the promise he had made us when he separated from us at the falls of the Columbia, he collected our horses on his return and took charge of them. That about this time The Cut Nose, or Neeshneparkkeook, and Tunnachemootoolt, or The Broken Arm, returned from a war excursion against the Shoshones on the South branch of Lewis's River, which had caused their absence when we were in this neighbourhood. That these men had become dissatisfied with him in consequence of our having confided the horses to his care, and that they were eternally quarreling with him insomuch that he thought it best, as he was an old man, to relinquish any further attention to the horses; that they had consequently become scattered; that most of the horses were near this place, a part were in the forks between the Chopunnish and

Kooskooskee Rivers, and three or four others were at the lodge of The Broken Arm, about half a day's march higher up the river.

He informed us with rispect to our saddles that on the rise of the water this spring, the earth had fallen from the door of the cache and exposed the saddles. He, being informed of their situation, had taken them up and placed them in another cache, where they were at this time. He said it was probable that a part of them had fallen into the water but of this he was not certain. The Twisted Hair said if we would spend the day tomorrow at his lodge, which was a few miles only from hence and on the road leading to The Broken Arm's lodge, he would collect such of our horses as were near this place, and our saddles; that he would also send some young men over the Kooskooskee to collect those in the forks and bring them to the lodge of The Broken Arm, to meet us. He advised us to go to the lodge of The Broken Arm, as he said he was a Cheif of great eminence among them, and promised to accompany us thither if we wished him.

We sent Drewyer to the Cut Nose, who also came to our fire and smoked with ourselves and The Twisted Hair. We took occasion in the course of the evening to express our regret that there should be a misunderstanding between these Cheifs. The Cut Nose told us in the presence of the Twisted Hair that he, the Twisted Hair, was a bad old man who wore two faces; that instead of taking care of our horses as he had promised us, that he had suffered his young men to ride them hunting and had injured them very much. The other made no reply.
—*Captain Lewis*

The camp of May 8th, 1806 was in the vicinity of present-day Orofino, Idaho, a few miles southeast of the "Canoe Camp" of the previous September-October. From here, the Corps left the Clearwater River and headed southeasterly overland, paralleling the southwest bank of the river.

May 9, 1806
We were detained untill 9 A.M. for our horses, which were much scattered, at which time we collected our horses and set out and proceeded on through a beautifull, open, rich country for 6 miles to the camp of the Twisted Hair. Before 2 P M all our hunters joined us, having killed only one deer which was lost in the river and a pheasent. Soon after we halted at the lodge of the Twisted Hair, he set out with two boys and Willard with a pack horse

down to the river near the place we made the canoes, for our saddles and a cannister of powder and some lead buried there; also a part of our horses which resorted near that place.

Late in the evening they returned with 21 of our horses and about half of our saddles, with the powder and ball. The greater part of the horses were in fine order, tho' five of them had been rode & worsted in such a manner last fall by the Indians that they had not recovered and are in very low order, and 3 with sore backs. We had all the recovered horses caught & hobbled. We procured some pounded roots of which a soup was made thick, on which we supped. The wind blew hard from the S.W. accompanied with rain from 7 oclock untill 9 P.M., when it began to snow and continued all night.

—*Captain Clark*

📖 *May 10, 1806*

This morning the snow continued falling until 1/2 after 6 A.M. We gathered our horses and, after taking a scant breakfast of roots, we set out. Our rout lay through an open plain for 16 miles.

At 4 in the afternoon, we descended the hills to Commearp Creek [now Lawyers Creek] and arrived at the village of Tunnachemootoolt, the Cheif at whose lodge we had left the flag last fall. This flag was now displayed on a staff placed at no great distance from the lodge. Underneath the flag, the Cheif met my friend Capt. C., who was in front, and conducted him about 80 yards to a place on the bank of the creek where he requested we should encamp.

I came up in a few minutes and we collected the Cheifs and men of consideration, smoked with them, and stated our situation with rispect to provision. The Cheif spoke to his people, and they produced us about two bushels of the quamash roots, dryed, four cakes of the bread of cowse, and a dryed salmon trout. We thanked them for this store of provision but informed them that, our men not being accustomed to live on roots alone, we feared it would make them sick, to obviate which we proposed exchanging a horse in reather low order for a young horse in tolerable order with a view to kill. The hospitality of the Cheif revolted at the idea of an exchange. He told us that his young men had a great abundance of young horses, and if we wished to eat them we should be furnished with as many as we wanted. Accordingly, they soon produced us two fat young horses, one of which we killed.

The other we informed them we would postpone killing untill we had consumed the one already killed.

A principal Cheif by name Ho-has-till-pilp, arrived with a party of fifty men mounted on elegant horses. He had come on a visit to us from his village, which is situated about six miles distant near the river. We invited this man into our circle and smoked with him; his retinue continued on horseback at a little distance. After we had eaten a few roots, we spoke to them as we had promised, and gave Tunnachemooltoolt and Hohastillpilp each a medal; the former one of the small size with the likeness of Mr. Jefferson, and the latter one of the sewing medals struck in the Presidency of Washington. We explained to them the design and the importance of medals in the estimation of the whites as well as the red men who had been taught their value. The Cheif had a large conic lodge of leather erected for our reception, and a parcel of wood collected and laid at the door; after which he invited Capt. C. and myself to make that lodge our home while we remained with him. We had a fire lighted in this lodge and retired to it, accompanied by the Cheifs and as many of the considerate men as could crowd in a circle within it. After we had taken a repast of some horse beef, we resumed our council with the Indians, which together with smoking the pipe, occupied the ballance of the evening.

—*Captain Lewis*

📖 *May 11, 1806*

The last evening we were much crowded with the Indians in our lodge, the whole floor of which was covered with their sleeping carcasses. At 8 A.M. a Cheif of great note among these people arrived from his village or lodge on the S. side of Lewis's River. This is a stout fellow of good countenance, about 40 years of age, and has lost the left eye. His name is Yoom-park-kar-tim. To this man we gave a medal of the small kind. Those with the likeness of Mr. Jefferson have all been disposed of except one of the largest size, which we reserve for some great Cheif on the Yellow Rock River.

We now pretty fully informed ourselves that Tunnachemootoolt, Neeshneparkkeook, Yoomparkkartirn, and Hohastillpilp were the principal Cheifs of the Chopunnish Nation and rank in the order here mentioned. As all those Cheifs were present in our lodge, we thought it a favourable time to repeat what had been said yesterday and to enter more minutely into the views of our government with rispect to the inhabitants of this western part of the continent; their intention of establishing trading houses for their relief; their wish to restore peace and harmony among the natives; the strength, power, and wealth of our Nation, &c.

To this end we drew a map of the country, with a coal on a mat in their way and, by the assistance of the Snake boy and our interpreters, were enabled to make ourselves understood by them, altho' it had to pass through the French, Minnetaree, Shoshone, and Chopunnish languages. The interpretation being tedious, it occupied nearly half the day before we had communicated to them what we wished. They appeared highly pleased. After this council was over we amused ourselves with showing them the power of magnetism, the spyglass, compass, watch, air gun, and sundry other articles equally novel and incomprehensible to them.

—Captain Lewis

📖 *May 12, 1806*

A fine morning. Great numbers of Indians flock about us as usial. After brakfast I began to administer eye-water and in a fiew minits had near 40 applicants with sore eyes, and maney others with other complaints, most common rheumatic disorders & weaknesses in the back and loins, particularly the womin.

The Indians had a grand council this morning, after which we were presented each with a horse by two young men at the instance of the Nation. We caused the Chiefs to be seated and gave them each a flag, a pint of powder, and 50 balls, to two young men who had presented the horses, we also gave powder and ball. The Broken Arm, or Tunnachemootoolt, pulled off his leather shirt, and gave me. In return, I gave him a shirt.

We retired into the lodge, and the nativs spoke to the following purpose: i.e., they had listened to our advice and that the whole Nation were deturmined to follow it; that they had only one heart and one tongue on this subject. Explained the cause of the war with the Shoshones. They wished to be at peace with all nations, &c. Some of their men would accompany us to the Missouri, &c., &c.

As a great number of men, womin, & children were waiting and requesting medical assistance, many of them with the most simple complaints which could be easily relieved, independent of maney with disorders entirely out of the power of medicine, all requesting

something, we agreed that I should administer, and Capt. L. hear and answer the Indians. I was closely employed untill 2 P.M., administering eye-water to about 40 grown persons, some simple cooling medicines to the disabled Chief, to several womin with rheumatic affections, & a man who had a swelled hip, &c., &c.

In the evening, three of our horses were brought, all in fine order. We have now only six remaining out. Those people are much afraid of the Blackfoot Indians, and the Big Bellies of Fort de Prarie establishment. Those Indians kill great numbers of this Nation whenever they pass over to hunt on the Missouri. One of our men bought a horse for a fiew small articles of an Indian. The Indians brought up a fat horse and requested us to kill and eate it, as they had nothing else to offer us to eate. The Cut Nose made a present of a horse to Drewyer at the same time the two horses were offered to Capt. Lewis & myself. The horses of those people are large, well formed and active. Generally in fine order. Sore backs caused by riding them either with out saddles, or with pads which does not prevent the weight of the rider pressing immediately on the back bone and withers of the horse.

The Indians formed two parties and played for their beeds. We gave the Twisted Hair a gun, powder & 100 ball, in part for taking care of our horses &c., and wish him to camp near us untill we crossed the mountains, which he agreed to do, and was much pleased. We have turned our attentions towards the Twisted Hair, who has several sons grown who are well acquainted as well as himself with the various roads through the Rocky Mountains, and will answer very well as guides to us through those mountains.

In the council to day the father of Hohastillpilp said the Chopunnish were fully convinced of the advantages of peace and ardently wished to cultivate peace with their neighbours. Early last summer 3 of their brave men were sent with a pipe to the Shoshones on the S.E. fork of Lewis's river in the Plains of Columbia; their pipe was disregarded and their 3 men murdered, which had given rise to the war expedition against that Nation last fall; that their warriors had fallen in with and killed 42 of the Shoshones with the loss of 3 men only on their part; that this had satisfied the blood of the deceased friends and they would never again make war against the Shoshones, but were willing to receive them as friends. That as we had not seen the Indians towards Fort de

Prarie, they did not think it safe to venture over to the Plains of the Missouri, where they would fondly go provided those Nations would not kill them. I gave a vial of eye water to the Broken arm for to wash the eyes of all who applied to him and told him when it was out we would replenish it again.

—*Captain Clark*

📖 *May 13, 1806*

A fine morning. I administered to the sick and gave directions. We collected all our horses and set out at 1 P.M. and proceeded down the creek to the Kooskooskee [Clearwater] River a short distance below the enterance of the creek. At this place we expected to have met the canoe which was promised to be furnished us, and for which an Indian set out very early this morning.

We halted at the river unloaded our horses and turned them out to feed. Several Indians accompanied us to the river and continued untill evening. The man who set out early this morning to the forks of this river for a canoe did not arive untill after sunset. We remained all night. In the evening we tried the speed of several of our horses. These horses are strong, active, and well formed. Those people have emence numbers of them, 50 or 60 or a hundred head is not unusual for an individual to possess.

The Chopunnish are in general stout, well formed, active men. They have high noses and many of them on the aquiline order, with cheerfull and agreeable countenances; their complexions are not remarkable. In common with other Indian Nations of America, they extract their beard, but the men do not uniformly extract their hair below; this is more particularly confined to the females. They appear to be cheerfull but not gay; they are fond of gambling and of their amusements, which consists principally in shooting their arrows at a target made of willow bark, and in riding and exercising themselves on horseback, racing &c. They are expert marksmen & good riders.

They do not appear to be so much devoted to baubles as most of the nations we have met with, but seem anxious always to receive articles of utility, such as knives, axes, kittles, blankets & mockerson awls. Blue beeds, however, may form an exception to this remark. This article among all the nations of this country may be justly compared to gold and silver among civilized nations.

They are generally well clothed in their stile. Their dress consists of a long shirt which reaches to the middle of the leg, long leggings which reach as high as the waist, mockersons & robe. Those are formed of various skins and are in all rispects like those of the Shoshone. Their ornaments consist of beeds, shells and pieces of brass variously attached to their dress, to their ears, arround their necks, wrists arms &c. A band of some kind usially surrounds the head; this is most frequently the skin of some fur animal as the fox, otter &c. I observed a tippet worn by Hohastillpilp, which was formed of human scalps and ornamented with the thumbs and fingers of several men which he had slain in battle. They also wear a collar or breastplate of otter skin ornamented with shells, beeds & quills. The women braids their hair in two tresses which hang in the same position of those of the men, which are sewed and hang over each sholder &c.

—*Captain Clark*

▲ *Waiting for Spring to Come to the Mountains*

The Expedition now began to set up a long-term camp, crossing over to the north-east bank of the Clearwater, about 2 miles north of the present-day town of Kamiah. Here they were to spend the next month waiting for the snows to melt on the high mountains and ridges of the Bitterroot Mountains, which they would need to cross over into Montana. Neither Lewis nor Clark attached a name to this camp, even though they spent a considerable time here. However, it has become popularly known as "Camp Chopunnish"—the name given to it by an early editor of the Journals.

📖 *May 14, 1806*

We had all our horses collected by 10 A.M.; during the time we had all our baggage crossed over the river, which is rapid and about 150 yards wide. After the baggage was over to the North side, we crossed our horses without much trouble and hobbled them in the bottom after which we moved a short distance below to a convenient situation and formed a camp around a very convenient spot for defence. This situation we concluded would be sufficently convenient to hunt the wood lands for bear & deer and for the salmon fish which we were told would be here in a fiew days, and also a good situation for our horses. The hills to the E. & N. of us are high, broken &

but partially timbered; the soil rich and affords fine grass. In short, as we are compelled to reside a while in this neighbourhood, I feel perfectly satisfied with our position.

Immediately after we had crossed the river, the Chief called the Broken Arm and another principal Chief arived on the opposit side and began to sing. We sent the canoe over and those Chiefs, the son of the Broken Arm and the son of a Great Chief who was killed last year by the Big Bellies of Saskashawan River. Those two young men were the two who gave Capt. Lewis and myself each a horse with great ceremony in behalf of the Nation a fiew days ago, and the latter a most elegant mare & colt the morning after we arived at the village. Hohastillpilp, with much ceremeony, presented Capt. Lewis with an elegant gray horse which he had brought for that purpose. Capt. Lewis gave him in return a handkerchief, two hundred balls and four pounds of powder, with which he appeared perfectly satisfied, and appeared much pleased. We made several attempts to exchange our stallions for geldings or mares without success. We even offered two for one. Those horses are troublesome and cut each other very much, and as we can't exchange them, we think it best to castrate them and began the operation this evening.

About Meridian, Shannon came in with two grouse & 2 squirrels common to this country. His mockersons worn out, obliged to come in early. Collins returned in the evening with the two bears which he had killed in the morning. We gave the Indians about us, 15 in number, two shoulders and a ham of the bear to eate, which they cooked in the following manner. To wit, on a brisk fire of dryed wood they threw a parcel of small stones from the river; when the fire had burnt down and heated the stone, they placed them leavel and laid on a parcel of pine boughs; on those they laid the flesh of the bear in flitches, placing boughs between each course of meat and then covering it thickly with pine boughs; after this they poured on a small quantity of water, and covered the whole over with earth to the depth of 4 inches. In this situation they suffered it to remain about 3 hours, when they took it out fit for use. This Nation esteem the killing of one of those tremendous animals equally great with that of an enemy in the field of action. We gave the claws of those bear which Collins had killed to Hohlstillpilp.

—*Captain Clark*

📖 *May 15, 1806*

This morning early Reuben Fields, in searching for his horse, saw a large bear at no great distance from camp; several men went in pursuit of the bear; they followed his trail a considerable distance but could not come up with him. Labiche and Shannon set out with a view to establish a hunting camp and continuing several days, two others accompanyed them in order to bring in the three bear which Labiche had killed. Drewyer and Cruzatte were sent up the river; Shields, R. Fields and Willard hunted in the hills near the camp; they returned in the evening with a few pheasants only and reported that there was much late appearance of bear, but believed that they had gone off to a greater distance. At 11 A.M. the men returned with the bear which Labiche had killed.

These bear gave me a stronger evidence of the various coloured bear of this country being one species only [grizzlies], than any I have heretofore had. In short, it is not common to find two bear here of this species precisely of the same colour; and if we were to attempt to distinguish them by their colours and to denominate each colour a distinct species, we should soon find at least twenty. Some bear nearly white have also been seen by our hunters at this place.

The most striking differences between this species of bear and the common black bear are that the former are larger, have longer talons and tusks, prey more on other animals, do not lie so long nor so closely in winter quarters, and will not climb a tree tho' ever so hardly pressed. The variegated bear I believe to be the same here with those on the Missouri, but these are not as ferocious as those, perhaps from the circumstance of their being compelled from the scarcity of game in this quarter to live more on roots, and of course not so much in the habit of seizing and devouring living animals. The bear here are far from being as passive as the common black bear; they have attacked and fought our hunters already, but not so fiercely as those of the Missouri. There are also some of the common black bear in this neighbourhood.

Frazier, J. Fields and Wiser complain of violent pains in their heads, and Howard and York are afflicted with the cholic. I attribute these complaints to their diet of roots which they have not been accustomed.

Tunnachemootoolt and 12 of his young men left us this morning on their return to their village. Hohastillpilp and three old men remained untill 5 in the evening. when they also departed. At 1 P.M. a party of 14 natives on horseback passed our camp on a hunting excursion; they were armed with bows and arrows and had decoys for the deer. These are the skins of the heads and upper portions of the necks of the deer extended in their natural shape by means of a frame of little sticks placed within. The hunter, when he sees a deer, conceals himself, and with his hand gives to the decoy the action of a deer at feed; and thus induces the deer within arrow shot; in this mode the Indians hunt on foot in the woodlands where they cannot pursue the deer with horses, which is their favorite method when the ground will permit.

We had all of our horses driven together today near our camp, which we have directed shall be done each day in order to familiarize them to each other. We had our baggage better secured under a good shelter formed of grass; we also strengthened our little fortification with pine poles and brush, and the party formed themselves very comfortable tents with willow poles and grass in the form of the awning of a wagon; these were made perfectly secure as well from the heat of the sun as from the rain. Had a bower constructed for ourselves under which we set by day, and sleep by night under the part of an old sail now our only tent, as the leather lodge has become rotten and unfit for use.

About noon the sun shines with intense heat in the bottoms of the river. The air on the bottom of the river hills or high plain forms a distinct climate, the air is much colder, and vegetation is not as forward by at least 15 or perhaps 20 days. The rains which fall in the river bottoms are snows on the plain. At the distance of fifteen miles from the river and on the eastern border of this plain, the Rocky Mountains commence and present us with winter in it's utmost extreme. The snow is yet many feet deep even near the base of these mountains; here we have summer spring and winter within the short space of 15 or 20 miles.

Hohastillpilp and the three old men being unable to pass the river, as the canoe had been taken away, returned to our camp late in the evening and remained with us all night.

—*Captain Lewis*

📖 *May 16, 1806*

Hohastillpilp and all the nativs left us at Meridian and went up the river with a view to cross some distance above where they expected to find a canoe.

We gave those people the head and neck of the largest bear, a part of which they ate, and the ballance they carefully took with them for their children. The Indians of this country seldom kill the bear. They are very much afraid of them and the killing of a White or Grizzly bear is as great a feat as two of their enemy. The fiew of those animals which they chance to kill is found in the leavel, open lands and pursued on horses & killed with their arrows. They are fond of the flesh of this animal and eate immoderately of it when they have a sufficiency to indulge themselves.

The men who were complainingof the head ache and cholic yesterday and last night are much better to day. Shabonos squar gathered a quantity of fenel roots, which we find very palatable and nurishing food. The onion we also find in abundance and boil it with our meat.

—*Captain Clark*

📖 *May 17, 1806*

It rained the greater part of the last night and this morning untill 8 oClock. The water passed through flimzy covering and wet our bed most perfectly; in short, we lay in the water all the latter part of the night. Unfortunately my chronometer, which for greater security I have worn in my fob for ten days past, got wet last night; it seemed a little extraordinary that every part of my breeches, which were under my head, should have escaped the moisture except the fob where the time piece was.

I opened it and found it nearly filled with water, which I carefully drained out, exposed it to the air and wiped the works as well as I could with dry feathers, after which I touched them with a little bears oil. Several parts of the iron and steel works were rusted a little, which I wiped with all the care in my power. I set her to going, and from her apparent motion hope she has sustained no material injury.

At 9 A.M. Sergt. Pryor and Collins returned. Sergt. Pryor brought the skin and flesh of a black bear which he had killed; Collins had also killed a very large variegated bear; but his horse having absconded last evening, was unable to bring it. They had secured this meat perfectly from the wolves or birds, and as it was at a considerable distance, we did not think proper to send for it today. Neither of these bear were in good order. As the bear are reather ferocious and we are obliged to depend on them pincipally for our subsistence, we thought it most advisable to direct at least two hunters to go together, and they accordingly paired themselves out for this purpose.

It rained moderately the greater part of the day and snowed as usual on the plain. Sergt. Pryor informed me that it was shoe deep this morning when he came down. We have been visited by no Indians today, an occurrence which has not taken place before since we left the Narrows of the Columbia. I am pleased at finding the river rise so rapidly; it no doubt is attributable to the melting snows of the mountains, that icy barrier which separates me from my friends and Country, from all which makes life esteemable.—patience, patience—.

—Captain Lewis

📖 *May 18, 1806*

Cloudy morning. 12 hunters turned out in different directions to the order of yesterday.

The squar wife to Shabono busied herself gathering the roots of the fenel, called by the Snake Indians *year-pah*, for the purpose of drying to eate on the Rocky Mountains. Those roots are very palatable either fresh roasted, boiled or dried, and are generally between the size of a quill and that of a mans finger, and about the length of the latter.

At 3 P.M. Jo. Field returned from the chase without killing anything, He complains of being unwell. Soon after, an old man and a woman arived, the man with sore eyes, and the woman with a gripeing and rheumatic affections. I gave the woman a dose of creme of tartar and flour of sulphur, and the man some eye water. A little before night, Rueben Fields, Drewyer and LaPage returned, having killed nothing but a large hawk. LaPage took a salmon from an eagle at a short distance below our camp. This is induces us to believe that the salmon is in this river, and most probably will be here in great numbers in the course of a fiew days.

—Captain Clark

📖 *May 19, 1806*

We sent Shabono, Thompson, Potts, Hall & Wiser over to the villages above to purchase some roots to eate with our pore bear meat, for which purchase we gave them a fiew awls, knitting pins, & arm bands, and directed them to proceed up on this side of the river opposit to the village and cross in the canoe which we are informed is at that place.

About 11 oClock 4 men and 8 women came to our camp with Thompson, who went to the village very early this morning. Those men

applied for eye water and the women had a variety of complaints, tho' the most general complaint was the rheumatism, pains in the back and the sore eyes. They also brought forward a very young child whome they said had been very sick. I administered eye water to all, two of the women I gave a carthartic; one whose spirits were very low and much depressed I gave 30 drops of laudanum, and to the others I had their backs, hips, legs, thighs & arms well rubbed with volitile liniment. All of those pore people thought themselves much benefited by what had been done for them, and at 3 P.M. they all returned to their villages well satisfied.

At 5 P.M. Potts, Shabono &c. returned from the village with about 6 bushels of the root the nativs call *cowse* and some bread of the same root. Rubin & Jos. Fields returned with the horse Capt. Lewis rode across the Rocky Mountains. We amused ourselves about an hour this afternoon looking at the men run their horses, several of them would be thought swift horses in the Atlantic States.

—Captain Clark

📖 *May 21, 1806*

We divided our store of merchandize amongst our party for the purpose of precuring some roots &c. of the nativs; to each mans part amounted to about an awl, knitting pin, a little paint and some thread & 2 needles, which is but a scanty dependence for roots to take us over those great snowy barriers (Rocky Mountains), which is and will be the cause of our detention in this neighbourhood, probably untill the 10 or 15 of June. They are at this time covered deep with snow. The plains on the high country above us is also covered with snow. We eate the last of our meat for dinner today, and our only certain dependence is the roots we can procure from the nativs for the fiew articles we have left. Those roots, with what game we can procure from the woods, will probably last us untill the arrival of the salmon. If they should not; we have a horse in store ready to be killed, which the Indians have offered to us

—Captain Clark

📖 *May 22, 1806*

A fine day. We exposed all our baggage to the sun to air and dry, also our roots which we have procured of the nativs. As the greater part of our men have not had any meat to eate for 2 days, and the roots they complain of not being accustomed to live on them altogether, we directed a large colt which was given to us by a young man with an elegant mare to be killed. This colt was fat and was handsome-looking meat. Late in the evening we were informed that the horse which Capt. L. rode over the Rocky Mountains had his hip out of place since that time, and could not walk. Capt. Lewis examined him and thought he could not recover.

At 5 P.M. two young men highly decorated in their way came to our camp and informed us that the fat fish were in great numbers in Lewis's River. Shabonos son, a small child, is dangerously ill. His jaw and throat is much swelled. We apply a poultice of onions after giving him some creme of tartar &c.

—Captain Clark

📖 *May 23, 1806*

The child is something better this morning than it was last night. We applied a fresh poultice of the wild onion, which we repeated twice in the course of the day. The swelling does not appear to increase any since yesterday. The 4 Indians who visited us today informed us that they came from their village on Lewis's River, two days ride from this place, for the purpose of seeing us and getting a little eye-water. I washed their eyes with some eye-water, and they all left us at 2 P.M. and returned to the villages on the opposit side of this river. The hunters informed us that they hunted with great industry all the country between the river and for some distance above and below without the smallest chance of killing any game.

—Captain Clark

📖 *May 24, 1806*

The child was very restless last night. It's jaw and back of it's neck is much more swollen than it was yesterday. I gave it a dose of creme of tartar and a fresh poultice of onions.

Ordered Shields, Gibson, Drewyer, Cruzat, Collins, and Joe & Reuben Fields to turn out hunting and if possible cross Collins Creek and hunt toward the quamash fields. W. Bratten is yet very low. He eats heartily, but he is so weak in the small of his back that he can't walk. We have made use of every remedy to restore him without it's having the desired effect. One of our party, John Shields, observed that he had seen men in similar situations restored by violent sweats, and Bratten requested that he might be sweated in the way Shields proposed, which we agreed to.

Shields dug a round hole 4 feet deep & 3 feet in diameter, in which he made a large fire so as to heat the hole, after which the fire was taken out, a seat placed in the hole. The patient was then set on the seat with a board under his feet and a can of water handed him to throw on the bottom & the sides of the hole, so as to create as great a heat as he could bear, and the hole covered with blankets supported by hoops. After about 20 minits, the patient was taken out and put in cold water a fiew minutes & returned to the hole, in which he was kept about an hour, then taken out and covered with several blankets, which was taken off by degrees untill he became cool. This remedy took place yesterday and Bratten is walking about today, and is much better than he has been.

At 11 A.M. a canoe came down with the Indian man who had applied for medical assistance while we lay at The Broken Arm's village. This man I had given a fiew doses of flowers of sulphur & creme of tartar and directed that he should take the cold bath every morning. He conceded himself a little better than he was at that time. He had lost the use of all his limbs, and his fingers are contracted. We are at a loss to deturmine what to do for this unfortunate man. I gave him a fiew drops of laudanum and some portable soup as medicine. 4 of our men crossed the river and went to the Broken Arms village and returned in the evening with a supply of bread and roots which they procured in exchange for awls which were made of pieces of cane.

—Captain Clark

📖 *May 25, 1806*

The child is not so well today as yesterday. I repeated the creme of tarter and the onion poultice.

I caused a sweat to be prepared for the Indian Chief in the same hole which Bratten had been sweated in two days past. We attempted to sweat the sick Indian than but could not succeed. He was not able either to set up or be supported in the place prepared for him. I therefore deturmined to inform the nativs that nothing but severe sweats would restore this disabled man, and even that doubtfull in his present situation.

—Captain Clark

📖 *May 26, 1806*

The child something better this morning, tho' the swelling yet continues. We still apply the onion poultice. I directed what should be done for the disabled man, gave him a fiew doses of creme of tartar & flower of sulphur, and some portable soup & directed that he should be taken home and sweated, &c. One of our men saw a salmon in the river today, and two others ate of salmon at the near village which was brought from Lewis's River.

—*Captain Clark*

📖 *May 27, 1806*

Shabono's child is much better today, tho' the swelling on the side of his neck, I believe, will terminate in an ugly imposthume, a little below the ear. The Indians were so anxious that the sick Chief (who has lost the use of his limbs) should be sweated under our inspection, they requested me to make a 2nd attempt today. Accordingly, the hole was enlarged, and his father a very good-looking old man performed all the drudgery, &c. We could not make him sweat as copiously as we wished, being compelled to keep him erect in the hole by means of cords. After the operation, he complained of considerable pain. I gave him 30 drops of laudanum, which soon composed him, and he rested very well.

I observe the strongest marks of parental affection. They all appear extreemly attentive to this sick man, nor do they appear to relax in their ascuity towards him, notwithstanding he has been sick and helpless for near five years. The Chopunnish appear to be very attentive & kind to their aged people and treat their women with more rispect than the nativs on the Missouri.

—*Captain Clark*

📖 *May 28, 1806*

We sent Goodrich to the village of the Broken Arm for hair to stuff saddle pads. Jo. & R. Fields set out this morning to hunt towards the mountains. At noon Shabono, York and LaPage returned; they had obtained 4 bags of the dried roots of cowse and some bread. In the evening Collins, Shannon & Colter returned with 8 deer. Deer were very abundant they informed us, but there was not many bear. The sick Chief is much better this morning; he can use his hands and arms and seems much pleased with the prospects of recovering. He says he feels much better than he has done for a great number of months. I sincerely wish that the sweats may restore him. Shabonos child is better this day than he was yesterday. He is free from fever. The imposthume is not so large but seems to be advanceing to maturity.

—*Captain Clark*

📖 *May 30, 1806*

LaPage and Charbono set out to the Indian villages early this morning in order to trade with them for roots. Sergt. Gass was sent this morning to obtain some goats hair to stuff the pads of our saddles. He ascended the river on this side and, being unable to pass the river to the village he wished to visit, returned in the evening unsuccessful. Shannon and Collins were permitted to pass the river in order to trade with the natives and lay in a store of roots and bread for themselves with their proportion of the merchandize as others had done. On landing on the opposite shore, the canoe was driven broadside, with the full force of a very strong current against some standing trees and instantly filled with water and sunk. Potts, who was with them, is an indifferent swimmer. It was with difficulty he made the land. They lost three blankets and a blanket capote and their pittance of merchandize.

In our bare state of clothing this was a serious loss. I sent Sergt. Pryor and a party over in the Indian canoe in order to raise and secure ours, but the depth of the water and the strength of the current baffled every effort. I fear that we have also lost our canoe. All our invalids are on the recovery. We gave the sick Cheif a severe sweat today, shortly after which he could move one of his legs and thighs and work his toes pretty well. The other leg he can move a little. His fingers and arms seem to be almost entirely restored. He seems highly delighted with his recovery. I begin to entertain strong hope of his recovering by these sweats.

—*Captain Lewis*

📖 *June 1, 1806*

Yesterday evening Charbono and LaPage returned, having made a broken voyage. They ascended the river on this side nearly opposite to a village eight miles above us. Here their led horse, which had on him their merchandize, fell into the river from the side of a steep clift and swam over. They saw an Indian on the opposite side whom they prevailed on to drive their horse back again to them. In swimming the river the horse lost a dressed elk skin of LaPages and several small articles & their paint was destroyed by the water. Here they remained and dryed their articles.

The evening of the 30th, the Indians at the village, learning their errand and not having a canoe, made an attempt yesterday morning to pass the river to them on a raft with a parcel of roots and bread in order to trade with the them. The Indian raft struck a rock, upset, and lost their cargo. The river having fallen heir to both merchandize and roots, our traders returned with empty bags.

This morning Drewyer, accompanied by Hohastillpilp, set out in search of two tomahawks of ours which we have understood were in the possession of certain Indians residing at a distance in the plains on the South side of the Kooskooskee; the one is a pipe tomahawk which Cap C. left at our camp on Musquetoe Creek and the other was stolen from us whilst we lay at the forks of this and the Chopunnish Rivers last fall.

—Captain Lewis

📖 *June 2, 1806*

McNeal and York were sent on a trading voyage over the river this morning. Having exhausted all our merchandize, we are obliged to have recourse to every subterfuge in order to prepare in the most ample manner in our power to meet that wretched portion of our journey, the Rocky Mountains, where hunger and cold in their most rigorous forms assail the wearied traveller. Not any of us has yet forgotten our suffering in those mountains in September last, and I think it probable we never shall.

Our traders McNeal and York were furnished with the buttons which Capt. C. and myself cut off our coats, some eye-water and basilican which we made for that purpose, and some phials and small tin boxes which I had brought out with phosphorus. In the evening they returned with about 3 bushels of roots and some bread, having made a successful voyage not much less pleasing to us than the return of a good cargo to an East India merchant.

—Captain Lewis

📖 *June 2, 1806*

Drewyer arived this evening with Neeshneparkkeeook and Hohashillpilp, who had accompanied him to the lodge of the person who had our tomahawks. He obtained both the tomahawks, principally by the influence of the former of those Chiefs. The one which had been stolen we prized most, as it was the private property of the late Sergt. Floyd and I was desirous of returning it to his friends. The man who had this tomahawk had purchased it from the man who had stolen it, and was himself at the moment of the arival just expiring. His relations were unwilling to give up the tomahawk, as they intended to

bury it with the deceased owner; but were at length induced to do so for the consideration of a handkerchief and two strands of beeds which Drewyer gave them, and two horses given by the Chiefs to be killed, agreeable to their custom at the grave of the deceased. The custom of sacrificing horses to the deceased appears to be common to all nations of the Plains of the Columbia. A wife of Neeshneeparkkeeook died some short time since, himself and her relations sacrificed 28 horses to her.

—Captain Clark

📖 *June 3, 1806*

Our invalids are all on the recovery; Bratten is much stronger and can walk about with considerable ease. The Indian Chief appears to be gradually recovering the use of his limbs; and the child is nearly well; the inflammation on his neck continues, but the swelling appears to subside. We still continue the application of the onion poultice.

Today the Indians dispatched an express over the mountains to Travellers Rest or to the neighbourhood of that creek on Clark's River in order to learn from a band of Flat-heads who inhabit that river and who have probably wintered on Clark's River near the enterance of Travellers Rest Creek, the occurences which have taken place on the East side of the mountains during last winter. This is the band which we first met with on that river. The mountains being practicable for this express, we thought it probable that we could also pass, but the Chiefs informs us that several of the creeks would yet swim our horses; that there was no grass and that the road was extreemly deep and slippery; they inform us that we may pass conveniently in twelve or fourteen days.

We have come to a resolution to remove from hence to the quawmash grounds beyond Collins Creek on the 10th, to hunt in that neighbourhood a fiew days, if possible lay in a stock of meat, and then attempt the mountains about the middle of this month. I begin to lose all hope of any dependence on the salmon, as this river will not fall sufficiently to take them before we shall leave it, and as yet I see no appearance of their running near the shore as the Indians informed us they would in the course of a fiew days.

—Captain Clark

🔱 Captain Clark has just made note of a group decision to pack up and move their camp about 10 miles to the north-northeast to the prairie near the hamlet of Weippe, Idaho. That was the site of their first encounter with the Chopunnish on September 20, 1805. In doing so, they'll once again pick up what would become the 'mainline' of the Lewis and Clark Trail.

📖 *June 4, 1806*

About noon the 3 Cheifs left us and returned to their villages. While they were with us, we repeated the promises we had formerly made them and invited them to the Missouri with us. They declined going untill the latter end of the summer, and said it was their intention to spend the ensuing winter on the East side of the Rocky Mountains. They gave us no positive answer to a request which we made, that two or three of their young men should accompany me to the Falls of the Missouri, and there wait my return from the upper part of Maria's River, where it was probable I should meet with some of the bands of the Minnetares from Fort de Prarie; that, in such case, I should endeavour to bring about a good understanding between those Indians and themselves, which when effected they would be informed of it through the young men thus sent with me; and that on the contrary, should I not be fortunate enough to meet with these people nor to prevail on them to be at peace, they would equally be informed through those young men, and they might still remain on their guard with rispect to them untill the whites had it in their power to give them more effectual relief. The Broken Arm invited us to his village and said he wished to speak to us before we set out, and that he had some roots to give us for our journey over the mountains.

—*Captain Lewis*

📖 *June 5, 1806*

Colter and Bratten were permitted to visit the Indian village today for the purpose of trading for roots and bread; they were fortunate and made a good return. We gave the Indian Chief another sweat today, continuing it as long as he could bear it; in the evening he was very languid but still continued to improve in the use of his limbs. The child is recovereing fast. I applied a plaster of salve made of the resin of the long-leafed pine, beeswax and bears oil mixed, which has subsided the inflammation entirely; the part is considerably swelled and hard. In the evening, Reuben Fields, G. Shannon, Labiche, & Collins returned from the chase and brought with them five deer and a brown bear.

—*Captain Clark*

📖 *June 6, 1806*

I visited the Broken Arm today, agreeable to my promise of the 4th. I was received in a friendly manner. The Broken Arm informed me that many of the small cheifs of the different bands of his Nation had not heard our word from our own mouths. Several of them were present and were glad to see me, &c. I repeated in part what had been said in council before. The Broken Arm told me that the Nation would not pass the mountains untill the latter part of the summer, and that with rispect to the young men who we had requested to accompany us to the Falls of the Missouri, they were not yet selected for that purpose, nor could they be so untill there was a meeting of the Nation in council. That would happen in the course of 10 or 12 days; that when they held a council they would select two young men. That if we set out previously to that time the men would follow us. We therefore do not calculate any assistance from them as guides, but depend more on engaging some of the Oat-lash-shoots on Clark's River in the neighbourhood of Travellers Rest Creek for that purpose.

—*Captain Lewis*

📖 *June 8, 1806*

The sick Chief is much mended, he can bear his weight on his legs and recovers strength. The child has nearly recovered. The Cut Nose and ten or 12 came over today to visit us; two of those were of the tribes from the plains of Lewis's river whome we had not before seen. One of those men brought a horse for which I gave a tomahawk which I had exchanged for with the Chief of the Clahclahlah's Nation below the great rapids of Columbia, and a broken-down horse which was not able to cross the mountains. We also exchanged 2 of our indifferent horses for sound-back horses.

In the evening, several foot races were run by the men of our party and the Indians; after which our party divided and played at prisoners base untill night. After dark the fiddle was played and the party amused themselves in dancing. One of those Indians informed us that we could not cross the mountains untill the full of the next moon, or about the 1st of July. If we attempted it sooner, our horses would be three days without eating, on the top of the Mountains. This information is disagreeable to us, inasmuch as it admits of some doubt as to the time most proper for us to set out. At all events, we shall set out at or about the time which the Indians seem to be generally agreed would be the most proper: about the middle of this month.

—*Captain Clark*

📖 *June 9, 1806*

This morning we had all the horses brought up and endeavoured to exchange five or six with the Indians in consequence to their having sore backs, but succeeded in exchanging one only. This evening our party obtained a very good horse for an indifferent one by giving the Indian an old leather shirt in addition. We ate the last of our meat yesterday evening and have lived on roots today. Our party seems much eleated witht the idea of moving on towards their friends and country; they all seem alert in their movements today; they have everything in readiness for a move.

—*Captain Lewis*

⛺ *Camp on the Kooskooskee to Travellers Rest*

📖 *June 10, 1806*

Rose early this morning and had all the horses collected except one of Whitehouses horses, which could not be found; an Indian promised to find the horse and bring him on to us at the quawmash fields, at which place we intend to delay a fiew days for laying in some meat, by which time we calculate that the snows will have melted more off the mountains and the grass, raised to a sufficient height for our horses to live.

We packed up and set out at 11 A.M. We set out with the party, each man being well mounted and a light load on a 2nd horse, besides which we have several supernumary horses in case of accident or the want of provisions, we therefore feel ourselves perfectly equipped for the mountains.

We ascended the hills which are very high and about three miles in extent. The pass of Collins Creek was deep and extreemly difficult, tho' we passed without sustaining further injury than wetting some of our roots and bread. The country through which we passed is extreemly fertile and generally free from stone, is well timbered with several species of fir, long-leafed pine and larch.

After we encamped this evening we sent out our hunters; Collins killed a doe on which we supped, much to our satisfaction. We had not reached the top of the river hills before we

were overtaken by a party of 8 Indians who informed me that they were going to the quawmash flats to hunt; their object, I believe, is the expectation of being fed by us in which, however kind as they have been, we must disappoint them at this moment, as it is necessary that we should use all frugality, as well as employ every exertion to provide meat for our journey. They have encamped with us.

—*Captain Clark*

🍂 Arriving at the quamash flats, i.e., Weippe Prairie, they stayed for three days to graze the horses and to do some hunting. Then they again headed east:

📖 *June 14, 1806*

We had all our articles packed up and made ready for an early departure in the morning. Our horses were caught and most of them hobbled and otherwise confined in order that we might not be detained. From hence to Traveller's Rest we shall make a forced march; at that place we shall probably remain one or two days to rest ourselves and horses and procure some meat. We have now been detained near five weeks in consequence of the snows, a serious loss of time at this delightfull season for traveling. I am still apprehensive that the snow and the want of food for our horses will prove a serious embarrassment to us, as at least four days journey of our rout in these mountains lies over bights and along a ledge of mountains never entirely destitute of snow. Everybody seems anxious to be in motion, convinced that we have not now any time to delay if the calculation is to reach the United States this season; this I am determined to accomplish if within the compass of human power.

—*Captain Lewis*

📖 *June 15, 1806*

We had some little difficulty in collecting our horses this morning; they had straggled off to a greater distance than usual. It rained very hard in the morning, and after collecting our horses we waited an hour for it to abate; but as it had every appearance of a settled rain, we set out at 10 A.M. We passed a little prarie at the distance of 8 1/2 miles to which we had previously sent R. Fields and Willard. We found two deer which they had killed and hung up. At the distance of 2 1/2 miles further we arrived at Collins's Creek, where we found our hunters. They had killed another deer and had seen two large bear together, the one black, and the other white. We halted at the creek, dined, and graized our horses.

—*Captain Lewis*

📖 *June 16, 1806*

The difficulty we met with from the fallen timber detained us untill 11 oClock before we reached this place. Here is a handsome little glade, in which we found some grass for our horses. We therefore halted to let them graize and took dinner, knowing that there was no other convenient situation for that purpose short of the glades on Hungary Creek, where we intended to encamp as the last probable place at which we shall find a sufficient quantity of grass for many days. This morning Windsor bursted his rifle near the muzzle.

Before we reached this little branch on which we dined, we saw in the hollows and N. hillsides large quantities of snow yet undissolved. In some places it was from two to three feet deep. The snow has increased in quantity so much that the greater part of our rout this evening was over the snow, which has become sufficiently firm to bear our horses; otherwise it would have been impossible for us to proceed, as it lay in immence masses, in some places 8 or ten feet deep. We found much difficulty in pursuing the road, as it was so frequently covered with snow.

The air was cold. My hands and feet were benumbed. We knew that it would require five days to reach the fish weirs at the entrance of Colt Killed Creek [at todays Powell, Idaho], provided we were so fortunate as to be enabled to follow the proper ridges of the mountains to lead us to that place. Of this, Drewyer, our principal dependence as a woodman and guide, was entirely doubtfull.

Short of that point we could not hope for any food for our horses, not even underwood itself, as the whole was covered many feet deep in snow. If we proceeded and should get bewildered in these mountains, the certainty was that we should lose all our horses and consequently our baggage, instruments, perhaps our papers, and thus eminently risk the loss of the discoveries which we had already made if we should be so fortunate as to escape with life. The snow bore our horses very well and the traveling was therefore infinitely better than the obstruction of rocks and fallen timber which we met with in our passage over last fall, when the snow lay on this part of the ridge in detached spots only.

Under these circumstances we conceived it madness in this stage of the expedition to proceed without a guide who could certainly conduct us to the fish weirs on the Kooskooskee, as our horses could not possibly sustain a journey of more than five days without food. We therefore came to the resolution to return with our horses while they were yet strong and in good order and endeavour to keep them so, untill we could procure an Indian to conduct us over the snowy mountains; and again to proceed as soon as we could procure such a guide, knowing from the appearance of the snow that, if we remained untill it had dissolved sufficiently for us to follow the road, we should not be enabled to return to the United States within this season.

Having come to this resolution, we ordered the party to make a deposit for all the baggage which we had not immediate use for and also all the roots and bread of cowse which they had, except an allowance for a few days to enable them to return to some place at which we could subsist by hunting untill we procured a guide. We left our instruments, papers, &c., believing them safer here than to risk them on horseback over the roads and creeks which we had passed.

Our baggage being laid on scaffolds and well covered, we began our retrograde march at 1 P.M., having remained about 3 hours on this snowy mountain. We returned by the rout we had come to Hungary Creek, which we ascended about 2 miles, and encamped. We had here more grass for our horses than the preceding evening, yet it was but scant. The party were a good deal dejected, tho' not as much so as I had apprehended they would have been. This is the first time since we have been on this long tour that we have ever been compelled to retreat or make a retrograde march. It rained on us most of this evening.

—*Captain Lewis*

🦌 The steep, timbered riverbanks on the upper Kooskooskee (Clearwater) had presented an almost impassible route for the Expedition as they had on the westward trek; that's why they were now again attempting to travel the snowy highlands north of the river. Travel along the river in that time wasn't as easy as it is today on the modern highway that has been bulldozed and blasted into the mountainsides just above the river's edge.

But now the lingering snows have stopped them cold (so to speak) in the highlands as well. Anyone who has ever had to turn back from a highly anticipated trip because of deep snow can appreciate what everyone in the party must have felt now.

As Lewis noted in the foregong entry, after stashing their gear, the Expedition returned to encamp in the lower mountains a dozen or so miles north of today's U.S. 12 and this next campground. From there they returned to the upper end of Collins Creek (now Lolo Creek) above the quamash flats (Weippe Prairie) on June 18th to wait for an Indian guide.

♠ Idaho 109

WILD GOOSE
Clearwater National Forest

Location: Northern Idaho east of Lewiston.

Access: From U.S Highway 12 at milepost 95 +.2 (21 miles northeast of Kooskia, 79 miles southwest of Lolo Pass), turn south into the campground.

Camping Facilities: 6 campsites; sites are medium-sized, reasonably level, with fair separation; parking pads are gravel, short to medium-length straight-ins; adequate space for tents; fire rings; some firewood is available for gathering in the area; water at central faucets; vault facilities; gravel driveway; limited to adequate supplies and services are available in Kooskia.

Day Use Facilities: None.

Activities & Attractions: Rafting, floating; fishing.

Natural Features: Located on a flat in a canyon along the north bank of the Clearwater River; the Lochsa and Selway Rivers join 2 miles east of the campground to form the Middle Fork of the Clearwater River; sites receive medium shade/shelter from conifers and hardwoods; a few sites are riverside; flanked by densely forested slopes; elevation 1500´.

Season, Fees & Phone: April to November; $8.00; (no fee if drinking water is not available); 14 day limit; Lochsa Ranger District ☎(208) 926-4275.

Camp Journal: Wild Goose is the westernmost national forest campground along this highway, and it is the only forest camp along the Clearwater River. (The others are on the Lochsa River, a major tributary of the Clearwater.) Also, it is usually one of the first camps (along with Wilderness Gateway) to be available in spring and the last to close in fall. (Because of the definite possibility of freezing temps in early spring and late summer, the drinking water system is turned on only from about Memorial Day to Labor Day.) This little riverside camp may evoke a certain sense of camaraderie among its namesake and the readers and writers of this book. All are long-distance travelers.

📖 *June 18, 1806*
This morning we had considerable difficulty in collecting our horses, they having straggled off to a considerable distance in search of food on the sides of the mountains among the thick timber. At 9 oClock we collected them all except one of Drewyers and one of Shields's. We set out, leaving Shields and LaPage to collect the two lost horses and follow us. We dispatched Drewyer and Shannon to the Chopunnish Indians in the plains beyond the Kooskooskee in order to hasten the arrival of the Indians who had promised to accompany us, or to procure a guide at all events and rejoin us as soon as possible. We sent by them a rifle, which we offered as a reward to any of them who would engage to conduct us to Travellers Rest. We also directed them, if they found difficulty in inducing any of them to accompany us, to offer the reward of two other guns to be given them immediately, and ten horses at the Falls of Missouri.

We had not proceeded far this morning before Potts cut his leg very badly with one of the large knives. He cut one of the large veins on the inner side of the leg. I found much difficulty in stopping the blood, which I could not effect untill I applied a tight bandage with a little cushion of wood and toe [a compress or tourniquet] on the vein below the wound. Colters horse fell with him in passing Hungary Creek and himself and horse were driven down the creek a considerable distance rolling over each other among the rocks. Fortunately he escaped without injury or the loss of his gun.

By 1 P.M., we returned to the glade on the branch of Hungary Creek, where we had dined on the 16th. Here we again halted and dined. As there was much appearance of deer about this place, we left R. and J. Fields with directions to hunt this evening and tomorrow morning at this place, and to join us in the evening at the meadows of Collins's Creek, where we intend remaining tomorrow in order to rest our horses and hunt. After dinner we proceeded on to Collins's Creek and encamped in a pleasant situation at the upper part of the meadows about 2 miles above our encampment of the 15th inst. We sent out several hunters, but they returned without having killed anything.

They saw a number of salmon trout in the creek and shot at them several times, without success. We directed Colter and Gibson to fix each of them a gig in the morning and endeavour to take some of the salmon trout. The hunters saw much fresh appearance of bear but very little of deer. We hope by means of the fish, together with what deer and bear we can kill, to be enabled to subsist untill our guide arrives, without the necessity of returning to the quamash flats. There is a great abundance of good food here to sustain our horses.

—*Captain Lewis*

📖 *June 19, 1806*

At 2 P.M. J. and R. Fields arrived with two deer. John Shields and LaPage came with them; they had not succeeded in finding their horses. Late in the evening Frazier reported that my riding horse, that of Capt. C., and his mule had gone on toward the quamash flats, and that he had pursued their tracks on the road about 2 1/2 miles. We determined to send out all the hunters in the morning, in order to make a fair experiment of the practicability of our being able to subsist at this place; and if not we shall move, the day after, to the quamash flats. The musquetoes have been excessively troublesome to us since our arrival at this place, particularly in the evening. Cruzatte brought me several large morels [big, ugly mushrooms] which I roasted and ate without salt, pepper, or grease. In this way, I had for the first time the true taste of the morel, which is truly an insipid, tasteless food. Our stock of salt is now exhausted except two quarts, which I have reserved for my tour up Maria's River, and that I left the other day on the mountain.

—*Captain Lewis*

📖 *June 20, 1806*

The hunters turned out early in different directions. Our giggers also turned out with two gigs, a bayonet fixed on a pole, a scooping net, & a snare made of horse hair. Near the ford of the creek, in a deep hole, we killed six salmon trout and two others were killed in the creek above in the evening. Reuben Fields killed a reddish brown bear which was very meager. The talons of this bear were remarkably short, broad at their base and sharply pointed. This was the species the Chopunnish call *yah-kar*. As it was in very low order, the flesh was indifferent.

Labiche and Cruzat returned late in the evening with one deer which the former had killed. The hunters assured us that their greatest exertions would not enable them to support us here more than one or two days longer, from the great scarcity of game and the difficult access of the country, the underbrush being very thick and great quantities of fallen timber.

As we shall necessarily be compelled to remain more than two days for the return of Drewyer & Shannon, we determined to return in the morning as far as the quamash flats and endeavour to lay in another stock of meat for the mountains, our former stock now being nearly exhausted as well as what we have killed on our rout. By returning to the quamash flats we shall sooner be informed whether or not we can procure a guide to conduct us through the mountains. Should we fail in precureing one, we are deturmined to risk a passage on the following plan immediately, because, should we wait much longer, or untill the snow disolves in such a manner as to enable us to follow the road, we cannot expect to reach the U. States this winter:

This is that Capt. L. or myself shall take four of our most expert woodsmen with 3 or four of our best horses and proceed two days in advance, taking a plentifull supplyof provisions. For this party to follow the road by the mark the Indians have made in many places with their baggage on the sides of the trees by rubbing against them, and to blaze the trees with a tomahawk as they proceed. That after proceeding two days in advance of Hungary Creek, two of those men would be sent back to the party, who by the time of their return to Hungary Creek would have reached that place. The men so returning would be enabled to inform the main party of the probable success of the proceeding party in finding the road, and of their probable progress, in order that, should it be necessary, the main party by a delay of a day or two at Hungary Creek, should give the advance time to make the road through before the main party could overtake them, and thus prevent delay on that part of the rout where no food is to be obtained for our horses.

Should it so happen that the advance should not find the road by the marks of the trees after attempting it for two days, the whole of them would return to the main party. In which sase we would bring back our baggage and attempt a passage over the mountains through the country of the Shoshones further to the South, by way of the main S.Westerly fork of Lewis's River and Madisons or Gallatins River's, where from the information of the Chopunnish, there is a passage where at this season of the year is not obstructed by snow, though the round is very distant and would require at least a month in it's performance. The Shoshones informed us when we first met with them that there was a passage across the mountains in that quarter but represented the difficulties ariseing from steep, rugged high mountains, and also an extensive and barren plain which was to be passed without game, as infinitely more difficult than the rout by which we came.

—*Captain Clark*

🌿 Captain Clark has just described an alternate plan to double-back to Lewis's River, i.e., the Snake River at Lewiston; then follow the Snake down along what is now the Idaho Washington-Oregon border, then easterly across the Snake River Plain in southern Idaho (the "extensive barren plain" noted in the foregoing paragraph); then northward back up to the Forks of the Missouri. Fortunately, as we'll read next, they did not have to resort to 'Plan B'. (Anyone who has traveled the Snake River Plain will readily understand the "forunately" part.)

📖 *June 21,1806*

We collected our horses early and set out on our return to the flats. We all felt some mortification in being thus compelled to retrace our steps through this tedious and difficult part of our rout, obstructed with brush and innumerable logs and fallen timber, which renders the traveling distressing and even dangerous to our horses. One of Thompson's horses is either choked this morning or has the distemper badly. I fear he is to be of no further service to us. An excellent horse of Cruzattes snagged himself so badly in the groin in jumping over a parcel of fallen timber that he will eventually be of no further service to us.

At the pass of Collins Creek, we met two Indians who were on their way over the mountains. They had brought with them the three horses and the mule which had left us and returned to the quamash ground. Those Indians returned with us about 1/2 a mile down the creek, where we halted to dine and graize our horses.

As well as we could understand the Indians, they informed us they had seen Geo. Drewyer & Shannon, and that they would not return

untill the expiration of two days. The cause why Drewyer & Shannon did not return with these men we are at a loss to account for. We pressed those Indians to remain with us and conduct us over the mountains on the return of Drewyer & Shannon. They consented to remain two nights for us and accordingly deposited their stores of roots & bread in the bushes at no great distance, and after dinner returned with us as far as the little prarie, about 2 miles distance from the creek. Here they halted with their horses and informed us they would remain untill we overtook them or at least 2 nights. At 7:00 in the evening we found ourselves once more at our old encampment, where we shall anxiously await the return of Drewyer & Shannon.

—*Captain Clark*

📖 *June 23,1806*

Apprehensive from Drewyer's & Shannons delay, that they had met with some difficulty in procuring a guide, and also that the two Indians, who had promised to wait two nights for us, would set out today, we thought it most advisable to dispatch Wiser and Frazier to them this morning, with a view if possible to detain them a day or two longer; and directed that, in the event of their not being able to detain the Indians, Sergt. Gass, Jo. and R. Fields, and Wiser should accompany the Indians by whatever rout they might take, to Travellers Rest, and blaze the trees well as they proceeded, and wait at that place untill our arrival with the party.

At 4 P.M. Shannon, Drewyer, & Whitehouse returned. Shannon & Drewyer brought with them three Indians who had consented to accompany us to the Falls of the Missouri, for the compensation of 2 guns. One of those men is the brother of the Cut Nose; and the other two are the same who presented Capt. L. and myself with a horse on a former occasion, at the lodge of the Broken Arm; and the two who promised to pursue us in nine nights after we left the river, or on the 19th. Those are all young men of good character and much respected by their Nation.

—*Captain Clark*

📖 *June 24, 1806*

We collected our horses early this morning and set out, accompanied by our 3 guides. Colter joined us this morning, having killed a bear, which, from his description of it's poverty and distance, we did not think proper to send after. We nooned it as usial at Collins Creek, where we found Frazier, solo; the other four men having gone in pursuit of the two Indians, who had set out from Collins Creek two hours before Fraziers arrival. After dinner we continued our rout to Fish Creek. Here we found Sergt. Gass, Wiser and the two Indian men whome they had prevailed on to remain at that place untill our arrival; Jos. & R. Fields had killed one small deer only, and of this they had been liberal to the Indians, insomuch that they had no provisions; they had gone on to the branch of Hungary Creek, at which we shall noon it tomorrow in order to hunt. We had fine grass for our horses this evening.

—*Captain Clark*

📖 *June 25, 1806*

Last evening the Indians entertained us with setting the fir trees on fire. They have a great number of dry limbs near their bodies, which, when set on fire, create a very sudden and emence blaze from top to bottom of those tall trees. They are a beautifull object in this situation at night. This exhibition reminded me of a display of fireworks. The nativs told us that their object in setting those trees on fire was to bring fair weather for our journey.

We collected our horses and set out at an early hour this morning. One of our guides complained of being unwell, a symptom which I did not much like, as such complaints with an Indian are generally the prelude to his abandoning any enterprise with which he is not well pleased. We left 4 of those Indians at our encampment. They promised to pursue us in a fiew hours. At 11 A.M. we arived at the branch of Hungary Creek, where we found Jo. and R. Fields. They had not killed anything. Here we halted and dined, and our guides overtook us. At this place the squar collected a parcel of roots of which the Shoshones eate. It is a small knob root a good deal in flavor and consistency like the Jerusalem artichoke.

After dinner we continued our rout to Hungary Creek and encamped about 1 1/2 miles below our encampment of the 16th. The Indians all continue with us and, I believe, are disposed to be faithful to their engagements.

—*Captain Clark*

📖 *June 26, 1806*

We collected our horses and set out early and proceeded on down Hungary Creek a fiew miles and ascended to the summit of the mountain where we deposited our baggage on the 17th. Found everything safe as we had left them. The snow, which was 10 feet 10 inches deep on the top of the mountain, had sunk to 7 feet, tho' perfectly hard and firm. We made some fire, cooked dinner, and dined, while our horses stood on snow 7 feet deep at least. After dinner we packed up and proceeded on.

The Indians hastened us off and informed us that it was a considerable distance to the place they wished to reach this evening, where there was grass for our horses. Accordingly we set out with our guides, who led us over and along the steep sides of tremendous mountains entirely covered with snow except about the roots of the trees, where the snow was partially melted and exposed a small spot of earth. We ascended and descended several steep, lofty heights, but, keeping on the dividing ridge of the Chopunnish & Kooskooskee rivers, we passed no stream of water.

Late in the evening, much to the satisfaction of ourselves and the comfort of the horses, we arived at the desired spot, and encamped on the steep side of a mountain convenient to a good spring. Here we found an abundance of grass for our horses. Soon after we had encamped, we were overtaken by a Chopunnish man who had pursued us with a view to accompany Capt. Lewis to the Falls of Missouri.

—*Captain Clark*

📖 *June 27, 1806*

We collected our horses early and set out. The road still continued on the heights of the dividing ridge on which we had traveled yesterday for 9 miles, or to our encampment of the 16th September last. About 1 mile short of the encampment, we halted by the request of the guides a fiew minutes on an elevated point and smoked a pipe. On this eminence the nativs have raised a conic mound of stones, 6 or 8 feet high, and erected a pine pole of 15 feet long. From hence they informed us that when passing over with their families some of the men were usually sent on foot by the fishery at the enterance of Colt Killed Creek in order to take fish and again meet the party at the quamash glade on the head of Kooskooskee River. From this place we had an extensive view of these stupendous mountains principally covered with snow like that on which we stood. We were entirely surrounded by those mountains, from which, to one unacquainted with them, it would have seemed impossible ever to have escaped. In short, without the assistance of our guides, I doubt much whether we who had once passed them could find our way to Travellers Rest, in their present situation; for the marked trees, on which we had placed considerable reliance are much fewer and more difficult to find than we had apprehended. Those Indians are most admirable pilots. We find the road wherever the snow has disappeared, tho' it be only for a fiew paces.

After having smoked the pipe and contemplating this scene sufficient to have dampened the spirits of any except such hardy travellers as we have become, we continued our march and at the distance of 3 miles descended a steep mountain and passed two small branches of the Chopunnish River just above their fork, and again ascended the ridge on which we passed. At the distance of 7 miles, arived at our encampment of 16th September last, passed 3 small branches, passed on a dividing ridge and we arived at a situation very similar to our situation of last night. Here we encamped for the night, having traveled 28 miles.

Our meat being exhausted, we issued a pint of bears oil to a mess, with which their boiled roots made an agreeable dish. Joe Potts leg, which had been much swollen and inflamed for several days, is much better this evening and gives him but little pain. We applied the pounded root and leaves of wild ginger, from which he found great relief.

—*Captain Clark*

⛰ Idaho 110

JERRY JOHNSON
Clearwater National Forest

Location: Northern Idaho east of Lewiston near Lolo Pass.

Access: From U.S. Highway 12 at milepost 150 +.3 (24 miles southwest of Lolo Pass, 76 miles northeast of Kooskia), turn north into the campground.

Camping Facilities: 15 campsites; sites are medium to large, with fair separation; parking pads are paved; adequate space for tents in most sites; fireplaces; plenty of firewood is available for gathering; water at hand pumps; vault facilities; paved driveway; nearest reliable source of limited to adequate supplies is in Kooskia, Idaho or Lolo, Montana, 60 miles northeast; nearest sources of complete supplies and services are Lewiston, Idaho, 150 miles west, or Missoula, Montana, 70 miles east.

Day Use Facilities: None.

Lochsa River, Clearwater National Forest

Activities & Attractions: Fishing (catch and release) on the Lochsa River, (a foot trail leads from the campground across the highway and down a steep bank to the water's edge); 4-wheel-drive trail leads north from the campground into the nearby primitive areas.

Natural Features: Located on a fairly level portion of a hillside above the Lochsa River, a major tributary of the Clearwater River, in the the Bitterroot Range; campground has moderate forestation without much underbrush; relatively low (for this region) timbered ridges flank the campground north and south; elevation 3000'.

Season, Fees & Phone: May to mid-September; $8.00; 14 day limit; Powell Ranger District ☎ (208) 942-3113.

Camp Journal: This spot is perhaps not as fully equipped as some of the other campgrounds along Highway 12, but it also tends to be less crowded (although "crowded" in this region really means "more than one-third occupied"). It may also be slightly more comfortable than some of the other camping areas near here, since it is positioned somewhat above the cold and dampness of the river level. Very few vehicles travel this winding highway through the Bitterroots between dusk and dawn; so a good night's sleep in this and other roadside camps, while not fully guaranteed, is a reasonable expectation.

The Expedition's camp on the night of June 27, 1806 was a half dozen miles northwest of this campground.

📖 *June 28, 1806*

We continued our rout along the dividing ridge over knobs & through deep hollows past our encampment of the 14 Sept. last, near the forks of the road leaving the one on which we had come to one leading to the fishery [at Powell, along the Lochsa River] to our right, immediately on the dividing ridge.

At 12 oclock we arived at an untimbered side of a mountain with a southern aspect just above the fishery. Here we found an abundance of grass for our horses as the guides had informed us. As our horses were hungary and much fatigued, and from information no other place where we could obtain grass for them was within the reach of this evening's travel we deturmined to remain at this place all night, having come 13 miles only. The water was distant from our encampment; we therefore melted snow and used the water.

The whole of the rout of this day was over deep snow. We find the travelling on the snow not worse than without it, as the easy passage it gives us over rocks and fallen timber fully compensates for the inconvenience of slipping; certain it is that we travel considerably faster on the snow than without it. The snow sinks from 2 to 3 inches with a horse, is coarse and firm and seems to be formed of the larger particles of the snow; the surface of the snow is reather harder in the morning than after the sun shines on it a fiew hours; but it is not in that situation so dense as to prevent the horses from obtaining good foothold.

—*Captain Clark*

🏕 Idaho 111

WHITEHOUSE
Clearwater National Forest

Location: Northern Idaho east of Lewiston near Lolo Pass.

Access: From U.S. Highway 12 at milepost 158 +.5 (16 miles west of Lolo Pass, 85 miles northeast of Kooskia); turn south off the highway into the campground. (Note that the driveway entrance may be difficult to see until you're almost past it.)

Camping Facilities: 14 campsites; campsites are large, level and reasonably well-spaced; parking pads are paved, medium to long enough for larger vehicles; nice, level tent spaces; fireplaces; firewood is available for gathering in the area; water at a hand pump; vault facilities; wide, paved driveway, with a narrow turnaround at the east end; camper supplies at a resort, 3 miles west; limited to adequate supplies are available in Kooskia, Idaho, 85 miles west, and Lolo, Montana, 51 miles east.

Day Use Facilities: None.

Activities & Attractions: Fairly good fishing on the Lochsa River; many 4 wheel drive and foot trails in the area.

Natural Features: Located in a forested canyon on the north bank of the Lochsa River; quite a few camp spots have river frontage, and most at least have a river view; campground vegetation consists mostly of tall pines combined with tall grass and hardwoods; campsites are moderately sheltered; Whitehouse Pond is in an adjacent clearing; dense conifer forest throughout this region; elevation 3300´.

Season, Fees & Phone: May to September; $8.00; 14 day limit; Powell Ranger District ☎(208) 942-3113.

Camp Journal: Whitehouse is nearly a twin of Wendover Campground, described in *Volume 1*. Whitehouse, however, has more sites with a river view, but a slightly less 'open' environment. The size of either camp is quite large in proportion to the relatively small number of sites, though.

One June 28, 1806 at midday, the Expedition stopped and camped for the night about six miles directly north of this campground, named, of course, for Corps member Joseph Whitehouse.

The following day they crossed Lolo Pass into Montana:

📖 *June 29, 1806*

We collected our horses and set out, having previously dispatched Drewyer & R. Fields to the Warm Springs [now Lolo Hot Springs in Montana] to hunt. We pursued the bights of the ridge on which we have been passing for several days; it terminated at the distance of 5 miles from our encampment, and we decended to & passed the main branch of Kooskooske 1 1/2 miles above the enterance of Glade Creek which falls in on the N.E. side. We bid *adieu* to the snow.

Near the river we found a deer which the hunters had killed and left us. This was a fortunate supply, as all our bears oil was now exhausted and we were reduced to our roots alone without salt. At noon we arived at the quawmash flats on Valley Creek [today's Lolo Creek] and halted to graize our horses and dined, having traveled 12 miles. Here is a pretty little plain of about 50 acres plentifully stocked with quawmash, and from appearance this forms one of the principal stages of the Indians who pass the mountains on this road.

After dinner we continued our march 7 miles further to the Warm Springs, where we arived early in the evening. The principal spring is about the temperature of the warmest baths used at the Hot Springs in Virginia. In this bath, which had been prepared by the Indians by stopping the river with stone and mud, I bathed and remained in 10 minits. It was with difficulty I could remain this long and it causd. a profuse sweat. Both the men and the Indians amused themselves with the use of the bath this evening. I observe after the Indians, remaining in the hot bath as long as they could bear it, run and plunge themselves into the creek, the water of which is now as cold as ice can make it; after remaining here a fiew minits, they return again to the warm bath, repeating the transition several times, but always ending with the warm bath. Saw the tracks of 2 barefooted Indians.

—*Captain Clark*

📖 *June 30, 1806*

Just as we had prepared to set out at an early hour, a deer came in to lick at the springs and one of our hunters killed it; this secured us our dinner, and we proceeded down the creek, sometimes in the bottoms and at other times on the top or along the steep sides of the ridge to the N. of the creek. At noon, having travelled 13 miles, we arrived at the entrance of a northern branch of the creek where we nooned it on the 12th of Septr. last. Here we halted, dined and graized our horses.

In descending the creek this morning on the steep side of a high hill, my horse slipped with both his hinder feet out of the road and fell; I also fell off backwards and slid near 40 feet down the hill before I could stop myself, such was the steepness of the declivity; the horse was near falling on me in the first instance, but fortunately recovered and we both escaped unhurt.

After dinner, we resumed our march. Soon after setting out Shields killed another deer, and in the course of the evening we picked up three others which Drewyer had killed along the road, making a total of six today. Deer are very abundant in the neighbourhood of Travellers Rest of both species [whitetails and mule deer], also some bighorns and elk.

A little before sunset we arrived at our old encampment on the S. side of the creek a little above it's entrance into Clark's River. Here we encamped with a view to remain two days in order to rest ourselves and horses & make our final arrangements for seperation. We found no appearance of the Ootlashshoots having been here lately. The Indians express much concern for them and apprehend that the Minnetares of Fort de Prarie have destroyed them in the course of the last winter and spring, and mention the tracks of the bearfooted Indians which we saw yesterday as an evidence of their being much distressed. Our horses have stood the journey suprisinly well, most of them are yet in fine order and only want a few days rest to restore them.

—*Captain Lewis*

⚑ **Montana 112**

LEE CREEK
Lolo National Forest

Location: Far Western Montana southwest of Missoula.

Access: From U.S Highway 12 at milepost 6 (6 miles east of Lolo Pass, 26.5 miles west of Lolo, Montana), turn south into the campground.

Camping Facilities: 22 campsites in 2 loops; sites in the lower section are large and well spaced; sites in the upper loop are smaller, sloped, a little closer together, but still well spaced; parking pads are gravel, medium to long straight-ins; most units are suitable for rv's, and about three-fourths are good for tents; fireplaces or fire rings; firewood is available for gathering; water at faucets throughout; vault facilities; gravel driveways; limited+ supplies and services are available in Lolo.

Day Use Facilities: None.

Activities & Attractions: Self-guiding nature trail along Lee Creek; fishing for small trout on Lolo Creek; small national forest visitor information center at Lolo Pass.

Natural Features: Located at the confluence of Lee Creek, a side stream, with Lolo Creek, the main stream in this watershed; the campground is situated in a moderately dense conifer forest; units 1-5 are streamside spots just as you enter the campground; the remainder of the sites are on a knoll directly to the east of the lower units; low timbered ridges lie north and south of the campground; elk and black bear are in the area; count on cool nights even in midsummer; elevation 4600´.

Season, Fees & Phone: May to early September; $8.00; 14 day limit; Missoula Ranger District ☎ (406) 329-3750.

Camp Journal: U.S. 12 was constructed less than a half-century ago. Prior to that time the only way to penetrate the wilderness in the Lolo Creek, Montana and Clearwater River, Idaho watersheds was on foot or horseback. Except for the sinuous strip of pavement that closely follows the main streams, not much has changed since Lewis and Clark forged their way through here on the way to and from the Coast two centuries ago.

📖 *July 1, 1806*

This morning early we sent out all hunters. Set Shields at work to repair some of our guns which were out of order.

Capt. Clark & myself consorted to the following plan, viz: From this place I determined to go with a small party by the most direct rout to the Falls of the Missouri, there to leave Thompson, McNeal, and Goodrich to prepare carriages and gear for the purpose of transporting the canoes and baggage over the portage; and myself and six volunteers to ascend Maria's River with a view to explore the country and ascertain whether any branch of that river lies as far North as Latd. 50, and again return and join the party who are to descend the Missouri, at the entrance of Maria's River. I now called for the volunteers to accompany me on this rout. I selected Drewyer, the two Fieldses, Warner, Frazier, and Sergt. Gass.

The other part of the men are to proceed with Capt. Clark to the head of Jefferson's River, where we deposited sundry articles and left our canoes. From thence, Sergt. Ordway and a party of 9 men are to descend the river with the canoe;. Capt. C., with the remaining ten, including Charbono and York, will proceed to the Yellowstone River at it's nearest approach to the Three Forks of the Missouri. Here he will build a canoe and descend the Yellowstone River with Charbono, the Indian woman, his servant York, and five others to the Missouri, where, should he arrive first, he will await my arrival. Sergt. Pryor with two other men is to proceed with the horses by land to the Mandans, and thence to the British posts on the Assiniboine with a letter to Mr.

Haney, whom we wish to engage to prevail on the Sioux Chiefs to join us on the Missouri and accompany them with us to the seat of the general government. These arrangements being made, the party were informed of our design and prepared themselves accordingly
—*Captain Lewis*

📖 *July 2, 1806*

All arrangements being now complete, we determined to set out in the morning. In the course of the day we had much conversation with the Indians by signs, our only mode of communicating our ideas. They informed us that they wished to go in search of the Oatslashshoots their friends and intended leaving us tomorrow morning. I prevailed on them to go with me as far as the East Branch of Clark's River and put me on the road to the Missouri. I gave the Cheif a medal of the small size; he insisted on exchanging names with me, according to their custom, which was accordingly done, and I was called Yo-me-kol-lick, which interpreted is the "white bear-skin folded".

In the evening the Indians run their horses, and we had several foot races between the natives and our party with various success. These are a race of hardy, strong, athletic, active men. Goodrich and McNeal are both very unwell with the pox, which they contracted last winter with the Chinnook women. This forms my inducement principally for taking them to the Falls of the Missouri, where during an interval of rest they can use the mercury freely.
—*Captain Lewis*

📖 *July 2, 1806*

The musquetors have been so troublesome day and night since our arrival in this valley that we are tormented very much by them and can't write, except under our biers [netting]. We gave the second gun to our guides, agreeable to our promise, and to each we gave powder and ball. Had all of our arms put in the most prime order. Two of the rifles have unfortunately bursted near the muzzle. Shields cut them off, and they shoot tolerably well. One which is very short we exchanged with the Indian who we had given a longer gun to induce them to pilot us across the mountains. We caused every man to fill his horn with powder & have a sufficiency of balls, &c.
—*Captain Clark*

Lewis on Maria's River *1806*

▲ *Travellers Rest to the Great Falls of the Missouri*

Captain Lewis now set out to explore first the lower part of Clark's River (the Bitterroot) to present-day Missoula; then a few miles along what they called the East Branch of Clark's River (now Clark Fork of the Columbia River) east of Missoula; then eastward up the Cokahlarishkit River (which would eventually be named the Blackfoot River) from the present milltown of Bonner, up and over Rogers Pass, and down the other side to the Medicine (now Sun) River to the Great Falls of the Missouri.

Lewis's route from Travellers Rest follows today's U.S. 93 to Missoula, then Interstate 90 for a few miles up to Bonner, then Montana State Highway 200 over to Great Falls.

The Lewis party's camp the first night would be near the east edge of today's city of Missoula.

📖 *July 3, 1806*

All arrangements being now completed for carrying into effect the several schemes we had planned for execution on our return, we saddled our horses and set out. I took leave of my worthy friend and companion, Capt. Clark, and the party that accompanied him. I could not avoid feeling much concern on this occasion, although I hoped this separation was only momentary.

I proceeded down Clark's River seven miles with my party of nine men and five Indians. Here the Indians recommended our passing the river, which was rapid and 150 yards wide. 2 miles above this place, I passed the entrance of the East Branch of Clark's River. As we had no other means of passing the river, we busied ourselves collecting dry timber for the purpose of constructing rafts. Timber being scarce, we found considerable difficulty in procuring as much as made three small rafts. We arrived at 11 A.M., and had our rafts completed by 3 P.M., when we dined and began to take over our baggage, which we effected in the course of three hours, the rafts being obliged to return several times. The Indians swam over their

horses, and drew over their baggage in little basins of deer skins, which they constructed in a very few minutes for that purpose. We drove our horses in after them, and they followed to the opposite shore.

I remained myself with two men who could scarcely swim untill the last. By this time the raft, by passing so frequently, had fallen a considerable distance down the river to a rapid and difficult part of it, crowded with several small islands and willow bars which were now overflowed. With these men, I set out on the raft and was soon hurried down with the current a mile and a half before we made shore. On our approach to the shore the raft sank, and I was drawn off the raft by a bush and swam on shore. The two men remained on the raft and fortunately effected a landing at some little distance below. I wet the chronometer by this accident, which I had placed in my fob, as I conceived for greater security.

I now joined the party and we proceeded with the Indians about 3 miles to a small creek and encamped at sunset. I sent out the hunters, who soon returned with three very fine deer, of which I gave the Indians half.

These people now informed me that the road which they showed me at no great distance from our camp would lead us up the East branch of Clark's River and to a river they called Cokahlarishkit, or the River of the Road to Buffaloe, and thence to Medicine River and the Falls of the Missouri, where we wished to go. They alleged that, as the road was a well-beaten track, we could not now miss our way, and as they were afraid of meeting with their enemies, the Minnetares, they could not think of continuing with us any longer; that they wished now to proceed down Clark's River in search of their friends the Shalees. They informed us that not far from the dividing ridge between the waters of this and the Missouri River, the roads forked. They recommended the left hand [Rogers Pass] as the best rout, but said they would both lead us to the Falls of the Missouri.

I directed the hunters to turn out early in the morning and endeavour to kill some more meat for these people, whom I was unwilling to leave without giving them a good supply of provision after their having been so obliging as to conduct us through those tremendous mountains.

The musquetoes were so excessively troublesome this evening that we were obliged to kindle large fires for our horses. These insects torture them in such manner, untill they placed themselves in the smoke of the fires, that I really thought they would become frantic.

—Captain Lewis

📖 *July 4, 1806*

I arrose early this morning and sent out Drewyer and the Fieldses to hunt. I gave a shirt, a handkerchief, and a small quantity of ammunition to the Indians. At half after eleven the hunters returned from the chase, unsuccessful. I now ordered the horses saddled, smoked a pipe with these friendly people, and at noon bid them *adieu*. They had cut the meat which I gave them last evening thin, and exposed it in the sun to dry, informing me that they should leave it in this neighbourhood untill they returned, as a store for their homeward journey.

These affectionate people, our guides, betrayed every emotion of unfeigned regret at separating from us. They said that they were confident that the Pahkees (the appellation they give the Minnetares) would cut us off.

I now continued my rout up the N. side of the Cokahlarishkit through a timbered country for 8 miles and encamped in a handsome bottom on the river where there was an abundance of grass for our horses. The evening was fine, air pleasant and no musquetoes.

—Captain Lewis

🔥 For the following five days, Lewis was preoccupied with courses and compass headings, as well as being on the lookout for hostiles; so he had little time for narrative entries in his journal. On the night of July 5, 1806, the party camped in the vicinity of the confluence of Warners Creek and the Cokahlarishkit River (today's Clearwater River and Blackfoot River, respectively).

⚕ Montana 113 ♿

CLEARWATER CROSSING

Clearwater Crossing Recreation Access Site

Location: Western Montana east of Missoula.

Access: From Montana State Highway 200 at milepost 31 +.5 (30 miles east of Bonner, 0.5 mile west of Clearwater Junction, i.e., junction of State Highways 200 & 83), turn north into the recreation site.

Camping Facilities: 5 camp/picnic sites; sites are very large, tolerably level, with fair visual separation but very good spacing; parking surfaces are gravel/grass, medium to long straight-ins or pull-offs; plenty of grassy tent space; fire rings; b-y-o firewood is suggested; no drinking water; vault facilities; gravel driveway; gas and camper supplies+ at Clearwater Junction.

Day Use Facilities: Shared with campers.

Activities & Attractions: Trout fishing (good to excellent); canoe/raft launch area.

Natural Features: Located on a grassy flat along the east bank of the Clearwater River, 3 miles above its confluence with the Blackfoot River; sites are minimally to lightly sheltered by scattered cottonwoods and a few tall conifers; bordered by forested hills and distant peaks; elevation 4100´.

Season, Fees & Phone: Open all year, subject to weather conditions, with limited services October to May; $5.00; 7 day limit; Montana Department of Fish Wildlife and Parks Region 2 Office, Missoula ☎ (406) 542-5500.

Camp Journal: Check out the view up the Clearwater Valley from here! You could fit a scout troop in each of these campsites. (Well, if it wasn't for the people-per-site limit you could.)

⚕ Montana 114 ♿

HARPERS LAKE

Harpers Lake Recreation Access Site

Location: Western Montana east of Missoula.

Access: From Montana State Highway 83 at milepost 1 +.2 (1 mile north of Clearwater Junction, i.e., junction of State Highways 83 & 200), turn west onto a gravel access road and proceed 0.4 mile to a fork (just past the information station); take the left fork onto the loop drive and go 0.5 mile to the first group of sites.

Camping Facilities: 14 camp/picnic sites in several sections; sites are medium to large, essentially level, with nominal to excellent separation; parking pads are gravel, long pull-throughs or pull-offs; large tent areas; fire rings; b-y-o firewood; vault facilities; gravel driveways; gas and camper supplies+ at Clearwater Junction.

Day Use Facilities: Medium-sized picnic and parking area; vault facilities.

Activities & Attractions: Good trout fishing on the river and the lake; handicapped access fishing pier; motorless boating; boat ramp.

Natural Features: Located on lightly forested flats in a valley near the east bank of the Clearwater River; sites are lightly to moderately sheltered by tall conifers; small Harpers Lake is a couple hundred yards east of the camp area; bordered by a sage flat and forested hills, with lofty mountains rising a couple of miles east; elevation 4100´.

Season, Fees & Phone: Open all year, subject to weather conditions, with limited services October to May; $5.00; 7 day limit; Montana Department of Fish Wildlife and Parks Region 2 Office, Missoula ☎(406) 542-5500.

Camp Journal: Terrific distant panoramas east and south from this area. Some really dandy campsites—lots of elbow room. The loop drive is a mile long, so keep looking for campsites as you peruse the recreation area.

Special Note: *The following four state park and national forest campgrounds are off the main route followed by the Lewis party. They're along Montana Highway 83 in the majestically scenic Clearwater Valley. Since the farthest is only a little more than a dozen miles from Lewis's itinerary, and they are within our 20-mile Trail corridor, any or all are decidedly worth visiting or camping in.*

♣ **Montana 115** ⓓ

SALMON LAKE
Salmon Lake State Park

Location: Western Montana northeast of Missoula.

Access: From Montana State Highway 83 at milepost 7 (7 miles north of the junction of State Highways 83 & 200, 8 miles south of the community of Seeley Lake), turn west onto a gravel park access road and go 0.4 mile to a fork; bear left at the fork into the campground.

Camping Facilities: 21 campsites; sites are small+, with nominal to fair separation; parking pads are gravel, acceptably level, medium-length straight-ins, plus some long pull-throughs; medium to large tent areas; fire rings; b-y-o firewood is recommended; water at

several faucets; restrooms; gravel driveways; limited supplies and services are available in Seeley Lake.

Day Use Facilities: Medium-sized picnic area, drinking water, vault facilities, small parking areas in the main day use area; very small picnic area, vaults and small parking space in a secondary day use area.

Activities & Attractions: Boating; boat launch and dock; fishing; designated swimming area; trail along the Lake shore.

Natural Features: Located along the east shore of Salmon Lake; some picnic sites are on the lake shore; campground is a few yards inland, on a gently rolling flat, with a moderately dense cover of conifers, underbrush and grass; the lake lies in the long, narrow Clearwater River Valley, flanked by densely forested mountains to the east and west; 42 acres; elev. 3800´.

Season, Fees & Phone: May to November; 14 day limit; $9.00 (includes park entry fee); phone c/o Montana Department of Fish Wildlife & Parks Region 2 Office, Missoula, ☎(406) 542-5500.

Camp Journal: Four-mile long, quarter-mile wide Salmon Lake comes complete with several, small, tree-covered islands (some of which are inhabited) that award added interest to an already scenic location. Several picnic sites in the park's main day use area are at the end of a small point of land. If you use just a drop or two of imagination, you can be picnicking on an 'island'.

♣ **Montana 116** ⓓ

PLACID LAKE
Placid Lake State Park

Location: Western Montana east of Missoula.

Access: From Montana State Highway 83 at milepost 10 +.1 (10 miles north of the junction of State Highways 200 & 83, 5 miles south of the community of Seeley Lake), turn west onto North Placid Lake Road (gravel); travel west for 3.1 miles (the access road takes a left/right jog at 2.8 miles from the highway), then turn south (left) into the main park area; or continue westerly for another 1.5 miles, then swing south (left) into a secondary park unit. (Note: The highway turnoff point is a bit difficult to see on the approach until you're almost on top of it.)

Camping Facilities: 42 campsites; sites are small+, with nominal to fairly good separation; parking pads are gravel, medium-length straight-ins, plus some long pull-throughs; some pads will require additional leveling; many good tent spots; fire rings; b-y-o firewood is recommended; water at central faucets; restrooms, plus auxiliary vault facilities; gravel driveways; limited supplies and services are available in Seeley Lake.

Day Use Facilities: Small picnic area and small parking area in the main park; other facilities are shared with the campground; very small picnic area and parking lot in the secondary park unit.

Activities & Attractions: Boating; boat launch and dock in the main park, small dock in the secondary unit; designated swimming area; fishing.

Natural Features: Located on a forested flat along the north shore of Placid Lake in the Clearwater River Valley; the lake is nestled at the foot of high, heavily timbered mountains; park vegetation consists of tall conifers, some hardwoods, moderate underbrush and grass; elevation 4100´.

Season, Fees & Phone: May to November; 14 day limit; $9.00 (includes park entry fee); phone c/o Montana Department of Fish Wildlife & Parks Region 2 Office, Missoula, ☎(406) 542-5500.

Camp Journal: The 90-mile Clearwater River-Swan River corridor along Highway 83 is one of the most popular recreation areas in Montana. Because Placid Lake is a bit removed from the mainstream of traffic, a site here is slightly more likely to be available than in some of the other camping areas in the valleys. The setting at Placid Lake is certainly just as beautiful as any of the others, though!

♣ **Montana 117**

RIVER POINT
Lolo National Forest

Location: Western Montana northeast of Missoula.

Access: From Montana State Highway 83 at milepost 14 (south of midtown Seeley Lake, 14 miles north of the junction of State Highways 83 & 200), turn west onto Boy Scout Camp Road (paved, signed for "West Side Seeley Lake Recreation Sites"); proceed west-northwest for 2.1 miles to the recreation area.

Camping Facilities: 27 campsites; sites are small+ or better in size, generally level, and most are well separated; parking pads are hard-

surfaced, medium-length straight-ins; small to medium+ tent spots; fireplaces; plenty of firewood is available for gathering in the surrounding area; water at several faucets; vault facilities; gravel driveways; limited+ supplies and services are available in Seeley Lake.

Day Use Facilities: Small picnic area; drinking water; vault facilities; small parking area.

Activities & Attractions: Fishing; boating; boat ramp at nearby Seeley Lake Campground; foot trail to the beach; Clearwater River Canoe Trail; Seeley Lake Game Preserve, adjacent.

Natural Features: Located in a valley near the southwest shore of Seeley Lake, surrounded by the forested slopes of the Rocky Mountains; the Clearwater River exits Seeley Lake at this point; campground vegetation consists of towering timber dripping with moss, and brush which separate the sites nicely; elevation 4000´.

Season, Fees & Phone: June to September; $9.00; 14 day limit; Seeley Lake Ranger District ☎(406) 677-2233.

Camp Journal: As it departs Seeley Lake, the Clearwater is a wide, deep stream worthy of its name. If you have a shallow-draft vessel, you may be able to explore the waters for quite a distance downstream. You may also be able to tie up your craft a few yards from one of several campsites near the riverbank.

♣ **Montana 118** ♿

SEELEY LAKE
Lolo National Forest

Location: Western Montana northeast of Missoula.

Access: From Montana State Highway 83 at milepost 14 (on the south side of the town of Seeley Lake, 14 miles north of the junction of State Highways 83 & 200), turn west onto Boy Scout Camp Road (paved, signed for "West Side Seeley Lake Recreation Sites"); proceed west-northwest for 3.3 miles (past River Point) to the recreation area.

Camping Facilities: 29 campsites in 2 loops; sites are medium to large, level, with good separation; parking pads are hard-surfaced, and most pads are of the straight-in variety spacious enough to accommodate larger rv's; many nice large, level, grassy spots for tents; fire rings; firewood is available for gathering in the area; water is available at several faucets; restrooms; paved driveways; limited+ supplies are available in Seeley Lake.

Day Use Facilities: Small picnic area; drinking water; restrooms; small parking area.

Activities & Attractions: Boating; boat ramp; fishing; a short foot trail leads from the campground down to a sandy beach with a designated swim zone and the picnic area.

Natural Features: Located near the middle-west shore of Seeley Lake in a Rocky Mountain valley; vegetation consists of moderately dense tall conifers, moderate underbrush and grass; elevation 4000´.

Season, Fees & Phone: June to September; $9.00; 14 day limit; Seeley Lake Ranger District ☎ (406) 677-2233.

Camp Journal: To a good number of campers familiar with the Seeley Lake resort area, this campground has an edge over its neighbor, River Point. It does have a couple of advantages, including a number of sites with lake views through the trees. It's very popular on summer weekends, so you'll probably want to plan to arrive early. Whichever camp you choose, there's a good chance your neighborhood will be visited by one or several of the many deer which reside in the surrounding dense forest.

Continuing along the Cokahlarishkit River on July 6, the Lewis party passed the following state park recreation sites. In his notebook, Lewis remarked:

📖 *July 6, 1806*

The river passes through and extensive and handsome plain on Warners Creek, leaving a high praries hill to the right separating the plain from the river. Saw two swan on this beautifull creek.

July 6, 1806, continued below

⛺ Montana 119

RUSSELL M. GATES
Russell M. Gates Recreation Access Site

Location: Western Montana east of Missoula.

Access: From Montana State Highway 200 at milepost 35 +.5 (3.5 miles east of the junction of State Highways 200 & 83 at Clearwater Junction, 0.1 mile west of the Missoula-Powell county line, 37 miles west of Lincoln,) turn south and go 0.3 mile down a gravel access road to the campground.

Camping Facilities: 12 campsites; sites are small, level, with fair separation; parking pads are gravel, mostly medium-length straight-ins; small to medium-sized tent spots; fire rings; limited firewood is available for gathering in the area, b-y-o is reccommended; water at a hand pump; vault facilities; gravel driveway; limited + supplies and services are available in Lincoln.

Day Use Facilities: Shared with campers.

Activities & Attractions: Fishing; rafting and canoeing.

Natural Features: Located on a flat along the north bank of the Blackfoot River; sites are moderately shaded/sheltered by tall conifers; bordered by forested hills and mountains; elevation 4200´.

Season, Fees & Phone: Open all year, subject to weather conditions, with limited services October to May; 7 day limit; $5.00; phone c/o Montana Department of Fish Wildlife & Parks Region 2 Office, Missoula, ☎ (406) 542-5500.

Camp Journal: Beautiful river views. The Blackfoot is one of the most pleasantly scenic streams in the Northern Rocky Mountains. This dandy little wayside camp is adjacent to the Blackfoot River Recreation Corridor, which includes a number of fishing and boating access points. (The Blackfoot was the setting for the classic novella and subsequent film, *A River Runs Through It*, which was centered around trout fishing and family life in early twentieth century Montana. However, the outdoor footage for the film was actually shot on the Gallatin River south of Bozeman.)

📖 *July 6, 1806*, continued from above

Continued to the entrance of a large creek called Seamans Creek [Monture Creek]. This course with the river, the road passes through an extensive high prarie rendered very uneven by a vast number of little hillocks and sinkholes. At the head of the creeks, high, broken mountains stand at the distance. We encamped on the lower side of the last creek just before it's entrance. Here a war party had encamped about 2 months since and concealed their fires.

—*Captain Lewis*

⛺ Montana 120 ♿

MONTURE CREEK
Monture Creek Recreation Access Site

Location: Western Montana east of Missoula.

Access: From Montana State Highway 200 at milepost 40 +.2 (// miles east of Clearwater Junction, 5 miles west of Ovando) turn south into the recreation site; 3 sites are just off the highway; or swing southwesterly (right) and go down the gravel access road for 0.2 mile to the lower section.

Camping Facilities: 6 camp/picnic sites in 2 areas, plus 'overflow' room for additional campers in adjacent areas; sites are medium to large, with nominal to good separation (better in the lower section), parking surfaces are gravel/grass, somewhat sloped in the upper section, level in the lower loop, short to medium-length straight-ins or pull-offs; medium to large areas for tents; fire rings; b-y-o firewood is suggested; no drinking water; vault facilities; gravel driveways; gas and camper supplies at Clearwater Junction.

Day Use Facilities: Shared with campers.

Activities & Attractions: Trout fishing (good to very good).

Natural Features: Located on a grassy bench above, and on a flat along, Monture Creek, a tributary of the Blackfoot River; upper sites are unsheltered, lower sites are sheltered by some tall timber, hardwoods and lots of streamside brush; surrounded by high mountains; elevation 4300´.

Season, Fees & Phone: Open all year, subject to weather conditions; no fee (subject to change); 7 day limit; Montana Department of Fish Wildlife and Parks Region 2 Office, Missoula ☎(406) 542-5500.

Camp Journal: The upper section has excellent distant views, but definitely check out the streamside sites before settling in. Monture Creek was originally named Seaman Creek by Captain Lewis for his faithful canine companion.

On July 7th, 1806, Lewis's party "Set out at 7 A.M." In one long day (they had 18 hours of daylight in which to travel at that time of year), they passed the present community of Lincoln, as well as the site of Aspen Campground (below), crossing over the Continental Divide at Rogers Pass late in the day and camping just east of the Divide—their first camp east of the Rockies since August 1805 at the forks of Jefferson's (Beaverhead) River.

♠ Montana 121 &

HOOPER PARK
Lincoln Community Park

Location: Western Montana east of Missoula.

Access: From Montana State Highway 200 near milepost 72 on the east end of the community of Lincoln, turn south into the park entrance and go 100 yards to the campground.

Camping Facilities: 25 campsites, including 7 with partial hookups; sites are small to small+, level, with nominal separation; parking pads are gravel, medium-to long straight-ins; ample space for tents; fire rings; firewood is usually for sale, or b-y-o; water at central faucets; restrooms; gravel driveways; limited+ to adequate supplies and services are available in Lincoln.

Day Use Facilities: Medium-sized picnic area; other facilities are shared with campers.

Activities & Attractions: Sports field; horsheshoe pits; playground.

Natural Features: Located on a timbered flat; sites are very well sheltered by tall conifers above a grassy surface; the town is bordered by Helena National Forest and Lincoln State Forest, in the Rocky Mountains west of the Continental Divide; elevation 4600´.

Season, Fees & Phone: Open all year, with limited services October to April; $6.00 for a standard site, $12.00 for a partial hookup site; 14 day limit; (no phone).

Camp Journal: A pleasant 'in-town' stop. The park is named for Joseph Hooper, an early settler, who, with his wife Rose, lived over 70 years in the Lincoln area.

♠ Montana 122

ASPEN GROVE
Helena National Forest

Location: Western Montana northwest of Helena.

Access: From Montana State Highway 200 at milepost 78 +.7 (7 miles east of Lincoln, 4 miles west of the junction of Montana State Highway 200 and County Highway 279), turn south onto a gravel access road; proceed 0.5 mile to the campground.

Camping Facilities: 19 campsites in 2 loops; sites are medium-sized, with fair to good separation; parking pads are gravel, basically level short to medium-length straight-ins, and some are double-wide; many really good tent-pitching spots; fireplaces; firewood is available for gathering in the surrounding area; water at several faucets; vault facilities; gravel driveways; limited supplies and services are available in Lincoln.

Day Use Facilities: Small picnic are with vault facilities and a small parking lot is located 0.3 mile east of the campground.

Activities & Attractions: Fishing; hiking; access to several mountain lakes is gained by driving north on nearby Copper Creek Road.

Natural Features: Located along the Blackfoot River on the edge of a sage flat in the Rocky Mountains; steep canyon walls rise to the south, across the river, and a more open valley lies to the north; sites are situated among aspens, scattered conifers and tall grass; elevation 4800´.

Season, Fees & Phone: June to September; $8.00; 14 day limit; Lincoln Ranger District ☎(406) 362-4265.

Camp Journal: There are some super vast vistas all up and down this valley.

From their camp on the Continental Divide for the night of July 7, 1806, Lewis's party started on down the east slope towards the Medicine (now Sun) River on the high plains west of present Great Falls. Lewis resumes his Journal narratives:

📖 *July 9, 1806*
Set out early and had not proceeded far before it began to rain. The air extreemly cold. Halted a few minutes in some old lodges untill it ceased to rain in some measure. We then proceeded and it rained without intermission. Wet us to the skin.

—*Captain Lewis*

🔥 On the night of July 9th, they camped on the Medicine River about 5 miles northwest of the future site of the city of Great Falls.

📖 *July 10, 1806*
The ground is rendered so miry by the rain which fell yesterday that it is excessively fatiguing to the horses to travel. We came 10 miles and halted for dinner, the wind blowing down the river in the forepart of the day was unfavourable to the hunters. They saw several gangs of elk, but they having the wind of them ran off. In the evening the wind set from the West and we fell in with a few elk. of which

R. Fields and myself killed 3, one of which swam the river and fell on the opposite side, so we therefore lost it's skin. I sent the packhorses on with Sergt. Gass, directing them to halt and encamp at the first timber, which proved to be about 7 miles. I retained Frazier to assist in skining the elk. We were about this time joined by Drewer. A large brown bear swam the river near where we were and Drewyer shot and killed it.

By the time we butchered the 2 elk and b'ar it was near dark. We loaded our horses with the best of the meat and pursued the party and found them encamped as they had been directed in the first timber. We did not reach them until 9 P.M. They informed us that they had seen a very large bear in the plains which had pursued Sergt. Gass and Thompson some distance, but their horses enabled them to keep out of it's reach. They were affraid to fire on the bear, lest their horses should throw them, as they were unaccustomed to the gun. We killed five deer, 3 elk and a bear today. Saw vast herds of buffaloe in the evening below us on the river. We heard them bellowing about us all night. Vast assemblages of wolves. Saw a large herd of elk making down the river. Passed a considerable rapid in Medicine River after dark. The river, about a hundred yards wide, is deep, and in many parts rapid, and today has been much crowded with islands.

—*Captain Lewis*

📖 *July 11, 1806*
I sent the hunters down Medicine River to hunt elk and proceeded with the party across the plain to the White Bear Islands [on the Missouri River]. It is now the season at which the buffaloe begin to copulate, and the bulls keep a tremendous roaring. We could hear them for many miles, and there are such numbers of them that there is one continual roar. Our horses had not been acquainted with the buffaloe. They appeared much allarmed at their appearance and bellowing.

When I arrived in sight of the White Bear Islands, the Missouri bottoms on both sides of the river were crowded with buffaloe. I sincerely believe that there were not less than 10 thousand buffaloe within a circle of 2 miles around that place. I met with the hunters at a little grove of timber opposite to the island where they had killed a cow and were awaiting our arrival. They had met with no elk.

I directed the hunters to kill some buffaloe, as well for the benefit of their skins to enable us to pass the river as for their meat for the men I meant to leave at this place. We unloaded our horses and encamped opposite to the islands; had the cow skinned and some willow sticks collected to make canoes of the hides.

By 12 oClock they killed eleven buffaloe, most of them in fine order. The bulls are now generally much fatter than the cows and are fine beef. I sent out all hands with the horses to assist in butchering and bringing in the meat. By 3 in the evening we had brought in a large quantity of fine beef and as many hides as we wanted for canoes, shelters, and gear. I then set all hands to prepare two canoes. The one we made after the Mandan fashion, with a single skin in the form of a basin, and the other we constructed of two skins, on a plan of our own.

—*Captain Lewis*

📖 *July 12, 1806*

We arrose early and resumed our operations in completing our canoes, which we completed by 10 A.M. About this time, two of the men whom I had dispatched this morning in quest of the horses returned with seven of them only. The remaining ten of our best horses were absent and not to be found. I fear that they are stolen. I dispatched two men on horseback in search of them. The wind blew so violent that I did not think it prudent to attempt passing the river. At noon Warner returned, having found three others of the horses. Sergt. Gass did not return untill 3 P.M., not having found the horses. He had been about 8 miles up Medicine River. I now dispatched Joseph Fields and Drewyer in quest of them. The former returned at dark, unsuccessfull, and the latter continued absent all night. At 5 P.M. the wind abated and we transported our baggage and meat to the opposite shore in our canoes, which we found answered even beyond our expectations. We swam our horses over also and encamped at sunset. The grass and weeds are much more luxuriant than they were when I left this place on the 13th of July 1805

—*Captain Lewis*

📖 *July 13, 1806*

Removed above to my old station opposite the upper point of the White Bear Island. Formed our camp and set Thompson, etc., at work to complete the gear for the horses. Had the cache opened, found my bear skins entirely destroyed by the water, the river having risen so high that the water had penetrated. All my specimens of plants also lost. The chart of the Missouri fortunately escaped. Opened my

trunks and boxes and exposed the articles to dry. Found my papers damp and several articles damp. The stopper had come out of a phial of laudanum and the contents had run into the drawer and destroyed a great part of my medicine in such manner that it was past recovery. Waited very impatiently for the return of Drewyer. He did not arrive.

—*Captain Lewis*

📖 *July 14, 1806*

Had the carriage wheels dug up. Found them in good order. The iron frame of the boat had not suffered materially. Had the meat cut thinner and exposed to dry in the sun. The old cache being too damp to venture to deposit my trunks &c. in, I sent them over to the large island and had them put on a high scaffold among some thick brush and covered with skins. I take this precaution, lest some Indians may visit the men I leave here before the arrival of the main party and rob them. The hunters killed a couple of wolves, the buffaloe have almost entirely disappeared. Saw the bee martin. The wolves are in great numbers, howling around us and lolling about in the plains in view at the distance of two or three hundred yards.

—*Captain Lewis*

📖 *July 15, 1806*

Dispatched McNeal early this morning to the lower part of the portage in order to learn whether the cache and white perogue remained untouched, or in what state they were. The men employed in drying the meat, dressing deer skins, and preparing for the reception of the canoes.

At 1 P.M., Drewyer returned without the horses and reported that, after a diligent search of 2 days, he had discovered where the horses had passed Dearborn's River, at which place there were 15 lodges that had been abandoned about the time our horses were taken; he pursued the tracks of a number of horses from these lodges to the road which we had traveled over the mountains, which they struck about 3 miles South of our encampment of the 7th, and had pursued this road Westwardly.

I have no doubt but they are a party of the Tushapahs who have been on a buffaloe hunt. Drewyer informed that their camp was in a small bottom on the river of about 5 acres enclosed by the steep and rocky and lofty clifts of the river, and that so closely had they kept themselves and horses within this little spot, that there was not a track to be seen of them within a quarter of a mile of that place. Every spire of grass was eaten up by their horses near their camp, which had the appearance of their having remained here some time.

His horse being much fatigued with the ride he had given him and finding that the Indians had at least 2 days the start of him, he thought it best to return. His safe return has relieved me from great anxiety. I had already settled it in my mind that a white bear had killed him, and should have set out tomorrow in search of him, and if I could not find him to continue my rout to Maria's River. I knew that if he met with a bear, in the plains even, he would attack him; and that, if any accident should happen to separate him from his horse in that situation, the chances in favour of his being killed would be as 9 to 10. I felt so perfectly satisfied that he had returned in safety that I thought but little of the horses, although they were seven of the best I had.

This loss, great as it is, is not entirely irreparable or at least does not defeat my design of exploring Maria's River. I have yet 10 horses remaining, two of the best and two of the worst of which I leave, to assist the party in taking the canoes and baggage over the portage, and take the remaining 6 with me. These are but indifferent horses, most of them, but I hope they may answer our purposes. I shall leave three of my intended party, Gass, Frazier, and Warner, and take the two Fieldses and Drewyer. By having two spare horses, we can relieve those we ride. Having made this arrangement, I gave orders for an early departure in the morning. Indeed, I should have set out instantly, but McNeal rode one of the horses which I intend to take and has not yet returned.

A little before dark, McNeal returned with his musket broken off at the breach, and informed me that on his arrival at Willow Run [on the portage], he had approached a white bear within ten feet without discovering him, the bear being in the thick brush. The horse took the allarm and, turning short, threw him immediately under the bear. This animal raised himself on his hind feet for battle, and gave him time to recover from his fall, which he did in an instant, and with his clubbed musket he struck the bear over the head and cut him with the guard of the gun and broke off the breach. The bear, stunned with the stroke, fell to the ground and began to scratch his head with his feet. This gave McNeal time to climb a willow tree which was near at hand and thus fortunately made his escape. The bear waited

at the foot of the tree untill late in the evening before he left him.

When McNeal ventured down and caught his horse, which had by this time strayed off to the distance of 2 miles, and returned to camp. These bear are a most tremendous animal; it seems that the hand of Providence has been most wonderfully in our favour with rispect to them, or some of us would long since have fallen a sacrifice to their ferocity. There seems to be a certain fatality attatched to the neighbourhood of these falls, for there is always a chapter of accidents prepared for us during our residence at them. The musquetoes continue to infest us in such manner that we can scarcely exist; for my own part I am confined by them to my bier [netting] at least 3/4ths of my time. My dog even howls with the torture he experiences from them; they are almost insupportable; they are so numerous that we frequently get them in our throats as we breath.

—*Captain Lewis*

📖 *July 16, 1806*

I dispatched a man early this morning to drive up the horses as usual; he returned at 8 A.M. with one of them only. Allarmed at this occurrence, I dispatched one of my best hands on horseback in search of them. He returned at 10 A.M. with them and I immediately set out. Sent Drewyer and R. Fields with the horses to the lower side of Medicine River, and proceeded myself with all our baggage and J. Fields down the Missouri to the mouth of Medicine River in our canoe of buffaloe skins. We were compelled to swim the horses above the White Bear Island and again across Medicine River, as the Missouri is of great width below the mouth of that river.

Having arrived safely below Medicine River, we immediately saddled our horses and proceeded down the river to the handsome fall of 47 feet, where I halted about 2 hours and took a hasty sketch of these falls; in the meantime, we had some meat cooked and took dinner, after which we proceeded to the grand falls where we arrived at sunset. On our way we saw two very large bear on the opposite side of the river. As we arrived in sight of the little wood below the falls, we saw two other bear enter it; this being the only wood in the neighbourhood, we were compelled of course to contend with the bear for possession, and therefore left our horses in a place of security and entered the wood, which we searched in vain for the bear; they had fled.

Here we encamped, and the evening having the appearance of rain, made our beds and slept under a shelving rock. These falls have abated much of their grandure since I first arrived at them in June 1805, the water being much lower at present than it was at that moment; however they are still a sublimely grand object.

—*Captain Lewis*

Å *Great Falls to Camp Disappointment*

📖 *July 17, 1806*

I arrose early this morning and made a drawing of the falls, after which we took breakfast and departed. It being my design to strike Maria's River about the place at which I left it on my return to it's mouth in the beinning of June 1805, I steered my course through the wide and level plains which have somewhat the appearance of an ocean, not a tree nor a shrub to be seen. The land is not fertile, at least far less so than the plains of the Columbia or those lower down this river. We killed a buffaloe cow as we passed through the plains and took the hump and tongue, which furnish ample rations for four men one day.

At 5 P.M., we arrived at Rose [now Teton] River, where I proposed remaining all night, as I could not reach Maria's River this evening, and unless I did there would be but little probability of our finding any wood, and very probably no water either. On our arrival at the river we saw where a wounded and bleeding buffaloe had just passed and concluded it was probable that the Indians had been running them and were near at hand. The Minnetares of Fort de Prarie and the Blackfoot Indians rove through this quarter of the country; and as they are a vicious, lawless, and reather abandoned set of wretches, I wish to avoid an interview with them if possible. I have no doubt but they would steal our horses if they have it in their power, and finding us weak, should they happen to be numerous, will most probably attempt to rob us of our arms and baggage; at all events, I am determined to take every possible precaution to avoid them if possible.

I hurried over the river to a thick wood and turned the horses to graize; sent Drewyer to pursue and kill the wounded buffaloe in order to determine whether it had been wounded by the Indians or not, and proceeded myself to reconnoiter the adjacent country, having sent R. Fields for the same purpose a different rout. I ascended the river hills, and by the help of my glass examined the plains but could make no discovery; in about an hour I returned to camp, where I met with the others who had been as unsuccessfull as myself. Drewyer could not find the wounded buffaloe. J. Fields, whom I had left at camp, had already roasted some of the buffaloe meat and we took dinner, after which I sent Drewyer and R. Fields to resume their resurches for the Indians, and set myself down to record the transactions of the day.

—*Captain Lewis*

📖 *July 18, 1806*

We set out this morning a little before sunrise, ascended the river hills and continued our rout as yesterday through the open plains. We passed immence herds of buffaloe on our way; in short, for about 12 miles it appeared as one herd only, the whole plains and valley being covered with them

After dinner we proceeded about 5 miles across the plain to Maria's River, where we arrived at 6 P.M. Being now convinced that we were above the point to which I had formerly ascended this river, and fearing that a fork of this stream might fall in on the North side between this place and the point to which I had ascended it, I directed Drewyer, who was with me on my former excursion, and Joseph Fields, to decend the river early in the morning to the place from whence I had returned, and examine whether any stream fell in or not. I keep a strict lookout every night; I take my tour of watch with the men.

—*Captain Lewis*

📖 *July 19, 1806*

Drewyer and J. Fields set out early this morning in conformity to my instructions last evening. They returned at 1/2 after 12 oClock and informed me that the course of the river, from hence downwards as far as they were, is N. 80. E. We set out, ascended the river hills, having passed the river, and proceeded through the open plains up the N. side of the river 20 miles and encamped. At 15 miles we passed a large creek on the N. side a little above it's entrance; there is but little running water in this creek at present, it's bed is about 30 yds. wide and appears to come from the Broken Mountains [now Sweetgrass Hills, rising to nearly 7000´], so called from their ragged and irregular shape. There are three of them extending from East to West almost unconnected, the center mountain terminates in a conic spire and is that which I have called the Tower Mountain. They are destitute of timber. The plains are beautifull and level but the soil is but thin.

—*Captain Lewis*

📖 *July 22, 1806*

We continued up the river on it's South side for 17 miles, when we halted to graize our horses and eat; there being no wood, we were compelled to make our fire with the buffaloe dung, which I found answered the purpose very well. We cooked and ate all the meat we had except a small piece of buffaloes meat which was a little tainted.

After dinner we passed the river and took our course through a level and beautifull plain on the N. side. The country has now become level, the river bottoms wide, and the adjoining plains but little elevated above them; the banks of the river are not usually more than from 3 to four feet, yet it does not appear ever to overflow them. We found no timber untill we had traveled 12 miles further when we arrived at a clump of large cottonwood trees in a beautifull and extensive bottom of the river about 10 miles below the foot of the Rocky Mountains, where this river enters them. As I could see from hence very distinctly where the river entered the mountains and the bearing of this point being S. of West, I thought it unnecessary to proceed further and therefore encamped, resolving to rest ourselves and horses a couple of days at this place and take the necessary observations.

This plain on which we are is very high; the Rocky Mountains to the S.W. of us appear but low from their base up, yet are partially covered with snow nearly to their bases. There is no timber on those mountains within our view; they are very irregular and broken in their form and seem to be composed principally of clay, with but little rock or stone. the river appears to possess at least double the volume of water which it had where we first arrived on it below; this no doubt proceeds from the evaporation caused by the sun and air and the absorbing of the earth in it's passage through these open plains.

I believe that the waters of the Saskachewan approach the borders of this river very nearly. I now have lost all hope of the waters of this river ever extending to N. Latitude 50°, though I still hope and think it more than probable that both White Earth River and Milk River extend as far North as latd. 50°. We

have seen but few buffaloe today, no deer and very few antelopes; game of every description is extreemly wild, which induces me to believe that the Indians are now, or have been lately, in this neighbourhood. We wounded a buffaloe this evening but our horses were so much fatigued that we were unable to pursue it with success.

—*Captain Lewis*

⚜ Lewis and his party have come as far north as today's city of Cut Bank, along what is now Cut Bank Creek, one of the principal headwaters of Marias River. He has finally come to the realization that his vision of finding a route up Marias River to the Saskatchewan River has been in vain. Cut Bank Creek rises in Glacier National Park, as does its sister tributary Two Medicine River.

For the next three, cloudy, rainy days, the party hunted and explored the local digs, while Lewis impatiently waited to make some celestial observations to document his findings and conclusions.

While they were in this camp, Lewis sent out Drewyer and Fields on hunting and 'recon' trips farther west up Cut Bank Creek. Although they didn't make it quite into the high country that later would become Glacier National Park, the future national reserve was "right over there". The following two excellent camps are close enough to Lewis's 'side trip' that we have included them as *Side Trips* in this volume.

▲ **Montana Side Trip** ♿

CUT BANK
Glacier National Park

Location: Northwest Montana in southeast Glacier Park

Access: From U.S Highway 89 at milepost 17 +.3 (17 miles northwest of Browning, 14 miles south of St. Mary), head west on Cut Bank Creek Road (gravel) for 5 miles to the campground.

Day Use Facilities: None.

Camping Facilities: 18 campsites; sites are small, level or nearly so, with nominal to fair separation; parking pads are gravel, mainly short straight-ins; medium to large tent spots; fireplaces; b-y-o firewood; water at a central fdaucet; vault facilities; gravel driveway; gas and groceries+ in St. Mary, adequate supplies and services are available in Browning.

Activities & Attractions: Hiking trails; stream fishing.

Natural Features: Located along the North Fork of Cut Bank Creek in a small valley nestled near the foot of the east slope of the Rocky Mountains; sites receive shelter from tall conifers; the valley is flanked by high, forested mountains and craggy peaks; elevation 5000´.

Season, Fees & Phone: June to September; $8.00; 7 day limit; Glacier National Park Headquarters, West Glacier, ☎(406) 888-5441.

Camp Journal: This small, semi-primitive camp is sequestered in a pretty, little valley that's off the well-worn track. It's bordered by classic, towering Northern Rockies peaks.

▲ Montana Side Trip ♿

TWO MEDICINE
Glacier National Park

Location: Northwest Montana in southeast Glacier Park.

Access: From Montana State Highway 49 at a point 4 miles north of East Glacier and 8 miles south of the junction of Highway 49 & U.S. 89 west of Browning, turn west onto Two Medicine Road; travel 7.5 miles to the campground.

Camping Facilities: 99 campsites in 3 loops; sites are small+ to medium-sized, with good separation; parking pads are packed gravel, medium+ to long pull-throughs; many pads will require additional leveling; ample spaces for tents, but many are sloped; fireplaces; b-y-o firewood is suggested; water at central faucets; restrooms in each loop; holding tank disposal station; paved driveways; camper supplies at the camp store; limited supplies and services are available in East Glacier.

Day Use Facilities: Small picnic area; drinking water; restrooms; medium-sized parking lot

Activities & Attractions: Hiking trails; limited boating (10 hp max.); boat launch; ranger-guided activities; scenic launch tours on Two Medicine Lake (extra charge).

Natural Features: Located along Two Medicine River just east of the shore of Two Medicine Lake in the Rocky Mountains; a trio of lakes—Lower Two Medicine, Two Medicine, and Upper Two Medicine—are nestled at the base of 9513´ Rising Wolf Mountain; some sites are on a riverside flat, most are on slopes above the stream; campground vegetation varies from open grassy sections to medium-dense stands of conifers; most sites are moderately sheltered/shaded; elevation 5200´.

Season, Fees & Phone: Mid-June to early September; $10.00; 7 day limit; Glacier National Park Headquarters, West Glacier, ☎(406) 888-5441.

Camp Journal: There are majestic peaks *all over the place* here! Unlike Logan Pass and the Going-to-the-Sun Road, Two Medicine is one of those places in the park that doesn't get a lot of hoopla and holler. But it's in a truly unforgettable setting.

Lewis and his small party now broke camp and headed back to their rendezvous with the rest of the men at the confluence of Maria's River and the Missouri, as previously arranged. However, they are about to experience what would become one of the most notable events of the course of the Expedtion: Their encounter with the Blackfoot.

⛺ *Brief Battle with the Blackfoot*

📖 *July 26, 1806*

The morning was cloudy and it continued to rain as usual, tho' the cloud seemed somewhat thinner. I therefore postponed setting out untill 9 A.M. in the hope that it would clear off; but finding the contrary result, I had the horses caught and we set out, bidding a lasting *adieu* to this place, which I now call Camp Disappointment.

I took my rout through the open plains S.E. 5 miles, passing a small creek at 2 miles from the mountains, when I changed my direction to S. 75 E. for 7 miles further and struck a principal branch [Two Medicine River] of Maria's River 65 yds. wide, not very deep. I passed this stream to it's South side and continued down it 2 miles on the last mentioned course when another branch [Birch Creek] of nearly the same dignity formed a junction with it, coming from the S.W. I passed the S. branch just above it's junction and continued down the river which runs a little to the N. of E. 1 mile and halted to dine and graize our horses. Here I found some Indian lodges which appeared to have been inhabited last winter in a large and fertile bottom well stocked with cottonwood timber. During our stay at this place, R. Fields killed a buck, a part of the flesh of which we took with us.

After dinner I continued my rout down the river to the North of East about 3 miles when the hills put in close on the S. side. I determined to ascend them to the high plain, which I did accordingly, keeping the Fieldes with me; Drewyer passed the river and kept down the valley of the river. I had intended to decend this river with it's course to it's junction with the fork which I had ascended and from thence have taken across the country obliquely to Rose [Teton] River and decend that stream to it's confluence with Maria's River.

The country through which this portion of Maria's River passes to the fork which I ascended appears much more broken than that above and between this and the mountains. I had scarcely ascended the hills before I discovered, to my left, at the distance of a mile, an assemblage of about 30 horses. I halted and used my spyglass, by the help of which I discovered several Indians on the top of an eminence just above them, who appeared to be looking down toward the river, I presumed, at Drewyer. About half the horses were saddled.

This was a very unpleasant sight. However, I resolved to make the best of our situation and to approach them in a friendly manner. I directed J. Fields to display the flag which I had brought for that purpose, and advanced slowly toward them. About this time they discovered us and appeared to run about in a very confused manner as if much allarmed. Their attention had been previously so fixed on Drewyer that they did not discover us untill we had begun to advance upon them. Some of them descended the hill on which they were, and drove their horses within shot of it's summit and again returned to the height as if to wait our arrival or to defend themselves.

I calculated on their number being nearly or quite equal to that of their horses, that our running would invite pursuit, as it would convince them that we were their enemies, and our horses were so indifferent that we could not hope to make our escape by flight. Added to this, Drewyer was separated from us, and I feared that his not being apprised of the Indians in the event of our attempting to escape, he would most probably fall a sacrifice.

Under these considerations, I still advanced toward them. When we had arrived within a quarter of a mile of them, one of them mounted his horse and rode full speed toward us, which when I discovered, I halted and alighted from my horse. He came within a hundred paces, halted, looked at us, and turned his horse about, and returned as briskly to his party as he had advanced.

While he halted near us, I held out my hand and beckoned him to approach, but he paid no attention to my overtures. On his return to his party, they all descended the hill and mounted their horses, and advanced toward us, leaving other horses behind them. We also advanced to meet them. I counted eight of them, but still supposed that there were others concealed, as there were several other horses saddled.

I told the two men with me that I apprehended that these were the Minnetares of Fort de Prarie, and from their known character I expected that we were to have some difficulty with them; that if they thought themselves sufficiently strong, I was convinced that they would attempt to rob us; in which case, be their numbers what they would, I should resist to the last extremity, preferring death to being deprived of my papers, instruments, and gun; and desired that they would form the same resolution, and be alert and on their guard.

When we arrived within a hundred yards of each other, the Indians, except one, halted. I directed the two men with me to do the same and advanced singly to meet the Indian, with whom I shook hands and passed on to those in his rear, as he did also to the two men in my rear. We now all assembled and alighted from our horses. The Indians soon asked to smoke with us, but I told them that the man whom they had seen pass down the river had my pipe and we could not smoke untill he joined us. I requested, as they had seen which way he went, that they would one of them go with one of my men in search of him. This they readily consented to, and a young man set out with R. Fields in search of Drewyer.

I now asked them by signs if they were the Minnetares of the North, which they answered in the affirmative. I asked if there was any cheif among them, and they pointed out 3. I did not believe them. However, I thought it best to please them and give to one a medal, to a second a flag, and to the third a handkerchief, with which they appeared well satisfied. They appeared much agitated with our first interview, from which they had scarcely yet recovered. In fact, I believe they were more allarmed at this accidental interview than we were.

From no more of them appearing, I now concluded they were only eight in number, and became much better satisfied with our situation, as I was convinced that we could manage that number should they attempt any hostile measures. As it was growing late in the evening, I proposed that we should remove to the nearest part of the river and encamp together. I told them that I was glad to see them and had a great deal to say to them.

We mounted our horses and rode toward the river, which was at but a short distance. On our way we were joined by Drewyer, Fields, and the Indian. We descended a very steep bluff about 250 feet high to the river, where there was a small bottom of nearly 1/2 a mile in length. In this bottom, there stand three solitary trees, near one of which the Indians formed a large semicircular camp of dressed buffaloe skins and invited us to partake of their shelter, which Drewyer and myself accepted, and the Fieldses lay near the fire in front of the shelter.

With the assistance of Drewyer, I had much conversation with these people in the course of the evening. I learned from them that they were a part of a large band which lay encamped at present near the foot of the Rocky Mountains, on the main branch of Maria's River, 1 1/2 days march from our present encampment; that there was a white man with their band; that there was another large band of their Nation hunting buffaloe near the broken mountains and were on their way to the mouth of Maria's River, where they would probably be in the course of a few days.

They also informed us that from hence to the establishment where they trade on the Saskachewan River is only 6 days easy march, or such as they usually travel with their women and children, which may be estimated at about 150 miles. That from these traders they obtain arms amunition, spiritous liquor, blankets &c. in exchange for wolves and some beaver skins.

I told these people that I had come a great way from the East, up the large river which runs towards the rising sun; that I had been to the great waters where the sun sets and had seen a great many Nations, all of whom I had invited to come and trade with me, on the rivers on this side of the mountains; that I had found most of them at war with their neighbours and had succeeded in restoring peace among them. That I was now on my way home and had left my party at the Falls of the Missouri with orders to descend that river to the entrance of Maria's River and there wait my arrival, and that I had come in search of them in order to

prevail on them to be at peace with their neighbours, particularly those on the West side of the mountains, and to engage them to come and trade with me when the establishment is made at the entrance of this river; to all of which they readily gave their assent, and declared it to be their wish to be at peace with the Tushepahs whom they said had killed a number of their relations lately, and pointed to several of those present who had cut their hair as an evidence of the truth of what they had asserted.

I found them extreemly fond of smoking and plyed them with the pipe untill late at night. I told them that if they intended to do as I wished them, they would send some of their young men to their band with an invitation to their chiefs and warriors to bring the white man with them and come down and counsel with me at the entrance of Maria's River, and that the ballance of them would accompany me to that place, where I was anxious now to meet my men, as I had been absent from them some time and knew that they would be uneasy untill they saw me. That if they would go with me, I would give them 10 horses and some tobacco. To this proposition they made no reply.

I took the first watch tonight and sat up untill half after eleven. The Indians by this time were all asleep. I roused up R. Fields and lay down myself. I directed Fields to watch the movements of the Indians, and if any of them left the camp, to awake us all, as I apprehended they would attempt to steal our horses.

This being done, I fell into a profound sleep and did not wake untill the noise of the men and Indians awoke me a little after light, in the morning.

—*Captain Lewis*

▲ Montana 123 &

LAKE FRANCIS
City of Valier Recreation Area

Location: North-central Montana northwest of Great Falls.

Access: From Montana State Highway 44 at milepost 13 +.8 on the west edge of the city of Valier (14 miles west of Interstate 15 Exit 348, 14 miles east of U.S. 89), turn west onto Teton Avenue; drive west (past the airport) for 0.4 mile, then the road curves south for 0.6 mile; turn west (right) into the campground.

Camping Facilities: Approximately 20 camp/picnic sites; sites are medium-sized, level, with nominal separation; parking pads are gravel/earth, small to large pull-offs or straight-ins; good tent-pitching opportunities; fireplaces; b-y-o firewood; water at a central faucet; restrooms; holding tank disposal station; gravel driveways; gas and groceries+ are available in Valier.

Day Use Facilities: Facilities are shared with campers.

Activities & Attractions: Boating; boat launch; fishing for warm-water species; sports/play areas.

Natural Features: Located on the east shore of Lake Francis on the west edge of the Great Plains; a line of bushes and medium-sized hardwoods serve as a wind break and very light shade for some sites; (b-y-o shade); the Northern Rockies rise about 35 miles west; typically breezy; elevation 3600´.

Season, Fees & Phone: Open all year, subject to weather conditions, with limited services October to May; $8.00; weekly rates available; Valier City Hall ☎(406) 279-3721.

Camp Journal: Lake Francis and its campground are situated in the middle of a vast prairie that stretches for miles and miles and miles in every direction. From your campsite, looking westward across the lake and the plains beyond, you can view the peaks of the Rockies rising above the horizon.

📖 *July 27, 1806*

This morning at daylight the Indians got up and crowded around the fire. J. Fields, who was on post, had carelessly laid his gun down behind him, near where his brother was sleeping. One of the Indians, the fellow to whom I had given the medal last evening, slipped behind him and took his gun and that of his brother, unperceived by him. At the same instant two others advanced and seized the guns of Drewyer and myself.

J. Fields, seeing this, turned about to look for his gun and saw the fellow just running off with her and his brother's. He called to his brother, who instantly jumped up and pursued the Indian with him, whom they overtook at the distance of 50 or 60 paces from the camp, seized their guns and wrested them from him; and R. Fields, as he seized his gun, stabbed the Indian to the heart with his knife. The fellow ran about 15 steps and fell dead. Of this I did not know untill afterward. Having

recovered their guns, they ran back instantly to the camp.

Drewyer, who was awake, saw the Indian take hold of his gun and instantly jumped up and seized her and wrested her from him, but the Indian still retained his pouch. His jumping up and crying, "Damn you, let go my gun!" awakened me.

I jumped up and asked what was the matter, which I quickly learned when I saw Drewyer in a scuffle with the Indian for his gun. I reached to seize my gun, but found her gone. I then drew a pistol from my holster and, turning myself about, saw the Indian making off with my gun. I ran at him with my pistol and bid him lay down my gun, which he was in the act of doing when the Fieldses returned and drew up their guns to shoot him, which I forbid, as he did not appear to be about to make any resistance or commit any offensive act.

He dropped the gun and walked slowly off. I picked her up instantly. Drewyer, having about this time recovered his gun and pouch, asked me if he might not kill the fellow, which I also forbid, as the Indian did not appear to wish to kill us. As soon as they found us all in possession of our arms, they ran and endeavoured to drive off all the horses.

I now hallooed to the men and told them to fire on them if they attempted to drive off our horses. They accordingly pursued the main party who were driving the horses up the river, and I pursued the man who had taken my gun, who, with another, was driving off a part of the horses which were to the left of the camp. I pursued them so closely that they could not take twelve of their own horses, but continued to drive one of mine with some others. At the distance of three hundred paces, they entered one of those steep niches in the bluff with the horses before them. Being nearly out of breath, I could pursue no further. I called to them, as I had done several times before, that I would shoot them if they did not give me my horse, and raised my gun.

One of them jumped behind a rock and spoke to the other, who turned around and stopped at the distance of 30 steps from me, and I shot him through the belly. He fell to his knees and on his right elbow, from which position he partly raised himself and fired at me and, turning himself about, crawled in behind a rock, which was a few feet from him. He overshot me. Being bareheaded, I felt the wind of his bullet very distinctly.

Not having my shot pouch, I could not reload my piece, and as there were two of them behind good shelters from me, I did not think it prudent to rush on them with my pistol, which had I discharged. I had not the means of reloading untill I reached camp. I therefore returned leisurely toward camp. On my way, I met with Drewyer who, having heard the report of the guns, had returned in search of me and left the Fieldses to pursue the Indians. I desired him to hasten to the camp with me and assist in catching as many of the Indian horses as were necessary, and to call to the Fieldses, if he could make them hear, to come back, that we still had a sufficient number of horses. This he did, but they were too far to hear him. We reached the camp and began to catch the horses and saddle them and put on the packs.

The reason I had not my pouch with me was that I had not time to return about fifty yards to camp, after getting my gun, before I was obliged to pursue the Indians or suffer them to collect and drive off all the horses. We had caught and saddled the horses and begun to arrange the packs when the Fieldses returned with four of our horses. We left one of our horses and took four of the best of those of the Indians.

While the men were preparing the horses, I put four shields, and two bows and quivers of arrows, which had been left, on the fire with sundry other articles. They left all their baggage at our mercy. They had but 2 guns, and one of them they left. The others were armed with bows and arrows and *eyedaggs* [short axes]. The gun we took with us. I also retook the flag, but left the medal about the neck of the dead man, that they might be informed who we were.

We took some of their buffaloe meat and set out, ascending the bluffs by the same rout we had descended last evening, leaving the ballance of nine of their horses, which we did not want. The Fieldses told me that three of the Indians whom they pursued swam the river, one of them on my horse; and that two others ascended the hill and escaped from them with a part of their horses; two I had pursued into the niche, one lay dead near the camp; and the eighth we could not account for but suppose that he ran off early in the contest.

Having ascended the hill, we took our course through a beautifull level plain a little to the S. of East. My design was to hasten to the entrance of Maria's River as quick as possible, in the hope of meeting with the canoes and party at that place, having no doubt but that the Indians would pursue us with a large party, as there was a band near the Broken Mountains. No time was therefore to be lost, and we pushed our horses as hard as they would bear.

At 3 P.M. we arrived at Rose River, having traveled by my estimate about 63 miles. Here we halted an hour and a half took some refreshment and suffered our horses to graize; Our whole rout so far was as level as a bowling green, with but little stone and few prickly pears.

After dinner we pursued the bottoms of Rose River, but finding it inconvenient to pass the river so often, we again ascended the hills on the S.W. side and took the open plains; by dark we had traveled about 17 miles further. We now halted to rest ourselves and horses about 2 hours; we killed a buffaloe cow and took a small quantity of the meat.

After refreshing ourselves we again set out by moonlight and traveled leasurely; heavy thunderclouds lowered around us on every quarter but that from which the moon gave us light. We continued to pass immence herds of buffaloe all night, as we had done in the latter part of the day. We traveled untill 2 oClock in the morning, having come by my estimate after dark about 20 miles.

We now turned out our horses and laid ourselves down to rest in the plain, very much fatigued as may be readily conceived. My Indian horse carried me very well, in short, much better than my own would have done and leaves me with but little reason to complain of the robbery

—*Captain Lewis*

📖 *July 28, 1806*

The morning proved fair. I slept sound, but fortunately awoke as day appeared. I awakened the men and directed the horses to be saddled. I was so sore from my ride yesterday that I could scarcely stand. And the men complained of being in a similar situation; however, I encouraged them by telling them that our own lives, as well as those of our friends and fellow travellers, depended on our exertions at this moment. They were alert, soon prepared the horses, and we again resumed our march.

I now told them that it was my determination that, if we were attacked in the plains on our way to the point, that the bridles of the horses should be tied together and we would stand

and defend them, or sell our lives as dear as we could.

We had proceeded about 12 miles on an East course when we found ourselves near the Missouri. We heard a report which we took to be that of a gun but were not certain. Still continuing down the N.E. bank of the Missouri about 8 miles further, being then within about five miles of the grog spring, we heard the report of several rifles very distinctly on the river to our right. We quickly repaired to this joyful sound and, on arriving at the bank of the river, had the unspeakable satisfaction to see our canoes coming down. We hurried down from the bluff on which we were and joined them, stripped our horses and gave them a final discharge, embarking without loss of time with our baggage.

I now learned that they had brought all things safe, having sustained no loss, nor met with any accident of importance. Wiser had cut his leg badly with a knife and was unable, in consequence, to work. We descended the river opposite to our principal cache, which we proceeded to open after reconnoitering the adjacent country. We found that the cache had caved in and most of the articles buried therein were injured. I sustained the loss of two very large bear skins, which I much regret. Most of the fur and baggage belonging to the men were injured. The gunpowder, corn, flour, pork and salt had sustained but little injury. The parched meal was spoiled, or nearly so.

Having no time to air these things, which they much wanted, we dropped down to the point to take in the several articles which had been buried at that place in several small caches. These we found in good order, and recovered every article except 3 traps belonging to Drewyer, which could not be found. Here, as good fortune would have it, Sergt. Gass and Willard, who brought the horses from the Falls, joined us at 1 P.M. I had ordered them to bring down the horses to this place in order to assist them in collecting meat, which I directed them to kill and dry here for our voyage, presuming that they would have arrived with the perogue and canoes at this place several days before my return.

Having now nothing to detain us, we passed over immediately to the island in the entrance of Maria's River to launch the red perogue, but found her so much decayed that it was impossible with the means we had to repair her, and therefore merely took the nails and other iron works about her which might be of service to us and left her. We now reembarked

on board the white perogue and five small canoes and descended the river about 15 miles and encamped on the S.W. side near a few cottonwood trees.

—*Captain Lewis*

⚑ *Down the Missouri to Meet Clark's Yellowstone Party*

🐾 In late July and early August, the Missouri nowadays is usually a fairly gentle stream, having a current of about 3 knots and few obstructions—perfect for an easy downstream passage. Lewis's party thus cruised effortlessly down the great river, whose swift, springtime current they had labored against on the way upstream. They floated along at a speed of 4 to 6 knots, since there were no upriver dams to regulate the water flow then, through the scenic Missouri Breaks area, west of today's U.S. 191, during July 29-31.

📖 *July 29, 1806*

Shortly after dark last evening a violent storm came on from the N.W., and continued the greater part of the night. Not having the menans of making a shelter, I lay in the water all night. The rain continued without inbtermission. We set out early, and the current being strong, we proceeded with great rapidity. At 11 A. M.we passed that very interesting part of the Missouri where the natural walls appear, particularly described in my outward bound journey.We continued our rout untill late in the evening and encamped on the N. E. side of the river at the same place we had encamped on the 29th of May 1805.

—*Captain Lewis*

📖 *July 30, 1806*

The rain still continued this morning. I consequently set out early as usual and pursued my rout downwards. The current being strong and the men anxious to get on, they plyed their oars faithfully and we went at the rate of about seven miles an hour. We halted several times in the course of the day to kill some bighorns, being anxious to procure a few more skins and skeletons of this animal; I was fortunate enough to procure one other male and female for this purpose, which I had prepared accordingly. We arrived this evening at an island about 2 miles above Goodriches Island and encamped on it's N. E. side. The rain continued without intermission all day; the

ALAMEDA FREE LIBRARY

air is cold and extreemly disagreeable.
Nothing extraordinary happened today.

July 31, 1806

The rain still continuing, I set out early and proceeded on as fast as possible. The bottoms in the latter part of the day became wider, better timbered and abound in game. The river is still rising and excessively muddy, more so I think than I ever saw it. We experienced some very heavy showers of rain today. We have been passing high pine hills all day. Late in the evening we came to on the N.E. side of the river and took shelter in some Indian lodges built of sticks.

—*Captain Lewis*

The Lewis party camped in the vicinity of the next campground, James Kipp, on the night of July 31, 1806.

Missouri Breaks, Upper Missouri National Wild and Scenic River

---

⚑ Montana 124 ♿

JAMES KIPP
Public Lands/BLM Recreation Area

Location: Central Montana along the Missouri River southwest of Malta.

Access: From U.S. Highway 191 at milepost 87 + .4 (52 miles northeast of Lewistown, 69 miles southeast of Malta), at the south end of the Robinson Bridge across the Missouri River, turn east onto the recreation area access road and proceed 0.25 mile down to the recreation area; turn left and go another 0.2 mile to the campground.

Camping Facilities: 34 campsites in 3 loops; most sites are medium to large, level, with nominal to fair separation; parking pads are gravel, medium+, wide straight-ins; good spots

for tents in some sites, may need to use the parking pad in many sites; fire rings; b-y-o firewood is suggested (unless you're willing do some brush-busting); water at several faucets; vault facilities; gravel driveways; camper supplies at Mobridge, 3 miles south; next-nearest sources of supplies and services (adequate) are Malta and Lewistown.

Day Use Facilities: Medium-sized picnic area; drinking water; vault facilities; medium-sized parking lot.

Activities & Attractions: Interpretive displays about local history and wildlife; fishing, mainly in spring for paddlefish; boat ramp; Charles M. Russell National Wildlife Refuge; self-guided auto nature trail begins at the north end of the Robinson Bridge.

Natural Features: Located on a grassy flat in a large grove of cottonwoods on the south bank of the Missouri River in the Missouri Breaks area; mature cottonwoods and dense undercover provide good shade for most campsites; deer and waterfowl are commonly seen; dry climate with hot (and somewhat buggy) summers, cold winters, near-perfect in spring and fall; high bluffs and hills flank both sides of the river; elevation 2300´.

Season, Fees & Phone: Open all year, with limited services October to April; 14 day limit; $6.00; Bureau of Land Management Lewistown District Office ☎(406) 538-7461.

Camp Journal: The Missouri Breaks area hasn't changed all that much since the days of Lewis and Clark and the fur trade. This might be a good opportunity to take some time to explore the beautiful backcountry in this vast, sparely populated region. James Kipp was the first fur trader to establish a base up here on what is still the Wild and Scenic Missouri. He founded Fort Piegan at the confluence of the Missouri and Marias Rivers in 1831.

August 1, 1806

The rain still continuing, I set out early as usual and proceeded on at a good rate. At 11 A.M. we passed the entrance of Mussel Shell River. At 1 in the evening [1:00 P.M.}, we arrived at a bottom on S.W. side where there were several spacious Indian lodges built of sticks and an excellent landing. As the rain still continued with but little intermission, and appearancess seemed unfavorable to it's becomeing fair shortly, I determined to halt at this place at least for this evening and indeavour to dry my skins of the bighorn, which had every appearance of spoiling, an event which I would not should happen on any consideration, as we have now passed the country in which they are found and I therefore could not supply the deficiency were I to loose these I have. I halted at this place being about 15 miles below Mussel Shell River, had fires built in the lodges, and my skins exposed to dry. Shortly after we landed the rain ceased, tho' it still continued cloudy.

—*Captain Lewis*

📖 *August 2, 1806*

The morning proved fair and I determined to remain all day and dry the baggage and give the men an opportunity to dry and air their skins and fur. Had the powder, parched meal and every article which wanted drying exposed to the sun. The day proved warm fair and favourable for our purpose. I permitted the Fieldses to go on a few miles to hunt. By evening we had dryed our baggage and repacked it in readiness to load and set out early in the morning. Nothing remarkable took place today. We are all extreemly anxious to reach the entrance of the Yellowstone River, where we expect to join Capt. Clarks party.

—*Captain Lewis*

📖 *August 3, 1806*

I arrose early this morning and had the perogue and canoes loaded and set out at half after 6 A.M. We soon passed the canoe of Colter and Collins, who were on shore hunting. The men hailed them but received no answer. We proceeded, and shortly after overtook J. and R. Fields, who had killed 25 deer since they left us yesterday. Deer are very abundant in the timbered bottoms of the river and extreemly gentle. We did not halt today to cook and dine as usual, having directed that in future the party should cook as much meat in the evening after encamping as would be sufficient to serve them the next day. By this means we forward our journey at least 12 or 15 miles per day. We encamped this evening on N.E. side of the river, 2 miles above our encampment of the 12th of May 1805. Collins and Colter did not overtake us this evening.

—*Captain Lewis*

⛰ Montana 125

HELL CREEK
Hell Creek State Park

Location: Eastern Montana northwest of Miles City.

Access: From Montana State Highway 200 in Jordan (67 miles west of Circle, 129 miles east of Lewistown), head north on a local gravel road for 24 miles to the park. (Note: The surface of the access road is transformed into gumbo in wet weather.)

Camping Facilities: Approximately 20 camp/picnic sites; sites are medium-sized, with nominal separation; parking pads are gravel , medium-length straight-ins; ample space for large tents; fire rings; b-y-o firewood; water at central faucets; restrooms and vault facilities; gravel driveways; gas and camper supplies at the marina; limited supplies and services are available in Jordan.

Day Use Facilities: Medium-sized picnic/camp area with shared facilities.

Activities & Attractions: Fishing for walleye, also northerns, sauger, bass, several varieties of trout, crappie, perch, channel cat; boating; boat launch; marina; annual walleye derby.

Natural Features: Located on a peninsula on the middle-south shore of Fort Peck Lake overlooking the Hell Creek Arm of the lake; vegetation principally consists of prairie grass dotted with evergreens and hardwoods; bordered by hills and the distant Piney Buttes which rise 600´ above the lake; Fort Peck Lake, a major reservoir on the Missouri River, is 130 miles long, has 1500 miles of shoreline, a maximum depth of about 200´ and covers 375 square miles; elevation 2300´.

Season, Fees & Phone: Open all year, subject to weather and road conditions; principal season is April to October; 14 day limit; camping $8.00 (includes park entry fee); phone c/o Montana Department of Fish Wildlife & Parks, Miles City, ☎(406) 232-0900.

Camp Journal: Montana is really two states in one. In Western Montana are those lofty locations that have made the state renowned for its natural beauty. In the 'other' Montana—Eastern Montana—are plains and buttes and low, isolated mountain ranges which admirers say *really* gave rise to Montana's nickname as "Big Sky Country". There are thousands of bays, coves, inlets, canyons and coulees to explore along Fort Peck's shoreline. Other nearby areas are comprised of badlands where anyone from Southern California, Nevada, Utah, or Arizona would feel right at home. Most people think all of Montana is supposed to look like Glacier National Park. Only a few recognize that the wild, rugged, open, unpopulated country bordering Fort Peck Lake has its own style of handsomeness.

The Lewis party camped in the Hell Creek area on the night of August 2, 1806.

On August 4, the party passed the confluence of the Missouri and the Milk River, a few miles downstream of the present location of Fort Peck Dam

📖 *August 4, 1806*

Ordway and Willard delayed so much in hunting today that they did not overtake us untill about midnight. They killed one bear and two deer. In passing a bend just below the gulf, it being dark, they were drawn by the current in among a parcel of sawyers, under one of which the canoe was driven and threw Willard, who was steering, overboard. He caught the sawyer and held by it. Ordway, with the canoe, drifted down about half a mile among the sawyers under a falling bank. The canoe struck frequently but did not overset. He at length gained the shore, and returned by land to learn the fate of Willard, who, he found, was yet on the sawyer. It was impossible for him to take the canoe to his relief.

Willard at length tied a couple of sticks together which had lodged against the sawyers on which he was, and set himself adrift among the sawyers, which he fortunately escaped, and was taken up about a mile below by Ordway with the canoe.

—*Captain Lewis*

📖 *August 7, 1806*

At 4 P.M. we arrived at the entrance of the Yellowstone River. I landed at the point and found that Capt. Clark had been encamped at this place and from appearances had left it about 7 or 8 days. I found a paper on a pole at the point, which merely contained my name in the hand wrighting of Capt. Clark. We also found the remnant of a note which had been attached to a piece of elk horn in the camp. From this fragment I learned that game was scarce at the point and musquetoes troublesome, which were the reasons given for his going on. I also learnt that he intended halting a few miles below, where he intended waiting for my arrival.

I now wrote a note directed to Colter and Collins, provided they were behind, ordering them to come on without loss of time. This note I wrapped in leather and attached to the same pole which Capt. C. had planted at the point. This being done, I instantly re-embarked and descended the river in the hope of reaching Capt. C's camp before night.

About 7 miles below the point on the S.W. shore I saw some meat that had been lately fleeced and hung on a pole. I directed Sergt. Ordway to go on shore and examine the place; on his return, he reported that he saw the tracks of two men which appeared so recent that he believed they had been there today; the fire he found at the place was blazing and appeared to have been mended up afresh or within the course of an hour past. He found at this place a part of a Chinnook hat, which my men recognized as the hat of Gibson. From these circumstances we concluded that Capt. C's camp could not be distant and pursued our rout untill dark with the hope of reaching his camp. In this, however, we were disappointed; and night coming on compelled us to encamp on the Northeast shore in the next bottom above our encampment of the 23rd and 24th of April, 1805. As we came to, a herd of buffaloe assembled on shore, of which we killed a fat cow.

—*Captain Lewis*

📖 *August 8, 1806*

Believing from the recent appearances about the fire which we passed last evening, that Capt. Clark could be at no great distance below, I set out early; the wind hard from the N.E., but by the force of the oars and current we travelled at a good rate untill 10 A.M., by which time we reached the center of the beaver bends, about 8 miles by water and 3 by land, above the entrance of the White Earth River.

Not finding Capt. Clark, I knew not what calculation to make with rispect to his halting, and therefore determined to proceed as tho' he was not before me and leave the rest to the chapter of accidents. At this place I found a good beach for the purpose of drawing out the perogue and one of the canoes, which wanted corking and repairing.

The men with me have not had leisure, since we left the West side of the Rocky Mountains, to dress any skins or make themselves clothes, and most of them therefore are extreemly bare. I therefore determined to halt at this place untill the perogue and canoe could be repaired and the men dress skins and make themselves the necessary clothing. We encamped on the N.E. side of the river. We found the musquetoes extreemly troublesome, but in this rispect there is but little choice of camps from hence down to St. Louis. From this place to the Little Missouri there is an abundance of game. I shall therefore, when I leave this place, travel at my leisure and avail myself of every opportunity to collect and dry meat untill I provide a sufficient quantity for our voyage, not knowing what provision Capt. C. has made in this rispect. I formed a camp, unloaded the canoes and perogue, had the latter and one of the canoes drawn out to dry, fleeced what meat we had collected and hung it on poles in the sun, after which the men busied themselves in dressing skins and making themselves clothes.

—*Captain Lewis*

August 10, 1806

I hastened the repairs which were necessary to the perogue and canoe, which were completed by 2 P.M. Those not engaged about this business employed themselves as yesterday. At 4 in the evening, it clouded up and began to rain, which, putting a stop to the operation of skin dressing, we had nothing further to detain us. I therefore directed the vessels to be loaded, and at 5 P.M. we got under way. We descended this evening as low nearly as the entrance of White Earth River and encamped on the southwest side.

—*Captain Lewis*

August 11, 1806

We set out very early this morning, it being my wish to arrive at the Burnt Hills by noon in order to take the latitude of that place, as it is the most northern point of the Missouri. I informed the party of my design and requested that they would exert themselves to reach the place in time, as it would save us the delay of nearly one day. Being as anxious to get forward as I was, they plyed their oars faithfully, and we proceeded rapidly.

We saw but little game untill about 9 A.M., when we came up with a buffaloe swimming the river, which I shot and killed; leaving the small canoes to dress it and bring on the meat, I proceeded. We had gone but little way before I saw a very large grizzly bear and put to in order to kill it, but it took wind of us and ran off. The small canoes overtook us and informed that the flesh of the buffaloe was unfit for use and that they had therefor left it.

Half after 11 A.M., we saw a large herd of elk on the N.E. shore, and I directed the men in the small canoes to halt and kill some of them, and continued on in the perogue to the Burnt Hills. When I arrived here, it was about 20 minutes after noon, and of course, the observation of the sun's Meridian altitude was lost.

Just opposite to the Burnt Hills, there happened to be a herd of elk on a thick willow bar, and finding that my observation was lost for the present, I determined to land and kill some of them. Accordingly, we put to, and I went out with Cruzatte only. We fired on the elk. I killed one and he wounded another. We reloaded our guns and took different routs through the thick willows in pursuit of the elk.

I was in the act of firing on the elk a second time when a ball struck my left thigh about an inch below my hip joint. Missing the bone, it passed through the left thigh and cut the thickness of the bullet across the hinder part of the right thigh. The stroke was very severe. I instantly supposed that Cruzatte had shot me in mistake for an elk, as I was dressed in brown leather and he cannot see very well. Under this impression I called out to him, "Damn you, you have shot me", and looked toward the place from whence the ball had come. Seeing nothing, I called Cruzatte several times as loud as I could, but received no answer.

I was now persuaded that it was an Indian that had shot me, as the report of the gun did not appear to be more than 40 paces from me and Cruzatte appeared to be out of hearing of me. In this situation, not knowing how many Indians there might be concealed in the bushes, I thought it best to make good my retreat to the perogue, calling out as I ran for the first hundred paces as loud as I could to Cruzatte to retreat, that there were Indians, hoping to allarm him in time to make his escape also. I still retained the charge in my gun which I was about to discharge at the moment the ball struck me.

When I arrived in sight of the perogue, I called the men to their arms, to which they flew in an instant. I told them that I was wounded but I hoped not mortally, by an Indian I believed, and directed them to follow me, that I would return & give them battle and relieve Cruzatte if possible, who I feared had fallen into their hands.

The men followed me as they were bid and I returned about a hundred paces, when my wounds became so painfull and my thigh so stiff that I could scarcely get on. In short, I was compelled to halt, and ordered the men to proceed and, if they found themselves overpowered by numbers, to retreat in order, keeping up a fire. I now got back to the perogue as well as I could, and prepared myself with a pistol, my rifle, and air gun, being determined, as a retreat was impracticable, to sell my life as dearly as possible.

In this state of anxiety and suspense I remained about 20 minutes, when the party returned with Cruzatte and reported that there were no Indians nor the appearance of any. Cruzatte seemed much allarmed, and declared if he had shot me it was not his intention, that he had shot an elk in the willows after he left or separated from me. I asked him whether he did not hear me when I called to him so frequently, which he absolutely denied. I do not believe that the fellow did it intentionally but after finding that he had shot me, was anxious to conceal his knowledge of having done so.

The ball had lodged in my breeches, which I knew to be the ball of the short rifles such as that he had; and there being no person out with me but him and no Indians that we could discover, I have no doubt in my own mind of his having shot me. With the assistance of Sergt. Gass, I took off my clothes and dressed my wounds myself as well as I could, introducing tents of patent lint into the ball holes. The wounds bled considerably, but I was happy to find that it had touched neither bone nor artery.

I sent the men to dress the two elk which Cruzatte and myself had killed, which they did in a few minutes, and brought the meat to the river. My wounds being so situated that I could not, without infinite pain, make an observation, I determined to relinquish it and proceeded on. At 4 P.M. we passed an encampment which had been evacuated this morning by Capt. Clark. Here I found a note from Capt. C. informing me that he had left a letter for me at the entrance of the Yellowstone River, but that Sergt. Pryor, who had passed that place since he left it, had taken the letter; that Sergt. Pryor having been robbed of all his horses, had descended the Yellowstone River in skin canoes and had overtaken him at this encampment.

—*Captain Lewis*

📖 *August 12, 1806*
Being anxious to overtake Capt. Clark, who from the appearance of his camps could be at no great distance before me, we set out early and proceeded with all possible expedition.

At 8 A.M. the bowsman informed me that there was a canoe and a camp, he believed of white men, on the N.E. shore. I directed the perogue and canoes to come to at this place, and found it to be the camp of two hunters from the Illinois, by name Joseph Dickson and Forest Hancock. These men informed me that Capt. C. had passed them about noon the day before. They also informed me that they had left the Illinois in the summer of 1804, since which time they had been ascending the Missouri, hunting and trapping beaver; that they had been robbed by the Indians, and the former wounded last winter by the Tetons of the Burnt Woods; that they had hitherto been unsuccessful in their voyage, having as yet caught but little beaver, but were still determined to proceed.

I gave them a short description of the Missouri, a list of distances to the most conspicuous streams and remarkable places on the river above, and pointed out to them the places where the beaver most abounded. I also gave them a file and a couple of pounds of powder with some lead. These were articles which they assured me they were in great want of. I remained with these men an hour and a half, when I took leave of them and proceeded.

While I halted with these men, Colter and Collins, who separated from us on the 3rd, rejoined us. They were well, no accident having happened. They informed me that after proceeding the first day and not overtaking us, they had concluded that we were behind and had delayed several days in waiting for us, and had thus been unable to join us untill the present moment.

My wounds felt very stiff and sore this morning but gave me no considerable pain. There was much less inflammation than I had reason to apprehend there would be. I had, last evening, applied a poultice of Peruvian barks.

At 1 P.M. I overtook Capt. Clark and party and had the pleasure of finding them all well. As wrighting in my present situation is extreemly painfull to me, I shall desist untill I recover, and leave my friend Capt. C. the continuation of our journal.

—*Captain Lewis*

Clark on the Yellowstone 1806

▲ Travellers Rest to Camp Fortunate

Captain Clark headed south, upstream along the banks of Clark's (Bitterrroot) River, with Sergeant Ordway, Sergeant Pryor, Bratton, Collins, Colter, Cruzatte, Gibson, Hall, Howard, Labiche, Lepage, Potts, Shannon, Shields, Weiser, Whitehouse, Willard, Windsor, his servant York, Charbonneau , Sagagawea and her son, Jean Baptiste.

📖 *July 3, 1806*

We collected our horses, and after brakfast I took my leave of Capt. Lewis and the Indians, and at 8 A.M. set out with several men, interpreter Shabono and his wife and child (as an interpreter and interpretress for the Crow Indians, and the latter for the Shoshone) with fifty horses. We proceeded on through the Valley of Clarks River, on the West side of the river nearly South 18 miles, and halted on the upper side of a large creek, having crossed 8 streams, 4 of which were small. This valley is from 10 to 15 miles in width, tolerably leavel, and partially timbered with long leaf & pitch pine, some cotton wood, birch, and sweet willow on the borders of the streams. I observed 2 species of clover in this valley, one the white clover common in the Western parts of the U. States, the other species which is much smaller than either the red or white. Both it's leaf & blossom the horses are excessively fond of this species.

After letting our horses graize a sufficient length of time to fill themselves, and taking dinner of venison, we again resumed our journey up the valley which we found more beautifully diversified with small open plains covered with a great variety of sweet scented plants, flowers & grass. This evening we crossed 10 streams, 8 of which were large creeks which come rolling their currents with velocity into the river. Those creeks take their rise in the mountains to the West, which mountains is at this time covered with snow for about 1/5 of the way from their tops downwards. Our course this evening was nearly South, 18 miles, making a total of 36 miles today. We encamped on the N. side of a large creek, where we found tolerable food for our horses. Musquetors very troublesome. One man, Jo Potts, very unwell this evening owing to riding a hard-trotting horse; I gave him a pill of opium, which soon relieved him.

—*Captain Clark*

🔥 This first camp was probably on Blodgett Creek, a couple of miles north of the present city of Hamilton, Montana.

▲ Montana 126

CHARLES WATERS
Bitterroot National Forest

Location: Western Montana south of Missoula.

Access: From U.S. Highway 93 at milepost 70 +.4 (4.5 miles south of Florence, 3.5 miles north of Stevensville), turn west onto Bass Creek Road (paved, but narrow); continue west for 2 miles to the recreation area entrance, then an additional 0.1 mile to the campground.

Camping Facilities: 17 campsites; most sites are large, level, fairly well separated, and would be excellent for either tents or rv's; most parking pads are gravel straight-ins; plenty of tent space; fireplaces or fire rings; some firewood is available for gathering in the area; water at faucets throughout; vault facilities; most driveways are paved; limited supplies in Florence; adequate supplies in Stevensville; complete supplies and services are available in Missoula, 24 miles north.

Day Use Facilities: Small parking area; other facilities are shared with campers.

Activities & Attractions: Nature trail and fitness trail; Bass Creek Trailhead (access to the Selway-Bitterroot Wilderness) just west of the campground.

Natural Features: Located on a lightly forested flat, nestled up against the eastern foothills of the Bitterroot Range; large open grassy areas, with a profusion of wildflowers during most of the summer; black bears have been sighted near the campground, so safeguard your vittles; elevation 3600´.

Season, Fees & Phone: May to October; $8.00; 14 day limit; Stevensville Ranger District ☎ (406) 777-5461.

Camp Journal: The members of the Corps of Discovery certainly must have been impressed with the spectacular scenery as they walked or paddled through the Bitterroot Valley. This recreation area is named after a prominent University of Montana forestry professor and researcher who used this locale as an outdoor laboratory. Nice place.

📖 *July 4, 1806*

I ordered three hunters to set out early this morning to hunt & kill some meat, and by 7 A.M. we collected our horses, took brakfast, and set out. Proceeded on up the valley on the West side of Clarks River, crossing three large, deep and rapid creeks, and two of a smaller size, to a small branch in the spurs of the mountain and dined. The last creek or river which we passed was so deep and the water so rapid that several of the horses were swept down some distance and the water run over several others, which wet several articles.

After crossing this little river, I observed in the road the tracks of two men whome I presume is of the Shoshone Nation. Our hunters joined us with 2 deer in tolerable order. On the side of the hill near the place we dined, saw a gange of Ibex or big horn animals. I shot at them running and missed. This being the day of the Declaration of Independence of the United States and a day commonly celebrated by my country, I had every disposition to celebrate this day, and therefore halted early and partook of a sumptious dinner of a fat saddle of venison and mush of cowse roots.

After dinner we proceeded on about one mile to a very large creek, which we ascended some distance to find a ford to cross. In crossing this creek several articles got wet; the water was so strong, alto' the depth was not much above the horses belly, the water passed over the backs and loads of the horses. Those creeks are emencely rapid, have great descent; the bottoms of the creek as well as the low lands on each side is thickly covered with large stone. After passing this creek, I inclined to the left and fell into the road on which we had passed down last fall near the place we had dined on the 7th of Sept. and continued on the road passing up on the W. side of Clarks

River 13 miles to the West Fork of said river, and encamped on an arm of the same.

Sent out 2 men to hunt, and 3 in search of a ford to pass the river. At dark they all returned and reported that they had found a place that the river might be passed, but with some risk of the loads getting wet. I order them to get up their horses and accompany me to those places &c. Our hunters killed 4 deer today. We made 30 miles today on a course nearly South, valley from 8 to 10 miles wide. Contains a good portion of pitch pine. We passed three large, deep rapid creeks this afternoon.

—*Captain Clark*

♠ Montana 127

LAKE COMO
Bitterroot National Forest

Location: Western Montana south of Missoula.

Access: From U.S. Highway 93 at milepost 34 +.8 (4 miles north of Darby, 12 miles south of Hamilton), turn west onto Lake Como Road Road (paved); travel 3 miles to an intersection; bear right and continue for another 0.7 miles to a second intersection; swing left to a 'T', then left again and go down 0.1 mile to the lower RV camp loop; or from the 'T' go right for another 0.5 mile (past the day use area) to the po' folks section in the upper camp loop.

Camping Facilities: *RV Loop:* 10 campsites with partial hookups (a small group site is also available, by reservation); sites are medium sized, with fair to good separation; parking pads are paved, super-long pull-throughs; additional leveling will be needed on many pads; adequate space for tents; fire rings and barbecue grills; b-y-o firewood is reccommended; water at sites; vault facilities; paved driveway; *Upper Loop:* 10 campsites in a single large loop; most sites are spacious, with good to very good separation; parking pads are gravel, short to medium-length straight-ins; large tent spots; pads and tent areas a reasonably level even though the campground is on a hill; fire rings; some firewood is available for gathering in the area; water at a hand pump; vault facilities; gravel driveway; gas and groceries+ in Darby, 4.7 miles south of the Lake Como turnoff; limited supplies in Darby, virtually complete supplies and services are available in Hamilton.

Day Use Facilities: Small picnic area; drinking water; vault facilities; medium-sized parking area.

Activities & Attractions: Designated swimming area with a sandy/gravel beach; fishing; boating; boart ramp; campground loop trail; foot trail around the lake.

Natural Features: Located along the northeast shore of Lake Como, below the foothills and peaks of the rugged Bitterroot Range; lower RV camp is on a lightly timbered slope; upper camp is on a knoll in a moderately dense conifer forest, with some low vegetation; a marsh with lily pads is in the center of the upper camp loop; a great variety of animals and birds, particularly migratory waterfowl reside near, or visit the lake; elevation 4200´.

Season, Fees & Phone: May to October; $12.00 in the lower loop, $7.00 in the upper loop; 14 day limit; Darby Ranger District ☎(406) 821-3913.

Camp Journal: Lake Como's recreation area offers some breathtaking vistas across the lake's deep blue waters to the craggy peaks of the Bitterroots, including Trapper Peak. At 10,157´, Trapper Peak is the highest mountain in the 200-mile-long Bitterroot Range. Montana's beautiful lake was named by Father Anthony Ravalli for Lake Como in northern Italy. The lakeside city of Como was the home town of Father Ravalli, the pioneering Jesuit missionary to Montana's Flathead Indians; he was also Montana's first medical doctor and pharmacist. Father Ravalli walked the mountains and valleys of Western Montana from 1845 to 1884.

⚑ Montana 128 ♿

HANNON MEMORIAL
Hannon Memorial Recreation Access Site

Location: South western Montana south of Missoula.

Access: From U.S. Highway 93 at milepost 26 +.9 (5 miles south of Darby, 3 miles north of Conner), turn west onto a gravel access road and go 0.1 mile to the camping area.

Camping Facilities: 5 campsites; sites are small to medium-sized, level, with fair to quite good separation; parking pads are gravel, short straight-ins or pull-offs; small to medium-sized tent spots; fire rings; some firewood is available for gathering; no drinking water; vault facilities; gravel driveway; limited supplies and services are available in Darby.

Day Use Facilities: Small picnic and parking area, vault facilities, on the east side of the highway.

Activities & Attractions: Trout fishing.

Natural Features: Located on a wooded flat along the east bank of the Bitterroot River; most sites receive midday and late-day shade from cottonwoods and some tall conifers; the lofty Bitterroot Range rises a few miles to the west; elevation 4000´.

Season, Fees & Phone: Open all year, with limited services October to April; no fee (subject to change); 7 day limit; Montana Department of Fish Wildlife and Parks Region 2 Office, Missoula ☎(406) 542-5500.

Camp Journal: You know that angling for trophy trout is BIG around here when you see signs and bumper stickers proclaiming:

> Fishing isn't a matter of life and death.
> It's more important than that.

This recreation site is named for early settlers Thomas and Hessie Hannon, who arrived in the Bitterroot Valley in 1879 and homesteaded in the Conner area.

⚑ Montana 129 ♿

WARM SPRINGS
Bitterroot National Forest

Location: South Western Montana south of Missoula.

Access: From U.S. Highway 93 at milepost 15 +.7 (16 miles north of Lost Trail Pass, 5 miles north of Sula, 7 miles south of Conner), turn westerly onto Medicine Springs Road (hard surfaced) and proceed 1.2 miles; turn southerly (left) onto an access road for 0.2 mile (past the summer homes and the picnic area) to the campground.

Camping Facilities: 14 campsites; sites are small to medium+, with fair to quite good separation; parking pads are gravel, mostly medium-length straight-ins; a little additional leveling will be needed on some pads; tent space varies from small to large; fire rings; some firewood is available for gathering; water at several faucets; vault facilities; paved driveway; gas and camper supplies in Conner and Sula.

Day Use Facilities: Small picnic and parking area, vault facilities.

Activities & Attractions: Hiking trail nearby; good fishing on the East Fork of the Bitterroot River, nearby.

Natural Features: Located on a gentle slope in a forested canyon along clear, rushing Warm Springs Creek in the foothills of the Bitterroot Range; campsite shade/shelter varies from light to quite dense, courtesy of tall timber, some hardwoods, and high ground cover; elevation 4400´.

Season, Fees & Phone: May to October; $8.00; 14 day limit; Sula Ranger District ☎(406) 821-3201 or Darby Ranger District (406) 821-3913.

Camp Journal: Some pretty nice campsites here, complemented by a clear, rushing stream. Not much to do in and around the camp; but there's fairly good fishing just a mile back down on the highway at Spring Gulch.

📖 *July 5, 1806*

I rose at daylight this morning. Dispatched Labiche after a buck, which he killed late last evening; and I, with the three men who I had sent in search of a ford across the West fork of Clarks River, examined each ford. Neither of them I thought would answer to pass the fork without wetting all the loads. Near one of those places pointed out by Colter I found a practicable ford and returned to camp.

Ordered everything packed up, and after brakfast we set out. Passed 5 channels of the river ,which is divided by small islands; in passing the 6th & last channel, Colter's horse swam and with some difficulty he made the opposit shore. Shannon took a different derection from Colter, reined his horse up the stream and passed over very well. I derected all to follow Shannon and pass quartering up the river, which they done and passed over tolerably well, the water running over the back of the 2 smaller horses only. Unfortunately, my trunk & portmanteau containing sea otter skins, flags, some curiosities & necessary articles in them got wet; also an assortment of medicine, and my roots. About 1 mile we struck the East Fork, which had fallen and was not higher than when we passed it last fall; we had not proceeded up this fork more than 1 mile, ere we struck the road by which we passed down last fall and kept it at one mile.

We crossed the river at a very good ford and continued up on the East side to the foot of the mountain nearly opposit Flower Creek & halted to let our horses graize and dry our wet articles. I saw fresh sign of two horses, and a fire burning on the side of the road. I presume

that those Indians are spies from the Shoshones. Shannon & Cruzat killed each a deer this morning and J. Shields killed a female Ibex or bighorn on the side of the mountain; this animal was very meager. Shannon left his tomahawk at the place he killed his deer. I derect him to return for it and join me in the valley on the East side of this mountain. Gave Shields permission to proceed on over to the 1st valley and there hunt untill my arrival this evening at that place.

After drying every article, which detained us untill 1/2 past 4 P.M., we packed up and crossed the mountain into the valley [Ross Hole] where we first met with the Flatheads. Here I overtook Shields; he had not killed any thing. I crossed the river, which heads in a high-peaked mountain covered with snow N.E. of the valley at about 20 miles. Shields informed me that the Flathead Indians passed up the small creek which we came down last fall about 2 miles above our encampment of the 4th & 5th of September. I proceeded up this South branch 2 miles and encamped on the E. side of the creek, and sent out several men to examine the road.

Shields returned at dark and informed me that the best road turned up the hill from the creek 3 miles higher up, and appeared to be a plain beaten path. As this rout of the Oatlashshoots can be followed, it will evidently shorten our rout at least 2 days; and as the Indians informed me last fall, a much better rout than the one we came out. At all events, I am deturmined to make the attempt and follow their trail if possible; if I can pursue it, my rout will be nearer and much better than the one we came from the Shoshones, & if I should not be able to follow their road, our rout can't possibly be much worse. The hunters killed two deer this evening. The after part of the day we only come 8 miles, making a total of 20 miles. Shannon came up about sunset having found his tomahawk.

—*Captain Clark*

🔥 Clark's party spent the night of July 5-6 in Ross Hole, headed on up into Gibbons Pass, then dropped down into Big Hole.

📖 *July 6, 1806*

Some frost this morning; the last night was so cold that I could not sleep. We collected our horses, which were much scattered, which detained us untill 9 A. M., at which time we set out and proceeded up the creek on which we camped 3 miles, and left the road which we came on last fall to our right and ascended a ridge with a gentle slope to the dividing mountain which seperates the waters of the Middle Fork of Clarks River from those of Wisdom and Lewis's river, and passed over, pursuing the rout of the Oatlashshoot band which we met last fall to the head of Glade Creek, a branch of Wisdom R., and down the said branch, crossing it frequently on each side of this handsome glades, in which I observe great quantities of quawmash just beginning to bloom on each side of those glades; the timber is small and a great proportion of it killed by the fires. I observe the appearance of old buffalow roads and some heads on this part of the mountain. The snow appears to lying in considerable masses on the mountain from which we decended on the 4th of September last. I observe great numbers of the whistleing squirrel, which burrows their holes, scattered on each side of the glades through which we passed. Shields killed a hare of the large mountain species.

The after part of the day we passed on the hillside N of the creek for 6 miles. and entered an extensive open, leavel plain in which the Indian trail scattered in such a manner that we could not pursue it. The Indian woman, wife to Shabono, informed me that she had been in this plain frequently and knew it well; that the creek which we decended was a branch of Wisdom River, and when we ascended the higher part of the plain we would discover a gap in the mountains in our direction to the canoes, and when we arived at that gap we would see a high point of a mountain covered with snow in our direction to the canoes.

We proceeded on 1 mile and crossed a large creek from the right, which heads in a snow mountain, and Fish Creek, over which there was a road thro' a gap. We ascended a small rise and beheld an open, beautifull, leavel valley or plain [Big Hole] of about 15 Miles wide and near 30 long, extending N & S., in every direction around which I could see high points of mountains covered with snow. I discovered one at a distance very high, covered with snow, which bore S. 8o° E. The squar pointed to the gap through which she said we must pass, which was S 56° E. She said we would pass the river before we reached the gap.

We had not proceeded more than 2 miles in the last creek, before a violent storm of wind accompanied with hard rain from the S.W. immediately from off the snow mountains; this rain was cold and lasted 1 1/2 hours. I discovered the rain, wind as it approached and halted and formed a solid column to protect ourselves from the violency of the gust. After it was over, I proceeded on about 5 miles to some small dry timber on a small creek and encamped, made large fires and dryed ourselves. Here I observed some fresh Indian signs where they had been gathering quawmash. (This is the great plain where Shoshones gather quawmash & cowse &c.; our woman had done so. Many beaver.)

—*Captain Clark*

♣♣ Montana 130

MAY CREEK
Beaverhead National Forest

Location: Southwest Montana west of Wisdom.

Access: From Montana State Highway 43 at milepost 9 +.4 (9 miles east of Lost Trail Pass, 16.5 miles west of Wisdom), turn south onto a gravel access road and go 0.1 mile to the campground.

Camping Facilities: 21 campsites; sites are generally large, level and well separated; most parking pads are gravel, medium to long straight-ins; large, well cleared tent spots; fire rings and barbecue grills; a limited amount of firewood is available for gathering in the vicinity; water at several faucets; vault facilities; gravel driveways; limited supplies and services are available in Wisdom.

Day Use Facilities: None

Activities & Attractions: Foot trails; fishing for small trout on nearby streams; Big Hole National Battlefield and Visitor Center, 8 miles east.

Natural Features: Located in a valley at the confluence of Joseph, May and Stevenson Creeks; tall conifers with very little underbrush shelter the camp area; the campground is bordered by a lush mountain meadow on the west, timber on the east; many sites look out across the meadow; densely forested hills and mountains lie in the surrounding area; elevation 6400´.

Season, Fees & Phone: June to mid-September; $5.00; 14 day limit; Wisdom Ranger District ☎ (406) 689-3243.

Camp Journal: The scenery in this region changes dramatically in just a few miles: very fertile and forested near May Creek Campground and to the west; much drier and more rugged a dozen miles east near Big Hole. The historical significance of the route that passes the campground is twofold: Captain

Clark passed about a couple of miles east of this campground after spending that frigid night in Ross Hole, mentioned in the foregoing journal entry. The Expedition camped the following evening in Big Hole, where years later 800 Nez Percé, fleeing from Oregon in the summer of 1877, engaged in a major encounter with a makeshift local U.S. Army force of 200 soldiers.

📖 *July 7, 1806*

This morning our horses were very much scattered; I sent out men in every direction in search of them. They brought all, except 9, by 6 oClock, and informed me that they could not find those 9. I then ordered 6 men to take horses and go different directions and at a greater distance. Those men all returned by 10 A.M., and informed me that they had made circles in every direction to 6 or 8 miles around camp and could not see any signs of them. That they had reasons to believe that the Indians had stolen them in the course of the night, and founded their reasons on the quality of the horses, all being the most valuable horses we had, and several of them so attached to horses of inferior quality which we have, they could not be separated from each other when driving with their loads on in the course of the day.

I thought it probable that they might be stolen by some skulking Shoshones; but, as it was yet possible that they might have taken our back rout or rambled to a greater distance, I deturmined to leave a small party to hunt for them today and proceed on with the main party and all the baggage to the canoes, raise them out of the water, and expose them to the sun to dry by the time this party should overtake me. I left Sergt. Ordway, Shannon, Gibson, Collins, and Labiche, with directions to hunt this day for the horses without they should discover that the Indians had taken them into the mountains, and pursue our trail, &c.

At 1/2 past 10 A.M. I set out and proceeded on through an open rich valley, crossing four large creeks with extensive low and mirey bottoms, and a small river, keeping the course I had set out on S. 56° E. After crossing the river, I kept up on the N.E. side, sometimes following an old road which frequently disappeared; at the distance of 16 miles we arived at a boiling spring [just West of the present-day hamlet of Jackson] situated about 100 paces from a large easterly fork of the small river, in a leavel, open, valley plain and nearly opposit & E. of the 3 forks of this little river, which heads in the snowy mountains to the S.E. & S.W. of the springs.

This spring contains a very considerable quantity of water, and actually blubbers with heat for 20 paces below where it rises. It has every appearance of boiling, too hot for a man to endure his hand in it 3 seconds. I direct Sergt. Pryor and John Shields to put each a piece of meat in the water of different sizes. The one about the size of my 3 fingers cooked done in 25 minits, the other much thicker was 32 minits before it became sufficiently done. This water boils up through some loose, hard, gritty stone. A little sulphurish.

After taking dinner and letting our horses graize 1 hour and a half, we proceeded on, crossed this easterly branch and up on the N. side of this middle fork 9 miles; crossed it near the head of an easterly branch and passed through a gap of a mountain, on the easterly side of which we encamped near some beautifull springs which fall into Willards Creek. I directed that the rambling horses should be hobbled, and the sentinel to examine the horses after the moon rose. Emence beaver sign.

This extensive valley surrounded with mountains covered with snow is extremly fertile, covered with esculent plants &c; and the creeks which pass through it contains emence numbers of beaver &c. I now take my leave of this beautifull, extensive valley which I call the Hot Spring Valley, and behold one less extensive and much more rugged on Willards Creek for near 12 miles in length. Remarkable cold night.

—*Captain Clark*

⚘ Montana 131

BANNACK
Bannack State Park

Location: Southwest Montana west of Dillon.

Access: From Montana Secondary Highway 278 near milepost 17 (17 miles west of Interstate 15 Exit 59 in Dillon, 26 miles southeast of Jackson), turn south onto a local paved road (well-signed for the state park) and travel south for 3 miles; turn easterly (left) onto a gravel park access road for 0.3 mile to the park boundary; continue ahead for 1 mile, then turn south (right) to the campground.

Camping Facilities: 25 campsites in two sections; (a small group site is available, nearby); sites are average in size, generally level, with nominal separation; parking areas are gravel or dirt, of assorted types and lengths; large, grass/earth tent spots; fire rings; b-y-o firewood; water at hand pumps; vault facilities; gravel/dirt driveways; horse corrals; adequate+ supplies and services are available in Dillon.

Day Use Facilities: Small picnic area; shelter; drinking water; vault facilities; restrooms (at the park visitor center) and vault facilities.

Activities & Attractions: Historic ghost town of Bannack; visitor center; Bannack Days are annually celebrated during the third weekend in July; the three-day gathering includes frontier cooking, quilting, blacksmithing, gold panning, cross-town telegraphy, black powder shoots and other demos related to the frontier lifestyle).

Natural Features: Located in a small valley on the north bank of Grasshopper Creek; dense, brushy, hardwood vegetation lines the creek; campsites are on a creekside flat and are lightly shaded by large cottonwoods; the surrounding terrain consists primarily of sage plains and very high, dry hills and mountains in all directions; elevation 5900´.

Season, Fees & Phone: Open all year, with limited services October to May; 14 day limit; $11.00 (includes park entry fee); park office ☎(406) 834-3413.

Camp Journal: Bannack was born after a placer strike in 1862, and the new town quickly became Montana's first major gold camp. In 1864, Bannack became Montana's first territorial capital. The town's population of some 3,000 souls were well-served by a self-sufficient community which offered not only the usual general stores, saloons, and assorted specialty shops, but also included a brewery, a bowling alley and a Chinese restaurant. But Bannack went the way of so many Western boomtowns. In less than a year, many of the town's residents—as well as the territorial capital—had moved to richer diggin's at Alder Gulch in Virginia City.

Bannack is now a ghost town, preserved in a state of arrested decay. About two-dozen major historic buildings, and a dozen or more lesser structures remain. There are literally hundreds of ghost towns throughout the American West, but most are in ruins. Only a handful have been set aside and preserved as public parks. Bannack could be one of the best.

What is now Grasshpper Creek was originally named Willards Creek by Lewis and Clark for Alexander Willard, a member of the Expedition who was one of Clark's men on this route. In the following entry, Clark details his route along Willards Creek, then along the "west branch of Jefferson's River" (now Horse Prairie Creek, west branch of the Beaverhead River) back to the site of Camp Fortunate of the previous August.

It might also be noted here that throughout his original journal entries, Clark uses his own version—"*Rochejhone*"—of French explorers' name for the Yellowstone—*Rochejaune (roche,* being "rock" or "stone", *jaune* meaning "yellow"). It is pronounced somewhat like "*rosh-hone´* ", with two long *o*'s). The name "Yellowstone" didn't become widely used until several years after the Expedition's return

Grasshopper (Willards) Creek, Bannack State Park

📖 *July 8, 1806*

Our horses being scattered we were detained untill 8 A.M. before we set out. We proceeded on down Willards Creek on the S.W. side about 11 miles, near which the creek passes through the mountain. We then steered S. 20° E. to the West branch of Jeffersons River in Snake Indian Cove, about 7 miles and halted two hours to let the horses graize.

After dinner we proceeded on down the fork, which is here but small, 9 miles, to our encampment of 17th August, at which place we sunk our canoes, and buried some articles as before mentioned. The most of the party with me being chewers of tobacco, became so impatient to be chewing it that they scarcely gave themselves time to take their saddles off their horses before they were off to the deposit.

I found every article safe, except a little damp. I gave to each man who used tobacco about two feet off a part of a roll, took one third of the ballance myself, and put up 2/3 in a box to send down with the most of the articles which had been left at this place, by the canoes to Capt. Lewis. As it was late, nothing could be done with the canoes this evening. I examined them and found them all safe except one of the largest, which had a large hole in one side and split in bow.

The country through which we passed today was diversified–high, dry, and uneaven stoney open plains and low bottoms, very boggy, with high mountains on the tops and North sides of which there was snow; great quantities of the species of hysoop [big sage] & shrubs common to the Missouri plains are scattered in those valleys and hillsides. The road which we have traveled from Travellers Rest Creek to this place an excellent road. And with only a fiew trees being cut out of the way would be an excellent wagon road; one mountain of about 4 miles over excepted, which would require a little digging. The distance is 164 miles. Shields killed an antelope.

—*Captain Clark*

📖 *July 9, 1806*

Rose early; had the horses brought up, after which I had the canoes raised, washed, brought down and drawn up on shore to dry and be repaired. Set several men to work digging for the tobacco which Capt. Lewis informed me had had buried in the place the lodge stood when we lay here last summer. They searched diligently without finding anything. At 10 A.M. Sergt. Ordway and party arived with the horses we had lost. He reported that he found those horses near the head of the creek on which we encamped, making off as fast as they could, and much scattered. Nothing material took place with his party in their absence.

I had the canoes repaired, men & loads apportioned ready to embark tomorrow morning. I also formed the party to accompany me to the River Rochejhone [Yellowstone] from applicants, and apportioned what little baggage I intended to carry, as also the spare horses. This day was windy and cold. The squar brought me a plant the root of which the nativs eate. This root most resembles a carrot in form and size and something of it's colour, being of a paler

yellow than that of our carrot, the stem and leaf is much like the common carrot, and the taste not unlike. It is a nativ of moist land. John Shields and Collins each killed a deer this morning. The wind dried our canoes very much; they will be sufficiently dry by tomorrow morning to set out in them down the river.

—*Captain Clark*

⚕ Montana 132 ⚕

BEAVERHEAD
Clark Canyon Reservoir Recreation Area

Location: Southwest corner of Montana south of Dillon.

Access: From Interstate 15 Exit 44 for Clark Canyon Dam (18 miles south of Dillon, 44 miles north of the Montana-Idaho border), from the west side of the freeway, go a few yards, then turn south (left) onto a gravel access road and go 0.2 mile down to the recreation area, then swing west (right) into the campground.

Camping Facilities: 30 campsites; sites are medium to large, with nominal visual separation but good spacing; parking pads are gravel, medium to long straight-ins or pull-offs; a little additional leveling will be needed on many pads; acres of grassy tent space, though it's mostly a bit sloped; sun shelters for several sites; fire rings; b-y-o firewood; water at a hand pump; vault facilities; gravel driveways; adequate+ supplies and services are available in Dillon.

Day Use Facilities: Medium-sized picnic and parking area, 0.3 mile south.

Activities & Attractions: Fishing; boating; boat ramp; marina nearby; designated swimming beach nearby; Camp Fortunate Overlook and Interpretive Area, 2 miles west.

Natural Features: Located on a westward-facing slope along the northeast shore of Clark Canyon Reservoir, an impoundment on the Beaverhead River, at the confluence of Red Rock River and Horse Prairie Creek; sites receive minimal to very light shade from planted hardwoods on mown grass; the reservoir is encircled by grassy, tree-dotted hills and mountains; the dam lies directly along the 45th Parallel of latitude; elevation 5800´.

Season, Fees & Phone: Open all year, with limited services October to April; no fee (subject to change); 14 day limit; U.S. Bureau of Reclamation Field Office ☎(406) 683-6472.

Camp Journal: On July 8, 1806, Captain Clark and the Yellowstone party returned here to the forks of the Beaverhead, the site of their historic meeting with Sacagawea's people in August of 1805. Upon arrival, they hastily commenced to unearth the goods they had previously cached for the trip home. Of crucial importance to some of the men was the retrieval of the tobacco that had been stashed here, (along with items of lesser consequence, like the canoes).

⛺ *Camp Fortunate to the River Rochejhone*

📖 *July 10, 1806*

Last night was very cold and this morning everything was white with frost and the grass stiff frozen. I had some water exposed in a basin in which the ice was 3/4 of an inch thick this morning. I had all the canoes put into the water, and every article which was intended to be sent down put on board, and the horses collected and packed with what fiew articles I intend taking with me to the River Rochejhone, and after brakfast we all set out at the same time & proceeded on down Jeffersons River on the East side through Service Berry Valley and Rattle Snake Mountain and into that beautifull and extensive valley, open and fertile, which we call the Beaver Head Valley, which is the Indian name; in their language *Har na Hap pap Chah*, from the number of those animals in it & a point of land resembling the head of one. I saw on the sides of the rock in Rattle Snake Mountain 15 big horn animals; those animals feed on the grass which grow on the sides of the mountain, and in the narrow bottoms on the water courses near the steep sides of the mountains on which they can make their escape from the pursuit of wolves, bear &c.

At Meridian, I halted to let the horses graize, having come 15 miles. I ordered the canoes to land. Sergt. Ordway informed me that the party with him had come on very well and he thought the canoes could go as fast as the horses, &c. As the river now becomes wider and not so shoal, I determined to put all the baggage, &c., which I intend taking with me to the R.iver Rochejhone in the canoes and proceed on down with them myself to the 3 Forks, or Madison's and Gallatin's Rivers, leaving the horses to be taken down by Sergt. Pryor; and 6 of the men of the party to accompany me to the River Rochejhone; and directed Sergt. Pryor to proceed on

moderately and, if possible, encamp with us every night.

After dinner had my baggage put on board and set out, and proceeded on tolerably well to the head of the 3000 Mile Island on which we had encamped August last. The canoes passed six of my encampments ascending; opposit this island I encamped on the East side. The musquetors were troublesome all day and untill one hour after sunset, when it became cool and they disappeared. In passing down in the course of this day we saw great numbers of beaver lying on the shores in the sun. I saw several large rattle snakes in passing the Rattle Snake Mountain; they were fierce.

—*Captain Clark*

⛺ Montana 133 ♿

BARRETTS
Clark Canyon Reservoir Recreation Area

Location: Southwest corner of Montana south of Dillon.

Access: From Interstate 15 Exit 56 (6 miles south of Dillon, 12 miles north of Clark Canyon Dam), go to the east side of the freeway, then a few yards to a 4-way intersection; turn south (right) onto a paved frontage road and proceed 0.5 mile, then turn east (left), cross the RR tracks, then swing south (right) onto a gravel access road for a final 0.1 mile to the recreation site.

Camping Facilities: 12 campsites; sites are medium to large, level, with nominal separation; parking is mainly in the medium-large gravel lot adjacent to the camp area; very good opportunity for tent camping; fire rings; b-y-o firewood; water at a hand pump; vault facilities; gravel driveway; adequate+ supplies and services are available in Dillon.

Day Use Facilities: Small picnic area; shelter; hand pump; vault facilities.

Activities & Attractions: Fishing; floating; small boat ramp for hand launching.

Natural Features: Located on a grassy, cottonwood-dotted flat along the west bank of the Beaverhead River in Beaverhead Canyon (also called Ryan's Canyon); not much shade for rv's in the parking lot, tent sites are lightly shaded; bordered by grassy hills and bluffs, and Rattlesnake Cliffs (see *Camp Journal*); elevation 4600´.

Season, Fees & Phone: Open all year, with limited services October to April; no fee (subject to change); 14 day limit; U.S. Bureau of Reclamation Field Office ☎ (406) 683-6472.

Camp Journal: While the camping area here is OK, the picnic site, accessible via a footbridge across the Beaverhead, would be a great place to hang out during the day. Lots of watered, mown grass and shade over there. Contemporary geographical names and the Journals are somewhat at odds in this region: Lewis and Clark considered the present Beaverhead River to be the main stream of the Jefferson River. Since then, mapmakers have chosen to 'shorten' the Jefferson considerably, marking its beginning about 35 miles north of here at Twin Bridges. In his entry of July 10th, Clark refers to "Rattle Snake Mountain", which the previous August they had named and mapped as "Rattle Snake Clifts". Whatever. They are the impressive escarpments which rise from the river at this recreation site.

📖 *July 11, 1806*

Sent on 4 of the best hunters in 2 canoes to proceed on a fiew miles ahead and hunt untill I came up with them. After an early brackfast, I proceeded on down a very crooked channel; at 8 a. m I overtook one canoe with a deer which Collins had killed; at Meridian passed Sergt. Pryors camp near a high point of land on the left side, which the Shoshones call the Beavers Head. The wind rose and blew with great violence from the S.W. immediately off some high mountains covered with snow. The violence of this wind retarded our progress very much; and the river being emencely crooked, we had it immediately in our face nearly every bend. At 6 P M I passed Philanthrophy River, which I perceived was very low. The wind shifted about to the N.E. and blew very hard, tho' much warmer than the forepart of the day.

At 7 P M I arived at the enterance of Wisdom River and encamped in the spot we had encamped the 6th of August last. Here we found a bayonet which had been left & the canoe quite safe. I directed that all the nails be taken out of this canoe and paddles to be made of her sides, & here I came up with Gibson & Colter, whom I had sent on ahead for the purpose of hunting this morning; they had killed a fat buck and 5 young geese nearly grown. Wisdom River is very high and falling. I have seen great numbers of beaver on the banks and in the water as I passed down today, also some deer and great numbers young geese, sand hill cranes &c. &c. Sgt. Pryor left a deer on the shore.

—*Captain Clark*

📖 *July 12, 1806*

Sergt. Pryor did not join me last night; he has proceeded on down. The beaver was flacking their tails in the river about usial the last night. This morning I was detained untill 7 A.M. making paddles and drawing the nails of the canoe to be left at this place and the one we had before left here. After completing the paddles &c and taking some brackfast, I set out, the current I find much stronger below the forks than above and the river tolerably straight as low as Panther Creek, when it became much more crooked. The wind rose and blew hard off the snowey mountains to the N.W. and renderd it very difficult to keep the canoes from running against the shore.

At 2 P.M. the canoe in which I was in was driven by a sudden puff of wind under a log which projected over the water from the bank, and the man in the stern, Howard, was caught in between the canoe and the log and a little hurt. After disengaging ourselves from this log, the canoe was driven immediately under a drift which projected over and a little above the water; here the canoe was very near turning over. We, with much exertion after takeing out some of the baggage, hauled her out, and proceeded on without receiving any damage. The men in the other canoes, seeing our situation, landed and come with as much speed as possible thro' the briers and thick brush to our assistance, but from the thickness of the brush did not get up to our assistance untill we had got clear.

At 3 P M we halted at the enterance of Fields Creek and dined here. Willard and Collins overtook us with two deer which they had killed this morning, and by takeing a different side of an island from which we came, we had passed them. After dinner I proceeded on and encamped a little below our encampment of the 31st of July last. The musquetoes very troublesome this evening. Some old buffalow signs. I killed 4 young geese and Collins killed 2 beaver this evening.

—*Captain Clark*

⚑ Montana 134 ♿

CHARBONNEAU
Charbonneau Recreation Access Site

Location: South Central Montana west of Bozeman.

Access: From Montana State Highway 2 at milepost 93 +.7 (2 miles west of the town of

Three Forks, 0.5 mile east of the junction of Highway 2 & U.S. Highway 287); turn northerly onto a gravel access road and proceed 0.1 mile to the recreation site. (Note: If you're traveling Interstate 90, eastbound, take Exit 274 then 2 miles south and east to the recreation site; or if westbound, take Exit 278, then 2 miles west, through town, to the site.)

Camping Facilities: Primitive 'open' camping for approximately 5 campers, parking surfaces are gravel/dirt, level, pull-offs or straight-ins, with enough space for medium to long vehicles; ample room for medium to large tents; some fire rings; b-y-o firewood; no drinking water; vault facilities; gravel driveway; pack-it-in-pack-it-out trash removal; (reportedly, camping facilities may be improved over the next several years); adequate supplies and services are available in Three Forks.

Day Use Facilities: Shared with campers

Activities & Attractions: Fishing; floating; small, carry-down boat ramp.

Natural Features: Located on a riverside flat along the east bank of the Jefferson River at the west end of the Valley of the Three Forks of the Missouri (regionally just called "Gallatin Valley"); camping area is minimally to lightly sheltered by cottonwoods; some grassy and brushy areas; bordered by woodland, cropland and rolling plains, surrounded by near and distant mountains; elevation 4200´.

Season, Fees & Phone: Open all year; no fee (subject to change); 7 day limit; Montana Department of Fish Wildlife and Parks Region 3 Office, Bozeman ☎ (406) 994-4042.

Camp Journal: This humble spot is, of course, named (with the 'correct' spelling for Touissant Charbonneau, the Expedition's chief interpreter and husband of Sacagawea. Interestingly, two camps along the Expedition's route are named for little-known Charbonneau, while only one (Lake Sakakawea State Park in North Dakota) is named for his legendary wife. If you're running late along the Interstate and just need a place to park or pitch for the night, this might do the trick.

📖 *July 13, 1806*

Set out early this morning and proceeded on very well to the enterance of Madisons River at our old encampment of the 27th July last, at 12 oClock, where I found Sergt. Pryor and party with the horses. They had arived at this place one hour before us. His party had killed 6 deer and a white bear. I had all the horses driven across Madison and Gallatin Rivers and halted to dine, and let the horses feed immediately below the enterance of Gallatin. Had all the baggage of the land party taken out of the canoes, and after dinner the 6 canoes and the party of 10 men under the direction of Sergt. Ordway set out. Previous to their departure I gave instructions how they were to proceed, &c. I also wrote to Capt. Lewis by Sergt. Ordway. My party now consists of the following persons, viz: Sergeant N. Pryor, Jo. Shields, G. Shannon, William Bratton, Labiche, Windsor, H. Hall, Gibson, interpreter Shabono, his wife & child, and my man York, with 49 horses and a colt. The horses' feet are very sore, and several of them can scarcely proceed on.

At 5 P.M. I set out from the head of Missouri at the 3 forks, and proceeded on nearly East 4 miles and encamped on the bank of Gallatins River, which is a beautifull navigable stream. Saw a large gange of Elk in the plains and deer in the river bottoms. I also observe beaver and several otter in Gallatins River as I passed along. Gibson killed an otter, the fur of which was much longer and whiter than any which I had seen. Willard killed 2 deer this morning; all the meat I had put into the canoes except a sufficiency for supper.

The country in the forks between Gallatins & Madisons Rivers is a beautifull, leavel plain covered with low grass on the lower or N E. side of Gallatins River; the country rises gradually to the foot of a mountain which runs nearly parallel. Those plains are indifferent or the soil of which is not very rich; they are stoney & contain several stratas of white rock. The current of the river is rapid, and near the mouth contains several islands; it is navigable for canoes. I saw several antelope, common deer, wolves, beaver, otter, eagles, hawks, crows, wild geese both old and young, does &c. &c. I observe several leading roads which appear to pass to a gap of the mountain in a E.N.E. direction about 18 or 20 miles distant.

The Indian woman, who has been of great service to me as a pilot through this country, recommends a gap in the mountain more South, which I shall cross.

—*Captain Clark*

🪓 Sacagawea was again about to prove her value as a guide. The "gap of a mountain in the E.N.E" probably was Flathead Pass, which appears as a very pronounced notch in the mountains; Flathead Pass is within the Bridger Range, northeast of the city of Bozeman. The "gap in the mountain more south" is Bozeman Pass; Bozeman Pass is in a break between the

Bridger & Gallatin Ranges east of town. To this day, the way via Flathead Pass is a winding, muddy route through a narrow, forested canyon; Interstate 90 traverses the somewhat lower, much more open passage of Bozeman Pass. The latter is also the route chosen by John M. Bozeman, who drove the first cattle into Montana Territory to feed hungry gold miners in the 1860's. Although John B. received history's credit for the mountain pass, Sacagawea Peak, the highest point in the Bridger Range, rising to 9665´, honors Clark's knowledgeable pathfinder.

📖 *July 14, 1806*

Sent Shields ahead to kill a deer for our brakfast, and at an early hour set out with the party. Crossed the Gallatin River, which makes a considerable bend to the N.E. and proceeded on nearly S. 78° E. through an open leavel plain. At 6 miles I struck the river and crossed a part of it and attempted to proceed on through the river bottoms, which were several miles wide at this place. I crossed several channels of the river running through the bottom in different.directions. I proceeded on about two miles, crossing those different channels, all of which were dammed with beaver in such a manner as to render the passage impracticable, and after being swamped, as I may say, in this bottom of beaver, I was compelled to turn short about to the right, and after some difficulty made my way good to an open, low, but firm plain which was an island, and extended nearly the course I wished to proceed.

Here the squar informed me that there was a large road passing through the upper part of this low plain from Madison River through the gap, which I was steering my course to. I proceeded up this plain 4 miles, and crossed the main channel of the river, having passed through a skirt of cotton timber to an open low plain on the N.E. side of the river and nooned it. The river is much divided, and on all the small streams innumerable quantities of beaver dams, tho' the river is yet navigable for canoes. I overtook Shields soon after I set out. He had killed a large fat buck. I saw elk, deer, and antelopes, and a great deal of old signs of buffalow. Their roads are in every direction.

The Indian woman informs me that a fiew years ago buffalow were very plenty in those plains and valleys, quite as high as the head of Jeffersons River, but fiew of them ever come into those valleys of late years, owing to the Shoshones, who are fearful of passing into the plains West of the mountains, and subsist on what game they can catch in the mountains, principally, and the fish which they take in the East fork of Lewis's River. Small parties of Shoshones do pass over to the plains for a fiew days at a time and kill buffalow for their skins and dryed meat, and return immediately into the mountains.

After dinner we proceeded on a little to the South of East through an open leavel plain to the three forks of the E. branch of Gallatins River; at about 12 miles, crossed the most southerly of those forks, and struck an old buffalow road (the one our Indian woman meant) which I kept, continuing nearly the same course up the middle fork, crossed it and camped on a small branch of the middle fork on the N. E. side at the commencement of the gap of the mountain. The road leading up this branch, several other roads all old, come in from the right & left. Emence quantities of beaver on this fork quite down, and their dams very much impede the navigation of it from the 3 forks down, tho' I beleive it practicable for small canoes by unloading at a fiew of the worst of those dams. Deer are plenty. Shannon, Shields and Sergt. Pryor each killed one which were very fat, much more so than they are commonly at this season of the year. The main fork of Gallatins River turns South and enters them mountains which are yet covered with snow. Madisons River makes a great bend to the East and enters the same mountain; a leavel plain between the two rivers below the mountain.

—*Captain Clark*

🏕 Clark's party has camped a few miles East of present-day Bozeman, and now began the relatively easy crossing of the pass:

📖 *July 15, 1806*

We collected our horses and after an early brackfast at 8 A M set out and proceeded up the branch to the head, thence over a low gap in the mountain thence across the heads of the N E branch of the 3 forks of Gallatin's River, which we camped near last night, passing over a low dividing ridge to the head of a water course which runs into the Rochejhone, pursuing an old buffalow road which enlarges by one which joins it from the most easterly branch of the East Fork of Gallatins R., proceeding down the branch a little to the N. of East, keeping on the North side of the branch to the River Rochejhone, at which place I arived at 2 P M.

The distance from the three forks of the easterly fork of Gallatins River (from whence it may be navigated down with small canoes), to the River Rochejhone is 18 miles on an excellent high, dry, firm road with very inconsiderable hills. From this river to the nearest part of the main fork of Gallatin is 29 miles, mostly through a leavel plain. From the head of the Missouri at the 3 forks, 48 miles through a leavel plain.

In the early evening, after the usial delay of 3 hours to give the horses time to feed and rest, and allowing ourselves time also to cook and eate dinner, I proceeded on down the river on an old buffalow road. At the distance of 9 miles below the mountains. Shields River discharges itself into the Rochejhone on it's N.W. side above a high rocky clift; this river is 35 yards wide, deep, and affords a great quantity of water; it heads in those snowy mountains to the N. W. with Howards Creek; it contains some timber, such as cotton & willow, in it's bottoms, and great numbers of beaver; the river also abounds in those animals as far as I have seen. Passed the creek and over a high rocky hill and encamped in the upper part of a large bottom.

The horses' feet are very sore; many of them can scarcely proceed on over the stone and gravel. In every other respect they are sound and in good spirits. I saw two black bear on the side of the mountains this morning. Several gangs of elk, from 100 to 200 in a gang, on the river. Great numbers of antelopes.

July 15, 1806, continued below

⛺ Montana 135 ♿

SHEEP MOUNTAIN
Sheep Mountain Recreation Access Site

Location: South Central Montana east of Livingston.

Access: From Interstate 90 Exit 340 for U.S. 89/White Sulphur Springs (7 miles east of Livingston), travel north on U.S Highway 89 for 1.3 miles; turn east (right) onto Convict Grade Road (paved for the first 0.8 mile, then gravel) and proceed 3.3 miles; turn south (right) onto a gravel recreation access road and go 0.2 mile to the recreation site.

Camping Facilities: 3 campsites, sites are very small, basically level, and closely spaced; parking surfaces are sandy, small straight-ins or pull-offs; (pretty tight for larger motorhomes or vehicles with trailers); space for small tents; fire rings; b-y-o firewood; no drinking water; vault facilities; sand/gravel driveway; (reportedly, the

facilities may be improved over the next several years); adequate supplies and services are available in Livingston.

Day Use Facilities: Shared with campers

Activities & Attractions: Trout fishing; river floating/canoeing; Yellowstone National Park is 60 miles south.

Natural Features: Located in a stand of mature cottonwoods along the north bank of the Yellowstone River; sites are generally well-sheltered; rugged Sheep Mountain rises a few miles north of the recreation site, the craggy Crazy Mountains a few miles farther north; the lofty Absaroka Range rises to the south-southeast; elevation 4500´.

Season, Fees & Phone: Open all year; $5.00; 7 day limit; Montana Department of Fish Wildlife and Parks Region 3 Office, Bozeman ☎ (406) 994-4042.

Camp Journal: Sheep Mountain, with its impressive south face known as Sheep Cliffs, isn't visible from within the recreation site (due to some intervening low hills). But there's a commanding view of the Absaroka (regionally pronounced *ab soar´ kuh*) Range, which is along Yellowstone National Park's northern boundary.

In the July 15th Journal entry, Clark described the Sheep Cliffs ("a high, rocky clift"), and the two streams which he named for Yellowstone party member John Shields, and Thomas Howard, who Clark sent with Sergeant Ordway down the Missouri from Three Forks to join Captain Lewis. Their camp on the night of July 15th was on the north side of the Yellowstone, probably within a couple hundred yards of Sheep Mountain recreation site.

📖 *July 15, 1806,* continued from above
The Roche passes out of a high rugged mountain [Absaroka Range] covered with snow. The bottoms are narrow within the mountains, but widen from 1/2 a mile to 2 miles in the valley below; those bottoms are subject to overflow; they contain some tall cotton wood, and willow rose bushes & rushes, honey suckle &c.; a second bottom on the N.E. side, which rises to about 20 feet higher than the first & is 1 mile wide, this bottom is coarse gravel, pebbles & sand, with some earth on which the grass grows very short, and at this time is quite dry; this 2nd bottom overflows in high floods. On the opposit side of the river, the plain is much higher and extends quite to the foot of the mountain. The mountains to the S.S.E., on the

East side of the river, is rocky, rugged, and on them are great quantities of snow. A bold snow mountain which bears East & is immediately at & NW of the 3 forks of the East fork of Gallatins River may be seen; there is also a high rugged mountain [Crazy Mountains], on which is snow bearing North 15 or 20 miles. But fiew flowers to be seen in those plains; low grass in the high plains, and the common coarse grass, rushes and a species of rye is the growth of the low bottoms. The mountains have some scattering pine on them, and on the spurs and hillsides there is some scrubby pine. I can see no timber sufficiently large for a canoe which will carry more than 3 men and such a one would be too small to answer my purpose

—*Captain Clark*

▲ *Trek Along the Yellowstone to Clark's Fork*

♣ Montana 136 ♿

SPRINGDALE BRIDGE
Springdale Bridge Recreation Access Site

Location: South Central Montana east of Livingston.

Access: From Interstate 90 Exit 354 for Springdale (21 miles east of Livingston, 14 miles west of Big Timber), from a 'T' intersection on the north side of the freeway, head west (left) and north on Montana Secondary Route 563 for 0.6 mile into the hamlet of Springdale; continue northerly for another 0.5 mile; at a point just before reaching the river bridge, turn easterly onto a gravel access road into the recreation site; go through the small parking lot, then east (right) into the camp area.

Camping Facilities: 3 campsites, plus overflow room for a couple of additional campers in the parking area; sites are very small, basically level, with very little separation; parking surfaces are small, sandy pull-offs or straight-ins; small tent spots; fire rings; b-y-o firewood is suggested; no drinking water; vault facilities; gravel driveway; adequate supplies and services are available in Big Timber.

Day Use Facilities: Mostly shared with campers; small parking area.

Activities & Attractions: Trout fishing; floating; small launch area; sizeable sandy beach.

Natural Features: Located on a wooded flat on the south bank of the Yellowstone River; sites are moderately shaded by tall cottonwoods and smaller hardwoods; good views of the craggy Crazy Mountains to the north, the Sheep Cliffs are northwest; elevation 4300´.

Season, Fees & Phone: Open all year, with limited services October to April; $5.00; 7 day limit; Montana Department of Fish Wildlife and Parks Region 3 Office, Bozeman ☎ (406) 994-4042.

Camp Journal: *Very* little turnaround room in the camp area. Anyone with an outfit longer than a mini mo'home might do well to take a walk-in tour before trying to maneuver in the tight, sandy camp. One campsite is so close to the river's edge that you might be splashed during high water. The Crazy Mountains, in full view several miles north, take their name from a frontier incident. A woman traveling with a wagon train became separated from the group and wandered for many days until she was finally found by searchers amid the rugged peaks. The ordeal drove the unfortunate woman to madness, and the peaks were henceforth called Crazy Woman Mountains, which was eventually shortened to the present name.

📖 *July 16, 1806*

I gave Labiche permission to proceed on early this morning ahead and kill a fat elk or buffalow. Our horses having rambled to a long distance down the river detained us much later than common. We did not set out untill 9 A.M. We had not proceeded on far before I saw a buffalow & sent Shannon to kill it; this buffalow proved to be a very fat bull. I had most of the flesh brought on and a part of the skin to make mockersons for some of our lame horses. Proceeded on down the river without finding any trees sufficently large for a canoe about 10 miles and halted, having passed over to an island on which there was good food for our horses to let them graize & dine. I have not seen Labiche as yet.

Saw a large gang of about 200 elk and nearly as many antelope; also two white or gray bears in the plains. One of them I chased on horseback about 2 miles to the rugged part of the plain, where I was compelled to give up the chase; two of the horses were so lame, owing to their feet being worn quite smooth and to the quick. The hind feet were much the worse. I had mockersons made of green buffalo skin and put on their feet, which seems to relieve them very much in passing over the stoney plains.

After dinner I proceeded on. Soon after I had set out, Labiche joined us with part of a fat elk which he had killed. I passed over a stoney point at which place the river runs close to the high land on the N.W. side, crossed a small creek and encamped on the river a little below it's enterance. Saw emence herds of elk feeding on the opposit side of the river. I saw a great number of young geese in the river. One of the men brought me a fish of a species I am unacquainted; it was 8 inches long, formed like a trout. It's mouth was placed like that of the sturgeon, a red streak passed down each side from the gills to the tail. The rocks which the high lands are faced with and which may also be seen in perpendicular stratas in the high plains, is a dark freestone. The greater part of this rock is of an excellent grit for grindstones, hard and sharp. Observe the silkgrass, sunflower & wild indigo all in bloom. But fiew other flowers are to be seen in those plains. The river and creek bottoms abound in cotton wood trees, tho' none of them sufficiently large for canoes. And the current of the Rochejhone is too rapid to depend on skin canoes. (which are not so easy managed & we did not know the river). No other alternative for me but to proceed on down untill I can find a tree sufficently large &c. to make a canoe.

—*Captain Clark*

♣ Montana 137 &

GREY BEAR
Grey Bear Recreation Access Site

Location: South Central Montana east of Livingston.

Access: From Interstate 90 Exit 362 for DeHart (29 miles east of Livingston, 7 miles west of Big Timber), from a 'T' at the north side of the freeway, turn east (right) onto a paved local road and proceed 0.7 mile; turn northerly (a sharpish left) onto a rough gravel road and go 0.7 mile (across a set of RR tracks); turn westerly (left) onto the recreation site access road and proceed 0.15 mile (bear left at the two forks) to the camp area.

Camping Facilities: 6 campsites; sites are medium to large, essentially level, with fairly good separation; parking surfaces are gravel/grass, generally long enough for big rigs; lots of space for tents; fire rings or barbecue grills; some firewood is available for gathering; no drinking water; vault facilities; pack-it-in-pack-it-out trash removal; gravel driveway; adequate supplies and services are available in Big Timber.

Grey Bear State Recreation Access Site

Day Use Facilities: Shared with campers.

Activities & Attractions: Fishing; floating; launch ramp.

Natural Features: Located on a large flat along the south bank of the Yellowstone River; sites are nicely shaded by tall cottonwoods, brush willows, and other hardwoods above tall grass; Crazy Mountains rise in the north, Absaroka Range lies to the west; elevation 4200´.

Season, Fees & Phone: Open all year, with limited services October to April; no fee (subject to change); 7 day limit; Montana Department of Fish Wildlife and Parks Region 5 Office, Billings ☎ (406) 247-2940.

Camp Journal: Wow! Magnificent views north across the Yellowstone and westerly, upriver, from here. A gem of a setting. Now *this* place is worth camping in.

Clark's camp on the night of July 16th was about 3 miles downstream of this recreation site.

In the following entry, Clark describes the countryside around the present-day town of Big Timber. His "Rivers Across" are Big Timber Creek and the Boulder River.

📖 *July 17, 1806*

The rain of last night wet us all. (having no tent, & no covering but a buffalow skin). I had the horses all collected early and set out, proceeded over the point of a ridge and through an open, low bottom, crossed a large creek which heads in a high, snow-topped mountain to the N.W. Immediately opposit to the enterance of the creek, one something larger falls in from the high snow mountains to the S.W. & South; those creeks I call "Rivers Across"; they contain some timber in their valleys. At the distance of several miles by water we arive at the enterance of two small rivers or large creeks which fall in nearly opposit to each other; the one on the N.E. side is 30 yards wide. I call it Otter River; the other Beaver River. Below the enterance of this creek I halted as usial to let the horses graize &c. I saw a single pelican, which is the first which I have seen on this river.

July 17, 1806 continued below

⚜ Montana 138 ♿

PELICAN
Pelican Recreation Access Site

Location: South Central Montana west of Billings.

Access: From Interstate 90 Exit 377 for Greycliff (10 miles east of Big Timber, 30 miles west of Columbus), from the north side of the freeway pick up a paved local road and go east for 0.6 mile into the hamlet of Greycliff; continue easterly on the paved road for another 0.8 mile; turn northerly (left) onto another paved local road (which becomes gravel after crossing the railroad tracks) and proceed 0.3 mile; turn easterly (right) onto a gravel recreation access road for 0.1 mile down into the recreation site.

Camping Facilities: 'Open' camping with enough room for a half dozen campers; camp areas are small to medium sized, level, with zip separation; parking/tent surfaces are grass or gravel, adequate enough for medium to large rv's or a pickup and a tent; some fire rings; b-y-o firewood; no drinking water; vault facilities; gravel driveways; adequate supplies and services are available in Big Timber.

Day Use Facilities: Shared with campers.

Activities & Attractions: Fishing; floating/canoeing; small boat launch; Greycliff Prairie Dog Town State Park, on the south side of I-90 at Exit 377.

Natural Features: Located in a valley on a grassy flat along the south bank of the Yellowstone river; sites are essentially unshaded, but there are lots of large cottonwoods adjacent; the valley is bordered by evergreen-dotted hills and bluffs; elevation 4000´.

Season, Fees & Phone: Open all year, with limited services October to April; no fee (subject to change); 7 day limit; Montana Department of Fish Wildlife and Parks Region 5 Office, Billings ☎ (406) 247-2940.

Camp Journal: Limited, albeit very pleasant, river-and-hill views from the campsites. Stroll a few yards up to the top of the bluff, and you'll enjoy an impressive vista of the craggy Crazy Mountains to the north; and Montana's highest point, 12,799´ Granite Peak, poking its snowy noggin up past the rim of local hills, in the not-too-distant south-southeast. Could it be that this small recreation site is named for the solitary pelican Clark noted in the previous Journal paragraph?

📖 *July 17, 1806*, continued from above

After dinner I proceeded on down the Rochejhone, passing over a low ridge through a small bottom, and on the side of a stoney hill for 2 miles, and through a small bottom, and again on the side of a high hill for 1 1/2 miles to a bottom in which we encamped opposit a small island. The high lands approach the river on either side much nearer than it does above and their sides are partially covered with low pine & cedar, none of which are sufficently large for canoes, nor have I seen a cotton tree in the low bottoms sufficently large for that purpose. Buffalow is getting much more plenty than they were above. Not so many elk & more deer. Shannon killed one deer.

I saw in one of those small bottoms which I passed this evening an Indian fort which appears to have been built last summer. This fort was built of logs and bark. The logs was put up very closely capping on each other about 5 feet high and closely chinked, around which bark was set up on end so as to cover the logs. The enterance was also guarded by a work on each side of it and facing the river. This work is about 50 feet diameter & nearly round. The squar informs me that when the war parties (of Minnits, Crows &c, who fight Shoshones) find themselves pursued, they make those forts to defend themselves in from the pursuers whose superior numbers might otherwise overpower them and cut them off, without receiving much injury on horseback &c.

—Captain Clark

♠ Montana 139

BRATTEN
Bratten Recreation Access Site

Location: South Central Montana west of Billings.

Access: From Interstate 90 Exit 392 for Reedpoint (22 miles east of Big Timber, 18 miles west of Columbus), drive north on a paved local road through Reedpoint for 0.3 mile to a 4-way intersection at the north end of town; turn west (left) onto a paved local road and travel 4.6 miles (to milepost 16 +.8); turn north (right) onto a gravel access road, cross the railroad tracks, and continue for 0.2 mile to the recreation site. **Alternate Access:** From Interstate 90 Exit Interstate 90 Exit 377 for Greycliff (10 miles east of Big Timber, 30 miles west of Columbus), from the north side of the freeway pick up a paved local road and go east for 0.6 mile into the hamlet of Greycliff; continue easterly on the paved road for another 9 miles to the access-road turnoff and continue as above.

Camping Facilities: 5 campsites; sites are medium sized, level, with nominal separation; parking pads are gravel, short to medium-length straight-ins or pull-offs; large, grassy areas for tents; fire rings; b-y-o firewood; no drinking water; vault facilities; gravel driveways; pack-it-in-pack-it-out trash removal; gas and groceries+ in Reedpoint; adequate supplies and services are available in Big Timber and Columbus.

Day Use Facilities: Shared with campers.

Activities & Attractions: Fishing; floating, canoeing.

Natural Features: Located on a large, grassy flat along the south bank of the Yellowstone River; most sites are unsheltered (but there's shade from tall cottonwoods nearby); the river is flanked by hills and bluffs dotted by pines and junipers; elevation 3900´.

Season, Fees & Phone: Open all year, with limited services October to April; no fee (subject to change); 7 day limit; Montana Department of Fish Wildlife and Parks Region 5 Office, Billings ☎(406) 247-2940.

Camp Journal: Bratten recreation site is named for William Bratton, one of the members of the Yellowstone party. Clark called a large stream that enters the Yellowstone about two miles upriver from this recreation site "Brattens Creek" for his fellow adventurer. The Captain's

original spelling, with an "e" instead of an "o", has been preserved. (The stream has since been renamed Bridger Creek for famed mountain man Jim Bridger.)

♠ Montana 140

INDIAN FORT
Indian Fort Recreation Access Site

Location: South Central Montana west of Billings.

Access: From Interstate 90 Exit 392 for Reedpoint 22 miles east of Big Timber, 18 miles west of Columbus), drive north on a paved local road through Reedpoint for 0.3 mile to a 4-way intersection at the north end of town; continue northerly (across the RR tracks) on a rough-surfaced/gravel road for another 0.4 mile to a point just across the rickety old trestle bridge that spans the river; turn westerly (left) onto the recreation site access road and proceed 0.6 mile to the camping area.

Camping Facilities: 10 campsites; sites are small to medium sized, basically level, with fair to very good separation; (if you don't require a table, look around for several small clearings which could be used as very private campsites); parking surfaces are grass or gravel, medium to large straight-ins or pull-offs; plenty of grassy space for tents; fire rings; b-y-o firewood; no drinking water; vault facilities; pack-it-in-pack-it-out trash removal; gravel driveways; gas and groceries+ in Reedpoint; adequate supplies and services are available in Big Timber and Columbus.

Day Use Facilities: Shared with campers.

Activities & Attractions: Fishing; floating, canoeing; small boat launch area.

Natural Features: Located on a wooded flat along the north bank of the Yellowstone River; sites are sheltered by light-medium to very dense hardwoods; bordered by rocky, evergreen-dotted hills and bluffs; elevation 3900´.

Season, Fees & Phone: Open all year, with limited services October to April; no fee (subject to change); 7 day limit; Montana Department of Fish Wildlife and Parks Region 5 Office, Billings ☎(406) 247-2940.

Camp Journal: The "Indian Fort" for which this site is named probably wasn't the same one Clark noted in his journal entry of July 17th. (That one is actually near the Bratten recreation site, several miles upriver from here.) As

Sacagawea had told Clark, fortifications built among the rocky blufftops were commonly used for defense and surveillance by the Indians. On the evening of July 17th, Clark's party camped on the north river bank, very close to this Indian Fort recreation site. The venerable old town of Reedpoint (or "Reed Point", pop. 96, more or less) bills itself as the "Sheep Drive Capital of the World" for the annual "Great Montana Sheep Drive" that draws thousands of visitors—two-legged as well as four-footed—on Labor Day Weekend.

📖 *July 18, 1806*

As we were about setting out this morning, two buffalow bulls came near our camp. Several of the men shot at one of them. Their being near the river, plunged in and swam across to the opposit side and there died. Shabono was thrown from his horse today in pursuit of a buffalow, the horse, unfortunately stepping into a braroe [badger] hole, fell and threw him over his head. He is a good deal bruised on his hip, sholder & face.

After brackfast I proceeded on as usial, passed over points of ridges so as to cut off bends of the river; crossed a small, muddy brook on which I found great quantities of the purple, yellow & black currants ripe. They were of an excellent flavour. I think the purple superior to any I have ever tasted. The river here is about 200 yards wide, rapid as usial, and the water gliding over coarse gravel and round stones of various sizes of an excellent grit for whetstones. The bottoms of the river are narrow. The hills are not exceeding 200 feet in height; the sides of them are generally rocky and composed of rocks of the same texture of a dark colour of grit, well calculated for grindstones &c. The high bottoms is composed of gravel and stone, like those in the channel of the river, with a mixture of earth of a dark brown colour. The country back from the river on each side is generally open, wavering plains. Some pine is to be seen in every direction in those plains on the sides of hills &c.

At 11 A.M., I observed a smoke rise to the S.S.E. in the plains toward the termination of the Rocky Mountains in that direction (which are covered with snow). This smoke must be raised by the Crow Indians in that direction, as a signal for us or other bands. I think it most probable that they have discovered our trail and, taking us to be Shoshone &c., in search of them; the Crow Indians (now at peace with them) to trade, as is their custom, have made this smoke to show where they are; or,

otherwise, taking us to be their enemy, made this signal for other bands to be on their guard.

I halted in a bottom of fine grass to let the horses graize. Shields killed a fat buck on which we all dined. After dinner and a delay of 3 hours to allow the horses time to feed, we set out at 4 PM. I set out and proceeded down the river through a beautifull bottom, passing a Indian fort on the head of a small island near the larbd. shore and encamped on a small island separated from the larbd. shore by a very narrow channel. Shields killed a buffalow this evening, which caused me to halt sooner than common to save some of the flesh, which was so rank and strong that we took but very little. Gibson, in attempting to mount his horse after shooting a deer this evening, fell on a snag and sent it nearly two inches into the muscular part of his thigh. He informs me this snag was about 1 inch in diameter, burnt at the end. This is a very bad wound and pains him exceedingly. I dressed the wound.

—*Captain Clark*

📖 *July 19, 1806*

I rose early and dressed Gibsons wound. He slept but very little last night and complains of great pain in his knee and hip as well as his thigh. There being no timber on this part of the Rochejhone sufficiently large for a canoe, and time is precious, as it is our wish to get to the U. States this season, conclude to take Gibson in a litter if he is not able to ride on down the river untill I can find a tree sufficiently large for my purpose. I had the strongest and gentlest horse saddled and placed skins & blankets in such a manner that, when he was put on the horse, he felt himself in as easy a position as when lying. This was a fortunate circumstance, as he could go much more at his ease than in a litter. Passed Rose Bud River on starbd. side (So called by Indians; i.e. *Itch-ke-pe* (Rose) *ar-ja* (river) about 40 yds; saw many rose buds, beautifull).

July 19, 1806, continued below

🏕 Montana 141 &

ITCH-KEP-PE
Columbus City Park

Location: South Central Montana west of Billings.

Access: From Interstate 90 Exit 408 for Columbus (40 miles west of Billings), from the south side of the interstate, head into town on Montana State Highway 78 for 0.8 mile to a 'T'; turn westerly, (right) continuing on Montana 78 through midtown for 0.7 mile; turn easterly (left, just before crossing the river) onto a paved access road for 50 yards down into the park.

Camping Facilities: 40 campsites; (additional campsites and a boat ramp are located a half mile east of the main park, via a connecting road); sites are small to medium-sized, level, with nominal to fair separation; parking pads are gravel are short to medium-length straight-ins or pull-offs; adequate space for a large tent in most sites; large central shelter; fire rings; b-y-o firewood; water at central faucets; restrooms; paved main driveway, gravel sub-drives; adequate supplies and services are available in Columbus.

Day Use Facilities: Shared with campers.

Activities & Attractions: Fishing; floating, canoeing; swimming pool, tennis courts, sports fields in other nearby parks.

Natural Features: Located on a well-wooded, grassy flat along the north bank of the Yellowstone River; most sites are well shaded by mature cottonwoods; bordered by tree-dotted bluffs; elevation 3700´.

Season, Fees & Phone: Open all year, with limited services October to April; no fee (donations are greatly appreciated, deposit box is located at the information station); Columbus City Clerk's Office ☎(406) 322-5313.

Camp Journal: *Itch-Kep-Pe* is the Crow word for "Rose", as Clark noted (with a minor variation in spelling) in his journal. The present-day Stillwater River, which enters the Yellowstone about a mile west of the park, was the stream Clark called "Rose Bud River". The camp fills up on most nights in midsummer. A pleasant, shady, very convenient stop.

📖 *July 19, 1806*, continued from above
I proceeded on about 9 miles, and halted to let the horses graize and let Gibson rest. His leg has become so numbed from remaining in one position as to render it extreemly painfull to him. I directed Shields to keep through the thick timber and examine for a tree sufficiently large & sound to make a canoe, and also hunt for some wild ginger for a poultice for Gibsons wound. He joined me at dinner with 2 fat bucks, but found neither tree or ginger. He informed me that 2 white bear chased him on horseback, each of which he shot from his horse &c. Currants are ripe and abundant, i.e,

the yellow, black & purple species. We passed over two high points of land from which I had a view of the Rocky Mountains to the W. & S.S.E. all covered with snow. I also saw a low mountain in an easterly direction. The high lands are particularly covered with pine and form perpendicular clifts on either side.

Afer dinner I proceeded on the high lands, become lower on either side, and those of the starbd. side form bluffs of a darkish yellow earth; the bottom widens to several miles on the starbd side. The timber, which cotton wood principally, scattered on the borders of the river, is larger than above. I have seen some trees which would make very small canoes. Gibsons thigh became so painfull that he could not set on the horse after riding about 2 hours and a half. I directed Sergt. Pryor and one man to continue with him under the shade of a tree for an hour and then proceed on to the place I should encamp, which would be in the first good timber for canoes for below. (It may be proper to observe that the emence swarms of grass hoppers have destroyed every sprig of grass for many miles on this side of the river, and appear to be progressing upwards about 4 miles below the place I left Sergt. Pryor with Gibson. Found some large timber near which the grass was tolerably good.

I encamped under a thick grove of those trees which was not sufficiently large for my purpose, tho' two of them would make small canoes. I took Shields and proceeded on through a large timbered bottom immediately below in search of better trees for canoes, found several about the same size with those at my camp. At dark I returned to camp. Sergt. Pryor had arived with Gibson. After my arrival at this place, the hunters killed seven elk, four deer, and I wounded a buffalow very badly near the camp immediately after I arived. In the forepart of the day, the hunters killed two deer, an antelope & shot two bear.

Shabono informed me that he saw an Indian on the high lands on the opposit side of the river, at the time I was absent in the woods. I saw a smoke in the same direction with that which I had seen on the 7th. It appeared to be in the mountains.

—*Captain Clark*

📖 *July 20, 1806*
I directed Sergt. Pryor and Shields, each of them good judges of timber, to proceed on down the river six or 8 miles and examine the bottoms, if any larger trees than those near

which we are encamped can be found, and return before twelve oClock. They set out at daylight. I also sent Labiche, Shabono, & Hall to bring the skin some of the flesh of the elk Labiche had killed last evening. They returned with one skin, the wolves having eaten the most of the other four elk. I also sent two men in search of wood suitable for ax handles. They found some choke cherry, which is the best wood which can be procured in this country. Saw a bear on an island opposit, and several elk.

Sergt. Pryor and Shields returned at half past 11 A.M., and informed me that they had proceeded down the timbered bottoms of the river for about 12 miles without finding a tree better than those near my camp. I determined to have two canoes made out of the largest of those trees and lash them together, which will cause them to be sturdy and fully sufficient to take my small party & self with what little baggage we have down this river. Had handles put in the 3 axes and after sharpening them with a file felled the two trees which I intended for the two canoes. Those trees appeared tolerably sound and will make canoes of 28 feet in length and about 16 or 18 inches deep and from 16 to 24 inches wide. The men with the three axes set in and worked untill dark.

Sergt. Pryor dressed some skins to make him clothes. Gibsons wound looks very well. I dressed it. The horses being fatigued and their feet very sore, I shall let them rest a fiew days. During which time the party intended for to take the horses by land to the Mandans, we will dress the skins and make themselves clothes to wear, as they are nearly naked. Shields killed a deer & buffalow, & Shannon a fawn and a buffalow, & York an elk; one of the buffalow was good meat. I had the best of him brought in and cut thin and spread out to dry.

—*Captain Clark*

🔥 This "Canoe Camp", as it has been called, was on the north bank of the Yellowstone, just south of present-day Park City, Montana.

📖 *July 21, 1806*
This morning I was informed that half of our horses were absent. Sent out Shannon, Bratten, and Shabono to hunt them. Shabono went up the river, Shannon down, and Bratten in the bottom near the camp. Shabono and Bratten returned at 10 A.M., and informed me that they saw no signs of the horses.

Shannon proceeded on down the river about 14 miles and did not return untill late in the evening. He was equally unsuccessful. Shannon informed me that he saw a remarkably large lodge about 12 miles below, covered with bushes, and the top decorated with skins, &c., and had the appearance of having been built about 2 years.

I sent out two men on horseback to kill a fat cow, which they did, and returned in 3 hours. The men work very diligently on the canoes; one of them nearly finished, ready to put in the water. Gibsons wound is beginning to heal. I am in great hope that it will get well in time for him to accompany Sergt. Pryor with the horses to the Mandans.

This evening late a very black cloud from the S.E. accompanied with thunder and lightning, with hard winds which shifted about, and was warm and disagreeable. I am apprehensive that the Indians have stolen our horses, and probably those who had made the smoke a fiew days past toward the S.W. I deturmined to have the ballance of the horses guarded, and for that purpose sent out 3 men. On their approach near, the horses were so allarmed that they ran away and entered the woods, and the men returned.

A great number of geese which raise their young on this river passed down frequently since my arrival at this place. We appear to be in the beginning of the buffalow country. The plains are beautifull and leavel, but the soil is but thin, stoney, and in many parts of the plains & bottoms there are great quantity of prickly pears. Saw several herds of buffalow since I arived at this camp, also antelopes, wolves, pigeons, doves, hawks, ravens, crows, larks, sparrows, eagles & bank martins &c. &c. The wolves which are the constant attendants of the buffalow are in great numbers on the scents of those large gangs which are to be seen in every direction in those praries

—*Captain Clark*

📖 *July 22, 1806*
The wind continued to blow very hard from the N.E. and a little before daylight was moderately cool. I sent Sergt. Pryor and Shabono in search of the horses, with directions to proceed up the river as far as the 1st narrows and examine particularly for their tracks. They returned at 3 P.M. and informed me that they had proceeded up the distance I directed them to go and could see neither horses nor tracks; the plains immediately out

from camp is so dry and hard that the track of a horse cannot be seen without close examination.

I therefore derected Sergt. Pryor, Shannon, Shabono, & Bratten to encircle the camp at some distance around and find the tracks of the horses and pursue them. They searched for tracks all the evening without finding which course the horses had taken, the plains being so remarkably hard and dry as to render it impossible to see a track of a horse passing through the hard parts of them.

I begin to suspect that they are taken by the Indians, and taken over the hard plains to prevent our following them. My suspicion is grounded on the improbability of the horses' leaving the grass and rushes of the river bottoms of which they are very fond, and takeing immediately out into the open, dry plains, where the grass is but short and dry. If they had continued in the bottoms, either up or down, their tracks could be followed very well. I directed Labiche, who understands tracking very well, to set out early in the morning and find what rout the horses had taken, if possible.

—*Captain Clark*

📖 *July 23, 1806*

Last night the wolves or dogs came into our camp and ate the most of our dryed meat, which was on a scaffold. Labiche went out early, agreeable to my directions of last evening. Sergt. Pryor and Windsor also went out. Sergt. Pryor found an Indian mockerson and a small piece of a robe, the mockerson worn out on the bottom & yet wet and has every appearance of having been worn but a fiew hours before. Those Indian signs are conclusive with me that they have taken the 24 horses which we lost on the night of the 20th, and that those who were about last night were in search of the ballance of our horses, which they could not find as they had fortunately got into a small prarie surrounded with thick timber in the bottom.

Labiche returned, having taken a great circle, and informed me that he saw the tracks of the horses making off into the open plains and were, by the tracks, going very fast. The Indians who took the horses bent their course reather down the river. The men finished both canoes by 12 oClock today, and I sent them to make oars & get poles, after which I sent Shields and Labiche to kill a fat buffalow out of a gang which has been within a fiew miles of us all day.

I gave Sergt. Pryor his instructions and a letter to Mr. Haney and directed that he, G. Shannon, & Windsor take the remaining horses to the Mandans, where he is to enquire for Mr. Haney. If at the establishments on the Assiniboine River, to take 12 or 14 horses and proceed on to that place, and deliver Mr. Haney the letter, which is with a view to engage Mr. Haney to prevail on some of the best-informed and most influential Chiefs of the different bands of Sioux to accompany us to the seat of our government, with a view to let them see our population and resources, &c., which I believe is the surest guarantee of savage fidelity to any Nation: that of a government possessing the power of punishing promptly every aggression.

Sergt. Pryor is directed to leave the ballance of the horses with the Grand Chief of the Mandans untill our arrival at his village; also to keep a journal of his rout, courses, distances, water course, soil production, & animals to be particularly noted. Shields and Labiche killed three buffalow, two of them very fat. I had as much of the meat saved as we could conveniently carry.

In the evening had the two canoes put into the water and lashed together, oars and everything fixed ready to set out early in the morning, at which time I have directed Sergt. Pryor to set out with the horses and proceed on to the enterance of the Big Horn River (which we suppose to be at no great distance), at which place the canoes will meet him and set him across the Rochejhone, below the enterance of that river.

—*Captain Clark*

Captain Clark's Speech for the Indians of the Rochejhone (Yellowstone) Valley

Clark prepared this speech in expectation of a council with the Crows somewhere on the Yellowstone. The reference to the theft of his horses on July 21st, still fresh in memory, seems to indicate that it was drafted while the men were making the two canoes.

Clark never had the opportunity to deliver his homily to the Crows. However, it has been included here to provide some insight into the prevailing (rather simplistic and paternalistic) perception which White people (particularly those in the government and the military) had of Red people during that era (and to this day).

Children: The Great Spirit has given a fair and bright day for us to meet together in his view that he may inspect us in this all we say and do. Children I take you all by the hand as the children of your Great Father, the President of the U. States of America, who is the Great Chief of all the white people towards the rising sun.

Children: This Great Chief who is benevolent, just, wise & bountifull, has sent me and one other of his chiefs (who is at this time in the country of the Blackfoot Indians) to all his red children on the Missouri and it's waters quite to the Great Lake of the West, where the land ends and the sun sets on the face of the great water, to know their wants and inform him of them on our return.

Children: We have been to the great lake of the West and are now on our return to my country. I have seen all my red children quite to that great lake and talked with them, and taken them by the hand in the name of their great father the Great Chief of all the white people.

Children: I have come across over high mountains and bad roads to this river to see the your Nation. I have come down the river from the foot of the great snowy mountain to see you, and have looked in every detection for you, without seeing you untill now.

Children: I heard from some of your people some nights past by my horses who complained to me of your people having taken 24 of their comrades.

Children: The object of my coming to see you is not to do you injury but to do you good; the Great Chief of all the white people, who has more goods at his command than could be piled up in the circle of your camp, wishing that all his red children should be happy, has sent me here to know your wants, that he may supply them.

Children: Your great father, the Chief of the white people, intends to build a house and fill it with such things as you may want and exchange with you for your skins & furs, at a very low price, & has directed me to enquire of you at what place would be most convenient for to build this house; and what articles you are in want of that he might send them imediately on my return.

Children: The people in my country are like the grass in your plains–numerous; they are also rich and bountifull, and love their red brethren who inhabit the waters of the Missouri.

Children: I have been out from my country two winters; I am pore, necked, and nothing to keep off the rain. When I set out from my country I had a plenty, but have given it all to my red children whom I have seen on my way to the Great Lake of the West, and have now nothing.

Children: Your Great Father will be very sorry to hear of the stealing the horses of his Chief's warriors whom he sent out to do good to his red children on the waters of Missouri. Those who close their ears to his good counsels he will shut them out and not let any goods & guns be brought to the red people; but to those who open their ears to his counsels, he will send everything they want into their country. and build a house where they may come to and be supplied whenever they wish.

Children: Your Great Father, the Chief of all the white people, has directed me to inform his red children to be at peace with each other, and the white people who may come into your country under the protection of the flag of your Great Father. Those people who may visit you under the protection of that flag are good people and will do you no harm

Children: Your Great Father has directed me to tell you not to suffer your young and thoughtless men to take the horses or property of your neighbours or the white people, but to trade with them fairly and honestly, as those of his red children below.

Children: The red children of your Great Father who live near him and have opened their ears to his counsels are rich and happy, have plenty of horses, cows & hogs, fowls bread &c.,&c., live in good houses, and sleep sound. And all those of his red children who inhabit the waters of the Missouri who open their ears to what I say and follow the counsels of their Great Father, the President of the United States, will in a fiew years be as happy as those mentioned &c.

Children: It is the wish of your Great Father, the Chief of all the white people, that some 2 of the principal Chiefs of this Nation should visit him at his great city and receive from his own mouth his good counsels, and from his own hands his abundant gifts. Those of his red children who visit him do not return with empty hands; he sends them to their Nation loaded with presents.

Children: If any one, two or 3 of your great Chiefs wishes to visit your Great Father and will go with me, he will send you back next summer loaded with presents and some goods for the nation. You will then see with your own eyes and hear with your own ears what the white people can do for you. They do not speak with two tongues nor promise what they can't perform.

Children: Consult together and give me an answer as soon as possible; your Great Father is anxious to hear from & see his red children who wish to visit him. I cannot stay but must proceed on & inform him &c.

—*Captain Clark*

☙ With the canoes finished, the Yellowstone party is once again ready to continue its trip. Probably about an hour after embarking, they will pass Clarks Fork of the Yellowstone, near present-day Laurel, Montana; later in the morning of July 24, they will float past the site of modern Billings, Montana:

⛺ *Clark's Fork to Joining Lewis on the Missouri*

📖 *July 24, 1806*

Had all our baggage put on board of the two small canoes which, when lashed together, is very sturdy and, I am convinced, will carry the party I intend taking down with me. At 8 A.M., we set out and proceeded on very well to a riffle about 1 mile above the enterance of Clarks Fork [of the Yellowstone River]. At this riffle the small canoes took in a good deal of water, which obliged us to land to dry out articles and bail the canoes. I also had buffalow skin tacked on, so as to prevent the water's flacking in between the two canoes.

This being a good place to cross the river, I deturmined to wait for Sergt. Pryor and put him across the river at this place. I observed a large lodge, the same which Shannon informed me of a fiew days past. This lodge, a council lodge, it is of a council form 60 feet diameter at it's base, built of 20 poles, each pole 2 1/2 feet in circumference and 45 feet long, built in the form of a lodge & covered with bushes. In this lodge I observed a cedar bush sticking up on the opposit side of the lodge fronting the door, on one side was a buffalow head, and on the other several sticks bent and stuck in the ground. A stuffed buffalow skin was suspended from the center with the back down. On the top of those poles were decorated with feathers of the eagle & calumet eagle, also several curious pieces of wood bent

in circular form with sticks across them in the form of a griddle hung on tops of the lodge poles, others in form of a large stirrup. This lodge was erected last summer. It is situated in the center of a beautifull island thinly covered with cotton wood, under which the earth which is rich is covered with wild rye and a species of grass resembling the bluegrass, and a mixture of sweet grass, which the Indian plat and wear around their necks for it's scent, which is of a strong sent like that of the vanilla.

After dinner, I proceeded on past the enterance of a small creek and some wood on the starbd. side, where I met with Sergt. Pryor, Shannon, & Windsor with the horses. They had but just arived at that place. Sergt. Pryor informed me that it would be impossible for the two men with him to drive on the horses after him without tiring all the good ones in pursuit of the more indifferent, to keep them on the course; that in passing every gang of buffalow, several of which he had met with, the loose horses, as soon as they saw the buffalow, would immediately pursue them and run around them. All those that had speed sufficient would head the buffalow, and those of less speed would pursue on as fast as they could.

He at length found that the only practicable method would be for one of them to proceed on and whenever they saw a gang of buffalow to scare them off before the horses got up. This disposition in the horses is no doubt owing to their being frequently exercised in chasing different animals by their former owners, the Indians, as it is their custom to chase every species of wild animal with horses, for which purpose they train all their horses.

I had the horses driven across the river, and set Sergt. Pryor and his party across. H. Hall, who cannot swim, expressed a willingness to proceed on with Sergt. Pryor by land, as another man was necessary to assist in driving the horses; but observing he was necked, I gave him one of my two remaining shirts, a pair of leather leggings, and 3 pairs of mockersons, which equipped him completely, and sent him on with the party by land to the Mandans.

I proceeded on the river much better than above the enterance of the Clarks Fork, deep and more navigable, the current regularly rapid from 200 to 300 yards in width, where it is all together much divided by islands, many of which are large and well supplied with cotton wood trees, some of them large. Saw emence number of deer, elk and buffalow on the banks. Some beaver. I landed on the larbd. side, walked out into the bottom and killed the fattest buck I every saw; Shields killed a deer and my man York killed a buffalow bull, as he informed me, for his tongue and marrow bones. For me to mention or give an estimate of the different species of wild animals on this river, particularly buffalow, elk, antelopes & wolves, would be increditable. I shall therefore be silent on the subject further. So it is we have a great abundance of the best of meat. We made 70 miles today. Current rapid and much divided by islands. Camped a little below Pryors River of 35 yds. on S.E.

—*Captain Clark*

🦌 They encamped just southwest of present-day Huntley, Montana. The "Pryors River" mentioned by Clark in the foregoing paragraph is now named Pryor Creek. It is a substantial stream which heads in the Pryor Mountains south of Billings and meets the Yellowstone River at Huntley. Pryor Creek is the principal watershed of the western fourth of the Crow Reservation; to the Reservation it is third in importance only to the Bighorn and Little Bighorn Rivers. The "Pryor" in both citations is, of course, Sergeant Nathaniel Pryor of the Yellowstone party.

📖 *July 25, 1806*

We set out at sunrise and proceeded on very well for three hours. Saw a large gang of buffalow on the larbd. bank. I concluded to halt and kill a fat one, during which time some brackfast was ordered to be cooked. We killed 2 buffalow and took as much of their flesh as I wished. Shields killed two fat deer, and after a delay of one hour and a half, we again proceeded on. And had not proceeded far before a heavy shower of rain poured down upon us, and the wind blew hard from the S.W. The wind increased and the rain began, continued to fall. I halted on the starbd. side; had some logs set up on end close together and covered with deerskins to keep off the rain, and a large fire made to dry ourselves. The rain continued moderately untill near twelve oClock when it cleared away and become fair.

The wind continued high untill 2 P.M. I proceeded on after the rain, lay a little, and at 4 P.M., arived at a remarkable rock situated in an extensive bottom on the starbd. side of the river and 250 paces from it. This rock I ascended and from it's top had a most extensive view in every direction. This rock,

which I shall call Pompys Tower, is 200 feet high and 400 paces in circumference, and only accessible on one side, which is from the N.E., the other parts of it being a perpendicular clift of lightish-coloured gritty rock. On the top there is a tolerable soil about 5 or 6 feet thick covered with short grass. The Indians have made two piles of stone on the top of this tower. The nativs have engraved on the face of this rock the figures of animals, &c., near which I marked my name and the day of the month & year.

From the top of this tower I could discover two low mountains and the Rocky Mountains covered with snow S.W. one of them appeared to be extensive and bore S. 15° E. about 40 miles. The other I take to be what the Indians call the Little Wolf Mtn. [present-day Bull Mountains, North of Billings]. I can only see the southern extremity of it, which bears N 55° W about 35 miles. The plains to the South rise from the distance of about 6 miles, the width of the bottom gradually to the mountains in that derection. A large creek with an extensive valley the direction of which is S. 25° E. meanders beautifully through this plain. A range of high land covered with pine appears to run in a N. & S. direction approaching the river below. On the northerly side of the river, high romantic clifts approach & jut over the water for some distance both above and below. A large brook, which at this time has some running muddy water, falls in to the Rochejhone immediately opposit Pompys Tower. Back from the river for some distance on that side, the hills are rugged & some pine back the plains are open and extensive.

July 25, 1806, continued below

🏕️ **Montana Side Trip** ♿

POMPEYS PILLAR
Pompeys Pillar National Monument

Location: South Central Montana northeast of Billings.

Access: From Interstate 94 Exit 23 for Pompeys Pillar (27 miles northeast of Billings), from the north side of the freeway proceed north and west on U.S. Highway 312 for 0.8 mile; turn northerly onto a gravel access road and go 0.7 mile to the parking lot.

Camping Facilities: None; nearest public camping area is Captain Clark State Recreation Access Site (see below).

Day Use Facilities: Medium-sized picnic area; drinking water; vault facilities; large, gravel parking lot.

Activities & Attractions: Small interpretive center; wooden steps (about 100 or so) lead up the north face to near the top of the sandstone column where Captain Clark inscribed his name and the date; short trail to the river.

Natural Features: Located on a tree-dotted plain along the south bank of the Yellowstone River; the impressive sandstone formation, Pompeys Pillar (Pompys Tower), rises from the level river plain; picnic sites are nicely shaded by mature cottonwoods; bordered by agricultural land; the river is flanked by tree-dotted hills and bluffs; elevation 3000´.

Season, Fees & Phone: General season is May to October, but may be available at other times, subject to weather; $3.00 per vehicle entry fee in summer; U.S. Bureau of Land Management Office, Pompeys Pillar National Monument ☎ (406) 896-5004.

Camp Journal: This solitary sandstone monolith was called by the Apsaalooka (Crow) people *Lishbiia Anaache*, "Place Where the Mountain Lion Dwells". The rock was a well-known landmark where Indians came to trade and exchange information. Apsaalooka legend says that the Pillar was once attached to the sandstone bluff on the north side of the river; at some time, the rock detached itself and rolled to its present location. To the Crow, the Yellowstone was the Elk River. This spot was a strategic, natural crossing of the great stream.

The origin of the name of the tower/pillar has been the subject of considerable speculation. The infant son of Touissant Charbonneau and Sacagawea had been formally named Jean Baptiste Charbonneau by his family. According to some sources, "pomp" was the Shoshone word for "first born". Captain Clark had taken a somewhat paternal liking for the infant, and nicknamed him "Pomp" or "Pompy" (perhaps similar to "Sonny" or "Buddy"). Other sources claim that "Pomp" was short for "Pompey", a common name for Southern slaves.

Nicholas Biddle, the first publisher of the history of the Expedition, changed the name from Clark's spontaneous "Pompys Tower" to a more classical-sounding "Pompeys Pillar". (Biddle tampered with a lot of the Expedition's written material.) That name has endured for nearly two centuries.

Pompeys Pillar/Pompys Tower has been the subject of some controversy in recent years. A scholar in the East proposed to Congress that the name of this national monument be changed back to the original, historically accurate "Pompys Tower". But an organized outcry from local citizens (including a letter-writing campaign by young school children) squelched the movement to rename the national monument.

Pompeys Pillar National Monument

📖 *July 25, 1806*, continued from above
After satisfying myself sufficiently in this delightfull prospect of the extensive country around, and the emence herds of buffalow, elk and wolves in which it abounded, I decended and proceeded on a fiew miles; saw a gang of about 40 big horn animals, fired at them and killed 2 on the sides of the rocks which we did not get. I directed the canoes to land, and I walked up through a crevice in the rocks almost inaccessible and killed 2 of those animals, one a large doe and the other a yearling buck. I wished very much to kill a large buck; had there been one with the gang I should have killed him.

During the time the men were getting the two big horns which I had killed to the river, I employed myself in getting pieces of the rib of a fish which was cemented within the face of the rock; this rib is about 3 inches diameter in cicumferance about the middle; it is 3 feet in length, tho' a part of the end appears to have been broken off. I have several pieces of this rib; the bone is neither decayed nor petrified but very rotten. The part which I could not get out may be seen, it is about 6 or 7 miles below Pompys Tower in the face of the larbd. clift about 20 feet above the water.

After getting the big horn on board &c., I proceeded on a short distance and encamped earlier than I intended on account of a heavy cloud which was coming up from the S.S.W. and some appearance of a violent wind. I

walked out and killed a small buck for his skin, which the party are in want of for clothes. About sunset the wind blew hard from the W. and some little rain. I encamped on the starbd. side immediately below the enterance of Shannons River [now Fly Creek], about 22 yards wide, and at this time discharges a great portion of water which is very muddy.
Emence herds of buffalow about our camp; as it is now running time with those animals, the bulls keep such a grunting noise which is a very loud and disagreeable sound, that we are compelled to scare them away before we can sleep. The men fire several shots at them and scare them away.

—Captain Clark

⛺ Montana 142 ♿

CAPTAIN CLARK
Captain Clark Recreation Access Site

Location: South Central Montana northeast of Billings..

Access: From Interstate 94 Exit 36 for Waco (13 miles northeast of the hamlet of Pompeys Pillar, 11 miles southwest of Custer), go to a 'T' intersection at the north side of the freeway, then turn east (right) onto a paved frontage road and proceed 2.2 miles to milepost 40 +.3; turn northerly (left) onto a narrow, gravel access road and proceed (the road curves westerly then northerly again, and crosses RR tracks) for 0.8 mile to the recreation site.

Camping Facilities: Open, primitive camping with enough room for several dozen campers; parking and tent surfaces are grassy and level; a few stone fire rings; b-y-o firewood; no drinking water; vault facilities; (an I-94 rest area with drinking water and restrooms is located about 2 miles east of Exit 36); pack-it-in-pack-it-out trash removal; gravel driveway; gas and camper supplies+ in Pompeys Pillar.

Day Use Facilities: Facilities are shared with campers.

Activities & Attractions: Boating/floating; small boat ramp; fishing; handicapped-access fishing pier.

Natural Features: Located on a large flat along the south bank of the Yellowstone River; a few large cottonwoods and Russian olives dot the flat, but most of the main area is unshaded; entensive pasture and crop lands lie to the east, west and south, tree-dotted bluffs closely flank the north bank of the river; elevation 2900´.

Season, Fees & Phone: Open all year, subject to weather conditions; 7 day limit; Montana Department of Fish Wildlife and Parks Region 5 Office, Billings ☎ (406) 247-2940.

Camp Journal: If Captain Clark and the Yellowstone party had needed a place to encamp about the time they floated past here on July 26, this would have been a pretty good choice. Indeed, there would have been plenty of room for the entire Corps of Discovery here: Several acres of level terrain, enough space right along the high river bank for a dozen campers, plus loads of room a few yards back from the edge. Sandstone bluffs rise steeply right from the north bank directly across the river from here; miles of distant views in other directions.

📖 *July 26, 1806*

Set out this morning very early, proceeded on past creeks very well. The current of the river regularly swift, much divided by stoney islands and bars, also handsome islands covered with cotton wood, the bottoms extensive on the starbd. side; on the larbd. the clifts of high land border the river; those clifts are composed of a whitish rock of an excellent grit for grindstones. The country back on each side is wavering lands with scattering pine. Passed 2 small brooks on the starbd. side and two large ones on the larbd. side. I shot a buck from the canoe and killed one other on a small island. And late in the evening passed a part of the river which was rock under the larbd. clifts. Fortunately for us, we found an excellent channel to pass down on the right of a stoney island half a mile below this bad place.

We arived at the enterance of Big Horn River on the starbd. side. Here I landed immediately in the point, which is a soft mud mixed with the sand and subject to overflow for some distance back in between the two rivers. I walked up the Big Horn 1/2 a mile and crossed over to the lower side, and formed a camp on a high point. I with one of my men, Labiche, walk up the N E side of Big Horn River 7 miles to the enterance of a creek which falls in on the N E side and is 28 yds. wide; some running water which is very muddy, this creek I call Muddy Creek. Some fiew miles above this creek the river bent around to the East of South.

The bottoms of the Big Horn River are extensive and covered with timber, principally cotton. It's current is regularly swift, like the Missouri; it washes away it's banks on one side, while it forms extensive sand bars on the other. Contains much less portion of large gravel than the River Rochejhone, and it's water more muddy and of a brownish colour, while that of the Rochejhone is of a lightish colour. The width of those two rivers are very nearly the same immediately at their enterances, the River Rochejhone much the deepest and contains the most water. I measured the depth of the Bighorn quite across at 1/2 a mile above it's junction and found it from 5 to 7 feet only, while that of the River Rochejhone is in the deepest part 10 or 12 feet; water on the lower side of the Bighorn is extensive, beautifull and leavel bottom thinly covered with cotton wood, under which there grows great quantities of rose bushes.

I am informed by the Minnetares Indians and others that this river [Bighorn] takes it's rise in the Rocky Mountains with the heads of the River Platte, and at no great distance from the River Rochejhone, and passes between the Cote Noir or Black Mountains and the most easterly range of Rocky Mountains. It is very long and contains a great proportion of timber, on which there is a variety of wild animals, particularly the big horn, which are to be found in great numbers on this river. Buffalow, elk, deer and antelopes are plenty, and the river is said to abound in beaver. It is inhabited by a great number of roving Indians of the Crow Nation, the Paunch Nation, and the Castahanas, all of those Nations who are subdivided, rove and pursue the buffalow, of which they make their principal food; their skins, together with those of the big horn and antelope, serve them for clothes. This river is said to be navigable a long way for perogues, without falls, and waters a fine rich open country.

I returned to camp a little after dark, having killed one deer; finding myself fatigued, went to bed without my supper. Shields killed 2 bulls & 3 elk.

—*Captain Clark*

♣ **Montana 143**

MANUEL LISA
Manuel Lisa Recreation Access Site

Location: South Central Montana northeast of Billings.

Access: From Interstate 94 Exit 49 for State Highway 87/Custer/Hardin (2 miles east of Custer, 44 miles west of Forsyth), go to a 'T' intersection at the north side of the freeway, then turn east (right) onto a paved frontage road and proceed 2.2 miles to the recreation site.

Camping Facilities: 3 campsites; sites are small, level, and closely spaced; parking surfaces are gravel, short to medium-length straight-ins or pull-offs; enough space for small to medium-sized tents; fire rings; b-y-o firewood; no drinking water; vault facilities; pack-it-in-pack-it-out trash removal; gravel driveway; gas and camper supplies+ are available in Custer.

Day Use Facilities: Small parking area.

Activities & Attractions: Boating/floating; small boat ramp; fishing.

Natural Features: Located on the west bank of the Bighorn River a few yards above its confluence with the Yellowstone; sites are lightly shaded by hardwooods; the rivers are flanked by tree-dotted hills and bluffs; elevation 2800´.

Season, Fees & Phone: Open all year, subject to weather conditions; 7 day limit; Montana Department of Fish Wildlife and Parks Region 5 Office, Billings ☎(406) 247-2940.

Camp Journal: This site is within a few yards of Captain Clark's camp on the bank of the Bighorn of July 26, 1806. Naturally speaking, this is a pleasant spot at a notable confluence that's good for a night or two. One potential drawback worth considering is its proximity to the Interstate—just a dozen or so yards below and north of the westbound lanes. Still, if you're inside a pickup topper, van, or rv, the limited nighttime traffic might not be a big bother. Manuel Lisa was a St. Louis entrepreneur and a business partner of Captain Clark in a short-lived trading enterprise on the Yellowstone.

📖 *July 27, 1806*
I marked my name with red paint on a cotton tree near my camp, and set out at an early hour and proceeded on very well; the river is much wider, from 4 to 600 yards, much divided by islands and sand bars. Passed a large dry creek (call Elk Creek) at 15 miles and halted at the enterance of a river 50 yards wide on the larbd side, I call River Labiche. Killed 4 buffalow and saved as much of their flesh as we could carry. Took brackfast. The buffalow and elk is astonishingly numerous on the banks of the river on each side, particularly the elk, which lay on almost every point in large gangs and are so gentle that we frequently pass within 20 or 30 paces of them without their being the least allarmed. The buffalow are generally at a greater distance from the river, and keep a continuing bellowing in every direction; much more

beaver sign than above the Bighorn. I saw several of those animals on the bank today. The antelopes are scarce, as also the big horns, and the deer by no means so plenty as they were near the Rocky Mountains. When we pass the Big Horn I take my leave of the view of the tremendous chain of Rocky Mountains white with snow, in view of which I have been since the 1st of May last.

About sunset I shot a very large, fat buck elk from the canoe, near which I encamped, and was near being bit by a rattle snake. Shields killed a deer & a antelope today for the skins which the party is in want of for clothes. This river below the Big Horn River resembles the Missouri in almost every particular, except that it's islands are more numerous & current more rapid, it's banks are generally low and falling in the bottoms on the starbd. side, low and extensive and covered with timber, near the river such as cotton wood, willow of the different species, rose bushes and grapevines, together with the red berry or buffalow grease bushes & a species of shoemake with dark brown back. Of those bottoms the country rises gradually to about 100 feet and has some pine. Back is leavel plains. On the larbd. side the river runs under the clifts and bluffs of high, which is from 70 to 150 feet in height, and near the river is some scattering low pine; back the plains become leavel and extensive. The clifts are composed of a light gritty stone which is not very hard. and the round stone which is mixed with the sand and forms bars is much smaller than they appeared from above the Bighorn, and may here be termed gravel. The colour of the water is a yellowish white and less muddy than the Missouri below the mouth of this river.

—*Captain Clark*

⛺ Montana 144 ♿

ROSEBUD EAST
Rosebud Recreation Access Site

Location: Southeast Montana near Forsyth.

Access: From Interstate 94 Exit 95 on the east edge of Forsyth (43 miles west of Miles City, 100 miles east of Billings), turn north onto East Main Street; (follow the sign for "Rosebud Recreation Area", ignore signs which indicate "camping" toward the south); follow East Main toward the west 0.5 mile to the intersection of Main Street and 15th Avenue; turn north onto 15th Avenue, and continue 6 blocks to the campground.

Camping Facilities: 22 campsites; most sites are fairly spacious, level, with good separation; parking pads are gravel, mostly long pull-throughs, plus a fiew straight-ins; good camping for tents; fireplaces, some barbecue grills; b-y-o firewood; water at central faucets; vault facilities; gravel driveways; adequate supplies and services are available in Forsyth.

Day Use Facilities: Small parking lot; other facilities are shared with campers.

Activities & Attractions: Fishing; boating; boat launch; Rosebud County Museum, a few blocks south, features items of regional Old West interest.

Natural Features: Located on the north bank of the Yellowstone River; tall hardwoods and dense low-level vegetation in the campground; rocky bluffs of the lower Yellowstone Valley border the river; semi-arid climate; elevation 2500´.

Season, Fees & Phone: Open all year, with limited services October to April; 14 day limit; $8.00 (includes park entry fee); phone c/o Montana Department of Fish Wildlife & Parks, Region 7 Office, Miles City, ☎(406) 232-0900.

Camp Journal: Here's a spot that's very handy for Interstate travelers. However, since it's right on the edge of town, you may experience a little residential noise (altho' the campground is closed to outside traffic from 10 pm until 6 am). This is principally a fishing access site that also offers basic camping. It may also be a little more populated and less desirable in midsummer than at other times. Clark's Yellowstone party camped about 9 miles west-northwest of here, just above the river's confluence with Big Porcupine Creek, on the night of July 27, 1806.

📖 *July 28, 1806*
Set out this morning at daylight and proceeded on gliding down this smooth stream, passing many islands and several creeks and brooks; at 6 miles passed a creek or brook of 80 yards wide (called by Indians Little Wolf River) [now Big Porcupine Creek] on the N.W. side, containing but little water. 6 miles lower passed a small creek 20 yds wide on the starbd. side; 18 Miles lower passed a large dry creek on the larbd. side; 5 Miles lower passed a river 70 yards wide containing but little water on the larbd. side, which I call Table Creek from the tops of several mounds in the plains to the N.W. resembling a table. Four miles still lower I arived at the enterance of a river 100 yards wide back of a small island on the South side. It contains some cotton wood timber and has a bold current, it's water, like

those of all other streams which I have passed in the canoes, are muddy. I take this river to be the one the Indians call the Little Big Horn River [now Rosebud Creek].

The clifts on the South side of the Rochejhone are generally composed of a yellowish, gritty, soft rock, whitest those of the N., is light-coloured and much harder. In the evening I passed stratas of coal in the banks on either side, those on the starbd. bluffs was about 30 feet above the water and in 2 veines from 4 to 8 feet thick, in a horizontal position. The coal contained in the larbd. bluffs is in several veines of different bights and thickness. This coal or carbonated wood is like that of the Missouri, of an inferior quality. Passed a large creek on the starbd. side between the 1st and 2nd coal bluffs; passed several brooks, the channel of them were wide and contained but little running water, and encamped on the upper point of a small island opposit the enterance of a creek 25 Yards wide (which the Indians call *Ma Shas-kap* river) on the starbd. side, with water.

—*Captain Clark*

📖 *July 29, 1806*

A slight rain last night with hard thunder and sharp lightening, accompanied with a violent N.E. wind. I set out early this morning, wind so hard ahead that we made but little way. In the forepart of the day, I saw great numbers of buffalow on the banks. The country on either side is like that of yesterday. Passed three large dry brooks on the starbd. side and four on the larbd. side. Great quantities of coal in all the hills I passed this day.

Late in the evening, I arived at the enterance of a river which I take to be the *Lazeka* or Tongue River. It discharges itself on the starbd. side and is 150 yards wide of water; the banks are much wider. I intended to encamp on an eligable spot immediately below this river, but finding that it's water so muddy and warm as to render it very disagreeable to drink, I crossed the Rochejhone and encamped on an island close to the larbd. shore.

The water of this river is nearly milk warm, very muddy and of a lightish brown colour. The current rapid and the channel contains great numbers of snags. Near it's enterance there is great quantities of wood, such as is common in the low bottoms of the Rochejhone and Missouri, tho' I believe that the country back thro' which this river passes is an open one where the water is exposed to the sun, which heats it in it's passage. It is shallow and

throws out great quantities of mud and some coarse gravel. Below this river and on the starbd. side at a fiew miles from the Rochejhone, the hills are high and rugged, containing coal in great quantities. Beaver is very plenty on this part of the Rochejhone. The river widens, I think it may be generally calculated at from 500 yards to half a mile in width, more sand and gravelly bars than above. Caught 3 catfish. They were small and fat. Also a soft shell turtle.

—*Captain Clark*

📖 *July 30, 1806*

Set out early this morning. At 12 miles arived at the commencement of shoals, the channel on the starbd. side near a high bluff. Passed a succession of those shoals for 6 miles, the lower of which was quite across the river and appeared to have a descent of about 3 feet. Here we were compelled to let the canoes down by hand, for fear of their striking a rock under water and splitting. This is by far the worst place which I have seen on this river from the Rocky Mountains to this place, a distance of 694 miles by water. A perogue or large canoe would with safety pass through the worst of those shoals, which I call the Buffalow Shoals, from the circumstance of one of those animals being in them. The rock which passes the river at those shoals appears hard and gritty, of a dark brown colour. The clifts on the starbd. side is about 100 feet in height; on the larbd. side the country is low, and the bottom rises gradually back. Here is the first appearance of burnt hills which I have seen on this river; they are at a distance from the river on the larbd. side.

I landed at the enterance of a dry creek on the larbd. side below the shoals and took brackfast. Those dry rivers, creeks &c., are like those of the Missouri which take their rise in, and are the conveyance of, the water from those plains. They have the appearanc of discharging emence torrents of water. The late rains which have fallen in the plains raised suddenly those brooks which receive the water of those plains, on which those sudden & heavy showers of rain must have fallen, several of which I have seen dischargeing those waters, while those below, heading or taking their rise in the same neighbourhood, as I passed them appear to have latterly been high. Those brooks discharge emencely of mud also, which contributes much to the muddiness of the river.

After brackfast proceeded on the river much narrower than above, from 3 to 400 yards wide only, and only a fiew scattering trees to be seen on the banks. At 20 miles below the Buffalow Shoals, passed a rapid which is by no means dangerous; it has a number of large rocks in different parts of the river, which causes high waves, a very good channel on the larbd. side. This rapid I call Bear Rapid, from the circumstance of a bear's being on a rock in the middle of this rapid when I arived at it. A violent storm from the N.W. obliged us to land immediately below this rapid, draw up the canoes, and take shelter in an old Indian lodge above the enterance of a river which is nearly dry. It has latterly been very high and spread over nearly 1/4 a mile in width. It's channel is 88 yards and in this there is not more water than could pass through an inch auger hole. I call it Yorks Dry River.

🔥 Buffalow Shoals are approximartely 8 miles northeast of midtown Miles City; the river passes about 2 miles north of the Business I-94 Exit in that vicinity. Yorks Dry River is now named Custer Creek. It rises in the Big Sheep Mountains north of the Yellowstone, and joins the main stream about 10 miles southwest of Terry, Montana.

After the rain and wind passed over, I proceeded on at 7 miles, passed the enterance of a river, the water of which is 100 yds wide, the bed of this river nearly 1/4 of a mile; this river is shallow and the water very muddy, and of the colour of the banks a darkish brown. I observe great quantities of red stone thrown out of this river, that from the appearance of the hills at a distance on it's lower side, induced me to call this Red Stone River. As the water was disagreeably muddy, I could not camp on that side below it's mouth. However, I landed at it's enterance and sent out and killed two fat cows, and took as much of the flesh as the canoes would conveniently carry, and crossed the river and encamped at the enterance of a brook on the larbd. side under a large spredding cotton tree. The river on which we passed today is not so wide as above, containing but fiew islands, with a small quantity of cotton timber. No timber of any kind to be seen on the high lands on either side.

—*Captain Clark*

🔥 Clark's Red Stone River is now named Powder River. This shallow stream of lore and legend rises in central Wyoming west of Casper and drains much of northeast Wyoming and southeast Montana. 'Thing is, the Powder River enters the Yellowstone with scarcely little more

water than it has at its head. The cowboys around Eastern Montana have an old whoop-n'-holler expression: "Powder River, let 'er buck! She's a mile wide and a foot deep!"

📖 *July 31, 1806*

I was much disturbed last night by the noise of the buffalow which were about me. One gang swam the river near our camp, which allarmed me a little for fear of their crossing our canoes and splitting them to pieces.

Set out as usial about sunrise. Passed a rapid which I call Wolf Rapid, from the circumstance of one of those animals being at the rapid. Here the river approaches the high, mountainous country on the N.W. side [Big Sheep Mountains]. Those hills appear to be composed of various coloured earth and coal, without much rock. I observe several conical mounds which appear to have been burnt. This high country is washed into curious formed mounds & hills and is cut much with ravines. The country again opens and at the distance of 23 miles below the Red Stone or *War-har-sah* River.

I landed in the enterance of a small river on the starbd. Side, 40 yards wide, shallow and muddy. It has lately been very high. Having passed the enterance of a river on the larbd. side 100 yards wide which has running water. this river I take to be the one the Minnitares call Little Wolf or *Sa-a-shah* River. The high country is entirely bare of timber. Great quantities of coal or carbonated wood is to be seen in every bluff and in the high hills at a distance on each side. Saw more buffalow and elk and antelopes this evening than usial.

18 miles below the last river on the starbd. side, I passed one 60 yards wide which had running water. This stream I call *Oak-tar-pon-er* or Coal River , has very steep banks on each side of it. Passed several large brooks; some of them had a little running water; also several islands, some high, black-looking bluffs and encamped on the starbd. side on a low point. The country, like that of yesterday, is open, extensive plains. As I was about landing this evening, saw a white bear and the largest I ever saw eating a dead buffalow on a sand bar. We fired two shot into him; he swam to the main shore and walked down the bank. I landed and fired 2 more shot into this tremendous animal without killing him. Night coming on, we could not pursue him; he bled profusely. Showers all this day.

—*Captain Clark*

♠ Montana 145 &

MAKOSHIKA
Makoshika State Park

Location: Eastern Montana south of Glendive.

Access: From Interstate 90 Exit 215 for Glendive (27 miles west of the Montana-North Dakota border, 37 miles northeast of Terry), travel south and west on Business Route I-94/Merrill Avenue through the center of town for 1.5 miles; at the far west end of Glendive, look for a very large Indian arrow pointing south (left); turn south, go through an underpass, and continue on a well-signed route south on Barry Street to Taylor, then west (right) on Taylor to Snyder, then south (left) on Snyder to the park.

Camping Facilities: 16 campsites adjacent to a small, paved parking lot; adequate space for large vehicles and tents; fire rings; b-y-o firewood; water at a central faucet; vault facilities; complete supplies and services are available in Glendive.

Day Use Facilities: Small picnic area; ramada; vault facilities; small parking area.

Activities & Attractions: Scenic views of badlands; Caprock Nature Trail (1 mile); Kinney Coulee Hiking Trail (1 mile, with moderately steep sections); amphitheater for interpretive programs during the summer; (a visitor center is planned).

Natural Features: Located in an area of rocky, colorful badlands; vegetation consists of sparse grass and scattered pines and junipers; elevation 2200´.

Season, Fees & Phone: Open all year, with limited services October to April; 14 day limit; camping $9.00 (includes park entry fee); park office ☎(406) 365-8596.

Camp Journal: Makoshika (Mah-*koh*-shih-kah) is a Sioux word which has been variously translated as "badlands", "bad earth" or "hell cooled over". (In midsummer, you can drop the "cooled over" part.) The park is best-known for its radical geology, but in recent years it also has been the scene of some serious dinosaur digging. If your itinerary allows you to plan on being here during a specific time of day, try to arrive before 10 a.m. or after 5:00 p.m. The myriad of shapes will be most striking and the colors most vibrant during those periods, especially when the early evening shadows accentuate the entire landscape with their 3-D effects. Interesting place, actually.

Clark's camp on July 31st was just a half dozen miles southwest of here. However, these badlands would not have been visible to him from down along the river.

📖 *August 1, 1806*

We set out early as usial; the wind was high and ahead, which caused the water to be a little rough and delayed us very much; added to this we had showers of rain repeatedly all day, at the intermission of only a fiew minits between them. My situation a very disagreeable one. In an open canoe, wet and without a possibility of keeping myself dry.

The country through which we passed is in every respect like that through which I passed yesterday. The brooks have all some water in them from the rain which has fallen. This water is excessively muddy. Several of those brooks have some trees on their borders as far as I can see up them. I observe some low pine and cedar on the sides of the rugged hills on the starbd. side, and some ash timber in the high bottoms. The river has more sand bars today than usial, and more soft mud. The current less rapid.

At 2 P.M. I was obliged to land to let the buffalow cross over. Notwithstanding an island of half a mile in width over which this gang of buffalow had to pass, and the channel of the river on each side nearly 1/4 of a mile in width, this gang of buffalow was entirely across and as thick as they could swim. The channel on the side of the island they went into the river, was crowded with those animals for 1/2 an hour, (I was obliged to lay to for one hour.) The other side of the island for more than 3/4 of an hour. I took 4 of the men and killed 4 fat cows for their fat and what portion of their flesh the small canoes could carry, that which we had killed a fiew days ago being nearly spoiled from the wet weather. Encamped on an island close to the larbd. shore. Two gangs of buffalow crossed a little below us, as numerous as the first.

—*Captain Clark*

♠ Montana 146 &

INTAKE DAM
Intake Dam Recreation Access Site

Location: Eastern border of Montana northeast of Glendive.

Access: From Montana State Highway 16 in the hamlet of Intake (16 miles northeast of Glendive, 36 miles southwest of Sidney), turn easterly onto a gravel access road and proceed 2 miles to the recreation site.

Camping Facilities: 5 campsites; sites are small, level, with nominal separation; parking surfaces are sandy gravel, short to medium-length pull-offs or straight-ins; small to medium-sized tent areas; fire rings; b-y-o firewood; water at a hand pump; vault facilities; gravel driveway; virtually complete supplies and services are available in Glendive.

Day Use Facilities: Small parking area.

Activities & Attractions: Boating; boat ramp; fishing.

Natural Features: Located on a wooded flat along the north-west bank of the Yellowstone River; sites receive light to medium shade from large cottonwoods; the river is flanked by tree-dotted hills and bluffs; elevation 2000´.

Season, Fees & Phone: Open all year, with limited services in October to May; 14 day limit; Montana Department of Fish, Wildlife & Parks, Region 7 Office, Miles City, ☎(406) 232-0900

Camp Journal: This segment of the river is especially noted for a unique type of angling: snagging for the elusive Yellowstone paddlefish. The paddlefish, which can weigh over 100 pounds, is a throwback to the age of dinosaurs and only inhabits a relatively few miles of streams in this region.

📖 *August 2, 1806*

Musquetors very troublesome this morning. I set out early, river wide and very much divided by islands and sand and mud bars. The bottoms more extensive and contain more timber such as cotton wood, ash, willow &c. The country on the N.W. side rises to a low plain and extends leavel for a great extent. Some high, rugged hills in the forepart of this day on the S.E. side on which I saw the big horns, but could not get near them. Saw emence numbers of elk, buffalow and wolves today. The wolves do catch the elk. I saw 2 wolves in pursuit of a doe elk which I believe they caught; they were very near her when she entered a small wood, in which I expect they caught her, as she did not pass out of the small wood during my remaining in view of it, which was 15 or 20 minits &c.

Passed the enterance of several brooks on each side, a small river 30 yds wide with steep banks on the starbd. side, which I call Ibex River. The river in this day's descent is less rapid, crowded with islands and muddy bars,

and is generally about one mile in width. As the islands and bars frequently hide the enterance of brooks &c. from me as I passed, many of them I have not noticed.

About 8 A.M. this morning, a bear of the large vicious species, being on a sand bar, raised himself up on his hind feet and looked at us as we passed down near the middle of the river. He plunged into the water and swam toward us, either from a disposition to attack or from the scent of the meat which was in the canoes. We shot him with three balls, and he returned to shore badly wounded. In the evening I saw a very large bear take the water above us. I ordered the boat to land on the opposit side with a view to attack him when he came within shot of the shore. When the bear was in a fiew paces of the shore, I shot it in the head. The men hauled her on shore, and it proved to be an old she, which was so old that her tusks had worn smooth, and much the largest female bear I ever saw.

I proceeded on and encamped a little above the enterance of Jos. Fields Creek on starbd. side, in a high bottom covered with low ash and elm. The musquetors excessively troublesome. I have noticed a great proportion of buck elks on this lower part of the river, and but very few above. Those above, which are emencely numerous, are females, generally. Shields killed a deer this morning during the time we were at brackfast. We were very near being detained by the buffalow today, which were crossing the river; we got through the line between 2 gangs.

—*Captain Clark*

🌿 Jos. Fields Creek was named for one of the members of the Expedition who was with Captain Lewis; nowadays it is called, for some uncertain reason, Charbonneau Creek; it enters the Yellowstone from North Dakota, just east of the Montana-North Dakota border. The Yellowstone makes a short sweep into Nor'Dakota just before it merges with the Missouri back inside Montana.

📖 *August 3, 1806*

Last night the musquetors was so troublesome that no one of the party slept half the night. For my part, I did not sleep one hour. Those tormenting insects found their way into my bier [net] and tormented me the whole night. They are not less numerous or troublesome this morning. At 2 miles, passed the enterance of Jo. Field's Creek, immediately above a high bluff which is falling into the river very fast. On the side of this bluff I saw some of the mountain big horn animals. I ascended the hill below the bluff. The musquetors were so numerous that I could not shoot with any certainty, and therefore soon returned to the canoes. I had not proceeded far before I saw a large gang of ewes & yearlins & fawns or lambs of the big horn, and at a distance alone I saw a ram. Landed and sent Labiche to kill the ram, which he did kill and brought him on board. This ram is not near as large as many I have seen. However he is sufficiently large for a sample. I directed Bratten to skin him, with his head, horns & feet to the skin, and save all the bone. I have now the skin & bone of a ram a ewe & a yearlin ram of those big horn animals.

At 8. A. M. I arived at the junction of the Rochejhone with the Missouri, and formed my camp immediately in the point between the two rivers, at which place the party had all encamped the 26th of April 1805. At landing, I observed several elk feeding on the young willows in the point, among which was a large buck elk which I shot & had his flesh dryed in the sun for a store down the river. Had the canoes unloaded and every article exposed to dry & sun. Many of our things were wet, and nearly all the store of meat which had been killed above spoiled. I ordered it to be thrown into the river. Several skins are also spoiled, which is a loss, as they are our principal dependence for clothes to last us to our homes &c.

The distance from the Rocky Mountains at which place I struck the River Rochejhone to it's enterance into the Missouri is 837 miles; 636 miles of this distance I descended in 2 small canoes lashed together, in which I had the following persons. John Shields, George Gibson, William Bratten, W. Labiche, Toust. Shabono, his wife & child, & my man York.

The Rochejhone or Yellow Stone River is large and navigable with but fiew obstructions quite into the Rocky Mountains, and probably to near it's source. The country through which it passes from those mountains to it's junction is generally fertile, rich open plains, the upper portion of which is rolling, and the high hills and hill sides are partially covered with pine and stoney. The middle portion, or from the enterance of Clarks Fork as low as the Buffalow Shoals, the high lands contain some scattering pine on the larbd. side. On the starbd. or S.E. side is some hills thickly supplied with pine. The lower portion of the river but fiew pines are to be seen, the country opens into extencive plains, river widens and

contains more islands and bars of coarse gravel, sand and mud.

The current of this river may be estimated at 4 miles and 1/2 per hour from the Rocky Mts. as low as Clarks Fork, at 3 1/2 Miles per hour from thence as low as the Bighorn, at 3 miles per hour from thence as low as the Tongue River, at 2 3/4 miles per hour from thence as low as Wolf Rapid, and at 2 1/2 miles per hour from thence to it's enterance into the Missouri. The colour of the water differs from that of the Missouri, it being of a yellowish brown, whilst that of the Missouri is of a deep drab colour, containing a greater portion of mud than the Rochejhone.

This delightfull river, from Indian information has it's extreme sources with the North River in the Rocky Mountains on the confines of New Mexico. It also most probably has it's westerly sources connected with those of the Multnomah and those of the main southerly branch of Lewis's River, while it's easterly branches head with those of Clark's River, the Bighorn and River Platte, and may be said to water the middle portion of the Rocky Mountains from N.W to S.E. for several hundred miles. The Indians inform us, that a good road passes up this river to it's extreme source, from whence it is but a short distance to the Spanish settlements. There is also a considerable falls [Yellowstone Falls] on this river within the mountains, but at what distance from it's source we never could learn. Like all other branches of the Missouri which penetrate the Rocky Mountains, all that portion of it lying within those mountains abound in fine beaver and otter, it's streams, also which issuing from the Rocky Mountains and discharging themselves above Clark's Fork inclusive, also furnish an abundance of beaver and otter and possess considerable portions of small timber in their valleys.

To an establishment on this river at Clarks Fork the Shoshones, both within and West of the Rocky Mountains, would willingly resort for the purposes of trade, as they would in a great measure be relived from the fear of being attacked by their enimies, the Blackfoot Indians and Minnetares of Fort de Prarie, which would most probably happen were they to visit any establishment which could be conveniently formed on the Missouri. I have no doubt but the same regard to personal safety would also induce many numerous nations inhabiting the Columbia and Lewis's River West of the mountains to visit this establishment in preference to that at the enterance of Maria's River, particularly during the first years of those western establishments. The Crow Indians, Paunch Indians, Castahanah's and others East of the mountains and South of this place would also visit this establishment; it may therefore be looked to as one of the most important establishments of the western fur trade. At the enterance of Clark's Fork there is a sufficiency of timber to support an establishment, an advantage that no position possesses from thence to the Rocky Mountains.

The banks of the Yellowstone River are bold, not very high, yet are not subject to be overflown, except for a fiew miles immediately below where the river issues from the mountain [at today's Livingston, MT, and it still floods there]. The bed of this river is almost entirely composed of loose pebble, nor is it's bed interrupted by chains of rock except in one place, and that even furnishes no considerable obstruction to it's navigation. As you decend with the river from the mountain, the pebble becomes smaller and the quantity of mud increases untill you reach Tongue River, where the pebble ceases and the sand then increases and predominates near it's mouth.

This river can be navigated to greater advantage in perogues than any other craft, yet it possesses sufficient depth of water for batteauxs even to the mountains; nor is there any of those moving sand bars so formidable to the navigation of many parts of the Missouri. The Bighorn R. and Clark's Fork may be navigated a considerable distance in perogues and canoes. Tongue River is also navigable for canoes a considerable distance.

—*Captain Clark*

📖 *August 4, 1806*

Musquetors excessively troublesome. So much so that the men complained that they could not work at their skins for those troublesome insects. And I find it entirely impossible to hunt in the bottoms, those insects being so numerous and tormenting as to render it impossible for a man to continue in the timbered lands, and our best retreat from those insects is on the sand bars in the river, and even those situations are only clear of them when the wind should happen to blow, which it did today for a fiew hours in the middle of the day. The evenings, nights, and mornings they are almost unendurable, particularly by the party with me, who have no bier [mosquito netting], to keep them off at night, and nothing to screen them but their blankets, which are worn and have many holes.

The torments of those musquetors and the want of a sufficiency of buffalow meat to dry—those animals not to be found in this neighbourhood—induce me to determine to proceed on to a more eligible spot on the Missouri below, at which place the musquetors will be less troublesome and buffalow more plenty. I ordered the canoes to be reloaded with our baggage & dryed meat which had been saved on the Rochejhone, together with the Elk killed at this place.

Wrote a note to Capt. Lewis, informing him of my intentions, and tied it to a pole which I had stuck up in the point. At 5 P.M., set out and proceeded on down to the 2nd point, which appeared to be an eligible situation for my purpose. On this point the musquetors were so abundant that we were tormented much worse than at the 1st point. The child of Shabono has been so much bitten by the musquetors that his face is much puffed up and swelled. I encamped on this extensive sand bar which is on the N.W. side.

—*Captain Clark*

📖 *August 5, 1805*

The musquetors were so troublesome to the men last night that they slept but very little. Indeed, they were excessively troublesome to me. My musquetor bier has a number of small holes worn, through which they pass in. I set out at an early hour, intending to proceed to some other situation. I had not proceeded on far before I saw a ram of the big horn animal near the top of a larbd. bluff. I ascended the hill with a view to kill the ram. The musquetors were so numerous that I could not keep them off my gun long enough to take sight, and by that means missed.

At 10 a.m. the wind rose with a gentle breeze from the N.W., which in some measure thinned the misquetors. I landed on a sand bar from the South point intending to form a camp at this place and continue untill Capt. Lewis should arive, and killed two buck elks and a deer, the best of their flesh & fat I had saved. Had all the dryed meat & fat put out to sun and continued at this place untill late in the evening. Finding that there were no buffalow or fresh sign, I determined to proceed on. Accordingly, set out at 4 P.M. and proceeded on but a fiew miles where I saw a bear of the white species walking on a sand bar. I with one man went on the sand bear and killed the bear, which proved to be a female very large and fat. Much the fattest animal we have killed on the rout, as this bear had got into the river before we killed her. I had her toed across to the South side under a high bluff where we formed a camp, had the bear skinned and fleeced. Our situation was exposed to a light breeze of wind, which continued all the forepart of the night from the S W. and blew away the misquetors.

—Captain Clark

📖 *August 6, 1806*

I rose very wet. About 11 P.M. last night the wind become very hard for a fiew minits, succeeded by sharp lightning and hard claps of thunder, and rained for about 2 hours very hard, after which it continued cloudy the ballance of the night. As we were about setting out, a female big horn animal came on the bluff immediately above us and looked down. I directed Labiche to shoot it, which he did. After skinning this animal, we set out and proceeded on to a sand bar on the S.W. side below the enterance of White Earth River, where I landed and had the meat, skins and bedding all put out to dry. Wind hard from the N.W. I halted on the N.W. side of this river in the bend above the White Earth River, where I saw where the Indians had been digging a root which they eate and use in soup, not more than 7 or 8 days past.

This morning a very large bear of the white species discovered us floating in the water and taking us, as I presume, to be buffalow, immediately plunged into the river and pursued us. I directed the men to be still. This animal came within about 40 yards of us and tacked about. We all fired into him without killing him, and the wind so high that we could not pursue him, by which means he made his escape to the shore, badly wounded. I have observed buffalow floating down, which I suppose must have been drowned in crossing above. More or less of those animals drown or mire in passing this river. I observed several floating buffalow on the River Rochejhone immediately below where large gangs had crossed.

The wind blew hard all the after part of the day. I derected the men to dress their skins, except one which I took with me, and walked. through the bottom to the foot of the hills. I killed five deer and the man with me killed 2. Four others were killed in the course of the day by the party; only 2 of those deer were fat, owing, as I suppose, to the musquetors which are so numerous and troublesome to them that they cannot feed, except under the torments of millions of those musquetors.

—Captain Clark

📖 *August 7, 1806*

Some hard rain this morning after daylight, which wet us all. I formed a sort of camp and delayed untill 11 A.M., when it stopped raining for a short time. I directed every thing put on board and proceeded on down. The rain continued at intervals all day, tho' not hard in the evening. Saw a bear on the bank but could not get a shot at it. At 6 P.M. I landed on a sand bar on the South side and camped. Soon after we landed the wind blew very hard for about 2 hours, when it lulled a little. The air was exceedingly clear and cold and not a misquetor to be seen, which is a joyfull circumstance to the party.

—Captain Clark

📖 *August 8, 1806*

A cool, windy morning. I derected Shields and Gibson to turn out and hunt this morning. At 8 A.M., Sergt. N. Pryor, Shannon, Hall, and Windsor came down the river in two canoes made of buffalow skins. Sergt. Pryor informed me that the second night after he parted with me on the River Rochejhone, he arived about 4 P.M. on the banks of a large creek which contained no running water. He halted to let the horses graize, during which time a heavy shower of rain raised the creek so high that several horses which had straggled across the channel of this creek was obliged to swim back. Here he determined to continue all night, it being in good food for the horses. In the morning he could see no horses.

In looking about their camp, they discovered several tracks within 100 paces of their camp, which they pursued. Found where the Indians had caught and driven off all the horses. They pursued on five miles. The Indians there divided into two parties. They continued in pursuit of the largest party five miles further. Finding that there was not the smallest chance of overtaking them, they returned to their camp and packed up their baggage on their backs, and steered a N.E. course to the River Rochejhone, which they struck at Pompy's Tower.

There they killed a buffalow bull and made a canoe in the form and shape of the Mandans and Ricares (the form of a basin), and made in the following manner. Viz: 2 sticks of 1 1/4 inch diameter is tied together so as to form a round hoop of the size you wish the canoe, or as large as the skin will allow to cover; two of those hoops are made, one for the top or brim and the other for the bottom, the depth you wish the canoe; then sticks of the same size are crossed at right angles and fastened with a thong to each hoop, and also where each stick crosses each other. Then the skin, when green, is drawn tight over this frame and fastened with thongs to the brim or outer hoop so as to form a perfect basin. One of those canoes will carry 6 or 8 men and their loads. Those two canoes are nearly the same size, 7 feet 3 inches diameter & 16 inches deep, 15 ribs or cross sticks in each. Sergt. Pryor informs me that the cause of his building two canoes was for fear of one's meeting with some accident in passing down the Rochejhone River, entirely unknown to either of them, by which means they might loose their guns and ammunition and be left entirely destitute of the means of procureing food. He informed me that they passed through the worst parts of the rapids & shoals in the river without taking a drop of water, and waves raised from the hardest winds does not effect them.

On the night of the 26th, the night after the horses had been stolen, a wolf bit Sergt. Pryor through his hand when asleep, and this animal was so vicious as to make an attempt to seize Windsor, when Shannon fortunately shot him. Sergt. Pryor's hand has nearly recovered. The country through which Sergt. Pryor passed after he parted with me is a broken, open country. He passed one small river, which I have called Pryor's River, which rises in a mountain to the South of Pompy's Tower.

The note I left on a pole at the mouth of the River Rochejhone Sergt. Pryor, concluding that Capt. Lewis had passed, took the note and brought it with him. Capt. Lewis, I expect, will be certain of my passing by the sign which I have made, and the encampment immediately in the point.

Sergt. Pryor, being anxious to overtake me, set out some time before day this morning, and forgot his saddlebags, which contain his papers, &c. I sent Bratten back with him in search of them.

I also sent Shannon over to hunt the bottom on the opposit side. Shields and Gibson returned at 10 A.M. with the skins and part of the flesh of three deer which they had killed in this bottom. I directed them to take one of the skin canoes and proceed down to the next bottom and wait untill my arrival, which will be this evening if Sergt. Pryor returns in time. My object is to procure as many skins as possible for the purpose of purchasing corn and beans of the Mandans. As we have now no article of merchindize nor horses to purchase with, our only resort is skins, which those people were very fond of the winter we were stationed near them.

After dark, Sergt. Pryor returned with his saddlebags, &c. They were much further up than he expected.

—*Captain Clark*

📖 *August 9, 1806*

A heavy dew this morning. Loaded the Canoes and proceeded on down about 6 miles and landed at the camp of the 2 hunters, Shields and Gibson, whom I had sent down to hunt last evening; they had killed five deer, two of which were in good order, which they brought in. Here I took brackfast and proceeded on a fiew miles and I walked on shore across a point of near 10 miles in extent in this bottom, which was mostly open. I saw some fiew deer and elk. I killed 3 of the deer, which were meager; the elk appeared fat. I did not kill any of them, as the distance to the river was too great for the men to carry the meat. At the lower part of this bottom a large creek of running water, 25 yds. Wide, falls in, which meanders through an open, rolling plain of great extent. In the low bottoms of this creek I observed some timber, such as cotton wood, ash & elm.

On my arrival at the lower part of the bottom, found that the canoes had been in waiting for me nearly two hours. The squar brought me a large and well flavoured goose berry of a rich crimson colour, and deep purple berry of the large cherry of the currant species which is common on this river as low as the Mandans; the engages call it the Indian currant.

I landed opposit to a high plain on the S.E. side late in the evening and walked in a grove of timber, where I met with an elk, which I killed. This elk was the largest buck I ever saw and the fattest animal which have been killed on the rout. I had the flesh and fat of this elk brought to camp and cut thin, ready to dry. The hunters killed nothing this evening.

—*Captain Clark*

📖 *August 10, 1806*

Had the flesh of the elk hung on poles to dry, and sent out the the hunters. Wind blew hard from the East all day. In the after part of the day it was cloudy & a fiew drops of rain. I finished a copy of my sketches of the River Rochejhone. Shields killed a black tail deer & an antelope. The other hunters killed nothing. Deer are very scarce on this part of the river.

I found a species of cherry in the bottom, the shrub or bush which are different from any which I have ever seen and not very abundant, even in this small tract of country to which it seems to be confined. The stem is compound erect and subdivided or branching, without any regular order. It rises to the height of 8 or 10 feet, seldom putting out more than one stem from the same root, not growing in copse as the choke cherry does. The bark is smooth and of a dark brown colour. The leaf is petalate, oval, acutely pointed at it's apex, from 1 and a 1/4 to 1 and a 1/2 inch in length and from a half to 3/4 of an inch in width, finely or minutely serrate, pale green and free from bubessance. The fruit is a globular berry about the size of a buck shot, of a fine scarlet red; like the cherries cultivated in the U. States, each is supported by a separate cylindric, flexible branch peduncle, which issues from the extremities of the boughs. The peduncle of this cherry swells as it approaches the fruit, being largest at the point of insertion. The pulp of this fruit is of an agreeable acid flavour and is now ripe. The stile and stigma are permanent. I have never seen it in bloom. It is found on the high, stiff lands or hill sides. The men dug a great parcel of the root which the nativs call *hankee* and the engages the breadroot or white apple, which they boiled and made use of with their meat. This is a large insipid root and very tasteless. The nativs use this root after it is dry and pounded in their soup.

—*Captain Clark*

📖 *August 11, 1806*

I set out early this morning. At 10 A.M. landed on a sand bar and brackfasted. During my delay at this place, which was 2 hours, had the elk meat exposed to the sun.

At Meridian I set out and had not proceeded more than 2 miles before I observed a canoe near the shore. I directed the canoes to land. Here I found two men from the Illinois, Jos. Dixon and Hancock. Those men are on a trapping expedition up the River Rochejhone. They inform me that they left the Illinois in the summer of 1804. The last winter they spent with the Tetons, in company with Mr. Coartong, who brought up goods to trade. The Tetons robbed him of the greater part of the goods and wounded this Dixon in the leg with a hard wad. The Tetons gave Mr. Coartong some fiew robes for the articles they took from him.

Those men further informed me that they met the boat and party we sent down from Fort Mandan, near the Kanzas River, on board of which was a Chief of the Ricares; that he met the Yankton Chiefs with Mr. Dorion, McClellen, and several other traders on their way down; that the Mandans and Minnetares were at war with the Ricaras and had killed two of the latter. The Assinniboins were also at war with the Mandans &c., and had prohibited the N.W. traders from coming to the Missouri to trade. They have latterly killed one trader near the Mouse River and are now in wait for Mr. McKenzie, one of the clerks who have been for a long time with Minnitares. Those difficulties, if true, will I fear be a bar to our expectations of having the Mandan, Minnetare & Ricara Chiefs to accompany us to the U. States. Tho' we shall endeavour to bring about a peace between Mandans, Minnetares & Ricaras and prevail on some of their Cheifs to accompany us to the U. States.

Proceeded on to a point on the S.W. side nearly opposit the enterance of Goat Pen Creek and encamped. Found the musquetors excessively troublesome

—*Captain Clark*

📖 *August 12, 1806*

I set out early this morning and had not proceeded on far before Shannon discovered he had lost his tomahawk. I directed him to land his skin canoe and go back to our camp of last night in search of it, and proceeded on myself with the two wood and one skin canoe to a large bottom on the N.E side above the head of an island and landed to take brackfast, as well as to delay untill Shannon & Gibson should arive. Sent out Shields & Labiche to hunt deer in the bottom. At 2 P.M. Shannon and Gibson arived, having found the tomahawk at our camp; they killed 3 elk &c. One of the canoes of buffalow skin by accident got a hole pierced in her of about 6 inches diameter. I directed two of the men to patch the canoe with a piece of elk skin over the hole, which they did and it proved all sufficient, after which the canoe did not leak one drop. The two hunters returned without haveing killed anything.

At Meridian, Capt. Lewis hove in sight with the party which went by way of the Missouri, as well as that which accompanied him from Travellers Rest on Clarks River. I was allarmed, on the landing of the canoes, to be informed that Capt. Lewis was wounded by an accident. I found him lying in the perogue. He informed me that his wound was slight and would be well in 20 or 30 days. This information relieved me very much. I examined the wound and found it a very bad flesh wound. The ball had passed through the fleshy part of his left thigh, below the hipbone, and cut the cheek of the right buttock for three inches in length, and the depth of the ball. Capt. L. informed me the accident happened the day before, by one of the men, Peter Crusat, mistaking him in the thick bushes to be an elk.

Capt. Lewis, with this Crusat and several other men, were out in the bottom shooting of elk, and had scattered in a thick part of the woods in persute of the elk. Crusat, seeing Capt L. passing through the bushes and taking him to be an elk from the colour of his clothes, which were of leather and very nearly that of the elk, fired, and unfortunately, the ball passed through the thigh as aforesaid. Capt. Lewis, thinking it Indians who had shot him, hobbled to the canoes as fast as possible and was followed by Crusat, the mistake was then discovered. This Crusat is near sighted and has the use of but one eye; he is an attentive, industrious man and one whom we both have placed the greatest confidence in during the whole rout.

At 2 P.M. Shannon & Gibson arived in the skin canoe with the skins and the greater part of the flesh of 3 elk, which they had killed a fiew miles above. The two men, Dixon & Hancock, the two men we had met above, came down intending to proceed on down with us to the Mandans.

At 3 P.M. we proceded on all together after having left the 2 leather canoes on the bank. A little below the enterance of Shabonos Creek, we came to on a large sand point from the S.E. side and encamped. The wind blew very hard from the S.W. and some rain. I washed Capt. L's. wound which has become sore and somewhat painfull to him.

—Captain Clark

🔥 An observant reader may notice that Clark's spelling improved in his Journal entries from about midway up the Columbia River. For the most part, since then he penned "very" and "Missouri", rather than "verry" and "Missourie", plus a few other words about half of the time. Probably during the winter at Fort Clatsop, either Lewis brought it to his attention, or he noticed the 'correct' spellings when reading Lewis's journal. Clark was the first to admit that 'rithmatic, rather than readin' and writin', was the strongest of his "3 R's".

Sacagawea and her son, Jean Baptiste ("Pompy"), North Dakota State Capitol, Bismarck

Homeward *1806*

▲ *Down the Missouri to the Land of the Mandans*

📖 *August 13, 1806*

We set out at sunrise and proceeded on very well with a stiff breeze astern the greater part of the day. Passed the Little Missouri River at 8 A.M. and at sunset encamped on the N.E. side, having come, by the assistance of the winds, the current and our oars, 86 miles.

—*Captain Clark*

🔺 North Dakota 147

LITTLE MISSOURI
Little Missouri State Park

Location: Western North Dakota north of Dickinson.

Access: From North Dakota State Highway 22 at a point 17 miles north of Kildeer and 3 miles south of the Little Missouri River Bridge, travel east on a county road for 6 miles to the park.

Camping Facilities: 25 campsites, including some with electrical hookups; sites are small+, with nominal separation; parking pads are gravel, mostly medium-length straight-ins; ample space for tents; fire rings; b-y-o firewood; water at central faucets; vault facilities; gravel driveways; complete supplies and services are available in Dickinson.

Day Use Facilities: Medium-sized picnic area; small group picnic shelters; drinking water; vault facilities; medium-sized parking area.

Activities & Attractions: Hiking and equestrian trails; horse-handling facilities; horse rentals (concession).

Natural Features: Located on rolling plains along the south bank of the Little Missouri River; grassy bluffs and colorful badlands border the river; park area is 5749 acres; elevation 2000´.

Season, Fees & Phone: Available all year, subject to weather and road conditions, with limited services October to May; 14 day camping limit; park entry $5.00, camping $5.00 for a standard site, $8.00 for a hookup site; park office ☎(701) 487-3315.

Camp Journal: Plenty of elbow room here. Little Missouri provides a different kind of wilderness experience than is found mostly in other places in the West. With more than 75 miles of trails you could walk for many hours without passing another traveler.

📖 *August 14, 1806*

Set out at sunrise and proceeded on. When we were opposit the Minnetares grand village, we saw a number of the nativs viewing us. We directed the blunderbusses be fired several times. Soon after, we came to at a crowd of the nativs on the bank opposit the village of the Shoe Indians, or Ma-har-has [Mahas], at which place I saw the principal Chief of the little village of the Minnetares & the principal Chief of the Ma-har-has. Those people were extreemly pleased to see us. The Chief of the little village of the Minnetares cried most immoderately. I enquired the cause and was informed it was for the loss of his son, who had been killed latterly by the Blackfoot Indians.

After a delay of a few minits, I proceeded on to the Black Cats village on the N.E. side of the Missouri, where I intended to encamp, but the sand blew in such a manner that we determined not to continue on that side, but return to the side we had left. Here we were visited by all inhabitants of this village who appeared equally as well pleased to see us as those above.

I walked up to the Black Cats village and smoked a pipe with him. This village, I discovered, had been rebuilt since I left and much smnaller than it was; enquiring as to the cause, was informed that a quarrel had taken place and a number of lodges had been removed to the opposit side.

I had, as soon as I landed, dispatched Charbono to the Minnetares, inviting the Chiefs to visit us, & Drewyer down to the lower village of the Mandans to ask Mr. Jessomme to come and interpret for us.

Mr. Jessomme arived and I spoke to the Chiefs of the villages, informing them that we spoke to them as we had done when we were with them last, and we now repeated our invitation to the principal Chiefs of all the villages to accompany us to the U. States &c.&c.

The Black Cat, Chief of the Mandans, spoke and informed me that he wished to visit the United States and his Great Father, but was afraid of the Sioux, who were yet at war with them and had killed several of their men since we had left them, and were on the river below and would certainly kill him if he attempted to go down.

I endeavoured to do away with his objections by informing him that we would not suffer those Indians to hurt any of our red children who should think proper to accompany us, and on their return they would be equally protected, and their presents, which would be very liberal, with themselves, conveyed to their own country at the expense of the U. States &c. &c. The Chief of the Mah-har-has told me if I would send with him he would let me have some corn. I directed Sergt Gass & 2 men to accompanyhim to his village; they soon returned loaded with corn.

—*Captain Clark*

🔥 In a Journal entry written the following day, Clark related additional details regarding the meeting with the chiefs on August 14th:

📖 *August 15, 1806*

After assembling the Chiefs and smokeing one pipe, I informed them that I still spoke the same words which we had spoken to them when we first arived in their country in the fall of 1804. We then envited them to visit their Great Father, the President of the U. States, and to hear his own counsels and receive his gifts from his own hands, as also to see the population of a government which can, at their pleasure, protect and secure you from all your enemies and chastise all those who will shut their ears to his counsels. We now offer to take you at the expense of our government and send you back to your country again with a considerable present in merchandize which you will receive of your Great Father.

The great Chief of the Minnetares spoke; he said he wished to go down and see his Great Father very much, but that the Sioux were in the road and would most certainly kill him or any others who should go down. They were bad people and would not listen to any thing

which was told them. When he saw us last we told him that we had made peace with all the nations below. Since that time the Sioux had killed 8 of their people and stole a number of their horses. He said that he had opened his ears and followed our councils; he had made peace with the Chyennes and Rocky Mountains Indians, and respected the same objections as mentioned. If the Sioux were at peace with them and could be depended on, he, as also other Chiefs of the villages, would be glad to go and see their Great Father; but as they were all afraid of the Sioux, they should not go down &c.

The Black Cat, Chief of the Mandans village on the North side of the Missouri, sent over and requested me to go over to his village. After taking a smoke, he informed me that as the Sioux were very troublesome and the road to his Great Father dangerous, none of the village would go down with us.

I told the Chiefs and warriors of the village who were then present that we were anxious that some of the village should go and see their Great Father and hear his good words & receive his bountifull gifts &c., and told them to pitch on some man on which they could rely on and send him to see their Great Father; they made the same objections which the Chief had done before. A young man offered to go down, and they all agreed for him to go down. The character of this young man I knew as a bad one and made an objection as to his age and character. At this time Gibson, who was with me, informed me that this young man had stole his knife and had it then in his possession; this I informed the Chief and directed him to give up the knife. He delivered the knife with a very faint apology for his having it in his possession.

I then reproached those people for wishing to send such a man to see and hear the words of so great a man as their Great Father; they hung their heads and said nothing for some time when the Chief spoke and said that they were afraid to send any one for fear of their being killed by the Sioux.

Being informed by one of our interpreters that the 2nd Chief of the Mandans, commonly called the Little Crow, intended to accompany us down, I took Chabono and walked to the village to see this Chief and talk with him on the subject. He told me he had determined to go down, but wished to have a council first with his people, which would be in the after part of the day.

Colter, one of our men, expressed a desire to join some trappers (the two Illinois men we met, & who now came down to us), who offered to become sharers with him and furnish traps &c. The offer was a very advantageous one to him, his services could be dispensed with from this place down; and as we were disposed to be of service to any one of our party who had performed their duty as well as Colter had done, we agreed to allow him the privilege, provided no one of the party would ask or expect a similar permission, to which they all agreed, that they wished Colter every success, and that as we did not wish any of them to separate untill we should arive at St. Louis, they would not apply or expect it &c.

A great number of the nativs of the different villages came to view us and exchange robes with our men for their skins. We gave John Colter some small articles which we did not want and some powder and lead. The party also gave him several articles which will be usefull to him on his expedition.

This evening Chabono informed me that our back was scarcely turned before a war party from the two Minnetare villages followed on and attacked and killed the Snake Indians whome we had seen, and in the engagement between them and the Snake Indians they had lost two men, one of which was the son of the principal Chief of the little village of the Minnetares. That they had also went to war from the Minnetares and killed two Ricaras. He further informed me that a misunderstanding had taken place between the Mandans & Minnetares and had very nearly come to blows about a woman; the Minnetares at length presented a pipe and a reconcilliation took place between them.

—*Captain Clark*

📖 *August 16, 1806*

As our swivel gun could no longer be servicable to us, as it could not be fired on board the largest perogue, we concluded to make a present of it to the Great Chief of the Minnetares (the One Eye), with a view to ingratiate him more strongly in our favour. I had the swivel gun charged and collected the Chiefs in a circle around it and addressed them with great ceremoney. Told them I had listened with much attention to what the One Eye had said yesterday and believed that he was sincere & spoke from his heart. I reproached them very severely for not attending to what had been said to them by us in council in the fall of 1804 and at different

times in the winter of 1804 & 5, and told them our backs were scarcely turned before a party followed and killed the pore defenceless Snake Indians whome we had taken by the hand & told them not to be afraid, that you would never them strike again &c. I also mentioned the Ricaras &c.

The little cheery old Chief of the Minnetares spoke as follows, viz: "Father, we wish to go down with you to see our Great Father, but we know the nations below and are afraid of the Sioux, who will be on the river and will kill us on our return home. The Sioux has stolen our horses and killed 8 of our men since you left us, and the Ricaras have also struck us. We stayed at home and listened to what you have told us. We at length went to war against the Sioux and met with Ricaras and killed two of them; they were on their way to strike us. We will attend to your word and not hurt any people. All shall be welcome and we shall do as you direct." The One Eye said his ears would always be open to the word of his Great Father and shut against bad council &c.

I then with a good deal of ceremony made a present of the swivel to the One Eye Chief, and told him when he fired this gun to remember the words of his Great Father which we had given him. After the council was over the gun was fired & delivered, the Chief appeared to be much pleased and conveyed it immediately to his village &c. We settled with and discharged Colter. We sent for Mr. Jessomme and told him to use his influence to prevail on one of the Chiefs to accompany us, and we would employ him. He informed us soon after that the Big White Chief would go if we would take his wife & son & Jessommes wife & 2 children, which we were obliged to agree to do

—*Captain Clark*

⛺ *Land of the Mandans to the River Quicurre*

📖 *August 17, 1806*

Settled with Touissant Chabono for his services as an enterpreter, the price of a horse and lodge purchased of him for public service, in all amounting to $500 33 1/2 cents. Directed two of the largest of the canoes be fastened together with poles tied across them so as to make them steady for the purpose of conveying the Indians and enterpreter and their families. We were visited by all the principal Chiefs of the Minnetares to take their leave of us.

At 2 oClock we left our encampment, after taking leave of Colter, who also set out up the river in company with Messrs. Dickson & Hancock. We also took our leave of T. Chabono, his Snake Indian wife and their child who had accompanied us on our rout to the Pacific Ocean in the capacity of interpreter and interpretess. T. Charbono wished much to accompany us in the said capacity if we could have prevailed upon the Minnetare Chiefs to decend the river with us to the U. States; but as none of those Chiefs of whose language he was conversant would accompany us, his services were no longer of use to the U. States, and he was therefore discharged and paid up. We offered to convey him down to the Illinois if he chose to go; he declined proceeding on at present, observing that he had no acquaintance or prospects of makeing a living below, and must continue to live in the way that he had done. I offered to take his little son, a beautifull promising child who is 19 months old to which they, both himself & wife, were willing, provided the child had been weaned. They observed that in one year the boy would be sufficiently old to leave his mother & he would then take him to me if I would be so friendly as to raise the child for him in such a manner as I thought proper, to which I agreed &c.

We dropped down to the Big White Chiefs Mandan village, 1/2 a mile below on the South side. All the Indians proceeded on down by land. And I walked to the lodge of the Chief whome I found surrounded by his friends; the men were setting in a circle smoking and the womin crying. He sent his baggage with his wife & son, with the interpreter Jessomme & his wife and 2 children, to the canoes provided for them. After smoking one pipe, and distributing some powder & lead which we had given him, he informed me that he was ready, and we were accompanied to the canoes by all the village. Maney of them cried out aloud.

As I was about to shake hands with the Grand Chiefs of all the villages there assembled, they requested me to set one minit longer with them, which I readily agreed to, and directed a pipe to be lit. The Chiefs informed that when we first came to their country they did not believe all we said, but they were now convinced that everything we had told them were true; that they should keep in memory every thing which we had said to them, and strictly attend to our advice, that their young

men should stay at home and should not go again to war against any nation; that if any attacked them they should defend themselves; that we might depend on what they said, and requested us to inform their Great Father. They also requested me to tell the Ricaras to come and see them, not to be afraid; that no harm should be done them; that they were anxious to be in peace with them. The Sioux, they said, they had no dependence in and should kill them whenever they came into their country to do them harm &c. I told them that we had always told them to defend themselves, but not to strike those nations we had taken by the hand, the Sioux with whome they were at war we had never seen; on our return we should inform their Great Father of their conduct towards his faithfull red children and he would take such steps as will bring about a lasting peace between them and his faithfull red children. I informed them that we should inform the Ricaras what they had requested &c. The Grand Chief of the Minnetares said that the Great Cheif who was going down with us to see their Great Father was as well as if he went also; and on his return he would be fully informed of the words of his Great Father, and requested us to take care of this Great Chief.

We then saluted them with a gun and set out and proceeded on to Fort Mandan, where I landed and went to view the old works; the houses, except one in the rear bastion, was burnt by accident; some picquits were standing in front next to the river.

—*Captain Clark*

⚕ North Dakota 148 ⚐

SAGLE
Cross Ranch State Park

Location: Central North Dakota northwest of Bismarck.

Access: From North Dakota State Highway 200A at the west edge of the hamlet of Hensler (5 miles west of the junction of Highway 200A & U.S. 83 in Washburn), travel south on an (unnamed) paved county road for 5.5 miles; turn east (left, signed for the park) onto another paved local road for 4.5 miles to a 'T' intersection; turn south (right) onto another local road and go a few yards, then swing east (left) and go east for a few yards, then southerly (parallel to the paved road) for a final 0.4 mile to the campground.

Alternate Access: From North Dakota State Highway 25 at a point 10 miles east of the community of Center and 19 miles north of I-94 Exit 47 just west of Mandan, head north on an unnamed paved local road for 5 miles to the signed park turnoff, and continue as above.

Camping Facilities: 15 campsites, including a half dozen walk-in tent sites; ('open' camping is available along the riverside beach); sites are smallish, basically level, with nominal to good separation; parking pads are gravel, short + straight-ins; medium to large areas for tents; fireplaces; b-y-o firewood; water at a central faucet; vault facilities; gravel driveway; limited + to adequate supplies and services are available in Washburn, 5 miles east.

Missouri River, Cross Ranch State Park

Day Use Facilities: Small picnic area; shelter; drinking water; vault facilities; small parking area.

Activities & Attractions: Visitor center; 14 miles of hiking trails; cross-country ski trails; naturalist-guided nature programs in summer; fishing, said to be fairly good, for small walleye, bass, northerns, cats; boat ramp; Centennial Buffalo Herd; annual Bluegrass Festival on Labor Day weekend.

Natural Features: Located on a flat along the west bank of the Missouri River; most sites are fairly well sheltered by hardwoods; bordered by sizeable meadows and prairie; elevation 1800´.

Season, Fees & Phone: Open all year, with limited services October to May; 14 day camping limit; park entry $5.00, camping $5.00; park office ☎(701) 794-3731.

Camp Journal: Very limited turnaround room at the end of the driveway, so this area is signed for "tent camping". But it is generally suitable for pickup and van campers as well, (too tight for trailers or mo'homes). The walk-down tent sites are kinda nice and cozy. The river views

here may not be quite as nice as those in the park's main campground (see *Volume 1*), but these sites are a little closer to the water's edge. The beach camp area is *very* close to the water's edge.

The Corps, with their new guests, headed downstream, passing the Heart River (near today's cities of Mandan-Bismarck) on August 18th.

⚑ North Dakota 149 ♿

FORT ABRAHAM LINCOLN
Fort Abraham Lincoln State Park

Location: Central North Dakota south of Mandan.

Access: From the intersection of Main Street (Business Route I-94) & 6th Avenue SE (North Dakota State Highway 1806) in midtown Mandan, turn south onto ND 1806 and travel 5.6 miles (0.35 mile past the park visitor center) to milepost 64 +.95; turn east (left), then swing north and proceed 0.2 mile to the campground. (Note: *Probably* the easiest access from Interstate 94 is Exit 33 at the *east* end of Mandan, then west for 0.7 mile onto Main Street; avoid the nooner and afternoon rush hours, and watch for the signs. Good Luck!)

Camping Facilities: 90 campsites, including about half with electrical hookups; sites are medium-sized, level, with nominal to fair separation; parking pads are long, gravel pull-throughs; large tent areas; fire rings; firewood is usually for sale, or b-y-o; water at several faucets; restrooms with showers; holding tank disposal station; paved driveways; complete supplies and services are available in Mandan/Bismarck.

Day Use Facilities: Large picnic area; drinking water; restrooms; large picnic area.

Activities & Attractions: Restored and reconstructed military post and Indian village; interpretive trails; museum; nature and historical programs; 17-mile Roughrider Trail (designated National Recreation Trail); x-c skiing; playground.

Natural Features: Located on a densely wooded flat at the confluence of the Heart and Missouri Rivers; elevation 1700´.

Season, Fees & Phone: Open all year, with limited services October to May; park entry $5.00, camping $8.00 for a standard site, $14.00 for a hookup site; reservations accepted, contact the park office ☎(701) 663-9571.

Camp Journal: The Seventh Cavalry, under General George Custer, departed from Fort Abraham Lincoln on its ill-fated expedition to thwart the forces of Crazy Horse and Sitting Bull at the Little Bighorn. The Cavalry and the Indians have finally come to compatible terms in this thousand-acre park. After viewing the great river's valley from on top of the park's bluffs, it will become apparent to you why the people of the frontier called it "The Wide Missouri".

📖 *August 19, 1806*

Capt. Lewis's wounds are healing very fast; I am much in hope of his being able to walk in 8 or 10 days. The wind rose and became very strong from the S.E., and a great appearance of rain. Jessomme, the interpreter, let me have a piece of a lodge, and the squars pitched or stretched it over some sticks; under this piece of leather I slept dry; it is the only covering which I have had sufficient to keep off the rain since I left the Columbia. It began to rain moderately soon after night.

—*Captain Clark*

🍂 They passed the mouth of the Cannon Ball River in south central North Dakota on August 20th, continuing homeward without incident.

📖 *August 21, 1806*

At 8 A.M. met three Frenchmen coming up; they proved to be three men from the Ricaras, two of them Reeves & Greinyea, wintered with us at the Mandans in 1804. We came to, those men informed us that they were on their way to the Mandans, and intended to go down to the Illinois this fall. One of them, quite a young lad, requested a passage down to the Illinois; we consented and he got into a canoe to ply an oar. Those men informed us that 700 Sioux had passed the Ricaras on their way to war with the Mandans & Minnetares, and that their encampment where the squars and children were was some place near the Big Bend of this river below. They also informed us that no trader had arived at the Ricaras this season, and that they were informed that the Ricara Chief who went to the United States last spring was a year, died on his return at some place near the Sioux River &c. Those men had nether powder nor lead. We gave them a horn of powder and some balls and after a delay of an hour we parted from them.

At half past 11 A.M. we arived in view of the upper Ricara villages, a great number of womin collecting wood on the banks; we saluted the village with four guns and they returned the salute by firing several guns in the village. I observed several very white lodges on the hill above the town, which the Ricaras from the shore informed me were Chyennes who had just arived. We landed opposit to the 2nd village and were met by the most of the men, women and children of each village, as also the Chyennes; they all appeared anxious to take us by the hand and much rejoiced to see us return. I was saluted by the two great Chiefs, whome we had made or given medals to as we assended this river in 1804.

I set myself down on the side of the bank and the Chiefs & brave men of the Ricaras & Chyennes formed a circle around me. After taking a smoke of Mandan tobacco, which the Big White Chief who was seated on my left hand furnished, I informed them, as I had before informed the Mandans & Minnetares, where we had been, what we had done and said to the different nations in their favour, and envited some of their chiefs to accompany us down and see their Great Father and receive from his own mouth his good councils and from his own hands his bountifull gifts &c., telling pretty much the same which I had told the Mandans and Minnetares. I told them not to be afraid of any nation below, that none would hurt them &c.

I also told the Ricaras that I was very sorry to hear that they were not on friendly terms with their neighbours the Mandans & Minnetares, and had not listened to what we had said to them but had suffered their young men to join the Sioux who had killed 8 Mandans &c. That their young men had stolen the horses of the Minnetares; in retaliation for those injuries, the Mandans & Minnetares had sent out a war party and killed 2 Ricaras. How could they expect other nations would be at peace with them when they themselves would not listen to what their Great Father had told them?

I further informed them that the Mandans & Minnetares had opened their ears to what we had said to them, but had stayed at home untill they were struck; that they were still disposed to be friendly and on good terms with the Ricaras; they then saw the Great Chief of the Mandans by my side who was on his way to see his Great Father, and was directed by his Nation & the Minnetares & Maharhas, to smoke in the pipe of peace with you and to tell you not to be afraid to go to their towns, or take the birds in the plains, that their ears were open to our councils and no harm should be done to a Ricara.

The sun being very hot, the Chyenne Chief invited us to his lodge, which was pitched in the plain at no great distance from the river. I accepted the invitation and accompanied him to his lodge, which was new and much larger than any which I have seen. It was made of 20 dressed buffalow skins in the same form of the Sioux and lodges of other nations of this quarter. About this lodge was 20 others, several of them nearly the same size. I enquired for the ballance of the Nation and was informed that they were near at hand and would arive on tomorrow and, when all together, amounted to 120 lodges.

After smokeing, I gave a medal of the small size to the Chyenne Chief &c., which appeared to allarm him; he had a robe and a fleece of fat buffalow meat brought and gave me with the medal back and informed me that he knew that the white people were all medicine and that he was afraid of the medal or any thing that white people gave to them. I had previously explained the cause of my giving him the medal & flag, and again told him the use of the medal and the cause of my giving it to him, and again put it about his neck, delivering him up his present of a robe & meat, informing him that this was the medicine which his Great Father directed me to deliver to all the great chiefs who listened to his word and followed his councils; that he had done so and I should leave the medal with him as a token of his sincerity &c. He doubled the quantity of meat, and received the medal in the evening.

The Great Chief requested that I would walk to his house which I did; he gave me about 2 carrots of tobacco, 2 beaver skins and a trencher of boiled corn & beans to eate (as it is the custom of all the nations on the Missouri to give something to every white man who enters their lodge, something to eate). This Chief informed me that none of his chiefs wished to go down with us; they all wished to see the Chief who went down return first, that the Chyennes were a wild people and were afraid to go. That they should all listen to what I had said. The interpreter informed me that the chiefs of those villages had no intention of going down. One the cheifs of the village on the island talked of going down.

I returned to the boat, where I found the principal Chief of the lower village, who had cut part of his hairand disfigured himself in such a manner that I did not know him; he informed me the Sioux had killed his nephew and that he was in tears for him &c.

We determined to proceed down to the island, and accordingly took the Chief on board and proceeded on down to the island village, at which place we arived a little before dark and were met as before by nearly every individual of the village. The one arm 2nd Cheif of this village, whome we had expected to accompany us down, spoke to the Mandan Cheif in a loud and threatening tone, which caused me to be somewhat allarmed for the safety of that Chief. I informed the Ricaras of this village that the Mandans had opened their ears to enfold our councils; that this Cheif was on his way to see their Great Father, the P. of U. S., and was under our protection; that if any injury was done to him by any nation, that we should all die to a man.

I at length went to the Grand Chiefs lodge by his particular invitation; the Mandan Chief stuck close to me. The Chief had prepared a supper of boiled young corn, beans & squashes, of which he gave me in wooden bowls. He also gave me near 2 quarts of the tobacco seed, & informed me lhe had always had his ears open to what we had said, that he was well convinced that the Sioux was the cause of all the trouble between the Mandans & them.

—*Captain Clark*

⚐ **South Dakota 150** ♿

INDIAN MEMORIAL
Lake Oahe/Corps of Engineers Park

Location: North-central South Dakota west of Mobridge.

Access: From U.S. Highway 12 at milepost 185 +.3 (0.4 mile west of the Missouri River bridge, 4 miles west of Mobridge, 25 miles southeast of McLaughlin), turn south onto a paved access road and proceed south, east, then south again for a total of 0.3 miles to the campground.

Camping Facilities: 81 campsites, most with electrical hookups, in 2 loops; sites are small to medium-sized, with limited to fair separation; most parking pads are paved or gravel, long, acceptably level straight-ins; medium to large tent areas; fire rings, plus a few barbecue grills; b-y-o firewood; water at central faucets; restrooms with showers; holding tank disposal station; mostly paved driveways; nearly complete supplies and services are available in Mobridge.

Day Use Facilities: Small parking areas.

Activities & Attractions: Boating; boat launches; fishing; playgrounds; amphitheater.

Natural Features: Located on a grassy bluff above the west shore of Lake Oahe on the Missouri River; most sites receive light to moderately dense shade/shelter from rows of large hardwoods, bushes and some evergreens; the lake is bordered by high, grassy, nearly treeless, windswept bluffs; elevation 1700´.

Season, Fees & Phone: Open all year, with limited services and no fee, November to April; $10.00 for a standard site, $14.00 for an electrical hookup site; 14 day camping limit; Lake Oahe CoE Project Office, Pierre, ☎(605) 224-5862 or (605) 845-2252.

Camp Journal: This segment of the Missouri resembles, to some degree, the middle Columbia River in central Washington State or even certain portions of the Colorado River along the Arizona-California border. Near this spot is the grave of Sitting Bull, the Sioux chief who led the winning team at the Little Bighorn.

📖 *August 22, 1806*

As I was about to leave the cheifs of the Chyennes lodge, he requested me to send some traders to them, that their country was full of beaver and they would then be encouraged to kill beaver; but now they had no use for them, as they could get nothing for their skins and did not know well how to catch beaver. If the white people would come amongst them, they would become acquainted and the white people would learn them how to take the beaver. I promised the Nation that I would inform their Great Father, the President of the U States, and he would have them supplied with goods, and mentioned in what manner they would be supplied &c. &c. I am happy to have it in my power to say that my worthy friend, Capt. Lewis, is recovering fast; he walked a little today for the first time. I have discontinud the tent in the hole the ball came out

—*Captain Clark*

⚐ South Dakota 151 ⚐

DOWNSTREAM: NORTH
Lake Oahe/Corps of Engineers Park

Location: Central South Dakota on the west edge of Pierre.

Access: From U.S. Highway 14 & South Dakota State Highway 34 at a point 1.2 miles west of the Missouri River Bridge and 3 miles west of Pierre, turn north onto State Highway 1806; proceed north for 4 miles; turn northeast (right) onto a paved project road; proceed 0.6 mile east to a 'T' intersection; turn south (right) and continue for 0.5 mile to the park.

Camping Facilities: 161 campsites, including 120 with electrical hookups; sites are medium to large, with nominal to fairly good separation; parking pads are paved, medium to very long straight-ins; minor additional leveling may be required; large, grassy tent spots; fireplaces; b-y-o firewood; water at central faucets; restrooms with showers; paved driveways; campground attendant; nearly complete supplies and services are available in Pierre.

Day Use Facilities: Medium-sized picnic area with shelter; drinking water; restrooms; large parking lot.

Activities & Attractions: Boating; marina; fishing; playground; amphitheater; Cottonwood Path Nature Trail; nearby archery and rifle ranges; Oahe Dam Visitor Center across the dam on the east bank.

Natural Features: Located on a gently rolling grassy flat near the west bank of the Missouri River; park vegetation consists of mown grass, huge cottonwoods, and some smaller hardwoods; surrounding terrain includes riverside marsh and barren bluffs which border the river; elevation 1400´.

Season, Fees & Phone: May to October; $10.00 for a standard site, $14.00 for an electrical hookup site; 14 day limit; Lake Oahe CoE Project Office, Pierre, ☎(605) 224-5862.

Camp Journal: There's plenty of room for big rv's and tents among the tall cottonwoods. You're camping in good company here: the Lewis & Clark Party lingered along this same riverbank on their trip West in 1804.

⚐ South Dakota 152 ⚐

DOWNSTREAM: SOUTH
Lake Oahe/Corps of Engineers Park

Location: Central South Dakota on the west edge of Pierre.

Access: From U.S. Highway 14 & South Dakota State Highway 34 at a point 1.2 miles west of the Missouri River Bridge and 3 miles west of Pierre, turn north onto State Highway 1806; proceed north for 4 miles; turn northeast (right) onto a paved project road; continue for 0.15 mile, then turn south/southeast (right) for 0.6 mile to the park.

Camping Facilities: 45 campsites in a loop and a string; sites are small to large, with average to good separation; parking pads are mostly paved (some are gravel), level, medium to huge, straight-ins or pull-throughs; large, level, grassy tent spots; fire rings; b-y-o firewood is recommended; water at central faucets; restrooms with showers; holding tank disposal station near the highway; paved driveways; camper supplies at a nearby marina; nearly complete supplies and services are available in Pierre.

Day Use Facilities: Medium-sized picnic area with shelter; drinking water; restrooms; large parking lot.

Activities & Attractions: Dam tours; boating; fishing (boat ramp and marina at Downstream North); playground; day use area with shelter; ORV area nearby off Highway 1806.

Natural Features: Located on the west bank of the Missouri River, just south of (below) Oahe Dam; most sites are situated on a grassy, tree-covered flat; some are along the riverfront; cottonwoods, grass and smaller planted trees comprise the vegetation; river views through the trees from most campsites; elevation 1400´.

Season, Fees & Phone: Open all year; $10.00; 14 day limit; Lake Oahe CoE Project Office, Pierre, ☎ (605) 224-5862.

Camp Journal: Of the two main parks in this area, Downstream South and Downstream North, the atmosphere is usually more 'relaxed' at South. (Many boaters prefer staying at Downstream North because it's 2 miles closer to the boat ramp/marina and there are electrical hookups available.) Downstream South is also known as "Campground 3".

Early on August 26th, the returning party passed the mouth of the Teton River, now known as the Bad River, at present-day Pierre, South Dakota:

📖 *August 26, 1806*

At 8 passed the place the Tetons were encamped at the time they attempted to stop us in Sept. 1804, and at 9 A.M. passed the enterance of Teton River. Saw several black tail or mule deer and sent out to kill them, but they were wild and the hunters could not get a shot at either of them. A fiew miles below the Teton River I observed a buffalow skin canoe lying on the S. shore and a short distance lower a raft, which induces me to suspect that the Tetons are not on the Missouri at the big bend as we were informed by the Ricaras, but up the Teton River. At 5 P.M. we landed at Louisels fort on Cedar Island; this fort is entire and every part appears to be in the same state it was when we passed it in Sept. 1804.

We proceeded on about 10 miles lower and encamped on the S.W. side. As we were now in the country where we were informed the Sioux were assembled, we were much on our guard, deturmined to put up with no insults from those bands of Sioux, all the arms &c. in perfect order. Capt. L. is still on the mending and he walks a little. We made 60 miles today, with the wind ahead greater part of the day.

—*Captain Clark*

📖 *August 29, 1806*

I ascended to the high country, and from an eminence I had a view of the plains for a great distance. From this eminence I had a view of a greater number of buffalow than I had ever seen before at one time. I must have seen near 20,000 of those animals feeding on this plain. I have observed that in the country between the nations which are at war with each other, the greatest numbers of wild animals are to be found.

—*Captain Clark*

📖 *August 30, 1806*

Capt. Lewis is mending slowly. I took 3 hunters and walked on the N.E. shore with a view to kill some fat meat. We had not proceeded far before I saw a large plumb orchard of the most delicious plumbs; out of this orchard 2 large buck elks ran; the hunters killed them. I stopped the canoes and brought in the flesh, which was fat and fine. Here the party collected as many plumbs as they could eate, and several pecks of which they put by &c. After a delay of nearly 2 hours, we again proceeded on downwards.

I saw several men on horseback which with the help of a spyglass I found to be Indians on the high hill to the N.E. We landed on the S.W. side, and I sent out two men to a village of barking squirrels [prairie dogs] to kill some of those animals.

Immediately after landing, about 20 Indians were discovered on an eminence a little above us on the opposit side. One of those men I took to be a French man, from his having a blanket, capote, &c., and a handkerchief around his head. Immediately after, 80 or 90 Indian men, all armed with fusees & bows & arrows, came out of a wood on the opposit bank, about 1/4 mile below us. They fired off their guns as a salute. We returned the salute with 2 rounds.

We were at a loss to deturmine of what nation those Indians were. From their hostile appearance, we were apprehensive they were Tetons, but from the country through which they roved we were willing to believe them either the Yanktons, Poncas, or Mahas, either of which Nations are well disposed toward the white people. I deturmined to find out who they were without running any risk of the party and Indians, and therefore took three French men who could speak the Maha, Pawnee, and some Sioux, and in a small canoe I went over to a sand bar which extended sufficiently near the opposit shore to converse.

Immediately after I set out, 3 young men set out from the opposit side and swam next me on the sand bar. I derected the men to speak to them in the Pania and Mahar languages first, neither of which they could understand. I then derected the man who could speak a fiew words of Sioux to enquire what nation or tribe they belong to. They informed me that they were Tetons and their Chief was the Black Buffalow. This Chief I knew very well to be the one we had seen with his band at Teton River, which band had attempted to detain us in the fall of 1804 as we ascended this river, and with whome we were near coming to blows.

I told those Indians that they had been deaf to our counsels, and ill-treated us as we ascended this river two years past; that they had abused all the whites who had visited them since. I believed them to be bad people & should not suffer them to cross to the side on which the party lay, and directed them to return with their band to their camp; that if any of them come near our camp we should kill them certainly. I left them on the bar and returned to the party and examined the arms, &c. Those Indians, seeing some corn in the canoe, requested some of it, which I refused, being deturmined to have nothing to do with those people.

Several others swam across, one of which understood Pania, and as our Pania interpreter was a very good one, we had it in our power to inform what we wished. I told this man to inform his Nation that we had not forgot their treatment to us as we passed up this river, &c.; that they had treated all the white people who had visited them very badly, robbed them of their goods, and had wounded one man whome I had seen. We viewed them as bad people and no more traders would be suffered to come to them, and whenever the white people wished to visit the nations above, they

would come sufficiently strong to whip any villainous party who dared to oppose them, and words to the same purpose.

I also told them that I was informed that a part of all their bands were going to war against the Mandans, &c., and that they would be well whipped, as the Mandans and Minnetares, &c., had a plenty of guns, powder and ball, and we had given them a cannon to defend themselves. And directed them to return from the sand bar and inform their chiefs what we had said to them, and to keep away from the river or we should kill every one of them, &c., &c. Those fellows requested to be allowed to come across and make comrades, which we positively refused, and I directed them to return immediately, which they did; and after they had informed the chiefs, &c., as I suppose, what we had said to them; they all set out on their return to their camps back of a high hill. 7 of them halted on the top of the hill and blackguarded us, told us to come across and they would kill us all, &c., of which we took no notice.

We all this time were extremely anxious for the arival of the 2 Fieldses & Shannon, whome we had left behind, and were somewhat concerned as to their safety. To our great joy, those men hove in sight at 6 P.M. Jo Fields had killed 3 black tail or mule deer.

We then set out, as I wished to see what those Indians on the hill would act; we steered across near the opposit shore. This notion put them in some agitation as to our intentions; some set out on the direction towards their camps, others walked about on the top of the hill, and one man walked down the hill to meet us and invited us to land, to which invitation I paid no kind of attention. This man I knew to be the one who had in the fall 1804 accompanied us 2 days, and is said to be the friend to the white people. After we passed him he returned on the top of the hill and gave 3 strokes with the gun (on the earth—this is swearing by the earth) he had in his hand. This, I am informed, is a great oath among the Indians.

—*Captain Clark*

South Dakota 153

BURKE LAKE
Burke Lake State Recreation Area

Location: South-central South Dakota near the South Dakota-Nebraska border near the town of Burke.

Access: From U.S. Highway 18 at milepost 286 +.2 (at the southern edge of Burke, 23 miles east of the junction of U.S. Highways 18 & 183, 45 miles west of the Missouri River near Pickstown), turn north onto Main Street; proceed north for 0.3 mile (5 blocks); turn east (right) onto 7th Street; continue for 0.8 mile, then turn south (right) onto a gravel access road; continue south for 1.55 miles (paved again after 1 mile of gravel) to the park.

Camping Facilities: 15 campsites; sites are quite roomy, level and well separated; parking pads are paved, medium to long straight-ins; some excellent tent-pitching opportunities; fireplaces; b-y-o firewood; water at central faucets; vault facilities; paved driveway; limited supplies and services are available in Burke.

Day Use Facilities: Small picnic area; small shelters; change house for beach users; drinking water; vault facilities; several small parking lots.

Activities & Attractions: Limited boating/sailing; boat launch; fishing for northern pike, largemouth bass, perch, bluegill; swimming beach; playground; hiking trail around the lake.

Natural Features: Located in a wooded glen in a grassy basin surrounded by miles of prairie and agricultural land; small, but picturesque, 25-acre Burke Lake is visible through the trees from many of the sites; pines and hardwoods provide a considerable amount of shelter and separation for the campsites; park area is 206 acres; elevation 2300´.

Season, Fees & Phone: Available all year, subject to weather conditions, with limited services October to May; 14 day camping limit; park entry $5.00, camping $6.00; phone c/o Snake Creek State Recreation Area, Platte, ☎(605) 337-2587.

Camp Journal: This is one of the nicest little hidden treasures in the state of South Dakota! It must surely be a welcome, forested retreat in the heat of the summer, and also a colorful scene in the autumn months. This a definite 'find'.

⚤ South Dakota 154 ⚤

RANDALL CREEK
Randall Creek State Recreation Area

Location: Southeast South Dakota near the South Dakota-Nebraska border.

Access: From U.S. Highway 18 at milepost 329 +.75 (at the west edge of the dam and the Missouri River Bridge, 45 miles east of Burke, 1.4 miles west of Pickstown), turn south onto a paved project road; continue south and east for 0.85 mile; turn south (right) and continue for 0.3 mile; turn right again to the park.

Camping Facilities: 133 campsites with electrical hookups, in several loops stretching for over a mile; sites are average to spacious, level, with fair to excellent separation; parking pads are paved, medium to very long straight-ins; most sites have large, grassy tent spots; fire rings and barbecue grills; b-y-o firewood is recommended; water at central faucets; restrooms with showers; holding tank disposal station; paved driveways; gas and camper supplies in Pickstown.

Day Use Facilities: Large picnic area; large shelters with chimneyed fireplaces/bbq facilities; drinking water; restrooms; large parking lot.

Activities & Attractions: Boating; boat launch for river access nearby; Lake Francis Case boat ramp across the highway to the north; fishing; playgrounds; team sports fields; Fort Randall ruins; dam tours.

Natural Features: Located on a wooded flat along the west bank of the Missouri River, just downstream of Fort Randall Dam and Lake Francis Case; lush grass and medium to tall hardwoods throughout the park; roughcut banks are visible across the river; there are a number of enormous riverside sites; elevation 1300´.

Season, Fees & Phone: Open all year; park entry $5.00; camping $11.00; 14 day camping limit; park office (605) 487-7046; reservations (800) 710-CAMP.

Camp Journal: Randall Creek is a superb facility...a real showplace. Obviously, a lot of planning and work went into creating this recreation complex. (The place is so big that you actually could get *lost* on a long walk away from your picnic spot or campsite.) Terrific.

▲ *River Quicurre*
to the Kanzas River

❧ The River Quicurre noted in the following section is now the Niobrara River. It is one of Nebraska's premier watersheds. The Niobrara rises hundreds of miles to the west near the Nebraska-Wyoming border.

📖 *September 1,1806*

At 9 A.M. we passed the enterance of River Quicurre, which had the same appearance it had when we passed up—water rapid and of a milky white colour.

September 1,1806, continued below

🏕 **Nebraska 155** ♿ ·

NIOBRARA
Niobrara State Park

Location: Northeast Nebraska northeast of O'Neill.

Access: From Nebraska State Highway 12 at milepost 159 +.3 (1.3 miles west of the junction of State Highways 12 and 14 near Niobrara, 9 miles east of Verdel), turn north into the main park entrance; then east for 0.2 mile to the main campground; or continue northerly for another mile to the cabin area and the picnic/campsites and viewpoints along the scenic loop. **Alternate Access:** From Highway 12 at a point 0.9 mile east of the main park entrance and 0.4 mile west of the Highways 12 & 14 junction, (just at the west end of the Niobrara River bridge), turn north into the (old) park entrance to the swimming pool and group area.

Camping Facilities: *Main Campground:* 69 campsites with electrical hookups; sites are small, acceptably level and closely spaced; parking pads are medium-length, gravel straight-ins; adequate space for a medium to large tent in most sites; fire rings; b-y-o firewood; water at several faucets; restrooms with showers; laundry facilities; holding tank disposal station; gravel driveways; *additional camping:* several dozen walk-in camp/picnic sites, some with shelters, are located within or near the large scenic loop drive; *Cabins:* 15 2-bedroom or 3-bedroom furnished housekeeping cabins; gas, camper supplies and a few limited services are available in the town of Niobrara, 2 miles northeast.

Day Use Facilities: Large picnic/camp area with shared facilities; group picnic shelters (reservable); lodge with kitchen for group conferences.

Activities & Attractions: Hiking trails; scenic loop drive with nearly a dozen roadside pullouts; observation/interpretive shelter with parking lot; swimming pool; hiking and horse trails; large boat launch for Niobrara River access, nearby; fishing for walleye, sauger, catfish; trail rides. .

Natural Features: Located mostly on grassy, windswept hills and bluffs above the confluence of Niobrara and Missouri Rivers; a portion of the park lies in bottomlands along the west bank of the Niobrara River; hardwoods and conifers shelter some of the picnic and campsites, but many sites have little shelter; the blufftops are dotted with trees; stands of mostly hardwoods are found in the ravines and bottomlands; elevation 1300´.

Season, Fees & Phone: Open all year, with limited services November to April; park entry $2.50, camping $6.00 for tents, $13.00-$14.00 for hookup sites; park office ☎(402) 857-3373.

Camp Journal: The attractively designed cabins are on a windswept blufftop with virtually unlimited views of the river valleys. Terrific!. Several nice little camping/picnicking sites near the ponds in the center of the scenic loop drive deserve special mention. As an option to staying in the main campground, virtually unlimited backpack/walk-in camping is available just about anywhere in the park. And there are really fabulous views of the valleys of the two rivers from just about any hilltop.

📖 *September 1,1806,* continued from above

About two miles below the Quicurre, 9 Indians ran down the bank and beckened to us to land. They appeared to be a war party, and I took them to be Tetons and paid no kind of attention to them further than an enquirey to what tribe they belonged. They did not give me any answer, I presume they did not understand the man who spoke to them as he spoke but little of their language. As one canoe was yet behind, we landed in an open, commanding situation out of sight of the Indians, determined to delay untill they came up.

About 15 minits after we had landed, several guns were fired by the Indians, which we expected was at the three men behind. I called out 15 men and ran up with a full determination to cover them if possible—let the number of the Indians be what they might. Capt. Lewis hobbled up on the bank and formed the remainder of the party in a situation well calculated to defend themselves and the canoes &c.

When I had proceeded to the point about 250 yards, I discovered the canoe about 1 mile above & the Indians where we had left them. I then walked on the sand beach and the Indians came down to meet me. I gave them my hand and enquired of them what they were shooting at. They informed me that they were shooting off their guns at an old keg which we had thrown out of one of the canoes and was floating down. Those Indians informed me they were Yanktons. One of the men with me knew one of the Indians to be the brother of young Dorion's wife.

Finding those Indians to be Yanktons, I invited them down to the boats to smoke. When we arived at the canoes they all eagerly saluted the Mandan Chief, and we all set and smoked several pipes. I told them that we took them to be a party of Tetons, and the firing I expected was at the three men in the rear canoe and I had went up with a full intention to kill them all if they had been Tetons & fired on the canoe as we first expected; but finding them Yanktons and good men we were glad to see them and take them by the hand as faithful children who had opened their ears to our counsels. One of them spoke and said that their Nation had opened their ears & done as we had directed them ever since we gave the medal to their great Chief, and should continue to do as we had told them. We enquired if any of their chiefs had gone down with Mr. Dorion. They answered that their great Chief and many of their brave men had gone down; that the white people had built a house near the Mahar village where they traded. We tied a piece of ribbon to each man's hair and gave them some corn of which they appeared much pleased. The Mandan Chief gave a pair of elegant leggings to the principal man of the Indian party, which is an Indian fashion (to make presents). The canoe & 3 men having joined us, we took our leave of this party, telling them to return to their band and listen to our counsels which we had before given to them. Their band of 80 lodges were on Plum Creek a fiew miles to the North. Those nine men had five fusees and 4 bows and quivers of arrows.

After we all came together we again proceeded on down to a large sand bar imediately opposit to the place where we met the Yanktons in council at the Calumet Bluffs, and which place we left on the 1st of Sept. 1804. I observed our old flagstaff or pole standing as we left it.

—*Captain Clark*

♣ Nebraska 156 ♿

BURBACH
Lewis and Clark Lake State Recreation Area

Location: Northeast Nebraska northwest of South Sioux City.

Access: From Nebraska State Highway 121 at milepost 73 +.8 (3 miles south of Gavins Point Dam, 7 miles north of Crofton), turn west onto Recreation Road 54-C (paved) and travel 4.4 miles; turn north (right) onto a paved access road for 0.6 mile to a 'T'; turn west (left) onto a gravel road; the recreation area stretches for the next mile along the access road.

Lewis and Clark State Recreation Area

Camping Facilities: Approximately 125 campsites; (a group camping area with hookups in located in the recreation area's Bloomfield section about 1 mile west of Burbach); sites are small to medium-sized, level, closely spaced, but with good visual separation; parking surfaces are short to medium-length, grass straight-ins; enough space for a small to medium-sized tent; barbecue grills; a small amount of firewood may be available early in the season, b-y-o is recommended; water at central faucets; restrooms; holding tank disposal station; gravel driveways; gas and camper supplies at the marina, 0.4 mile east, and in Crofton.

Day Use Facilities: Small picnic area; restrooms; parking areas.

Activities & Attractions: Fishing; boating; boat launch at the nearby marina.

Natural Features: Located close to the south shore of Lewis and Clark Lake on the Missouri River; park vegetation consists of long, wide rows of tall hardwoods, evergreens and large bushes, plus extensive open, grassy areas; Weigand Creek enters the lake at the east edge of the campground; glimpses of the lake through the trees from some campsites; elevation 1200´.

Season, Fees & Phone: Available all year, subject to weather conditions, with limited services October to May; 14 day camping limit; park entry $2.50, camping $4.00 for a primitive site, $9.00 for a standard site, $13.00 for a hookup site; park office ☎ (402) 388-4169.

Camp Journal: More privacy than you would first believe possible is provided at this enormous campground. Most of the campsites are in their own little wooded cubbyholes.

⚜ Nebraska 157 ♿

WEIGAND

Lewis and Clark Lake State Recreation Area

Location: Northeast Nebraska northwest of South Sioux City.

Access: From Nebraska State Highway 121 at milepost 73 +.8 (3 miles south of Gavins Point Dam, 7 miles north of Crofton), turn west onto Recreation Road 54-C (paved) and travel 4 miles; turn north (right) onto a paved access road for 0.25 mile to the campground; continue ahead, or turn left or right to the various camp sections.

Camping Facilities: Approximately 120 campsites, including about 30 with electrical hookups, in 9 short rows; sites are small, level, closely spaced, with fair visual separation; parking surfaces are short to medium-length, grass straight-ins; small to medium-sized areas for tents; fireplaces; b-y-o firewood is recommended; water at central faucets; restrooms; holding tank disposal station; gravel driveways; gas and camper supplies at the marina and in Crofton.

Day Use Facilities: Small picnic area; drinking water; restrooms; parking areas.

Activities & Attractions: Boating; boat launch, marina; fishing.

Natural Features: Located close to the south shore of Lewis and Clark Lake; rows of tall hardwoods and evergreens provide ample shelter/shade for most sites; Weigand Creek enters the lake at the west edge of the recreation area; a few sites are lakeshore, some others have glimpses of the lake; elevation 1200´.

Season, Fees & Phone: Available all year, subject to weather conditions, with limited services October to May; 14 day camping limit; park entry $2.50, camping $4.00 for a primitive site, $9.00 for a standard site, $13.00 for a hookup site; park office ☎ (402) 388-4169.

Camp Journal: Given a choice, most campers would probably choose one of the two-dozen or so lakeshore sites. But there are also a number of pleasant spots about 50 yards from the high tide mark, plus some near the mouth of the creek, that merit consideration. It might take a while to pick your way past the many rows of sites here. No matter. Great views are just a short walk from any spot.

⚜ Nebraska 158 ♿

NEBRASKA TAILWATERS

Lewis & Clark Lake/Corps of Engineers Park

Location: Northeast Nebraska northwest of South Sioux City.

Access: From Nebraska State Highway 121 at milepost 75 (0.6 mile east of Gavins Point Dam, 0.4 mile northeast of the CoE Gavins Point Visitor Center, 7 miles north of Crofton), turn northwest onto a paved access road and proceed 0.4 mile down and around to the campground. (Note: The highway makes several turns in this area; it might be easiest to think of the campground turnoff as being at an angle off Nebraska 121 at an east-south 'L' turn in the highway; at this 'L' a paved local road leads west to the dam.)

Camping Facilities: 52 campsites, most with electrical hookups; sites are small, slightly sloped, with very little separation; most parking pads are paved, medium to long straight-ins; small tent areas; handicapped-access unit; fireplaces; b-y-o firewood; water at central faucets; restrooms; holding tank disposal station on Highway 121, just above the campground; paved driveway; camper supplies, 0.5 mile east on Highway 121.

Day Use Facilities: Small parking area.

Activities & Attractions: Fishing; boating; boat launch.

Natural Features: Located on a slightly sloping flat on a short bench on the south bank of the Missouri River, just below Gavins Point Dam; large hardwoods provide limited wind shelter and some shade for most campsites; elevation 1200´.

Season, Fees & Phone: May to October; $12.00 for a standard site, $14.00 for an electrical hookup unit; 14 day limit; Lewis and Clark Lake/Gavins Point Dam CoE Project Office ☎ (402) 667-7873.

Camp Journal: Fishing from a boat is a popular (and productive) activity along the dam's outlet stream, and probably a major reason campers stay here. Because of the red tape relating to whether you need a Nebraska or South Dakota angling license to fish from a boat on a specific segment of the river here, it might be a good idea to carefully read the local regs before you embark.

📖 *September 3, 1806*

Passed the enterance of Redstone River on the N. E. side at 11 A.M., and at half past 4 P.M. we spied two boats & several men. Our party plyed their oars, and we soon landed on the side of the boats. The men of these boats saluted us with their small arms. I landed and was met by a Mr. James Aird from Mackinaw by way of Prarie de Chien and St. Louis. This gentleman is of the house of Dickson & Co., of Prarie de Chien, who has a license to trade for one year with the Sioux. He has 2 bateaux loaded with merchandize for that purpose. This gentleman received both Capt. Lewis and myself with every mark of friendship. He was himself at the time with a chill of the ague on him which he has had for several days.

Our first enquiry was after the President of our country, and then our friends, and the state of politics of our country, &c., and the state of Indian affairs, to all of which enquiries Mr. Aird gave us as satisfactory information as he had it in his power to have collected in the Illinois, which was not a great deal. Soon after we landed, a violent storm of thunder, lightning, and rain from the N.W., which was violent, with hard claps of thunder and sharp lightning which continued untill 10 P.M., after which the wind blew hard. I sat up late and partook of the tent of Mr. Aird, which was dry. Mr. Aird unfortunately had his boat sunk on the 25th of July last, by a violent storm of wind and hail, by which accident he lost the most of his useful articles, as he informed us.

This gentleman informed us of many changes and misfortunes which had taken place in the Illinois, amongst others the loss of Mr. Cady [Pierre] Chouteau's house and furniture by fire. For this misfortune of our friend Chouteau, I feel myself very much concerned, &c. He also informed us that General Wilkinson was the governor of the Louisiana and at St. Louis. 300 of the American troops had been cantoned on the Missouri a fiew miles above it's mouth. Some disturbance with the Spaniards in the Natchitoches country is the cause of their being called down to that country. The Spaniards had taken one of the U. States' frigates in the Mediterranean. Two British ships of the line had fired on an American ship in the port of New York and killed the captain's brother. 2 Indians had been hung in St. Louis for murder, and several others in jail. And that Mr. Burr and General Hamilton fought a duel, the latter was killed,

&c., &c. I am happy to find that my worthy friend Capt. Lewis is so well as to walk about with ease to himself, &c., and we made 60 miles today. The river much crowded with sand bars, which are very differently situated from what they were when we went up.

—*Captain Clark*

🏕 **Nebraska 159** ♿

PONCA
Ponca State Park

Location: Northeast corner of Nebraska northwest of South Sioux City.

Access: From Nebraska State Highway 12 in Ponca City (18 miles northwest of South Sioux City) turn north onto Nebraska Route 26-E Spur (S-26-E); take the grand tour through midtown Ponca, then north for 3 miles to the park entrance station.

Camping Facilities: 91 campsites, most with electrical hookups, in 2 loops; most sites are small, somewhat sloped, with minimal separation; parking pads are short, paved or packed gravel straight-ins; small (some medium) tent spots; barbecue grills; b-y-o firewood; water at several faucets; restrooms with showers; holding tank disposal station; paved/gravel driveways; *Cabins:* 14 2-bedroom, furnished, air-conditioned housekeeping cabins; limited supplies and services are available in Ponca.

Day Use Facilities: Large picnic area; shelter; drinking water; restrooms; large parking lot.

Activities & Attractions: Swimming pool; hiking trails; trail rides; cross-country skiing; fishing; boat launch.

Natural Features: Located on a hilltop and hillside several hundred yards from the Missouri River; campsites receive light to dense shelter/shade; dense hardwoods and cedars border the campground; (the river is within a short drive or a long hike, but is not within view); elevation 1200´.

Season, Fees & Phone: Open all year, with limited services October to May; park entry $2.50, camping $8.00 for tents, $12.00-$13.00 for hookup sites; park office ☎(402) 755-2284.

Camp Journal: You might be able to tuck a vehicle with a small trailer into some of the parking spaces here, but the campground really doesn't readily accommodate large outfits. Whoever designed the campground apparently decided that it was better to work with the terrain and the beautiful, dense forest rather than attempt to alter them.

📖 *September 4, 1806*

The musquetoes became troublesome early this morning. I rose at the usial hour, found all the party as wet as rain could make them. As we were in want of some tobacco, I proposed to Mr. Aird to furnish us with 4 carrots, for which we would pay the amount to any merchant of St. Louis. He very readily agreed to furnish us with tobacco, and gave to each man as much as it is necessary for them to use between this and St. Louis, an instance of generosity for which every man of the party appears to acknowledge. Mr. Aird also insisted on our accepting a barrel of flour. We gave to this gentleman what corn we could spare, amounting to about 6 bushels. This corn was well calculated for his purpose, as he was about to make his establishment and would have it in his power to hull the corn, &c. The flour was very acceptable to us. We have yet a little flour, part of what we carried up from the Illinois as high as Maria's River and buried it there untill our return, &c.

At 8 A.M., we took our leave and set out, and proceeded on very well. At 11 A.M., passed the enterance of the Big Sioux River, which is low, and at Meridian we came to at Floyd's Bluff below the enterance of Floyd's River, and ascended the hill with Capt. Lewis and several men. Found the grave had been opened by the nativs and left half covered. We had this grave completely filled up, and returned to the canoes, and proceeded on to the sandbar on which we encamped from the 12th to the 20th of August 1804 near the Mahar Village. Here we came to and directed every wet article put out to dry, all the bedding of the party and skins being wet. As it was late in the evening we deturmined to continue all night. Had issued to each man of the party a cup of flour. A little before night several guns were heard below and in a direction towards the Mahar village which induced us to suspect that Mr. McClellan, who we was informed was on his way up to trade with the Mahars, had arived at the creek below, and that those reports of guns was some of his party out hunting

—*Captain Clark*

⛺ Nebraska 160 ♿

SCENIC PARK
South Sioux City Park

Location: Northeast corner of Nebraska in South Sioux City.

Access: From U.S. Highways 75 & 77 at the far north end of South Sioux City (0.1 mile south of the Missouri River bridge, at the intersection of Dakota Avenue & East 6th Street) turn east onto East 6th Street; proceed 0.4 mile to E Street; turn north (left) onto E Street and continue for 0.1 mile, then turn east (right) for a final 0.15 mile to the campground. (Note that Dakota Avenue, which is the main drag that runs north-south through midtown, merges with Highways 75 & 77 here at the far north end the city.)

Camping Facilities: 25 campsites; sites are small to medium-sized, basically level, with fair separation; parking pads are gravel, medium to long straight-ins; adequate space for large tents; barbecue grills; b-y-o firewood; water at central faucets; restrooms with showers; holding tank disposal station; paved driveway; complete supplies and services are available in South Sioux City.

Day Use Facilities: Large picnic area; drinking water; restrooms; large parking lot.

Activities & Attractions: Swimming pool; playground; tennis courts.

Natural Features: Located along the south bank of the Missouri River at the northeast corner of a large city park complex; sites are moderately sheltered/shaded by mature hardwoods on a mown lawn; elevation 1100´.

Season, Fees & Phone: May to October; $11.00 for a standard site, $14.00 for an electrical hookup unit; 10 day limit; South Sioux City Parks Department ☎ (402) 494-2452.

Camp Journal: Even if you're a confirmed, country campground devotee, this spot may prove to be a useful, even welcome, stop someday. The riverfront has been pretty nicely maintained in this locale. And while there may not be rocky bluffs or towering mountains to view from your campsite, looking out across the Wide Missouri to the nighttime skyline of Sioux City, Iowa and the East, may still prove to be visually satisfying.

📖 *September 5, 1806*

The report of the guns which was heard must have been the Mahars who most probably have just arived at their village from hunting the buffalow. This is a season they usialy return to their village to secure their crops of corn, beens, punkins &c &c. Proceeded on very well passed the Blue Stone Bluff at 3 P.M.

—*Captain Clark*

⚐ Nebraska 161

SUMMIT LAKE
Summit Lake State Recreation Area

Location: East-central Nebraska north of Omaha.

Access: From U.S. Highway 75 at a point 1.5 miles south of Tekamah, 15 miles north of Blair, turn west onto a gravel road and proceed 3.2 miles; turn northwest (right), and proceed 1.2 miles around the south end of the lake to a point above the west side of the lake; turn north (right) into the recreation area. (Note: access is also possible from Nebraska State Highway 32 west of Tekamah, on gravel road to the north shore, then via a winding route to the park.)

Camping Facilities: 26 campsites; (a number of primitive sites are also available); sites are very small, with zip separation; parking pads are medium-length, gravel straight-ins which might require a little additional leveling; adequate space for a small to medium-sized tent in most sites; barbecue grills; b-y-o firewood; water at a hand pump; vault facilities; gravel driveways; limited to adequate supplies and services are available in Tekamah.

Day Use Facilities: Small picnic area; shelters; medium-sized parking area; certain other facilities are shared with campers.

Activities & Attractions: Fishing for catfish, bluegill, walleye, northern pike and crappie; limited boating (max. 5 mph); boat launch; fish cleaning station (on the north shore); designated swimming beach; hiking trail; day use area.

Natural Features: Located on a small, grassy flat at the west end of 190-acre Summit lake, in a basin ringed by grassy bluffs dotted with a few trees; sites lack shelter/shade; elevation 1100´.

Season, Fees & Phone: Open all year, subject to weather conditions, with limited services October to May; 14 day camping limit; park entry $2.50, camping $4.00-$9.00; phone c/o Nebraska Game & Parks Commission District III Office, Norfolk, ☎(402) 370-3374.

Camp Journal: The hiking trail and swimming beach are welcome add-ons, but this is still primarily a simple fishing camp. (Dead trees have been left standing just offshore of the campground. While this feature is certainly important in attracting fish, it's not a visual enhancement.)

📖 *September 6, 1806*

At the lower point of Pelican Island a little above the Petite River de Sioux, we met a trading boat of Mr. Auguste Chouteau, of St. Louis, bound to the River Jacques to trade with the Yanktons. This boat was in the care of a Mr. Henry Delorn. He had exposed all his loading to dry, and sent out five of his hands to hunt. They soon arived with an elk. We purchased a gallon of whiskey of this man (promised to pay Chouteau, who would not receive [accept] any pay), and gave to each man of the party a dram, which is the first spirituous liquor which had been tasted by any of them since the 4th of July, 1805. Several of the party exchanged leather for linen shirts, and beaver for coarse hats. Those men could inform us nothing more than that all the troops had moved from the Illinois and that General Wilkinson was preparing to leave St. Louis. We advised this trader to treat the Tetons with as much contempt as possible and stated to him where he would be benefited by such treatment, &c., &c., and at 1 P.M. set out. Those men gave us two shots from a swivel gun they had on the bow of their boat, which we returned in our turn.

Proceeded on about 3 miles and came up with two of the hunters. They had not killed anything. At 5 miles we overtook the canoe of the other hunters, with Shannon in it, floating down—the two Fieldses being in the woods behind.

The Chief & the squars & children are weary of their journey. Children cry &c.

—*Captain Clark*

🌿 "Mr. Auguste Chouteau", mentioned above, and his family became the most successful fur traders on the upper Missouri. The cities of Augusta, Montana and Chouteau, Montana are named for him.

⚐ Nebraska Side Trip ♿

FORT ATKINSON
Fort Atkinson State Historical Park

Location: Eastern border of Nebraska north of Omaha.

Access: From U.S. Highway 75 in the community of Fort Calhoun (9 miles north of the junction of U.S. 75 & Interstate 680 Exit 12 on the north side of Omaha, 9 miles southeast of Blair), go east to the park.

Camping Facilities: None; nearest public campground is in N.P. Dodge City Park, on the northeast corner of Omaha.

Day Use Facilities: Informal picnicking; drinking water; restrooms; large parking lot.

Activities & Attractions: Reconstructed buildings and grounds of an historic military post; comprehensive visitor center; interpretive displays and programs.

Natural Features: Located on a large, grassy flat on a bluff above the west bank of the Missouri River; the central fort area is bordered by hardwoods; elevation 1100´.

Season, Fees & Phone: Grounds open all year; buildings and visitor center open May to September, plus certain other spring and fall weekends; park entry fee $2.50; ☎(402) 468-5611.

Camp Journal: Founded in 1819, Fort Atkinson was the first and largest military post west of the Missouri River. Fifteen years previous, in early August 1804 on their way upriver, Lewis and Clark had held an impromptu powwow with local Indians on this bluff. The West's most dynamic duo later named the spot Council Bluffs and recommended the key location for a fort. During it's scant decade of active duty, Fort Atkinson was the portal to the great, rich expanses along the Upper Missouri and the Platte. But the place was given back to the prairie in 1827, and all surface traces of the historic site were eventually cleared away by agriculture.

Since the early 1960's, however, Fort Atkinson has been undergoing a steady reincarnation. Now the resurrected fort's long, chinked-log buildings and boardwalks stand in a simple square pattern around the huge central parade ground, just as they did nearly two centuries ago. The 'living history' demonstrations weave an invaluable fourth dimension into the geographical and structural aspects of the fort. The visitor center with its multi-faceted displays and multi-media presentations are unequivocally first rate. Definitely recommended.

♠ Nebraska 162 ♿

N.P. DODGE
Omaha City Park

Location: Eastern border of Nebraska in Omaha.

Access: From Interstate 680 Exit 13 for 30th Street (on the northeast tip of Omaha, 0.4 mile west of the Missouri River bridge), turn south off the freeway for 0.05 mile, then east (left) onto Dick Collins Road for 0.25 mile to a 'T' intersection; turn north (left), pass under the freeway, and travel north on John J. Pershing Drive for 1.1 miles; turn east (right) into the park for 0.5 mile, then south (right) for a final 0.2 mile to the campground. (Whew!)

Camping Facilities: 46 campsites, most with electrical hookups, in 2 loops; sites are small to medium-sized, with fair separation overall; parking pads are gravel, medium straight-ins or long pull-throughs; medium to large tent areas; barbecue grills; b-y-o firewood; water at central faucets; restrooms with showers; holding tank disposal station; gravel driveways; complete supplies and services are available within 3 miles.

Day Use Facilities: Very large picnic area; shelters; drinking water; restrooms; very large parking area.

Activities & Attractions: Paved bikeways and walkways; horse trails; boating; boat launches and moorings; fishing; tennis courts; soccer and baseball fields; playgrounds; Neale Woods Nature Center.

Natural Features: Located on a wooded flat within a very short walk of the west bank of the Missouri River; sites are nicely-sheltered/shaded by large hardwoods; expanses of grass adjoin the campground; elevation 1000´.

Season, Fees & Phone: Mid-May to mid-October; $6.00 for a tent in the tent area, $10.00 for a standard site, $14.00 for an electrical hookup site, $5.00 for disposal station use; 14 day limit; park office ☎(402) 444-4673.

Camp Journal: It goes without saying that it's often pretty busy in here. But N.P. Dodge is probably one of the nicest big city parks you'll encounter—and one of the largest at that. (Just the half-dozen or more soccer fields cover acres of turf). Lots of room to roam.

♣ Nebraska 163 ♿

GLENN CUNNINGHAM LAKE
Omaha City Recreation Area

Location: Eastern border of Nebraska in Omaha.

Access: From Interstate 680 Exit 9 for 72nd Street (on the north-central edge of Omaha), turn north onto 72nd Street and proceed 0.6 mile; turn west (left) onto Rainwood Road and continue for 0.8 mile; turn southwest (left) onto the campground access road (paved) and proceed 0.5 mile to the campground.

Camping Facilities: 58 campsites; sites are medium-sized with fair spacing and minimal visual separation; parking pads are sandy gravel straight-ins; about half of the pads may require a little additional leveling; large tent areas, may be slightly sloped; barbecue grills; b-y-o firewood; water at several faucets; restrooms with showers; holding tank disposal station; gravel driveways; complete supplies and services are available within 3 miles.

Day Use Facilities: Medium-sized picnic area drinking water; restrooms; medium-sized parking area.

Activities & Attractions: Fishing; boating; boat launch; playground; Fort Atkinson State Historical Park, with rebuilt structures and a top-notch visitor center, is a short drive away.

Natural Features: Located on a semi-open, gentle slope on a small bay on the east shore of Glenn Cunningham Lake, an impoundment on Little Papillion Creek; campground vegetation consists of mown lawns and hardwoods and pines which provide limited shelter/shade for some sites; elevation 1000´.

Season, Fees & Phone: Mid-May to mid-October; $12.00; 14 day limit; park office ☎ (402) 444-4627.

Camp Journal: Freeway *swoooosh* is slightly audible, and the neighbors in the subdivision on the hill overlooking the campground may drop in for tea, but otherwise it's not evident that this is a city park. This is a fairly new campground with very good facilities. For a more woodsy setting, check out Omaha's N. P. Dodge Park (see listing).

♣ Nebraska 164 ♿

TWO RIVERS: NORTH
Two Rivers State Recreation Area

Location: East-central Nebraska west of Omaha.

Access: From Nebraska State Highway 92 at milepost 464 +.4 (8 miles east of Mead, 14 miles west of Omaha), turn south onto County Road 96 (paved) and proceed 1 mile; turn west onto the park access road for 1.1 miles to the park entrance; turn north (right) and proceed around the main loop roadway to the day use and camp areas.

Camping Facilities: *Cottonwood Campground:* 50 campsites with electrical hookups; sites are good-sized, essentially level, with fairly good separation; parking pads are medium to long, sandy gravel pull-offs; adequate space for large tents; fire rings; b-y-o firewood; water at central faucets; restrooms with showers; sandy gravel driveways; *Goldenrod Campground:* approximately 50 standard ('primitive') campsites; sites are medium-sized, level, with moderate separation; parking pads are medium-length, sandy gravel straight-ins; large, grassy tent areas; fire rings; water at a hand pump; vault facilities; gravel driveways; *Riverside Campground:* small, more or less open, primitive tent camping, drinking water and vaults; *Oak Grove Campground:* Group camping area with 18 electrical hookups; holding tank disposal station near Fawn Meadow Campground, 0.5 mile south; gas and camper supplies on the main highway.

Day Use Facilities: Picnic spots scattered about the park; drinking water; restrooms; several small parking areas.

Activities & Attractions: Lake fishing for small trout (extra fee), plus lake and river fishing for standard warm-water species; handicapped-access fishing dock; lake swimming beach; playground.

Natural Features: Cottonwood and Riverside: located in a grove of enormous cottonwoods on a flat along the bank of the Platte River; sites are well sheltered/shaded; Goldenrod and Oak Grove: located on a grassy flat dotted with hardwoods by Lake No. 4; sites are moderately shaded; four small sandpit lakes are nearby; surrounding countryside is level farmland; elevation 1100´.

Season, Fees & Phone: Open all year, with limited services November to April; park entry

$2.50, camping $8.00-$9.00, add $3.00 for hookups; park office ☎(402) 359-5165.

Camp Journal: Two Rivers tends to fill up on most summer weekends, and Cottonwood is its most-favored campground. It seems to combine some of the more desirable attributes of the rec area's other principal campgrounds, Goldenrod and Fawn Meadows. Having a lot of riverfront real estate helps too. Four sandpit lakes are within a very short walk of any of the camps on this side of the park.

♣ **Nebraska 165** &

TWO RIVERS: SOUTH
Two Rivers State Recreation Area

Location: East-central Nebraska west of Omaha.

Access: From Nebraska State Highway 92 at milepost 464 +.4 (8 miles east of Mead, 14 miles west of Omaha), turn south onto County Road 96 (paved) and proceed 1 mile; turn west onto the park access road for 1.1 miles to the park entrance; just beyond the entrance, turn south (left) and continue to the Union Pacific Caboose Park and another 0.2 mile to Fawn Meadows Campground.

Camping Facilities: *Fawn Meadows Campground:* 23 full hookup units in a paved parking lot arrangement; sites are very small, level, with nearly nil separation; parking pads are medium-length, paved straight-ins; water at sites; restrooms; showers; holding tank disposal station; *Caboose Cabins:* 10 refurbished and furnished railroad cabooses; each car sleeps 6 persons; gas and camper supplies on the main highway.

Day Use Facilities: Very large bathhouse with showers near the Lake 2 beach; parking lot.

Activities & Attractions: Lake fishing ('put-and-take') for small trout, also for typical warm-water species; handicapped-access fishing dock; lakeside swimming beach; playground; bicycling.

Natural Features: Located on the edge of a meadow near Lake No.1; Fawn Meadow sites are lightly shaded; Cabooses are essentially unshaded, but somewhat sheltered from wind by a line of tall hardwoods; surrounding grounds are well-landscaped with acres of lawns, shrubs and trees; several other small lakes in the area; elevation 1100´.

Season, Fees & Phone: Open all year, with limited services November to April; park entry

$2.50, camping $8.00-$9.00, add $3.00 for hookups; park office ☎(402) 359-5165.

Camp Journal: The ten bright yellow cabooses were contributed to the park by the Union Pacific Railroad. They're lined up single file on their own rail 'siding'. The Caboose Park is truly unique among state park facilities in the West. Super neat idea!

♣ **Nebraska 166** &

HAWORTH
Bellevue City Park

Location: Eastern border of Nebraska south of Omaha.

Access: From Nebraska State Highway 370 at milepost 19 (at the far east edge of the city of Bellevue, at the west end of the Missouri River toll bridge to Iowa), turn south onto Payne Drive and proceed 0.2 mile, then east (left) for 0.1 mile; turn north (left) into the campground entrance.

Camping Facilities: 111 campsites, including 14 standard sites, 30 electrical hookup sites, and 67 partial hookup units, in 3 loops; sites are small to medium-sized, with minimal to fair separation; parking pads are reasonably level, medium to long, paved straight-ins; adequate room for medium to large tents; barbecue grills, plus some fire rings; b-y-o firewood; water at sites and at central faucets; restrooms with showers; holding tank disposal station; community shelters; paved driveways; complete supplies and services are available in Bellevue.

Day Use Facilities: Medium-sized picnic area; shelter; drinking water; restrooms; medium-sized parking lot.

Activities & Attractions: Playground; marina nearby; river tour boat in summer; athletic fields, adjacent; Strategic Air Command Museum and former SAC base in Bellevue.

Natural Features: Located on a large flat near the west bank of the Missouri River; campground vegetation consists of patches of grass, and large hardwoods which provide ample to excellent shelter/shade for most sites; elevation 1000´.

Season, Fees & Phone: Open all year, with limited services November to April; $8.00 for a tent, $10.00 for camping vehicles, plus $3.00 for electric use, $3.00 for disposal station use; 14 day limit; park manager ☎ (402) 291-3122.

Camp Journal: There are no really big attractions in the area that would explain this pleasantly nice camp's surprising popularity—it's just the most economical camp around here.

📖 *September 9, 1806*

Passed the enterance of the great River Platte, which is at this time low, the water nearly clear, the current turbulant as usial. The sand bars which choked up the Missouri and confined the river to a narrow, snakey channel are wasted way, and nothing remains but a fiew small remains of the bar which is covered with driftwood. Below the R. Platte the current of the Missouri becomes evidently more rapid than above, and the snags much more numerous and bad to pass.

Late in the evening we arived at the Bald-Pated Prarie and encamped immediately opposit our encampment of the16th and 17th of July 1804. Our party appears extremly anxious to get on, and every day appears to produce new anxieties in them to get to their country and friends. My worthy friend Capt. Lewis has entirely recovered. His wounds are heeled up and he can walk and even run nearly as well as ever he could. The parts are yet tender &c &c. The climate is every day perceptively warmer and air more sultry than I have experienced for a long time. The nights are now so warm that I sleep comfortable under a thin blanket, a fiew days past, 2 was not more than sufficient.

—*Captain Clark*

♣ Nebraska 167 ♿

LOUISVILLE
Louisville State Recreation Area

Location: East-central Nebraska southwest of Omaha.

Access: From Nebraska State Highway 50 at milepost 76 + .4 (abeam of midtown Louisville), turn west/north-west onto the park access road and proceed 0.1 mile to the entrance station; continue ahead 0.1 mile, then northeast (right) or southwest (left) to the camping areas.

Camping Facilities: 229 campsites, including 145 with electrical hookups, plus park n' walk tent sites, open camping, and a group camp, in a half-dozen major areas; sites are small to medium-sized, most are level, with nominal to fair separation; parking pads are medium-length straight-ins; medium to large tent areas; barbecue grills or fire rings; b-y-o firewood; water at central faucets; restrooms with showers; holding tank disposal station; gravel

loop driveways, paved main roadways; limited supplies and services are available in Louisville.

Day Use Facilities: Several small and medium-sized picnic areas; several shelters; drinking water; restrooms; several small parking areas; concession stand.

Activities & Attractions: Swimming beach; fishing; limited boating (electric motors, sail, human effort); x-c skiing.

Natural Features: Located along the shores of 5 small lakes (with a total of about 50 acres of water) and within a few yards of the south bank of the Platte River; park vegetation consists of light to medium-dense, large hardwoods and lots of grass; lake views from the majority of picnic and camp sites; low, well-wooded hills lie in the surrounding area; elevation 1100´.

Season, Fees & Phone: Open all year, with limited services November to May; park entry $2.50, camping $8.00-$9.00, add $3.00 for hookups; park office ☎(402) 234-6855.

Camp Journal: The three hookup loops are also referred to as the A.C. Nielsen camping areas as an acknowledgment of a grant by the Omaha company which funded much of the construction. Tent campers and picnickers didn't get short-changed, though there are some dandy lakeside tent and picnic sites as well. (Similar to several other Nebraska sra's, Louisville's sandpit lakes are numbered rather than named.) In some respects, this place looks more like a state park than 'just' a state recreation area.

♣ Nebraska 168

RIVERVIEW MARINA
Riverview Marina State Recreation Area

Location: Eastern border of Nebraska in Nebraska City.

Access: From U.S. Highways 73/75 (11th Street) on the north edge of Nebraska City, turn east onto 5th Avenue for 1 block to 10th Street; turn north (left) onto 10th Street for 2 blocks to 7th Avenue; turn east (right) onto 7th Avenue for 6 blocks to 4th Street; turn north (left) onto 4th Street and continue for 0.4 mile down the hill, then right for 0.2 mile to the recreation area. (Note: if you arrive at night, it's all too easy to launch your camper into the Missouri at the end of the parking lot. Get the drift?)

Camping Facilities: Approximately 20 campsites in a paved, semi-parking-lot arrangement, plus several park n' walks; sites are small, level, and closely spaced; parking spots are long straight-ins or pull-offs; medium to large, grassy tent spots; barbecue grills in some sites; b-y-o firewood; water at central faucets; restrooms; paved driveways; adequate supplies and services are available in Nebraska City.

Day Use Facilities: Picnic area; drinking water; restrooms; large parking lot, suitable for vehicles with boat trailers.

Activities & Attractions: Boating; boat launch; fishing.

Natural Features: Located on several wooded acres on the west bank of the Missouri River; elevation 1000´.

Season, Fees & Phone: Open all year, subject to weather conditions; park entry $2.50, camping $5.00-$9.00; .phone c/o Nebraska Game & Parks Commission District V Office, Lincoln, ☎(402) 471-0641.

Camp Journal: Well...it's like this: although camping is permitted here, it really is more of a boating/fishing access and day use area than a campground. The place does get pretty busy. But consider these points: (a) it's the only public camping area for many miles; (b) the charge for camping is only the cost of admission; (c) it still beats getting a room at the Shake N' Rattle Inn in Nebraska City, then listening to four 18-wheelers per minute rumble by all night long.

♠ **Nebraska 169**

BROWNVILLE
Brownville State Recreation Area

Location: Eastern border of Nebraska southeast of Nebraska City.

Access: From U.S. Highway 136 in midtown Brownville, at the west end of the Missouri River bridge to Iowa, turn south onto a paved local road; proceed 0.4 mile south, east, and south (past the day use area entrance); turn east (left) onto a paved driveway to the campground.

Camping Facilities: 14 campsites; sites are medium-sized, level, with nominal to fair separation; parking pads are medium-length, paved straight-ins; good tent-pitching possibilities; some sites lack tables; barbecue grills in most units; b-y-o firewood; water at a central faucet in the adjoining day use area; vault facilities in the day use area; paved driveways; gas and very limited groceries in Brownville.

Day Use Facilities: Picnic area; drinking water; vault facilities; parking area.

Activities & Attractions: Missouri River History Museum and tours aboard the sidewheeler *Captain Meriwether Lewis*, a riverboat formerly with the Corps of Engineers, moored alongside the day use area; boating; small boat launch.

Natural Features: Located on a flat along the west bank of the Missouri River; shelter/shade from large hardwoods varies from none to light; a heavily wooded, steep hill forms the western backdrop for the area; elevation 900´.

Season, Fees & Phone: Open all year, subject to weather conditions; park entry $2.50, camping $5.00-$9.00; park office ☎(402) 471-0641.

Camp Journal: This little park has real potential. Currently, it's use is probably better-suited to day users and self-contained campers (or tent campers who like a lot of exercise). The *Captain Meriwether Lewis* is one of the largest and neatest inland crafts most people might have an opportunity to examine—and it's berthed right in its original environment. A bit of history is associated with Brownville: the nation's first homestead claim was filed here after Abraham Lincoln signed the Homestead Act in 1862.

📖 *September 10, 1806*

We met a Mr. Alexander La Fass and three French men from St. Louis in a small perogue, on his way to the River Platte to trade with the Pania, Loup, or Wolf Indians. This man was extreemly friendly to us. He offered us anything he had. We accepted of a bottle of whisky only, which we gave to our party. Mr. La Fass informed us that General Wilkinson and all the troops had descended the Mississippi, and Mr. Pike and young Mr. Wilkinson had set out on an expedition up the Arkansaw River, or in that direction.

After a delay of half an hour, we proceeded on about 3 miles and met a large perogue and 7 men from St. Louis bound to the Mahas for the purpose of trade. This perogue was in charge of a Mr. LaCroix. We made some fiew enquiries of this man and again proceeded on through a very bad part of the river, crowded with snags & sawyers, and encamped on a sand bar about 4 miles above the Grand Nemaha. We find the river in this timbered country narrow and more moving, sands, and a much greater quantity of aawyers or anags than above. Great caution and much attention is required to steer clear of all those difficulties in this low state of the water.

—*Captain Clark*

⚑ Nebraska 170 ⚐

INDIAN CAVE
Indian Cave State Park

Location: Southeast corner of Nebraska north of Falls City.

Access: From Nebraska State Highway 67 at milepost 8 (18 miles north of Falls City), turn east onto Nebraska Route 64-E Spur (S-64-E) and travel 5.1 miles to the park entrance.

Camping Facilities: 134 campsites, including 104 with electrical hookups in the main campground; (a small tent camping area, and a score of backpack camps, some with Adirondack shelters, and group camp areas are also available); sites are small+, with fair separation; parking pads are mostly medium-length, paved, respectably level straight-ins; adequate space for small to medium-sized tents; barbecue grills or fire rings; b-y-o firewood; water at central faucets; restrooms with showers; disposal station; paved driveways; camper supplies near the park; adequate supplies and services are available in Falls City.

Day Use Facilities: Several small to medium-sized picnic areas; individual picnic shelters; group shelters; drinking water; restrooms; numerous small and medium-sized parking lots and roadside pull-outs.

Activities & Attractions: 20 miles of hiking trails; trail shelters; river access (foot traffic); historical sites, including the reconstructed mid-19th century settlement of St. Deroin; amphitheater; interpretive programs; fishing; summer weekend cookouts; cross-country skiing on 16 miles of marked trails; sledding.

Natural Features: Located on a steep hillside (main campground) and on a ridgetop (tent area) among the densely wooded hills along the Missouri River; elevation 1200´.

Season, Fees & Phone: Open all year, subject to weather; limited services November to April; park entry $2.50, camping $8.00-$9.00, $3.00 for hookups; park office ☎(402) 883-2575.

Camp Journal: 'Tell you what: Nebraska has a number of really nice state parks; a few of them are a trifle glitzy; but this one is for real, so to speak. True, Indian Cave does have a small share of programmed catfish frys and proposed swimming pools. But the park's main orientation seems to be, and hopefully will remain, in harmony with the philosophy of the individual who finds simple satisfaction in hills, trails, woodlands, and river lore. A fine place.

⚑ Nebraska 171 ⚐

VERDON LAKE
Indian Cave State Recreation Area

Location: Southeast corner of Nebraska northwest of Falls City.

Access: From U.S. Highway 73 at milepost 16 +.4 (0.8 mile west of the town of Verdon, 6 miles east of the junction of U.S. Highways 73 & 75 north of Dawson), turn north into the recreation area. (There's a short, steepish dropoff from the highway onto the gravel driveway, so 'easy does it' with a larger vehicle.)

Camping Facilities: Approximately 20 camp/picnic sites in 2 areas; sites are small, most are level, with minimal to fair separation; parking pads are gravel/grass, short to medium-length straight-ins or pull-offs; space for small to medium-sized tents in most sites; small, concrete pads for some table areas; barbecue grills; b-y-o firewood; water at a hand pump; vault facilities; gravel driveways; gas and limited groceries in Verdon; adequate supplies and services are available in Falls City, 12 miles southeast.

Day Use Facilities: Facilities are shared with campers

Activities & Attractions: Fishing for crappie, bluegill, largemouth bass, catfish; limited boating (electric, hand-propelled).

Natural Features: Located on the west and east shores of 30-acre Verdon Lake; most sites are along the lightly sheltered/shaded lake shore; a few sites are on a well sheltered hillside a few yards from the west shore; gently rolling hills lie in the surrounding area; elevation 1000´.

Season, Fees & Phone: Open all year, subject to weather conditions; parky entry $2.50, camping $5.00-$9.00; 14 day limit; phone c/o Nebraska Game & Parks Commission District V Office, Lincoln NE, ☎(402) 471-0641.

Camp Journal: This is the only highwayside stop in Nebraska's southeast corner. Although it probably serves principally as a day use area, one of the sites a little farther from the highway certainly would suffice for a short term stay that's within a few miles of the primary highway 'trail'. Simple, but very agreeable, setting

Special Note: *There are no Kansas campgrounds strictly within our designated 20-mile Trail 'corridor'. However, because Expedition members traveled and explored*

within Kansas's boundaries, it is important that the state be represented in this volume. The following two camps are the closest Kansas campgrounds to the Expedition's route. Their inclusion is especially fitting, since they were built by the U.S. Army Corps of Engineers, which surveyed and mapped much of the New West following the passage of their predecessors, Army Captains Lewis and Clark.

Kansas. The hills and bluffs seem a little higher and more forested. For a good view of the surroundings, you might check out the simple secondary camping area on a hill just north of the principal camp, on the opposite side of Highway 92. There are showers up there as well.

🔺 Kansas 172 &

OLD TOWN
Perry Lake/Corps of Engineers Park

Location: Northeast Kansas northeast of Topeka.

Access: From U.S. Highway 24 at milepost 383 +.1 (on the east edge of the community of Perry, 3 miles west of the junction of U.S. 24 & 59 northwest of Lawrence, 18 miles east of Topeka), turn north onto a paved road and travel 12 miles to Kansas State Highway 92; turn west onto Highway 92 and proceed 1 mile; turn south (left) for 0.15 mile to the main camping area.

Camping Facilities: 147 campsites; sites are small to medium-sized, with nominal separation; parking pads are medium to long, gravel straight-ins; a little additional leveling may be required; adequate space for large tents; barbecue grills; some firewood is available for gathering in the surrounding area; water at central faucets; restrooms with showers; holding tank disposal station; paved driveways; limited to adequate supplies and services are available in Perry.

Day Use Facilities: None.

Activities & Attractions: Fishing primarily for crappie and catfish, also bass, and walleye (best in spring); boating; boat launch; playground; closest campground to the north trailhead for Perry Lake Trail, a designated National Recreational Trail, 2 miles southwest.

Natural Features: Located at the mouth of a bay on the east shore of Perry Lake; most sites have at least some shelter/shade provided by scattered large hardwoods on a grassy surface; elevation 1000´.

Season, Fees & Phone: May to October; $11.00; 14 day limit; Perry Lake CoE Project Office ☎ (913) 597-5144.

Camp Journal: The shoreline of Perry Lake provides a little more in the way of scenic interest than some of the other lakes in eastern

🔺 Kansas 173 &

SLOUGH CREEK
Perry Lake/Corps of Engineers Park

Location: Northeast Kansas northeast of Topeka.

Access: From U.S. Highway 24 at milepost 383 +.1 (on the east edge of the community of Perry, 3 miles west of the junction of U.S. 24 & 59 northwest of Lawrence, 18 miles east of Topeka), turn north onto a paved road and travel 7.5 miles; turn south/southwest onto a paved access road for 1.7 miles; turn left and continue for 0.4 mile to the first loop; the others are along the next mile, all on the left.

Camping Facilities: 270 campsites in 5 loops; sites are medium-sized, with minimal to fair separation; parking pads are short to medium-length, gravel straight-ins, and many are extra wide; additional leveling will be required for about half of the pads; adequate space for a tent on a grassy surface or on parking pad extensions; fire rings; limited firewood is available for gathering in the general vicinity, b-y-o to be sure; restrooms with showers, plus auxiliary vault facilities; holding tank disposal station; paved driveways; limited to adequate supplies and services are available in Perry.

Day Use Facilities: Medium-sized picnic area; shelters; drinking water; restrooms; medium-sized parking lot.

Activities & Attractions: Fishing; boating; boat launches; hiking trail along the shore.

Natural Features: Located at the mouth of a long, narrow inlet (Big Slough Creek) on the east shore of Perry Lake; campsites are situated along a level shore or on the slope above the shore; campground vegetation consists of grass and scattered hardwoods; many sites are unsheltered; elevation 1000´.

Season, Fees & Phone: May to October; $11.00 for a standard site, $14.00 for an electrical hookup site, add $2.00 for a "prime" site; 14 day limit; Perry Lake CoE Project Office ☎ (913) 597-5144.

Camp Journal: There are some really nice campsites here, particularly in the Limestone Cove Loop (the one farthest from the entrance). However, you also get a great shot of the bare rock face of the dam. An extra tariff is collected for the "prime" sites—generally the ones closest to the lake.

📖 *September 12, 1806*

We set out at sunrise, the usial hour, and proceeded on very well. About 7 miles we met 2 perogues from St. Louis. One contained the property of Mr. Chouteau bound to the Panias, or River Platte; the other going up trapping as high as the Mahas. Here we met one of the French men who had accompanied us as high as the Mandans. He informed us that Mr. McClellan was a fiew miles below. The wind blew ahead. Soon after we passed those perogues, we saw a man on shore who informed us that he was one of Mr. McClellan's party, and that he was a short distance below. We took this man on board and proceeded on and met Mr. McClellan at the St. Michael's Prarie. We came to here.

Here we found Mr. Jo. Gravelin, the Ricare interpreter whom we had sent down with a Ricaras Chief in the spring of 1805; and old Mr. Dorion, the Sioux interpreter. We examined the instructions of those interpreters and found that Gravelin was ordered to the Ricaras with a speech from the President of the U. States to that Nation, and some presents which had been given the Ricara Chief who had visited the U. States, and unfortunately died at the city of Washington. He was instructed to teach the Ricaras agriculture and make every enquiry after Capt. Lewis, myself, and the party.

Mr. Dorion was instructed to accompany Gravelin and, through his influence, pass him with his presents &c., by the Teton bands of the Sioux, and to prevail on some of the principal Chiefs of those bands, not exceeding six, to visit the seat of the government next spring. He was also instructed to make every enquiry after us. We made some small additions to his instructions by extending the number of Chiefs to 10 or 12, or 3 from each band, including the Yanktons, &c. Mr. McClellan received us very politely, and gave us all the news and occurrences which had taken place in the Illinois within his knowledge. The evening proving to be wet and cloudy, we concluded to continue all night. We dispatched the two canoes ahead to hunt with 5 hunters in them.

—Captain Clark

📖 *September 13, 1806*

Rose early. Mr. McClellan gave each man a dram, and a little after sunrise we set out, the wind hard above from the S.E. At 8 A.M., we landed at the camp of the 5 hunters whome we had sent ahead. They had killed nothing. The wind being too high for us to proceed in safety through the immensity of snags which were immediately below, we concluded to lay by and sent on the small canoes a short distance to hunt and kill some meat. I felt myself very unwell, and detected a little chocolate which Mr. McClellan gave us, prepared of which I drank about a pint and found great relief.

—Captain Clark

📖 *September 14, 1806*

At 2 P. M., a little below the lower end of the old Kanzas village, we met three large boats bound to the Yanktons and Mahars, the property of Mr. Lacroy, Mr. Aiten & Mr. Choteau, all from St. Louis. Those young men received us with great friendship and pressed on us some whisky for our men, bisquit, pork and onions, & part of their stores. We continued near 2 hours with those boats, making every enquiry into the state of our friends and country &c. Those men were much afraid of meeting with the Kanzas. We proceeded on to an island near the middle of the river below our encampment of the 1st of July 1804, and encamped having decended only 53 miles to day. Our party received a dram and sung songs untill 11 oClock at night in the greatest harmony.

—Captain Clark

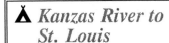

🏕 *Kanzas River to St. Louis*

🏕 **Missouri 174** ♿

BLUE SPRINGS LAKE
Fleming Park/Jackson County Park

Location: Western Missouri on the east side of Kansas City.

Access: From Interstate 470 Exit 14 (2 miles south of the Junction of I-470 & I-70 in Kansas City) proceed east on Bowlin Road for 0.3 mile; turn north (left) onto a paved local road (NE Campground Road) and go 0.5 mile to the campground.

Camping Facilities: 57 campsites, including 20 with full hookups and 17 with electrical hookups; sites are small to medium-sized, with minimal to nominal separation; parking pads are gravel, mainly medium-length straight-ins; additional leveling will be needed on most pads; medium to large areas for tents; fire rings; b-y-o firewood; water at central faucets; restrooms with showers; holding tank disposal station; paved driveways; adequate+ supplies and services are available within 3 miles.

Day Use Facilities: Numerous small to large picnic areas around the lake; shelters; drinking water; restrooms; numerous small and medium-sized parking lots and roadside pull-outs.

Activities & Attractions: Volleyball court; horseshoe pits; playground; swimming beach, picnic area, fishing, handicapped-access fishing pier, boating, boat launch, marina, all within 1.5 miles.

Natural Features: Located on an open hilltop above the west shore of Blue Springs Lake; the lake is a 700-acre Corps of Engineers flood-control impoundment on the East Fork of the Little Blue River, a tributary of the Missouri River; sites are unshaded to lightly shaded by hardwoods on mown grass; elevation 900´.

Season, Fees & Phone: Open all year, with limited services November to April (no water, chem vaults only) November to April; $11.00 for a standard site, $14.00 for an electrical hookup site, $19.00 for a full hookup site; 14 day limit; reservations accepted, recommended in midsummer, contact Jackson County Parks Department ☎(816) 229-8980, or (816) 795-8200.

Camp Journal: Pretty good distant views from this vantage point. Blue Springs Lake is the more popular of the two camps in Fleming Park (also see Lake Jacomo), as evidenced by a "reservations recommended" statement made by park personnel. It's got to be the views and the proximity to a variety of lakeside activities, rather than the amount of campsite shade here.

🏕 Missouri 175 ♿

Lake Jacomo
Fleming Park/Jackson County Park

Location: Western Missouri on the east side of Kansas City.

Access: From Interstate 470 Exit 10A (6 miles south of the Junction of I-470 & I-70 in Kansas City) drive east on Colbern Road for 1.7 miles;

turn north (left) onto Beach Drive and proceed 0.7 mile; turn westerly (left) onto the paved campground access road and go up a steep hill for 0.6 mile to the campground.

Camping Facilities: 60 campsites, including 10 with full hookups and 38 with electrical hookups; sites are small to medium-sized, with nominal to fair separation; parking pads are gravel, mostly medium-length straight-ins; additional leveling will be needed on many pads; medium to large areas for tents; fire rings; b-y-o firewood; water at central faucets; restrooms with showers; holding tank disposal station; paved driveways; adequate supplies and services are available within 5 miles.

Day Use Facilities: Several small to large picnic areas around the lake; shelters; drinking water; restrooms; numerous small and medium-sized parking lots.

Activities & Attractions: Nature trail; volleyball court; horseshoe pits; nature programs in summer; fishing; boating; marina nearby.

Natural Features: Located on a hill above the south-west tip of Lake Jacomo; sites receive light to medium shelter from large hardwoods on mown grass; the lake is bordered by low, wooded hills; elevation 900´.

Season, Fees & Phone: Open all year, with limited services (no water, chem vaults only) November to April; $11.00 for a standard site, $14.00 for an electrical hookup site, $19.00 for a full hookup site; 14 day limit; Jackson County Parks Department ☎(816) 229-8980, or (816) 795-8200.

Camp Journal: Nicely maintained shoreline 'landscaping' on this local lake. Lake Jacomo is the larger of the two lakes in Fleming Park (also see Blue Springs Lake). This campground is also called just "Jacomo".

📖 *September 16, 1806*
The day proved excessively warm and disagreeable, so much so that the men rowed but little. At 11 A. M. we met young Mr. Robidoux with a large boat of six oars and 2 canoes. The license of this young man was to trade with the Panias, Mahars and Otoes, reather an extraodinary a license for so young a man, and without the seal of the territory annexed. As General Wilkinson's signature was not to this instrument, we were somewhat doubtfull of it. Mr.Browns signature we were not acquainted with without the territorial seal. We made some enquirys of this young man and cautioned him against pursuing the steps

of his brother in attempting to degrade the American character in the eyes of the Indians.

—*Captain Clark*

📖 *September 17, 1806*

At 11 A.M., we met a Captain McClallan, late a Capt. of Artillery of the U. States Army, ascending in a large boat. This gentleman, an acquaintance of my friend Capt. Lewis, was somewhat astonished to see us return and appeared rejoiced to meet us. We found him a man of information and from him we received a partial account of the political state of our country. We were making enquiries and exchanging answers, &c., untill near midnight.

This gentleman informed us that we had been long since given up by the people of the U.S. generally, and almost forgotten. The President of the U. States had yet hopes of us. We received some civilities of Capt. McClallan. He gave us some bisquit, chocolate, sugar, and whiskey, for which our party were in want, and for which we made a return of a barrel of corn and much obliged to him.

Capt. McClallan informed us that he was on a reather speculative expedition to the confines of New Spain, with the view to introduce a trade with those people. His plan is to proceed up this river to the enterance of the River Platte, there to form an establishment from which to trade partially with the Panias & Otoes, to form an acquaintance with the Pawnees, and prevail on them. Some of their principal Chiefs to accompany him to Santa Fe, where he will appear in a stile calculated to attract the Spanish government in that quarter, and through the influence of a handsome present, he expects to be permitted to exchange his merchindise for silver & gold, of which those people abound. He has a kind of introductory speach from Govr. Wilkinson to the Panias and Otoes, and a quantity of presents of his own which he proposes distributing to the Panias with a view to gain their protection in the execution of his plans. If the Spanish government favours his plans, he proposes taking his merchendize on mules & horses, which can easily be procured of the Panias, to some point convenient to the Spanish Settlements within the Louisiana Territory, to which place the inhabitants of New Mexico may meet him for the purpose of trade &c. Capt. McClallans plan I think a very good one, if strictly persued &c.

—*Captain Clark*

♠ Missouri 176 ♿

VAN METER
Van Meter State Park

Location: North Central Missouri north of Marshall.

Access: From the junction of Missouri State Highways 41 & 122 (8 miles north of Marshall, 7 miles south of Miami), head west and north on Highway 122 for 4.5 miles to the park visitor center; continue for another 0.5 mile to a 3-way intersection; turn west (left) into the campground.

Camping Facilities: 20 campsites, including 12 with electrical hookups; sites are small to small+, level, with minimal to fair separation; parking pads are gravel, long straight-ins or pull-throughs; medium to large areas for tents; fire rings; firewood is usually for sale, or b-y-o; water at several faucets; restrooms with showers; paved driveway; complete supplies and services are available in Marshall.

Day Use Facilities: Medium-sized picnic area; large shelters; drinking water; restrooms; medium-sized parking lot.

Activities & Attractions: Missouri Indian mounds; small visitor center features a-v programs and exhibits; several hiking trails; Van Meter Forest Natural Area; sports field.

Natural Features: Located around the edge of a large, grassy clearing surrounded by dense woodland, 3 miles south of the Missouri River; many sites are lightly to moderately shaded by planted hardwoods, others receive good shade from big ol' walnut trees that encircle the camp loop; bordered by densely wooded hills and cropland; small Lake Wooldridge can be reached via a short trail from a parking area 1 mile northeast of the campground; elevation 700´.

Season, Fees & Phone: Open all year, with limited services October to April; $8.00 for a standard site, $14.00 for a hookup site; 15 day limit; visitor center ☎(816) 886-7537.

Camp Journal: North of the camp and picnic areas a series of ridges rise above the bottomland. Hundreds of years ago, Missouri Indians established a village on a ridge crest overlooking the Missouri River. At its peak, the village encompassed about 300 acres and had a population of about 5,000. Contact with European explorers in the 1700's resulted in disastrous outbreaks of smallpox and other mortal diseases. By the time the Expedition passed here, the village had been abandoned by the few hundred surviving Missouri.

September 18, 1806

Our party entirely out of provisions, subsisting on pawpaws. We divided the bisquit which amounted to nearly one bisquit per man, this in addition to the pawpaws is to last us down to the settlement which is 150 miles. The party appears perfectly contented and tell us that they can live very well on the pawpaws. We made 52 miles today only. One of our party, J. Potts, complains very much of one of his eyes which is burnt by the sun from exposing his face without a cover from the sun. Shannon also complains of his face & eyes &c.

—*Captain Clark*

September 19, 1806

We arived at the enterance of Osage River at dark and encamped on the spot we had encamped on the 1st & 2nd of June 1804, having came 72 miles. A very singular disorder is taking place amongst our party–that of the sore eyes. Three of the party have their eyes inflamed and swelled in such a manner as to render them extreemly painfull, particularly when exposed to the light. The eyeball is much inflamed, and the lid appears burnt with the sun. The cause of this complaint of the eye I can't account for. From it's sudden appearance, I am willing to believe it may be owing to the reflection of the sun on the water.

—*Captain Clark*

September 20, 1806

As three of the party was unabled to row from the state of their eyes, we found it necessary to leave one of our craft and divide the men into the other canoes. We left the two canoes lashed together which I had made high up the River Rochejhone. Those canoes we set adrift, and a little after daylight we set out and proceeded on very well. At meridian we passed the enterance of the Gasconde River, below which we met a perogue with 5 French men bound to the Osage village.

The party, being extreemly anxious to get down, ply their oars very well. We saw some cows on the bank, which was a joyful sight to the party and caused a shout to be raised for joy. We came in sight of the little French village called La Charrette. The men raised a shout and sprang upon their oars, and we soon landed opposit to the village. Our party requested to be permitted to fire off their guns, which was allowed, & they discharged 3 rounds with a hearty cheer, which was

returned from five trading boats which lay opposit the village. We landed and were very politely received by two young Scotch men from Canada—one in the employ of Mr. Aird, and the other, Mr. Reed. Two other boats, the property of Mr. Lacomb . All of those boats were bound to the Osage and Otoes. Those two young Scotch gentlemen furnished us with beef, flour, and some pork for our men, and gave us a very agreeable supper. As it was like to rain, we accepted of a bed in one of their tents. We purchased of a citizen two gallons of whiskey for our party, for which we were obliged to give eight dollars in cash, an imposition on the part of the citizen.

Every person, both French and Americans, seemed to express great pleasure at our return, and acknowledged themselves much astonished in seeing us return. They informed us that we were supposed to have been lost long since, and were entirely given out by every person, &c.

Those boats are from Canada in the batteaux form and wide in proportion to their length. Their length is about 30 feet and the width 8 feet & pointed bow and stern, flat bottom and rowing six oars only. The Schenectady form. Those bottoms are prepared for the navigation of this river. I believe them to be the best calculated for the navigation of this river of any which I have seen. They are wide and flat, not subject to the dangers of the rolling sands, which larger boats are on this river. The American inhabitants express great disgust for the government of this territory. From what I can learn it arises from a disappointment of getting all the Spanish grants confirmed.

—*Captain Clark*

September 21, 1806

Rose early this morning. Collected our men. Several of them had accepted of the invitation of the citizens and visited their families. At half after 7 A.M. we set out. Passed 12 canoes of Kickapoos ascending on a hunting expedition. Saw several persons, also stock of different kinds on the bank, which revived the party very much. At 3 P.M. we met two large boats ascending. At 4 P.M. we arived in sight of St. Charles. The party, rejoiced at the sight of this hospitable village, plied their oars with great dexterity, and we soon arived opposit the town.

This day being Sunday, we observed a number of gentlemen and ladies walking on the bank. We saluted the village by three rounds from our blunderbuss and the small arms of the party, and landed near the lower part of the town. We were met by great numbers of the inhabitants. We found them excessively polite. We received invitations from several of those gentlemen. Mr. Querie undertook to supply our party with provisions &c. The inhabitants of this village appear much delighted at our return, and seem to vie with each other in their politeness to us all. We came only 48 miles today. The banks of the river thinly settled, &c. Some new settlements since we went up.

—Captain Clark

📖 *September 22, 1806*

This morning being very wet and the rain still continuing hard, and our party being all sheltered in the houses of those hospitable people, we did not think proper to proceed on untill after the rain was over, and continued at the house of Mr. Proulx. I took this opportunity of wrighting to my friends in Kentucky, &c.. At 10 A.M. it ceased raining, and we collected our party and set out, and proceeded on down to the cantonment at Coldwater Creek, about 3 miles up the Missouri on it's Southern banks. At this place we found Colonel Hunt and a Lieut. Peters, and one company of artillery. We were kindly received by the gentlemen of this place. Mrs. Wilkinson, the lady of the Governor & General, we were sorry to find in delicate health. We were honored with a salute of guns and a hearty welcome. At this place there is a publick store kept in which I am informed the U.S. has $60,000 worth of Indian goods.

—Captain Clark

⚑ **Missouri 177** ♿

DR. EDMUND A. BABLER
Dr. Edmund A. Babler Memorial State Park

Location: Eastern Missouri on the west edge of Saint Louis.

Access: From Interstate 44 Exit 264 in Eureka (28 miles southwest of the Gateway Arch), head northerly on Missouri State Highway 109 for 10 miles; turn west (left) into the park entrance and proceed 0.6 mile on Guy Park Drive to a 4-way intersection; turn south (left) and go 0.3 mile to the campground. (Access is also possible from Interstate 70, but it's considerably more complicated; in short, from I-70, take I-64 south to Chesterfield, then state highways 340 and 100 to state highway 109; the park is 4 miles north of the junction of highways 100 & 109.)

Camping Facilities: 77 campsites, including 24 with electric hookups; sites are small to medium-sized, essentially level, with nominal to fair separation; parking pads are gravel, mostly short to medium-length straight-ins; nice grassy tent spots; fire rings; firewood is usually for sale, or b-y-o; water at several faucets; restrooms with showers; coin-op laundry; holding tank disposal station; paved driveways; complete supplies and services are available 4 miles south.

Day Use Facilities: Several small to large picnic areas; shelters; drinking water; restrooms; numerous small and medium-sized parking lots and pull-outs.

Activities & Attractions: Large visitor center with interpretive exhibits; naturalist programs on summer weekends; playground; campground amphitheater; swimming pool; tennis courts; trails; bike paths.

Natural Features: Located on the south side of the Missouri River Hills along the south bank of the river; sites receive light to medium shade from large hardwoods; elevation 600´.

Season, Fees & Phone: Open all year, with limited services October to April; $8.00 for a standard site, $14.00 for a hookup site; 15 day limit; park office ☎(314) 458-3813.

Camp Journal: While there aren't any Missouri River views from anywhere in the park, it's "just over the hill" from here. Dr. Edmund Babler was a prominent surgeon who operated one of the most successful private practices in St. Louis during the late 19th and early 20th centuries. He is memorialized in this 2400-acre wooded park because of his tireless work with the poor.

📖 *September 23, 1806*

We rose early. Took the Chief to the publick store and furnished him with some clothes, &c. Took an early brakfast with Colonel Hunt and set out. Descended to the Mississippi and down that river to St. Louis, at which place we arived about 12 oClock. We suffered the party to fire off their pieces as a salute to the town. We were met by all the village and received a hearty welcome from it's inhabitants, &c.

Here I found my old acquaintance, Major W. Christy, who had settled in this town in a publick line as a tavernkeeper. He furnished us with storerooms for our baggage, and we accepted of the invitation of Mr. Peter Chouteau and took a room in his house. We paid a friendly visit to Mr. Auguste Chouteau and some of our old friends this evening. As the post had departed from St. Louis, Capt. Lewis wrote a note to Mr. Hays in Cahokia to detain the post in that place untill 12 tomorrow, which is reather later than his usial time of leaving it.

—*Captain Clark*

📖 *September 24, 1806*

I slept but little last night. However, we rose early and commenced wrighting our letters. Capt. Lewis wrote one to the President, and I wrote Govr. Harrison and my friends in Kentucky, and sent off George Drewyer with those letters to Cahokia & delivered them to Mr. Hays &c. We dined with Mr. Choteau today, and after dinner went to a store and purchased some clothes, which we gave to a tailor and derected to be made. Capt. Lewis in opening his trunk found all his papers wet, and some seeds spoiled.

—*Captain Clark*

📖 *September 25, 1806*

Had all of our skins &c. sunned and stored away in a storeroom of Mr. Caddy Choteau. Paid some visits of form to the gentlemen of St. Louis. In the evening a dinner & ball.

—*Captain Clark*

📖 *September 26, 1806*

A fine morning. We commenced wrighting &c.

—*Captain Clark*

Epilogue

Captains Meriwether Lewis and William Clark and the Corps of Discovery thus concluded one of the most dramatic and significant episodes in American history.

The Lewis and Clark Expedition had traveled more than 8,000 miles over two years, four months and nine days. The Expedition's discoveries contributed an immense, rich body of knowledge about what, prior to their passage, had been a vast, unknown land.

Upon their return, the members of the Expedition received a 'bonus' for their successful endeavor. Congress granted each of the two officers 1600 acres of land; each enlisted man was awarded half a section of prime farmland, 320 acres. In addition, all of them received double pay.

Just as they held similar interests, yet were very different in many personal respects, Lewis's and Clark's lives diverged.

Lewis was appointed Governor of Louisiana Territory. He served but a brief, discontented term as governor. Often moody and withdrawn, he much preferred life in the wilderness to an existence in the political snakepit. Governor Lewis eventually became entangled in a long-running, long-distance dispute with federal bean counters and paper pushers. So he headed to Washington in the fall of 1809 to untangle the red tape in person. In a tragic twist of events, at a frontier farm near Hohenwald, Tennessee, Lewis died of pistol wounds to the chest and head on October 11, 1809—barely three years after completing that legendary journey. As he lay mortally wounded, Lewis was said to utter the phrase "So hard to die"—the same words he wrote in describing the death of a great grizzly bear on the upper Missouri in 1805. Most historians, as well as Thomas Jefferson and William Clark, surmise that the sketchy evidence, along with Lewis' personality profile, suggest the likelihood of a self-inflicted demise.

In contrast, Clark's life was a long and successful one. He was promoted to the rank of brigadier general and named Superintendant of Indian Affairs. As soon as he returned to civilization, he married his childhood sweetheart, Julia ("Judith") Hancock. Clark was appointed governor of Missouri Territory in 1813, and served in that capacity concurrently with his post as Chief of Indian Affairs. He later lost his governorship when Missouri was admitted to statehood, but continued as Superintendant of Indian Affairs until his death on September 1, 1838. Throughout all those years, "The Red Head Chief", as he was named by the Indians, is said to have maintained an esteemed mutual respect between himself and Native Americans, frontiersmen and settlers alike. He rests in the Clark family plot in Bellefontaine Cemetery, Saint Louis.

Two centuries later, the Journals of Lewis and Clark and the epic adventure story told across their pages stand tall among the greatest of our national legacies. They are an especially meaningful, integral contribution to the bold heritage of the West.

Appendix

The Corps of Discovery

Herewith are brief biographical sketches of the individuals who comprised the roster of the legendary Corps of Discovery. William Clark performed a 20-year follow-up study between the years 1825 to 1828 to determine who was still living and what pursuits they were engaged in; most of the information is based upon Clark's work. Little is known of many of them. For simplicity, the age for each that is listed is the approximate age of the individual during the summer of 1805, about midway through the 28-month duration of the Expedition.

Co-Commanders:

Meriwether Lewis and *William Clark*. Their biographical information is detailed in the *Forward* and *Epilogue* sections in the volumes.

Sergeants:

Patrick Gass, 34; a Pennsylvanian; elected sergeant after Charles Floyd's death in August 1804; after several more years in the Army, settled down in West Virginia and died in 1870; the last surviving member of the Expedtion.

John Ordway, 30; from New Hampshire, was considered the Expedition's First Sergeant; very reliable; also kept a journal of the trek; settled in Missouri, prospered, died in 1817.

Nathaniel Pryor, 33; a native Virginian; cousin of Charles Floyd; highly regarded for his character and ability by the Captains; received a commission, eventually promoted to captain; became a trader, married an Osage woman, lived with her tribe until his death in 1831.

Charles Floyd, a Kentuckian, died at age 22 as a member of the Expedition, probably of a ruptured appendix; his grave site in Sioux City, Iowa is marked with a tall obelisk.

Enlisted Men:

William Bratton, 27; a native Virginian, moved to Kentucky with his family at age 12; a skilled blacksmith; eventually married, lived in Ohio and Indiana, died and buried in Indiana in 1841.

John Collins, age unknown; born in Maryland; disciplined for tapping into the Corps whiskey supply while assigned to guard it; otherwise, he was a good worker; later joined famed explorer and trapper William Ashley; killed in a battle with the Arikaras in 1823.

John Colter, 30, born in Virginia, moved to Kentucky with his family as a youth; a skilled hunter; later became the first white man to see what would eventually become Yellowstone National Park; his tales of the geysers, hot springs, and paint pots caused the newspapers to dub the land "Colter's Hell"; he narrowly escaped a harrowing encounter with the Blackfeet at Three Forks in 1810, and became a legend in his own time; settled down to a tranquil life in Missouri, died there in 1813.

Pierre (Peter) Cruzatte, age unknown; French-Indian ancestry; the Expedition's nearsighted chief waterman; best known for his fiddle playing and his accidental shooting of Lewis; he is listed by Clark simply as "killed" by the mid-1820's, presumably in the wilderness.

Joseph Fields, 33; born in Virginia, moved to Kentucky when young; he and his brother were both highly regarded for their skill and courage by the Captains; listed as "killed" less than a year after the end of the Expedition.

Reuben Fields, 34; also a native Virginian, and later Kentuckian; both Fields brothers were crack marksmen and hunters; settled down in Kentucky, married, died in 1823.

Robert Frazer, age unknown; born in Virginia; accompnaied Lewis to Washington in 1806; settled in Missouri and died there in 1837.

George Gibson, age unknown; a native of Pennsylvania; a good hunter and skilled in sign language; died in St. Louis in 1809.

Silas Goodrich, age unknown; born in Massachusetts; the Captains commented about his preoccupation with fishing, at which he was very skilled; 're-upped' in the Army; listed by Clark as having died by the mid 1820's.

Hugh Hall, 33; another native of Massachusetts; along with Collins, was disciplined for boozing; lived in St. Louis for a while, then disappeared.

Thomas P. Howard, 26; Massachusetts native; except for some disciplinary problems, little is known of him; he may have stayed in the Army.

Francois (Francis) Labiche, age unknown; French-Indian or French-Negro ancestry; an experienced riverman, as well as an interpreter; accompanied Lewis and the Indian chiefs to Washington in 1806; listed by Clark as living in St. Louis in the mid-1820's.

John Baptiste Lepage, age unknown; French-Canadian; a skilled hunter and boatman; little else is known of him.

Hugh McNeil, age unknown; born and raised in Pennsylvania; not much else is known; listed by Clark as deceased by the mid-1820's.

John Potts, 29; a German immigrant; served in the Army in Tennessee prior to being assigned to the Corps; he was killed while with John Colter when they were bushwacked by the Blackfeet near Three Forks in 1808.

George Shannon, 20; born in Pennsylvania, as a teen moved with his family to Ohio; the youngest of the Army personnel; he was lost twice on the Expedition, and had a knack for losing his tomahawk as well; served as Clark's liaison during the preparation of the Journals for publication; he became a lawyer in Kentucky, and later was elected U.S. senator from Missouri; died and buried in Missouri in 1836.

John Shields, 36; a native Virginian; his skill and ingenuity in maintaining the arms and equipment of the Corps was highly praised a number of times by the Captains; following the Expedition's return, he trapped with Daniel Boone in Missouri for a while, then settled in Indiana, where he died and was buried in 1809.

John B. Thompson, age unknown; he apparently was a valuable assistant to Clark in charting courses and mapmaking; he may have been on an ill-fated expedition to the Rockies in 1807; Clark lists him as "killed" by the mid 1820's.

William Werner, age unknown; probably a native of Kentucky; his Corps service was acceptable but not stellar; Clark lists him as living in Virginia in the mid-1820's.

Joseph Whitehouse, 30; born in Virginia, moved to Kentucky at an early age; handy with a needle and thread; re-enlisted during the War of 1812, deserted in 1817, then disappeared.

Alexander Willard, 27; a New Hampshire native; after the long trek, he worked as a government blacksmith; had a wife and a dozen children; lived in Missouri and Wisconsin for many years; the family moved to California in 1852, where he died near Sacramento in 1865.

Richard Windsor, age unknown; one of the Expedition's best hunters; settled in Missouri for a while, then served another 10 years in the Army; Clark lists him as living in Illinois in the mid-1820's.

Peter Weiser, 24; born and raised in Pennsylvania; after the trek, he spent several years as a trapper and fur trader on the Missouri and the Yellowstone; the Weiser River and the city of Weiser, Idaho, are named after him. Clark lists him as "killed" by the mid-1820's.

Civilian Members:

Touissant Charbonneau, 47; French-Canadian; the Expedition's chief interpreter; lived among the Hidatsa and Mandan Indians for many years; after the big trek, he worked in the fur trade and as an interpreter for government and private enterprise; died in the early 1840's.

George Drouillard, age unknown; French-Canadian-Indian ancestry; he was a rugged *hombre*; the Expedition's best hunter and highly skilled in sign language; he later became a partner with Manuel Lisa in a fur-trading venture on the Missouri and the Yellowstone; killed at Three Forks by the Blackfeet in 1810.

Sacagawea, 17; Shoshone interpreter; she was captured by a Hidatsa raiding party near Three Forks at about age 12; lived among them until purchased by Charbonneau to be his wife; she proved to be a valuable asset as an interpreter, guide, and symbol of peaceful intentions, since a woman with a child never traveled with a war party; died of natural causes at a trading post in present-day South Dakota in 1812.

York, 34; servant to Captain Clark; a strong, burly, black man who was held in awe by the Indians; Clark issued his freedom in 1811; he operated a freight business in Kentucky and Tennessee for a number of years; he died about 1830 while enroute to rejoin Clark in St. Louis.

Jean Baptiste Charbonneau, age 6 months; son of Sacagawea and Touissant Charbonneau; by previous agreement, at age six he was sent to St. Louis to live with the Clark family and to be educated; as a young man, he spent six years traveling in Europe; returned to the U.S. and became a mountain man and fur trader, and a guide for several notable explorers of the day; he died in 1866 in Oregon while enroute from his home in California to Montana.

Arms, Equipage & Merchandize

Presented below is a list of most items carried by the Lewis and Clark Expedition at the start of its epic journey. The list was derived from official government invoices, vouchers, receipts and inventory documents involving the U.S. Army Quartermaster, plus private-enterprise sources of supplies and equipment. Arms were furnished by the famed Harpers Ferry Arsenal. For the most part, they were signed-for by Captain M. Lewis, as early as a year in advance of the launch date of the Expedition. Items listed as being acquired "From Public Store" indicate those supplies which Lewis or other Army personnel were to acquire from mercantiles, and then forward the invoices to Army disbursment offices for payment. Listed are the actual prices charged to Captain Lewis's account or billed to the government. "Ditto" is abbreviated "do.". Total startup costs: $3600.

Camp Equipage

4	Tin horns	$ 2.00
2	Tin lanthorns	2.00
2	Tin lamps	.50
32	Cannisters for portable soup	8.00
1	Box sqr. of small, astd.	1.00
3 doz:	Pint tumblers	4.20
125	Large fishg hooks	4.45
125	Fishg Lines assorted	18.09
1	Strand of fishg do. with hooks, complete	3.00
1	Sportsmans flaske	1.50
8 ps.	Cat gut for mosquito cart	15.50
6	Brass kettles & porterage	15.18
1	Block tin sauce pan	1.50
I	Corn mill	9.00
1	Set of Gold scales & wts.	2.33
1	Rule	.60
1 set	Iron weights	.75
2 pr.	Large shears	1.86
4 doz	packg. Needl & large awls	1.13
2 doz:	Table spoons	1.87
4 doz.	Drawing knives	1.20
3 doz:	Gimblets	3.60
17	Files & rasps & 1 shoe float	2.31
11/4 dz	Small cord	1.79
2	Small vices	1.67
3 pr.	Plyers	.97
1	Saw set	10.00
9	Chisels	1.77
2	Adzes	1.20
2	Hand saws	3.06
6	Augers astd.	1.64
2	Hatchets	.83
1	Wetstone	.47
2 p.	Pocket steel yards	.47
1 pkg	12 lbs Castile soap	1.68

From Rich. Wevill, prop. :

[Custom-made items]

8 oiled-linen tents & 45 oiled-Flanders sheeting bags (total 156 square yards mat'l)	$119.39

From Public Store:

8	Receipt Books [blank journals]	
48 ps.	Tape	
6	Brass Inkstands	
6	Papers Ink Powder	
1	Common Tent	
1 lb.	Sealing Wax	
100	Quils	
1	Packing Hogshead	

Mathematical Instruments

1 Spirit level	$ 4.00
1 Case platting Instruments	14.00
1 Two pole chain	2.00
1 Pocket Compas plated	5.00
1 Brass Boat Compass	1.50
3 Brass Pocket Compasses	7.50
1 Magnet	1.00
1 Hadleys Quadrant with Tangt Screw	22.00
1 Metal Sextant	90.00
1 Microscope to index of do	7.00
1 Sett of Slates in a case	4.00
4 oz of Talc	1.25
1 Surveying Compass wt extra needles (Pd by L)	23.50
1 Circular protractor & index do.	8.00
1 Six In: Pocket Telescope do.	7.00
1 Nautical Ephemeris do.	1.50
1 Requisite Tables do.	2.50
1 Kirwan's Mineralogy do.	5.00
1 Chronometer & Keys	250.75
1 Copy of Bartons Bottany (pd. by C. L.)	6.00
1 Kelleys Spherics do..	3.00

2 Nautical Ephemeris do.	4.00
1 Log line reel & log ship	1.95
1 Parrallel Glass for a Horison	1.00

Arms & Accoutrements & Ammunition

1 pair	Pocket pistols (Pd. by L.)	$ 10.00
176 lb.	Gun powder	155.75
52	Leaden cannisters for gunpowder.	26.33
15	Powder horns & pouches	26.25

[Extra rifles, blunderbusses, a large-calibre deck gun, and spare parts were furnished by the Harpers Ferry Arsenal; no paperwork exists.]

From Public Store:

15	Powder horns
18	Tomahawks
15	Scalping knives & belts
15	Gun slings
30	Brushes & wires
15	Cartouch boxes
15	Painted knapsacks
500	Rifle flints
125	Musket flints
50 lb	Best rifle powder
1 pr.	Horsemans pistols
420 lbs	Sheet lead

Medicines &c

| 1 box | Medicine & surgecal insts. | $90.69 |
| 2 lbs. | Tea & cannister | $3.80 |

Provisions &c

| 193 lbs. Portable Soup | $298.50 |

[Experimental Army C ration—ugh!]
30 Galls Spirits of Wine in 6 kegs [aaah!] 77.20

Clothing &c

| 45 Flannel Shirts | $ 71.10 |
| 16 Coatees | 246.00 |

From Public Store:

15	Blankets
15	Match Coats
15	Blue wool: overalls
36 prs.	Stockgs
20	Frocks
30	Shirts
20	pr Shoes

Indian Presents

12	Pipe tomahawks	$18.00
6 1/2 lbs.	Strips sheet iron	1.62
1 ps.	Red flannel 47 1/2 yds	14.94
11 ps.	Hanckercheifs assd	59.83
1 dz	Ivory Combs	3.33
1/2 catty	Inda. S. silk .	3.75
21 lbs.	Thread assd.	23.17
1 ps.	Scarlet cloth 22 yds	58.50
5 1/2 doz.	Fan: I Floss	18.87
6 gro:	Binding	11.79
2 cards	Beads	3.80
4 doz.	Butcher knives	5.33
12 doz.	Pocket looking glasses	5.19
15 doz.	Pewter do.	3.99
8 doz.	Burning do.	12.00
2 doz.	Nonesopretty	2.94
2 doz.	Red strip'd tapes	2.80
72 ps.	Strip'd silk ribbon	39.60
3 lbs.	Beads	2.01
6 papers	Small bells	4.02
1 box	100 larger do.	2.25
73 bunches	Beads assd.	41.00
3 1/2 doz:	Tinsel bands assd	3.75
1 doz:	Needle cases	.30
2 3/4 doz	Lockets	3.56
8 1/2 lbs.	Red beads	25.50
2 doz:	Earings	4.00
8	Brass kettles	10.67
12 lbs.	Brass strips	6.80
500	Broaches	62.07
72	Rings	6.00
2	Corn mills	20.00
15 doz:	Scissors	18.97
12 lbs.	Brass wire	7.80
14 lbs	Knitting pins	3.89
4600	Needles assd.	9.73
2800	Fish hooks assd	8.00
1 gro:	Iron combs	2.80
3 gro:	Curtain rings	1.87
2 gro:	Thimbles assd.	3.21
11 doz:	Knives	25.17
10 lbs.	Brads	1.00
8 lbs.	Red lead	.89
2 lbs.	Vermillion	3.34
130 rolls	Tobacco (pigtail)	14.25
48	Calico ruffled shirts	71.04
1	Trunk to pack sundry Ind. prests.	3.50
8 groce	Seat or mockasin awls	15.67

From Public Store:

| 15 | Blankets |

✓ Spelling Check

Meriwether Lewis and William Clark wrote rich, descriptive narratives of the scenes and events they experienced on their epic first-crossing of the continent. However, neither would win honors in a spelling bee, then or now. Clark, especially, was, shall we say, inconsistent in his spelling of even the most common words. However, certain words, such as those ending in an "or", as in *color, neighbor* and *favor*, were indeed spelled differently then. As the British, and to some extent the Canadians, still do, Lewis and Clark spelled them as "colour", "neighbour" and "favour".

The following table lists words which Lewis and/or Clark frequently and consistently spelled differently (or "creatively') than we do in 21st Century North America.

Modern Spelling	Lewis	Clark
alarmed	allarmed	allarmed
antelopes	antelopes	goats
Arikaras	—	Ricares, Ricaras
arrived	arrived	arived
balance	ballance	ballance
beads	beads, beeds	beeds, beads
beautiful	beautifull	beutifull, beautifull
biscuit	bisquit	bisquit
Blackfeet*	Blackfoot	Blackfoot
breakfast	breakfast	brakfast
breaking	breaking	brakeing
buffalo	buffaloe	buffalow
caulking	corking	corking
Charbonneau**	Charbono	Shabono, Chabono
cheerful	cheerfull	cheerfull
chiefs	cheifs#, chiefs	chiefs
Cheyenne	—	Chien, Chyenne
chokecherry	choke cherry	choke cherry
cliff	clift	clift
color	colour	colour
cottonwood	cottonwood	cotton wood
delightful	delightfull	delightful
determined	determined	deturmined
dried	dryed, dried	dryed, dried
Drouillard**	Drewyer	Drewyer
eat	eat	eate
endeavor	endeavour	endeavour
entrance	entrance	enterance
extremely	extreemly	extreemly
favor	favour	favour
few	few	fiew
graze	graize	graize
hungry	hungary	hungary
immense	immence	emence
inquire	enquire	enquire
invite	envite	envite, invite

its (possessive)	it's	it's
Kansas	—	Kanzas
kettle	kettle	kittle
Labiche**	Labuish, Labishe	Labeech, Labeesh
labor	labour	labour
lately	latterly	latterly
level	level	leavel
many	many	maney
merchandise	merchandize	merchandize, merchindize
minutes	minutes	minits
Missouri	Missouri	Missourie, Missouri
mocassins	mockersons	mockersons
mosquitoes	musquetoes	musqueters+
natives	natives	nativs
neighbor	neighbour	neighbour
o'clock	oClock	oClock
opposite	opposite	opposit
painful	painfull	painfull
Pawnees	—	Panies, Panias
pirogue	perogue	perogue
picketed	picquited	picquited
poor	poor	pore
prairie	prarie	prarie
rainy	rainy	rainey
rather	reather	reather
rattlesnake	rattle snake	rattle snake
respect	rispect	rispect
route	rout	rout
Sacagawea or Sagajawea	Sah-cah-gar-we-ah	The Indian Woman
service	service	sarviss
Saskatchewan	Saskachewan	Saskashawan
Shoshones	Shoshonees	Shoshonees, Sosonees
shoulder	sholder	sholder
smallpox	small pox	small pox
smoking	smoking	smokeing
squaw	squaw	squar
style	stile	stile
tow	toe	toe
traveler	traveller	traveller
usual	usual	usial
until	untill	untill
very	very	verry
whom	whom	whome
women	women	womin, women
writing	wrighting	wrighting

* An Indian Nation in Northwest Montana

** A member of the Expedition

Lewis had his own interpretation of the rule: "i before e except after c".

+ Clark spelled *mosquitoes* nearly 20 different ways

Map Legend

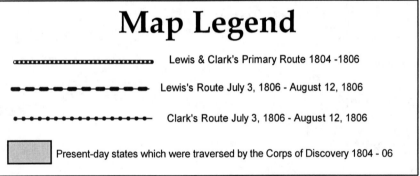

•••••••••••••••••••••••••••••• Lewis & Clark's Primary Route 1804 -1806

━ ━ ━ ━ ━ ━ ━ ━ ━ ━ Lewis's Route July 3, 1806 - August 12, 1806

•━•━•━•━•━•━•━•━• Clark's Route July 3, 1806 - August 12, 1806

Present-day states which were traversed by the Corps of Discovery 1804 - 06

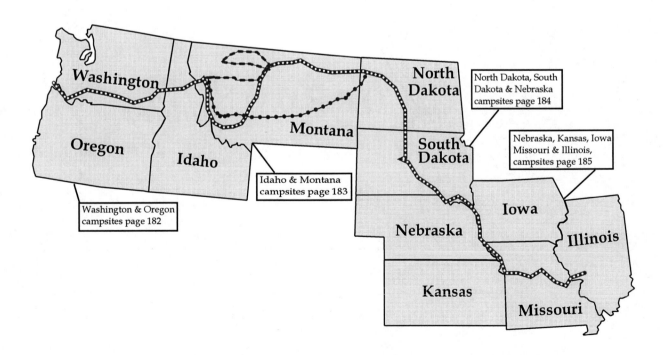

North Dakota, South Dakota & Nebraska campsites page 184

Nebraska, Kansas, Iowa Missouri & Illinois, campsites page 185

Idaho & Montana campsites page 183

Washington & Oregon campsites page 182

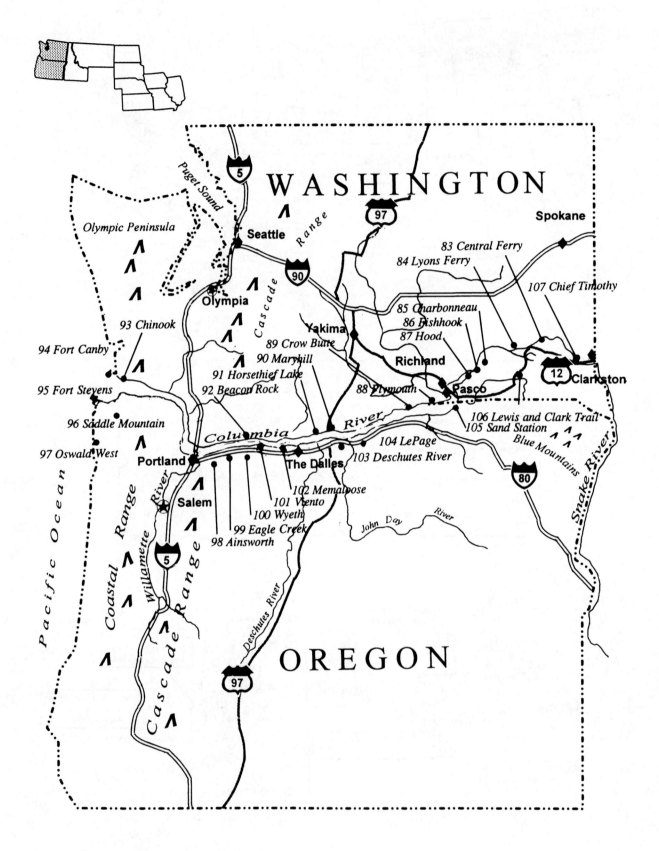

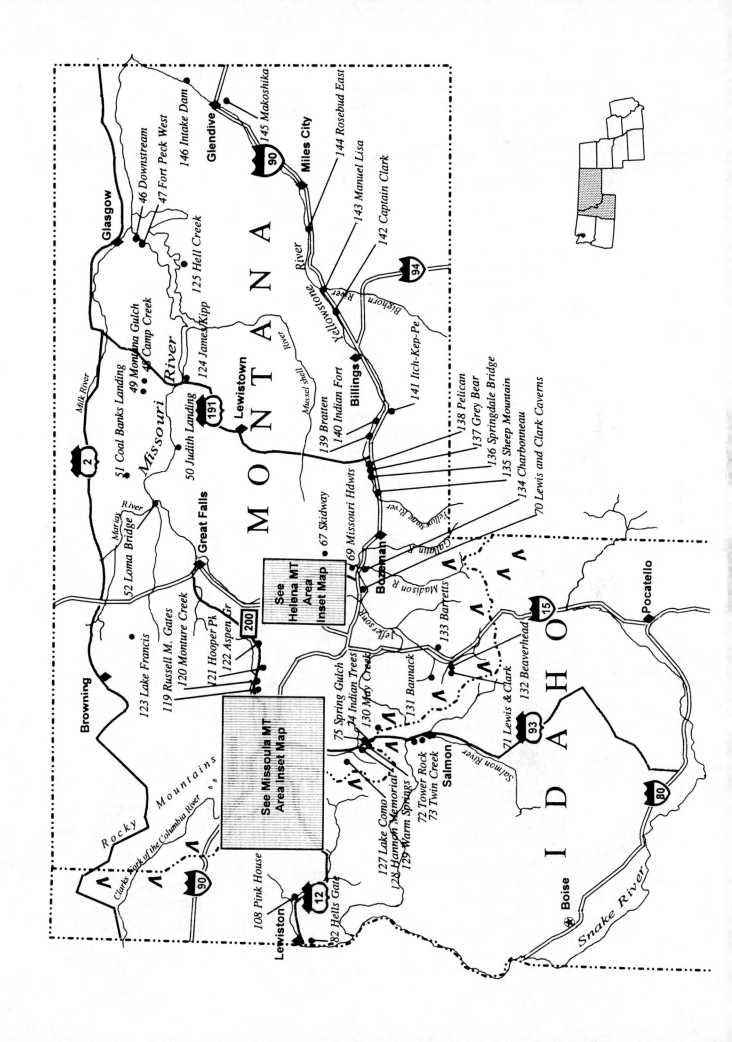

Glasgow

46 Downstream
47 Fort Peck West
146 Intake Dam

Glendive

145 Makoshika

Miles City

144 Rosebud East

143 Manuel Lisa

142 Captain Clark

49 Montana Gulch
48 Camp Creek
125 Hell Creek

51 Coal Banks Landing

124 James Kipp

Lewistown

Missouri River

Mussel shell River

191

50 Judith Landing

140 Indian Fort

139 Bratten

Billings

141 Itch-Kep-Pe

138 Pelican

137 Grey Bear

136 Springdale Bridge

135 Sheep Mountain

134 Charbonneau

70 Lewis and Clark Caverns

Milk River

2

Marias River

52 Loma Bridge

Great Falls

M O N T A N A

67 Skidway

69 Missouri Hdwts

Yellowstone River

Browning

Rocky Mountains

123 Lake Francis

119 Russell M. Gates

120 Monture Creek

121 Hooper Pk

122 Aspen Gr

200

See Helena MT
Area Inset Map

Bozeman

Madison R

Jefferson

Gallatin R

Yellowstone River

133 Barretts

Pocatello

15

Clarks Fork of the Columbia River

See Missoula MT
Area Inset Map

75 Spring Gulch

74 Indian Trees

130 May Creek

131 Bannack

132 Beaverhead

71 Lewis & Clark

93

128 Hannon Memorial

129 Warm Springs

72 Tower Rock

73 Twin Creek

Salmon

Salmon River

127 Lake Como

I D A H O

80

108 Pink House

12

Lewiston

82 Hells Gate

Boise

Snake River

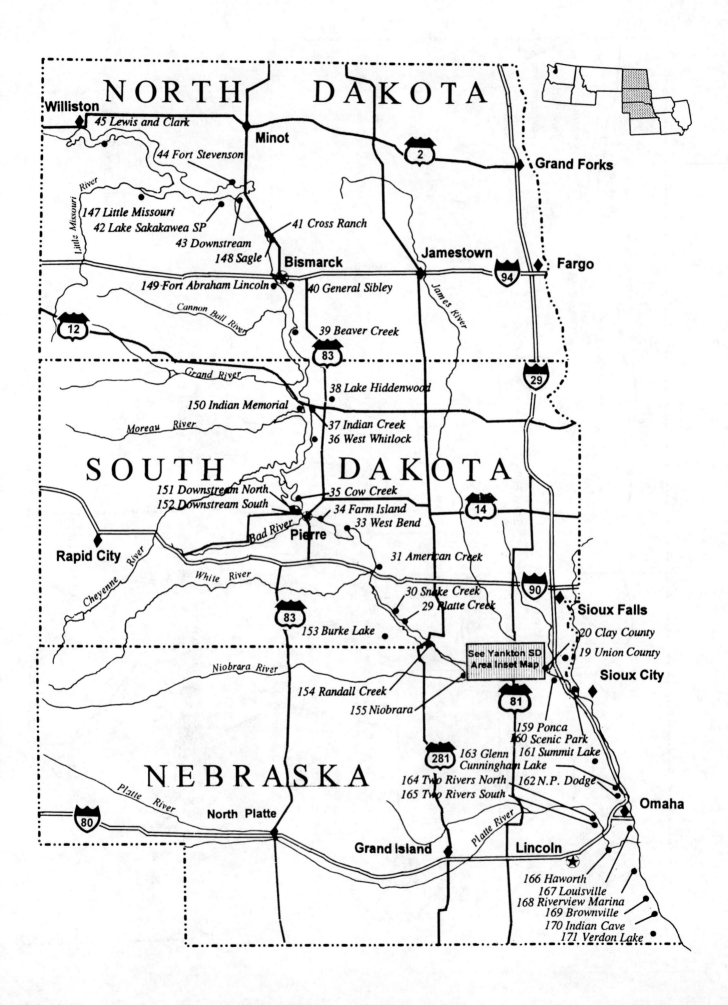

NORTH DAKOTA

Williston
45 Lewis and Clark
Minot
44 Fort Stevenson
2
Grand Forks
147 Little Missouri
42 Lake Sakakawea SP
41 Cross Ranch
43 Downstream
148 Sagle
Bismarck
Jamestown
94
Fargo
149 Fort Abraham Lincoln
40 General Sibley
Little Missouri River
Cannon Ball River
12
39 Beaver Creek
83
29
Grand River
38 Lake Hiddenwood
150 Indian Memorial
Moreau River
37 Indian Creek
36 West Whitlock
SOUTH DAKOTA
James River
151 Downstream North
35 Cow Creek
152 Downstream South
34 Farm Island
Bad River
Pierre
33 West Bend
14
Rapid City
31 American Creek
Cheyenne River
White River
30 Snake Creek
90
83
29 Platte Creek
Sioux Falls
153 Burke Lake
20 Clay County
19 Union County
Niobrara River
See Yankton SD Area Inset Map
Sioux City
154 Randall Creek
81
155 Niobrara
159 Ponca
160 Scenic Park
281
163 Glenn
161 Summit Lake
NEBRASKA
Cunningham Lake
164 Two Rivers North
162 N.P. Dodge
165 Two Rivers South
Platte River
North Platte
80
Platte River
Omaha
Grand Island
Lincoln
166 Haworth
167 Louisville
168 Riverview Marina
169 Brownville
170 Indian Cave
171 Verdon Lake

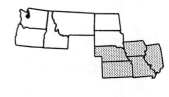

IOWA

Sioux Falls

Missouri River

18 Stone
159 Ponca
Sioux City
160 Scenic Pk
17 Snyder Bend
16 Brown's Lake
161 Summit Lake
15 Lewis and Clark
162 N.P. Dodge
163 Glenn
Cunningham Lake
14 Wilson Island

Platte River
Omaha
Council Bluffs
164-5
Two Rivers
13 Lake Manawa
166 Haworth

167 Louisville
168 Riverview Marina
12 Waubonsie

NE
11 Big Lake
169 Brownville
8 Smith's Fork
7 Camp Branch
6 Crows Creek
170 Indian Cave

171 Verdon Lake
St. Joseph
5 Watkins Mill
10 Lewis and Clark
176 Van Meter
9 Weston Bend
4 Arrow Rock

Topeka
3 Finger Lakes
2 Indian Glade
St. Louis
173 Slough Creek
Kansas City
172 Old Town
174 Blue Springs Lake
175 Lake Jacomo
Missouri River
1 Horseshoe Lake

Jefferson City

Emporia

177 Dr. Edmund A. Babler

KANSAS

MISSOURI

Des Moines

Davenport

ILLINOIS

Mississippi River

Helena MT Area Inset Map

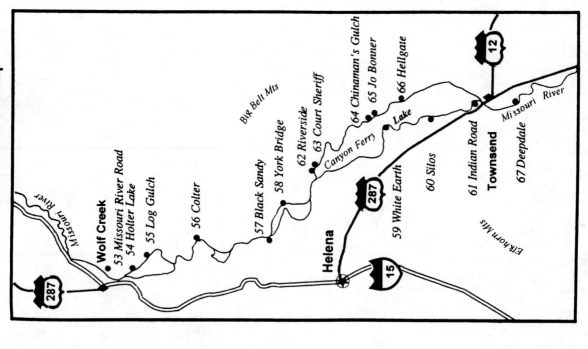

Big Belt Mts

Missouri River

53 Missouri River Road
54 Holter Lake
55 Log Gulch
56 Colter
57 Black Sandy
58 York Bridge
62 Riverside
63 Court Sheriff
64 Chinaman's Gulch
65 Jo Bonner
66 Hellgate

Wolf Creek

Canyon Ferry Lake

59 White Earth
60 Silos
61 Indian Road
67 Deepdale

Townsend

Helena

Elkhorn Mts

12
287
15
287

Missoula MT Area Inset Map

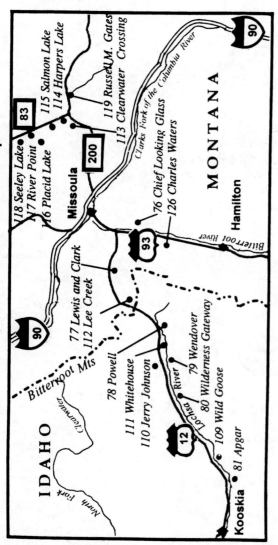

IDAHO

MONTANA

115 Salmon Lake
114 Harpers Lake
119 Russell M. Gates
113 Clearwater Crossing

Clark Fork of the Columbia River

118 Seeley Lake
117 River Point
116 Placid Lake

Missoula

76 Chief Looking Glass
126 Charles Waters

Hamilton

Bitterroot River

77 Lewis and Clark
112 Lee Creek

Bitterroot Mts

78 Powell
79 Wendover
80 Wilderness Gateway
111 Whitehouse
110 Jerry Johnson
109 Wild Goose
100 Apgar
81 Apgar

Lochsa River

North Fork (Clearwater)

Kooskia

90
83
200
93
90
12

Yankton SD Area Inset Map

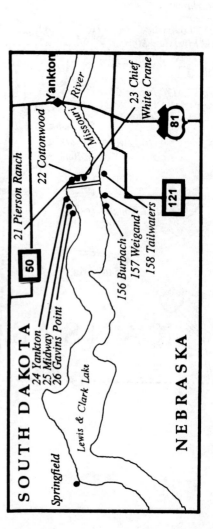

SOUTH DAKOTA

NEBRASKA

Yankton

Missouri River

23 Chief White Crane

22 Cottonwood

21 Pierson Ranch

24 Yankton
25 Midway
26 Gavins Point

156 Burbach
157 Weigand
158 Tailwaters

Springfield

Lewis & Clark Lake

50
81
121

INDEX

+ Indicates a "Side Trip"

* Indicates a thumbnail description of a nearby campground described in the *Camp Journal* section of a principal camp area

Volume 1

Idaho

Illinois

Iowa

Missouri

Montana

North Dakota

Volume 2

Idaho

Kansas

Missouri

Montana

America's Greatest Adventure!

The Double Eagle Guide to

Camping Along
The Lewis and Clark Trail

__*Volume 1* **Search for the Northwest Passage**   ISBN 1-932417-04-4
          May 1804 to November 1805   Hardcover $21.95*

__*Volume 2* **Return from the Distant Sea**   ISBN 1-932417-06-0
          November 1805 to September 1806   Hardcover $21.95*

* **Save $3.00** Softcover, spiral-bound editions are also available. Recommended for light-duty, personal use only. Subtract $3.00 from standard hardcover price and ✓here: ❏

Please add $4.00 for shipping the first volume, and $2.00 for each additional volume.

Please include your check/money order, and complete the shipping information in the indicated space below:

Total amount enclosed $_____

Name_____

Address_____

City_____ State_____ Zip_____

Please mail your completed order to:

Discovery Publishing   P.O. Box 50545   Billings, MT 59105   (Phone 1-406-245-8292)

Thank You Very Much For Your Order!

Prices, shipping charges, and specifications are subject to change.

(A photocopy or other reproduction may be substituted for this original form.)